BY THE EDITORS OF CONSUM
WITH IRA J. CHASNOFF, M.D.

Your Child: A Medical Guide

BEEKMAN HOUSE
New York

Library of Congress Catalog Card Number: 82-62853
ISBN: 0-517-38203-2

This edition published by:
Beekman House
Distributed by Crown Publishers, Inc.
One Park Avenue
New York, New York 10016

Medical consultant: Ira J. Chasnoff, M.D.

Illustrations: Teri J. McDermott,
M.A., Medical Illustrator

Page design: Ingeborg Jakobson

Cover design: Frank E. Peiler

Contents

Notice

In this book, the authors and editors have done their best to outline the indicated general treatment for various childhood conditions, diseases, ailments, and their symptoms. Also, recommendations are made regarding certain drugs, medications, and preparations.

Different people react to the same treatment, medication, or preparation in different ways. This book does not attempt to answer all questions about all situations that you or your child may encounter.

Neither the Editors of CONSUMER GUIDE® and PUBLICATIONS INTERNATIONAL, LTD., nor the authors or publisher take responsibility for any possible consequences from any treatment, action, or application of medication or preparation by any person reading or following the information in this book. The publication of this book does not constitute the practice of medicine, and this book does not attempt to replace your physician. The authors and publisher advise the reader to check with a physician before administering any medication or undertaking any course of treatment.

Introduction

Raising a healthy, happy child is always a challenge, and every parent knows that panicky feeling that comes with the knowledge—or even the suspicion—that a child is sick. Part of the problem is that it can be very difficult to assess the seriousness of a childhood illness. Does a stomachache indicate only that the child overate at a birthday party or is apprehensive about a school test, or does it mean something more serious? How bad does a cold have to be before you need to keep the child home from school? Should you treat a cut knee yourself or let a doctor take a look at it? What's the difference between a sprain and a fracture, and what should you do for each? The questions are endless, and no parent ever avoids all of them.

It's even harder for the brand-new parent with a first baby who suddenly develops an unexplained rash or a bad bout of colic. But even parents who have survived those first confusing days find that the childhood years hold all sorts of unexpected challenges. When a child gets hit on the head with a ball on the playground, could he have a concussion? When the child teases the cat until it scratches her badly, should the scratch be seen by the doctor? How do you treat a minor burn? What does a fever really mean? When should you give a child aspirin? What happens if the child is allergic to bee stings? What constitutes an emergency?

This book works on the principle that an informed parent who has done homework ahead of time is in the best possible position to deal with the minor—and major—medical crises of childhood. The book is a comprehensive guide to the problems that a parent is most likely to encounter, along with practical advice on recognizing, assessing, and dealing with each one. You will learn how to spot the signs that may mean the child is sick, and how to determine whether the child is tired because he or she has been playing hard or because the child is coming down with the virus that's currently going around the neighborhood. You'll learn how to judge when the child needs a doctor's care—and what information to give the doctor's office when you call. You'll find out when home treatment is called for—and what kind—and when to call the doctor right away.

The opening chapters of this book provide basic information that every parent needs to know. There's sensible advice on how to choose a doctor, what to expect from the doctor, and how to make sure you and the child's doctor work together to take good care of your child's health. You'll find out why vaccinations are vital; why routine checkups are so important and what the doctor looks for in the course of an examination; what you need to have in your medicine chest at home; what kinds of medications the doctor orders—and why it's important to understand what "four times a day" really means; and what medical tests involve and why the doctor needs them. There's also a reassuring section for parents on what to expect from a newborn and how to tell that the baby is developing normally.

The opening chapters include all this information. They are followed by individual articles of conditions and diseases that parents may have to cope with before a child grows up and becomes responsible for his or her own health care. The subjects covered range from the sort of everyday problems that are an inevitable part of childhood—colds, sore throats, stomachaches, cuts, and scrapes—to potentially life-threatening diseases that, fortunately, affect far fewer chidlren. Whether the condition is minor or major, you'll be better able to help your child if you understand what is involved and what you should do.

Not all the articles discuss diseases as such. Also covered are such matters as dyslexia and stuttering, which can cause the child and parent just as much pain and concern as an illness that is caused by an identifiable germ. You'll also get good information on unusual conditions you may have heard about but never really understood, such as Reye's syndrome, anorexia nervosa, and toxic shock syndrome. Most important of all, the information in this book is presented in clear, non-technical language.

All in all, *Your Child: A Medical Guide* is a thorough, up-to-date, and understandable book that can be a parent's best friend in many of the medical situations that occur as any child is growing up. Use it to help you play an informed, practical, competent role in caring for your child's most precious asset— good health.

Chart of symptoms

Here are some common childhood diseases (vertical column) and their symptoms (across the top). Key symptoms are indicated by a solid dot; possible symptoms are indicated by an open dot. To use this chart run your finger down the columns that correspond to each of your child's symptoms, and read the diseases (to the left) which cause each symptom. By a process of elimination you should be able to zero in on the possible causes of your child's illness. Then, turn to the section of the book relating to the various diseases. There you'll find both the information you need to further narrow down the diagnosis and the treatment recommended to relieve distress.

SIGNS AND SYMPTOMS

DISEASES	Unconsciousness	Vomiting	Visible deformity	Tenderness	Rash	Pain	Noisy breathing	Loss of function	Itching	Headache	Fever	Difficulty breathing	Diarrhea	Cough	Blueness	Abnormal discharge	Abnormal behavior
Appendicitis		○		●		●					●		○				
Arthritis			○	○	○	●		●			○						
Asthma							●					●		●	○		
Blood poisoning				●						○	●						
Boils				●		●											
Botulism		●				●					●	●					
Bronchiolitis							●				●	○		●	○		
Bronchitis							○	○			●			●			
Chicken pox					●				●		●						
Common cold							○	○		○	●			●		○	
Concussion	●	●						○		●							●
Convulsions with fever	●							○			●	●			●		
Convulsions without fever	●							○		○							●
Croup		○				○	●				●	●		●	○		
Cystic fibrosis							○					○		●	●	○	
Diphtheria						●	●				●	●		●			
Dysentery						●					●		●				
Earaches						●				○	○					○	
Encephalitis	○	●								●	●						●
Food allergies		○			○	●	○		○				○	●			
Food poisoning		●				●					●		●				
Fractures			●	●		●		●									
Gastroenteritis, acute		●		○		●					●		●				
Glands, swollen			●	○		○					○						
Gonorrhea						○										●	
Hand, foot, and mouth disease				○	●	●					●						
Hay fever							○		●	○						●	
Hepatitis		○				○				○	●						

● KEY SYMPTOMS   ○ POSSIBLE SYMPTOMS

SIGNS AND SYMPTOMS

DISEASES	Unconsciousness	Vomiting	Visible deformity	Tenderness	Rash	Pain	Noisy breathing	Loss of function	Itching	Headache	Fever	Difficulty breathing	Diarrhea	Cough	Blueness	Abnormal discharge	Abnormal behavior
Hernia			●	○		○											
Herpes simplex					○	●					○						
High blood pressure										○							
Impetigo					●				○								
Infectious mononucleosis					○	●				○	●						
Influenza		○				●				○	●		○	●			
Laryngitis								○			○			●			
Leukemia								○			●						
Measles					●				○		●			●	●		
Meningitis	○	●			○					●	●						●
Mumps			●	●	●					○							
Nephritis	○	○								○	●				●		
Pinworms					○				●						●		
Pneumonia					○		○			○	●	●		●	○		
Poisoning	○	○			○	○				○		○	○	○			○
Polio		○			●			●			●						
Rocky Mountain spotted fever					●	●				○	●						
Roseola	○				●						●				○		
Rubella					●						●						
Scabies					●				●								
Sinusitis				●		●				●	●			●		○	
Sore throat				○		●					○			○			
Stomachache, acute		○		○		●							○				
Stomachache, chronic		○		○		●					○		○				
Strep throat		○		○	○	●				○	●			○			
Swimmer's ear				●		●	○	○			○					●	
Tetanus	●					●		○	○								
Tonsillitis				○		●	○				●			○			
Ulcers		○		○		●										●	
Urinary tract infections		○		○		○					●		○			○	
Viruses		○			○	○	○		○	○	○	○	○	○			
Whooping cough		●					○				●			●	○		

● KEY SYMPTOMS   ○ POSSIBLE SYMPTOMS

Parent/physician partnership

Raising a child is a big responsibility, and it's always comforting to know that there's someone you can turn to when you have a problem. For advice on many of your concerns about your child you can call on your own parents, your family and friends, other parents, your child's teachers. But when it comes to your child's health the person you need is a physician.

CHOOSING A DOCTOR

To get the best from your child's doctor, you must first select the best doctor for your child. A pediatrician is a doctor who sees only children. The pediatrician has had an extra three to five years of special training in the physical, emotional, and educational needs of young people. Your family physician probably has comparable training in terms of years of study, but this study has been directed to people of all ages rather than just to children. The best pediatrician you can find should, in theory, know more about children than the best family doctor you can find.

The most important thing, however, is that you should be able to get along with the doctor who is caring for your child. If you feel more comfortable with your own family physician than with any pediatrician in your locality, you may decide to have the family physician take care of your child, too. You know what's best for you and the child, so trust your own decision.

Your child's doctor, who is a trained and experienced professional, should be a reliable and sympathetic source of information and advice throughout your child's growing years. Always remember, though, that the doctor is a medical adviser, not another parent. There are decisions about your child's well-being that only you can make, and a good doctor does not try either to make child-rearing decisions for you or to make you feel that you're not a competent parent. A good parent/doctor relationship is one in which each partner respects the other.

How do you find a good doctor? If the child is your first, the doctor who delivered your baby can give you names of local physicians and maybe recommend someone who is well thought of by other new parents. You may have a friend or neighbor with children who can recommend someone. If you've moved to a new area, consult a neighbor who has children, or call the local hospital or the local branch of the state medical society. Professional organizations will not give you recommendations as such; they will give you names and expect you to make your own inquiries. However, a phone call and a visit to a doctor's office should be enough to tell you whether or not that doctor is right for you and your child. It is also a good idea to visit the doctor even before your baby is born to become acquainted and to arrange for your baby's medical care.

WORKING TOGETHER

Once you've found a doctor whose medical ability you trust, there are practical steps you can take to maintain a good working relationship between the two of you.

For instance, when you call the doctor's office because your child is sick, you may not talk to the doctor but to a professional nurse practitioner who acts as the go-between in your communications with the doctor. You can have the same confidence in the nurse that you do in the doctor. The nurse is a qualified medical professional in his or her own right, and is well able to handle many of your questions. This means you don't have to wait for the doctor to get through with a patient before he or she can talk to you. Of course, if your child's condition does require the doctor's attention, the nurse will have the doctor talk to you on the phone, or help you set up an appointment to see the doctor.

Whether you talk directly to the doctor or to the nurse when you call the office, be prepared to give the following information:

- Your name and the child's name.

- Your child's approximate weight; this is important because medications are prescribed by body weight, and the dosage that is appropriate for a 100-pound teenager is very different from that given to a 25-pound toddler.

- Your child's temperature; whether or not the child is running a fever—and if so, how high a fever—is a clue to the child's condition. Use a thermometer to take the child's temperature. A guess based on flushed cheeks or a hot forehead isn't good enough.

- Information on any illnesses the child has been exposed to recently.

- Details of medications the child is allergic to.

- The name, phone number, and business hours of your pharmacist so that the doctor can phone in a prescription if necessary. (Although the nurse can handle many of your questions and perform some examinations and medical procedures, only a doctor can prescribe medication.)

Be sure to have a pencil and paper at hand so that you can write down any information or instructions the doctor or nurse gives you.

When you call the doctor's office you probably have an idea as to whether you just want some advice on the telephone, or whether you want to bring the child in to see the doctor. So tell the doctor or nurse what you have in mind—don't expect them to guess. If the doctor or nurse feels it's not necessary to bring the child in, you'll be told the reason for that advice. However, the decision is yours, and if you still want a personal consultation you're entitled to insist.

Another way to stay on good terms with your child's doctor is to plan ahead so that both you and the doctor know what an office visit is intended to achieve. A common cause of communication breakdown between parent and physician is the parent's complaint that the doctor was too busy, didn't answer questions, or cut the visit short.

To avoid this, at the time you make the appointment also tell the receptionist what the visit is for. If you feel you're going to need extra time with the doctor, make a point of saying this so that your request can be figured into the doctor's schedule. And, when you see the doctor, do not confuse the issue by trying to get a complete update on other family members' problems in the course of one appointment. Let the doctor examine your child and deal with the reason you brought the child into the office. If you have other concerns not directly related to the present one, make an appointment to come back another time.

ASKING QUESTIONS

One of the things you'll probably have checked out when you chose your doctor was his or her ability to speak language you understand. Doctors, like specialists in any field, are so familiar with their professional language that they sometimes forget how confusing it is to other people. So if your child's doctor slips into medical jargon that you don't understand, ask for a translation. Don't feel uncomfortable about asking, either. You must know what the doctor's instructions are before you can carry them out, and it's part of the doctor's responsibility to make sure you are fully informed about all matters that concern your child's health.

Sometimes you may find that you understand what the doctor is saying—but you don't agree with it. In this case don't hesitate to ask why the doctor has reached a certain decision, or what the alternatives are. If you still don't feel comfortable with the doctor's advice, don't argue. You may get the doctor to agree with your point of view, but this may not be in the child's best interests. If you and the doctor disagree on a diagnosis or a course of treatment, ask for a second opinion. This means going to another doctor and asking his or her professional advice on the issue. Your doctor may welcome this suggestion—or even make the suggestion before you do. A doctor may be hesitant to assume full responsibility for diagnosing and treating a difficult or unusual case. In such a situation it is common to have two or more consultants working together to determine the best course of treatment.

When you ask for a second opinion, your doctor should be able to suggest names of possible consultants. If you trust the doctor, you'll trust his or her choice of other professionals. If you don't, you'll be looking for another doctor anyway.

It sometimes happens that when communication between parent and physician does break down, the only responsible course the parent can take is to find another doctor.

HOUSE CALLS

Many people who are now parents remember the days when doctors made house calls. And they wonder why doctors today don't make house calls. Your modern physician will probably tell you that many wrong diagnoses resulted from examining sick children in their homes without adequate equipment. In the office, the doctor has a professionally set-up medical facility with all the equipment necessary for an accurate diagnosis. So whether or not a doctor makes house calls—and most don't—should not affect your opinion of his or her competence. If you trust your doctor, and if you're confident that he or she will always be available in an emergency, you've made a good choice.

A final word on the parent/physician partnership—and, again, it's partly a matter of courtesy. If your physician is taking good care of your child, express your appreciation; doctors like to be thanked, just the same as anyone else. And if you're not satisfied with the health care your child is receiving, the doctor should know that, too. A physician's failure to please you may be due to many factors other than professional inadequacy, and if the doctor knows there's a problem maybe he or she can correct it. If not, your best plan is to find another doctor.

Remember that although the doctor is your partner in caring for your child's health, you're still responsible for deciding just who this partner will be.

Fever

Everybody knows what a fever is, but many people don't know what it means. One common error is to assume that the higher the fever, the sicker the child. It is also commonly believed that fever is a child's enemy, that it should be fought and the temperature brought to normal as soon as possible.

The fact is that children past early infancy tend to develop high fevers with little provocation. Relatively harmless illnesses like roseola often cause temperatures as high as 106°F, whereas many serious diseases, such as leukemia and polio, may cause slight or no rise in temperature. Furthermore, it is not true that high fever causes "brain damage."

A child is as seriously sick as the illness warrants, not as a thermometer registers. A child with pneumonia or meningitis and a fever of 104°F is still quite ill even though the temperature has been artificially reduced to normal. A child with a strep throat and 101°F fever is no less sick than the same child with a strep throat and a temperature of 104°F. Other symptoms (such as exhaustion, confusion, difficulty in breathing) indicate the illness's severity, not the degree of fever.

It makes more sense, in fact, to regard a fever as a child's friend rather than as an enemy. A fever is an early warning signal that a child is ill and that you must look to find a cause. Fever also speeds up the body's metabolic processes (possibly including its resistance mechanisms) and in some instances may help the body's defenses overcome an illness.

Fever, together with other symptoms, also acts as a barometer to help you judge when an illness is ending. For example, the course of a fever may indicate whether or not an antibiotic is working effectively. Finally, the pattern of daily fluctuations in a fever may be characteristic of particular illnesses and may aid the parent or physician in making a correct diagnosis.

A high fever does have disadvantages, however. It makes a child feel uncomfortable and, as it develops, may cause chills. If a fever continues for days, it may weaken a child so that it takes longer for the child to recuperate. In susceptible younger children a fever may lead to convulsions (see *Convulsions with fever*). For all these reasons, it is sensible to reduce a fever. However, it is important not to confuse treating the fever with treating the illness, not to panic as a fever rises, and not to harm the child in your anxiety to fight the fever.

A MATTER OF DEGREE

At any given moment, different parts of the body are at different temperatures. Moreover, normal temperatures vary as much as two to three degrees Fahrenheit over the course of a day even when a child is healthy. A rectal temperature of 99.8°F or less, an oral temperature of 98.6°F or below, and an armpit temperature, though the least accurate, of 98°F or less are all considered normal.

Despite these variations, all thermometers are marked to indicate 98.6°F as normal. A rectal thermometer differs from an oral one only in having a more rugged bulb. (The most practical instrument for home use is a stubby bulb thermometer, which can be used to take a child's temperature in any of the preferred ways.)

For the most reliable readings at any age, the rectal thermometer is recommended, although it takes a little longer for the temperature to register.

No one can accurately estimate the degree of a fever by touch. If your child feels warm or appears ill, you must use a thermometer to register the accurate temperature that you and your doctor need to know in order to treat the child.

Before using the thermometer, shake it down to be certain the mercury column is below 98.6°F and the bulb is intact. Then spread the child's buttocks with the thumb and forefinger of one hand so the anal opening is clearly visible. Lubricate the bulb with petroleum jelly and insert it gently into the center of the anus. The child should feel no pain or discomfort. (Only the bulb portion of the thermometer needs to be inserted for the two to three minutes required to obtain an accurate reading.)

To take a baby's temperature, place the child face down on a solid surface and put the heel of your hand firmly on the lower back. An unwilling toddler can be firmly clasped between your thighs and bent forward over your leg so that you can take the temperature.

Although less reliable, an oral temperature reading is sufficient and can be taken in a child who is old enough to hold the bulb of the thermometer under the tongue with the mouth closed for three minutes. (If the thermometer breaks and the child accidentally swallows the mercury in the thermometer, don't fret. Thermometers contain elemental mercury, which is a nonpoisonous and harmless form of the metal.)

CARE OF YOUR THERMOMETER

After each use, the thermometer should be shaken down below "normal" and washed with soap and cold water. Sterilize the thermometer by soaking it in a solution of rubbing alcohol before storing it in its case. Place it back in the medicine cabinet where it will be handy the next time you need it. Do not let children treat the thermometer as a toy.

TREATMENT OF FEVER

The most reliable medications for lowering fever are aspirin and acetaminophen, a non-aspirin pain reliever found in some over-the-counter preparations. You can give one children's aspirin or the equivalent amount of acetaminophen for every 15 pounds of weight. This dose can be repeated every four hours. Other basic guidelines for administering aspirin or acetaminophen include:

1. Do not awaken the child to give aspirin or acetaminophen.
2. Do not mix aspirin and acetaminophen or alternate between the two.
3. Call the doctor if fever persists longer than 48 hours or if other signs of illness are present.

Keep a feverish child lightly clothed or covered to allow the body heat to escape. This, too, will help lower a fever.

Other methods of reducing a fever include placing the child in a lukewarm bath or encasing the naked child in a wet sheet. A child with a consistently high temperature should be under the care of a doctor.

Although giving the child aspirin has long been the accepted home treatment for lowering a fever, aspirin should not be used if the child has chicken pox or influenza. A condition called Reye's syndrome has been possibly linked to the use of aspirin in the treatment of chicken pox or influenza. Reye's syndrome is a relatively rare type of encephalitis, or inflammation of the brain, accompanied by changes in the liver, and it usually starts after the child has begun to recover from chicken pox or influenza.

It has not been proven that aspirin causes or promotes Reye's syndrome, but it is recommended that aspirin not be given to children with chicken pox or influenza. Instead, sponge baths and aspirin substitutes such as acetaminophen—which has not been linked to Reye's syndrome—should be used to manage the fever and other symptoms.

Related topics: Chicken pox, Convulsions with fever, Influenza, Reye's syndrome

Medications

Treating a sick child with medication is a two-way responsibility, and it's a perfect example of how parent and doctor work together in the interests of the child's health. The doctor is responsible for making an accurate diagnosis of the child's condition and prescribing the appropriate drug. But it's the parent's responsibility to make sure that the drug is administered correctly.

Some doctors estimate that 10 to 30 percent of cases in which medication apparently fails to work occur because the medication didn't get a chance to work—because it wasn't given properly. Whenever a doctor prescribes medication for your child, the doctor will also instruct you as to how the medicine should be taken. If you don't understand, ask. And don't rely on the scribble on the prescription. Prescriptions are written in a form of medical shorthand that is quite clear to a pharmacist but may not mean a thing to you. So make sure you know, before you leave the doctor's office or get off the phone, just how to give the child the medication.

How much. The quantity of medication the doctor prescribes for your child depends on the child's body weight and age. The dosage prescribed for a baby will be much different from that prescribed for an adolescent, even if the drug is the same and given for the same reason. It's important to give the child the exact amount prescribed, and that means you can't rely on hit-or-miss measurements. It's easy enough to give one or two pills, but liquid measures are more tricky. You can't use a kitchen teaspoon to administer a teaspoon of medication—you could be way off. One teaspoonful means 5.0 cc (cubic centimeters) of liquid. Half a teaspoonful means 2.5 cc—not what looks like half of the teaspoon you use to stir your coffee.

You can buy a specially marked measuring spoon for medication from any pharmacist. Keep it in the medicine chest and be sure to use it any time you're giving the child liquid medication. If you've got a child who insists on taking medication from his or her own special spoon, transfer the medication from the measuring spoon to the child's spoon *after* measuring.

Make sure the child takes all the medication. If the child vomits within 20 minutes of receiving medication, you can assume the medication was lost and should give another dose.

When. It's also important to follow the doctor's instructions about *when* medicine should be given. Different medications require longer or shorter periods of time to be absorbed by the body and start doing their work of helping the child get well. Some medications need to be given at very precisely regulated intervals. Make sure you understand the prescription, because "four times a day" and "every six hours" do *not* mean the same thing.

If the label on the medication tells you to give the medicine four times a day, it means that the child should have four doses within the waking hours at fairly equally spaced intervals.

On the other hand, "every six hours" means exactly what it says. Each dose must be given six hours after the last one, and the child must be awakened at the appropriate time if necessary. This instruction may also appear on the prescription as every six hours "around the clock."

How long. A mistake that is all too easy to make is to assume that because a child acts well, he or she *is* well. Taking a child off medication too soon can cause relapses and complications. The symptoms of an illness can subside long before the illness itself is over. The child's earache goes away, the fever drops, the appetite returns to normal, and the parent thinks the child is well again. In fact, the healing process may barely have begun. Strep infections, for example, require ten straight days of antibiotic treatment. Some infections—urinary tract and ear infections, for instance—often take even longer, even though the symptoms may disappear in a day.

Therefore, instructions such as "Give for ten full days," "Continue for two weeks," "Give until finished," are not just so many words. They are precise and necessary directions to you from the doctor. Consider such an instruction not as a request, but as an order.

How to. It's best to let your child find out early that taking medication is just one of those things children have to do now and then. It is one of those situations in which you are the boss and the child doesn't have a choice in the matter.

Every parent needs to know how to give a child medicine, and the parent who reports to the doctor that "my child just won't take your medication" is forcing the doctor to resort to another method of treatment which may be less effective. In extreme cases, a child who cannot be medicated at home must be hospitalized so that the appropriate medications can be given by professionals.

A young child, approached in a reassuring and matter-of-fact manner, will usually accept medication without any trouble. There are ways in which you can make it easy for both you and the child.

Liquid medicine can be given directly from the spoon (after carefully measuring)—in fact, many medications designed for children are specially flavored so that they are not unpleasant to taste. An alternative method is to use a nonglass medicine dropper to squirt the liquid slowly into the child's cheek. If you use this method you must be very careful not to direct the stream of liquid forcefully against the back of the throat and down the windpipe.

If the medicine doesn't taste good, give the child a sweet treat afterwards to take away the bad taste (or disguise the medicine in a little applesauce, ice cream, or juice). If you do this, however, make sure the child takes the entire portion.

Some infants and toddlers will accept medicine in the form of chewable tablets, or even regular tablets or capsules that can be swallowed whole. However, do not give pills and capsules to even a cooperative child under the age of five. Small children can easily choke to death on a bulky pill. If the medication for the young child is not available in liquid form, mash tablets or empty the contents of capsules into a small quantity of juice or food before giving them to the child. Again, you must watch to see the child gets the whole dose.

After the age of five or six your child can probably swallow tablets or capsules whole. You can help the child learn how to do this by taking advantage of occasions when he or she needs a nonprescription remedy—aspirin for a slight headache, perhaps. If the child is willing, show him or her how to put the pill on the back of the tongue and swallow it with a drink or with a half-teaspoonful of ice cream, applesauce, or jelly. It's also possible to buy a special glass that delivers the pill into the mouth automatically with the first gulp of liquid. Whenever a child is taking a pill, watch to be sure the medication goes down smoothly and the child is in no danger of choking.

A final word: don't ever try to fool a child into taking medication by saying it's "candy" or "just like candy." Very many cases of drug poisoning have occurred in children who helped themselves to medications that looked or tasted like candy. Many doctors even discourage the use of children's vitamin pills that are sweet-flavored, brightly colored, or shaped like cartoon characters. Such products blur the distinction in the child's mind between candy and drugs and the child may make a tragic mistake.

The medicine chest

Although most of the medications your child will take will be on a doctor's prescription, there are certain items every parent ought to have on hand at home. Some of these are nonprescription medications that you can buy over the counter at your drugstore. These are usually called OTC medications. Other items, like a thermometer, are basics of a home health care kit. You'll also need antiseptics, ointments, gauze pads, and bandages in preparation for the inevitable bangs, bruises, scrapes, cuts, and other minor crises of childhood.

When you're assembling this kit, however, remember a few safety rules:

- Do not buy or administer any but the most basic drugs without the advice of a doctor.

- Only buy medications in containers that have child-proof caps. Keep all medications in their original, clearly-labeled containers.

- Unless your child takes a prescription medication on a regular basis, do not keep leftover medicines. Flush liquids and pills or capsules down the toilet and throw out the containers.

- Keep all medications locked away from children. If you and your young child are visiting friends who do not have children, make sure that no dangerous substances are within reach of the child.

ASPIRIN AND ACETAMINOPHEN

Aspirin is probably the most commonly used home remedy of all and the one parents think of at once in the face of any crisis. Acetaminophen is a nonaspirin alternative with similar properties. Both are available as flavored, chewable tablets, and in liquid form, and aspirin is available in the form of rectal suppositories. Both come in different strengths, and when you buy you should check the label to make sure that the strength is appropriate to the age of your child. Aspirin or acetaminophen tablets can be crushed and mixed with a little applesauce, jelly, or ice cream to make them more acceptable to the child. Whenever you disguise a medicine this way, however, you must be careful to watch that the child takes the whole dose. Aspirin suppositories should not be used. Their rate of absorption is uneven, and they present a greater risk of aspirin poisoning than other forms of this drug.

Until recently, aspirin substitutes such as acetaminophen were used primarily when a child couldn't take aspirin for one reason or another. It has now been suggested, however, that the use of aspirin, especially when given to a child with chicken pox or the flu, may be associated with a condition known as Reye's syndrome. This is a relatively rare form of encephalitis (inflammation of the brain) that also involves the liver.

Although it has not been proven that aspirin causes or promotes Reye's syndrome, it is recommended that aspirin not be given to

The following alphabetical list of basic medical supplies for your home should see you through most nonemergency situations.

Acetaminophen
Adhesive bandages
  (assorted sizes)
Adhesive tape
Antibiotic ointment
Antiseptic solution and/or soap
Aspirin
Decongestant

Emetic—syrup of ipecac
Knitted roller bandage
Lubricant—petroleum jelly
Nasal aspirator
Nose drops
Sterile gauze pads (various sizes)
Steristrips
Thermometer

children with chicken pox or influenza. Acetaminophen, however, has not been linked to Reye's syndrome and is an acceptable substitute. If you are in any doubt about the use of aspirin or acetaminophen for your child, consult your doctor.

EMETIC

An emetic is used to induce vomiting in certain cases of swallowed poison. Every medicine chest should contain an emetic, and syrup of ipecac is recommended. It's convenient to have two small bottles, each containing a single dose of two to three teaspoonfuls for immediate use. Note, however, that vomiting should not be induced automatically in a case of poisoning. If the poison is an item not normally edible—such as gasoline, turpentine, cleaning fluid—you should *not* make the child vomit because the poison may do more harm on the way back. Refer to the section on *Poisoning* for more information.

NOSE DROPS, NASAL ASPIRATOR, AND DECONGESTANT

Along with aspirin and acetaminophen, these items are useful in treating the symptoms of common colds. Ask your doctor to recommend types and uses.

THERMOMETER AND LUBRICANT

A multipurpose, stubby-bulb thermometer, which can be used rectally, is most practical. Any lubricating ointment will serve to grease a thermometer for rectal use, but a water-soluble gel is superior because it readily washes off in cold water.

ADDITIONS

The following are useful for treating minor accidents: antiseptic solution, antibiotic ointment, sterile gauze pads (2 x 2 and 3 x 3 inches), rolls of knitted bandage (two-inch and three-inch wide), adhesive tape (one-quarter inch wide), steristrips, and adhesive bandages of assorted sizes.

Immunizations

Despite the availability of vaccines that effectively protect children against diseases that used to be killers, surveys repeatedly indicate that almost 50 percent of American children are inadequately protected against these diseases.

The seven potentially devastating diseases against which all children can and should be properly immunized are: diphtheria, tetanus, whooping cough (pertussis), polio, measles, mumps, and rubella.

There are two reasons why so many children go unprotected against these diseases. First, many parents believe that polio, diphtheria, and whooping cough no longer exist. Second, people don't realize how dangerous these and the other four diseases are. Children die or are permanently disabled each year as a result of these preventable diseases. The statistics prove that children *are* in danger from these diseases, and without immunization your child is also at risk.

Doctors use two types of immunization:

Active (live) immunization is done by injecting a weakened or killed virus or bacterium into the body. This stimulates the body's natural defense system. The body produces substances known as antibodies, carried in the bloodstream, which are tailor-made to fight the invading organisms. The antibodies remain in the body for years, sometimes a lifetime, to protect it against that particular disease.

Passive (dead) immunization involves injecting ready-made antibodies—usually extracted from the blood of animals that have been immunized for the purpose of producing antibodies to be used in passive immunization. Passive immunization is only temporary but serves to protect a person who may already be infected until the body has time to create its own antibodies.

The following sections explain how you can protect your child against these diseases. Refer to the appropriate article for full information on the symptoms, diagnosis and treatment of each one.

DIPHTHERIA, TETANUS, AND WHOOPING COUGH (PERTUSSIS)

In order to be protected against these three diseases, infants must receive three injections of the combined DTP (diphtheria, tetanus, pertussis) vaccine by the age of six months. The first injection is given at two months, followed by two more administered every other month. The child must receive a booster shot of DTP at age 18 to 24 months and another booster shot at age four to six years. Thereafter, a booster of diphtheria-tetanus vaccine is necessary every ten years for life.

Diphtheria. Diphtheria is a bacterial disease that is frequently fatal. It causes infection of the nose, throat, tonsils, and lymph nodes of the neck. The bacterium responsible can produce a toxin (poison) that causes heart damage and paralysis. Cases of diphtheria are reported in every state every year. For every case reported there are many other persons who are carriers of diphtheria. (A carrier is a person who harbors the disease without getting sick him- or herself, and who can transmit it to other people.)

Before the diphtheria vaccine came into general use 40 years ago, 80 percent of adult Americans were immune to diphtheria because they had had some form of the illness in childhood. This situation no longer exists, so adults should receive booster shots of diphtheria vaccine every ten years. Serious reactions to the diphtheria vaccine, which is a dead vaccine, are rare.

Tetanus. Tetanus, or lockjaw, is a disease of the nervous system that can enter the body through a wound—even a minor wound like a scratch or an insect bite. Like diphtheria, tetanus cases also occur every year. Although the vaccine is thoroughly safe and effective, its protection weakens over the years and booster shots are required. Medical opinion differs as to how often boosters should be given. The American Academy of Pediatrics states that after the age of four to six a child should receive a booster every ten years.

The American College of Surgeons believes that boosters are necessary every five years to insure protection from tetanus that results from the type of minor wound that is unlikely to be treated by a doctor. In general, clean wounds, such as those from kitchen utensils, require boosters every ten years; dirty wounds, such as those from rusty nails, barbed wire, and others that happen outdoors, require boosters every five years. For example, if your child has a wound from a rusty nail, check to see if he or she has received a booster within the last five years. Adults should receive boosters at least every ten years.

Whooping cough. Whooping cough is more common than many parents (and doctors) realize. It is a highly contagious infection of the respiratory tract, and it gets its name from the severe, strangling cough that develops as the disease progresses. Whooping cough vaccine is the most uncertain of the three components of the DTP vaccine, and it does not always give complete immunity. There have been extremely rare instances of brain damage following its use, but in some of these cases the damage was caused by faulty administration of the vaccine rather than by the vaccine itself. The vaccine may also cause a brief reaction of fever. For these reasons, routine boosters are not recommended after the child is four to six years old. However, the mortality rate among infants under age one who contract whooping cough and the possibility of complications in older children are high enough to exceed by far the minimal risk of the vaccine.

In England, serious reactions to the vaccine were sufficiently frequent at one point to persuade the medical profession to suspend its use. However, because of the increasing incidence of whooping cough and its severe complications, immunization has now been reinstituted in England.

POLIO

Polio, also known as poliomyelitis or infantile paralysis, is an infection of the spinal cord that can, in 1 to 2 percent of cases, lead to paralysis or death.

Outbreaks of polio do still occur in this country, and infants should receive two or three doses of live vaccine (Sabin, containing types 1, 2, and 3). The first dose should be given at two months, with the second and third doses separated by intervals of six weeks to two months. This vaccine is given by mouth, not as an injection. A booster series should be given at the age of one-and-a-half to two years, and again at four to six years. Children who were not immunized in infancy should receive a total of three or four doses, depending on their ages. The Sabin vaccine is undoubtedly safe for children.

Adults who are not immune and who plan to travel to a country where polio is uncontrolled should also be immunized. In fact, all adults should be immunized against this disease. Some medical authorities believe that the risk of an adult being exposed to polio within the United States is minimal, and therefore adult immunization is unnecessary. However, too many cases of polio have occurred in adults over the age of 30 to make this argument acceptable.

The Sabin vaccine does carry a slight risk of polio for adults. However, the Salk vaccine (which is a dead vaccine) does not. Adults who are not immune should receive an initial series of Salk vaccine to acquire temporary immunity, followed by a full series of Sabin vaccine for permanent protection.

MEASLES, MUMPS, RUBELLA

The live triple measles-mumps-rubella (MMR) vaccine should be given to children after the age of 15 months. It confers long-term—probably lifelong—immunity against all three diseases.

Measles. Measles is a contagious viral disease that affects mainly the respiratory system, the eyes, and the skin. It is considered dangerous mainly because its complications can include pneumonia (infection of the lungs), encephalitis (inflammation of the brain), and ear infections. Because children are now vaccinated against it, measles is seldom seen today. The risk of a child contracting encephalitis from the vaccine is less than one in a million, and pneumonia and ear infections are never seen with immunization.

Mumps. Mumps is a contagious viral disease that causes swelling of the parotid glands, which are the saliva glands beneath the ear. Mumps can be painful and uncomfortable, but seldom has long-term complications. The most serious complication of mumps is encephalitis (inflammation of the brain) which can be followed by hearing loss or deafness. The mumps vaccine, which is included in the MMR vaccine, is harmless to the child and is 95 percent effective in preventing the disease.

Rubella. Rubella, or German measles, is a contagious viral disease that produces mild, cold-like symptoms and a short-lived rash. The disease is not usually dangerous except when it is contracted by a pregnant woman. In the first three to four months of the pregnancy, rubella can affect the unborn child and cause serious, lifelong problems. Now that the vaccine is available and routinely given to young children, rubella is fairly uncommon. The last major outbreak was in 1964–65. However, a pregnant woman should take care to avoid exposure to the disease, and a child who contracts rubella should be kept away from anyone who is or might be pregnant. Very rarely, the rubella vaccine causes transient (temporary) arthritis in older children.

SMALLPOX

Vaccination against smallpox, a highly contagious disease that used to appear in epidemics, is no longer practiced in the United States. The risk of the live vaccine, although minimal, is still greater than the risk of contracting smallpox. It is anticipated that smallpox will be eradicated from the entire world in the near future.

OTHER VACCINES

Vaccines against typhoid, typhus, yellow fever, influenza, Rocky Mountain spotted fever, meningitis, and pneumonia are presently available. None of these is yet recommended for children except in instances when the child will be at special risk. Consult your doctor if you are in doubt. A vaccine against chicken pox is being worked on but is not yet available.

Related topics: Diphtheria, Influenza, Measles, Meningitis, Mumps, Pneumonia, Polio, Rocky Mountain spotted fever, Rubella, Tetanus, Whooping cough

The physical examination

The medical care of a child is usually aimed at preventing serious illness. This is why children should be examined regularly by a doctor or other health professional. The child need not be ill at the time of these visits. In fact, if the child is sick, the routine examination may be delayed until the child has recovered. These routine visits to the doctor are sometimes called "well-child" or "well-baby" checkups. They are often planned at the same times as required immunization.

Although they are extremely important, immunizations are only a small part of keeping your child healthy. At the time of the checkup the child also should be examined thoroughly, have routine tests, be measured to find out if he or she is growing normally, and have his or her physical and mental development evaluated.

For a baby or a small child, the measurements include height or length, weight, and also head circumference. The changes in these measurements as the child grows can be charted on a graph, and compared to the normal range of child development. If the child is not growing normally over a period of time, the doctor will check to see if the problem is caused by a growth disorder or by some other disease or abnormality. If such problems are found early, they can sometimes be corrected before any lasting damage is done.

THE FIRST VISIT

A baby's first visit to the doctor's office is usually between two and four weeks after birth, and this visit serves several purposes. For one thing, it gives the parent, the doctor, and the child an opportunity to meet together and begin a relationship. The parent can get to know the doctor and the customs of the practice, the doctor can get basic information about the family, and the child's general health can be evaluated. At this first visit the doctor will take the baby's physical measurements. This initial information is necessary so that the child's development can be followed from the beginning of life. The doctor will also examine the baby for abnormalities. Some babies are born with physical problems and abnormalities that are obvious right away. Other inborn problems do not show up until a few weeks after birth.

At the first visit, the doctor will ask questions about the parents' health and health history as well as examine the baby. Some medical problems can be inherited, and some can run in families. It is important for the new baby's medical record to show such background information. If the child later shows signs of problems that have appeared before in the family, the doctor will be able to make a diagnosis more quickly.

The first visit will also include checking to see that the umbilical cord is healing as it should, that the circumcision (if it was done) is healing, and that the child has had no ill effects from labor and delivery. Feeding schedules, vitamins, and immunizations will be discussed as well. Usually a schedule of regular return visits is made up at the first visit. The number and spacing of the visits will depend on the baby's health, the parents' needs and wishes, and when the baby should have immunizations.

If the baby's health and development seem to be normal, some or all of the later visits may be handled by a pediatric nurse practitioner, a physician's assistant, or another health professional. These people are specially trained to be an extension of the doctor. They can work with you to clear up any questions you have about taking care of your baby. Of course, any question or problem that the nurse or assistant cannot handle is referred to the doctor.

LATER VISITS

As the child grows past babyhood, questions will come up about how to handle toilet training, rivalries with brothers and sisters, obedience, temper tantrums, and the like. These are areas where your doctor and the staff can help. Go ahead and ask about them. A child's doctor is not concerned only with the child's physical body. Social and psychological development are also a part of every child's growth and affect health in many ways.

THE DOCTOR'S PROCEDURES

In a complete physical examination, the doctor uses a combination of his or her senses and knowledge of the body to check over your child, system by system. The doctor uses instruments to extend the senses. For example, the stethoscope magnifies sounds, and the otoscope (for examining the ears) and ophthalmoscope (for examining the eyes) have lights and magnifying lenses in them to extend the doctor's vision.

In the process of an examination, the doctor will look at the child's skin, ears, eyes, nose, bone structure, and body openings. He or she will feel the lymph nodes and other organs that can be felt through the skin. The doctor will tap body cavities and listen to the sounds that result. He or she will also listen to the sounds made by the heart, the lungs, and the digestive system. A blood pressure reading is an important part of the child's examination from an early age.

The doctor's senses are further extended by laboratory tests. Some of these tests are routine, such as vision and hearing tests, hemoglobin and hematocrit blood tests, and urinalysis. These tests are discussed elsewhere in this book. Other tests may be done if the doctor finds a possible problem.

Each physical examination your child has will vary, depending on the child's age, stage of development, and state of health. During the first six months the doctor will be giving particular attention to the baby's growth and development, including how well the baby is learning to move and control his or her muscles. The doctor will also check to be sure the hips are stable and listen for heart murmurs, which may be normal or may indicate heart problems. The doctor will take the pulse at the baby's groin (the femoral pulses) to be sure that there is no obstruction to blood flow in the aorta (the main artery carrying blood to the lower part of the body). The baby's developing language skills are also an important part of growth, and the doctor will ask about progress in that area.

After about six months, the child may begin to be afraid of the doctor. The child may just cry, or may be actively uncooperative. This will, of course, make the physical examination and conversation more difficult for the doctor, but a doctor who deals with children every day knows what to expect. You can help make the examination go more smoothly by trying to reassure or distract your child. If your efforts and the doctor's fail, the doctor will get as much information as possible under the circumstances.

THE PARENT'S ROLE

Especially with younger children and babies, you will play an important role in the examination. Most of the time, the doctor will want you to be present. Your presence has two main purposes: you can learn about your child's health; and you can comfort and reassure your child during the examination. An infant is often examined on the parent's lap, and you may also be asked to help with measuring the child and taking his or her temperature.

If you have questions during the examination, be sure to ask them, even if you think they may sound silly, or feel that you ought to know the answers already. Part of the doctor's job is answering your questions. The more you know about how to care for your child, the better off both you and the child will be. You will, after all, be responsible for carrying out the doctor's instructions when your child is sick. The doctor needs you to be well informed.

Medical tests

Laboratory tests are used by doctors to help identify illnesses, to determine what particular type of infectious organism is causing a problem, and to learn how serious a disease may be. Some procedures can be performed right in the doctor's office; others must be done in a laboratory where more complex equipment is available. Some common tests and procedures are described here.

URINALYSIS

Urinalysis means analysis of a specimen of urine, the liquid form of body waste. Urine tests can reveal infections in the kidneys, the bladder, and the rest of the urinary tract. The chemical and cell content of urine can also show how well the digestive system is working.

Urine can be tested in four different ways. First, it can be examined visually for color and texture. Normal urine is a clear yellow; if it is cloudy, reddish, or some other color, an infection or an injury may be present in the body. Second, the water content of the urine can be measured. This shows how well the kidneys are doing their job of filtering the body's wastes. Third, the chemical content of the urine can be analyzed, to find out if the body is discarding necessary chemicals that should be retained. Finally, the urine can be examined under a microscope to find out what cells, bacteria, and other material are present. This is done to identify an infection or disease more exactly.

Chemical analysis of urine is often used as a screening test for diabetes, a disease in which the body does not properly use the carbohydrates (sugars and starches) that are its chief sources of energy. To test for diabetes, the amount of glucose (a form of sugar) in the urine is measured by dipping a chemically treated stick in the urine and comparing the color of the stick with a color chart. If the glucose is above a certain level, diabetes may be the cause. Additional blood tests are then done to verify the diagnosis.

BLOOD TESTS

Blood circulates throughout the body, so the contents of the blood can provide information both about general health and about specific diseases. The blood to be tested is drawn out of a vein with a syringe, or taken by pricking a finger. The method used to take a sample or specimen depends on how much blood is needed for the tests that are to be done, and also how "clean" the specimen needs to be. A fingerstick sample is more likely to be contaminated by contact with the surface of the finger than is a sample taken by putting a sterile needle into a vein.

Many different tests can be done on the blood, and a few of the most common ones are described here. (More complex tests can be done to find out what chemicals are present in the blood.)

Hematocrit. This test is done to find out how much of the blood is made up of red blood cells, which carry oxygen to the body tissues. The blood sample is spun in a machine called a centrifuge, which makes it separate into red blood cells, white blood cells, and plasma. The red cells are the heaviest, so they sink to the bottom. The percentage of red cells is then determined and compared to the normal range.

Hemoglobin. Hemoglobin is a protein that gives red blood cells their red color; it also combines with oxygen so that the oxygen can be carried in the blood. A hemoglobin test is often done at the same time as a hematocrit. The amount of hemoglobin in the blood is tested by adding certain chemicals to the blood and then measuring the intensity of the red color that signifies hemoglobin.

These two tests are done to check for anemia, red blood cell deficiency.

White blood cell count. White blood cells are part of the body's defense against infection. Too many or too few of these cells in the blood may indicate an infection or a blood disorder. To count the white blood cells, a blood specimen is diluted and put in a counting chamber, which is a slide with a grid on it. The slide is examined under a microscope and the cells are counted. This test can be done in most doctor's offices.

Differential blood count. There are five different types of white blood cells; each type has a distinctive shape and appearance, and each one has a different function. To get more precise information about a disease, the doctor may need to know how many of each type of white blood cells are present in the blood. To do this, a stain is added to a blood specimen; because the stain affects each type of white blood cell differently, it is then easier to tell them apart. The stained specimen is examined under a microscope, and at least 100 white blood cells are identified and classified. The cells are also examined to see if they are a normal shape. In the course of this test the red blood cells can also be counted and checked for abnormalities.

Sedimentation rate. Sedimentation rate means the speed at which red blood cells move through the blood and settle in the bottom of a container. A rapid sedimentation rate is a sign of disease. To test the rate of settling, a chemical is added to a blood sample to keep it from clotting. Then the red cells are timed as they slowly move to the bottom of a specially marked test tube. This test is used to screen for diseases, but it does not identify exactly what is causing the cells to fall more quickly than normal. Keeping track of the sedimentation rate in successive tests can help a physician follow the progress of diseases that cause inflammation, including rheumatic fever and rheumatoid arthritis.

THROAT CULTURES

A throat culture is done to find out if a throat infection is being caused by bacteria and, if

so, to identify the specific bacteria. This can provide the doctor with important information. If the infection is due to a virus rather than to a bacterium, the doctor will know not to prescribe antibiotics because viruses don't respond to antibiotics; if a bacterium is the cause, knowing which one it is will enable the doctor to prescribe the correct antibiotic to treat that particular type of bacteria.

To collect material for the culture the doctor uses a swab tipped with cotton to scrape cells and discharge from the throat. This material is put into a growth medium, a solution that encourages bacteria to grow. The specimen is watched carefully, and the bacteria are identified. A throat culture is often sent to a laboratory for testing, so it may take 48 hours to get the results.

OTHER CULTURES

Although throat cultures are the most common cultures, bacteria from other sites can be identified by the same method. Cultures can be made from blood, discharge from an infected eye or ear, discharge coughed up from the lungs, bowel movements, urine, or discharge from infected cuts or wounds. As with a throat culture, material from the site is sent to a laboratory, then placed in a growth medium to see what types of bacteria grow and how many there are of each type.

ELECTROCARDIOGRAM (ECG OR EKG)

An electrocardiogram, or ECG, is a recording of the electrical impulses of the heart. These impulses are what makes the heart beat in a regular rhythm. To make such a record, an ECG machine is attached to the patient with electrodes, metal plates that are placed on the arms, legs, and chest. These electrodes pick up the electrical impulses that move through the body. The impulses cause a needle in the machine to move on a piece of paper, as the paper moves through the machine. Where the needle touches the paper, it makes a line. The physician studies the pattern on the paper to see if the heart rhythm is normal.

The ECG does not hurt the patient, but it is important for the patient to stay very still while the recording is done. All muscle movements, not just movements of the heart muscle, are caused by electrical impulses. Therefore, any movement can affect the ECG recording and give an inaccurate picture of the heartbeat.

An ECG is done to check for irregular heart rhythms (arrhythmias), an enlarged heart, heart valve disorders, heart malformations, and many other heart disorders. The test can be done in a doctor's office or an outpatient laboratory.

ELECTROENCEPHALOGRAM (EEG)

An electroencephalogram, or EEG, is a recording of electrical activity in the brain. It is a painless procedure similar to an ECG. The metal plates known as electrodes are attached to the patient's head and to an EEG machine. The electrodes pick up the brain's electrical impulses. These impulses activate a needle, which traces the pattern of the impulses on a piece of paper moving through the machine. The physician compares the pattern on the recording to patterns of normal brain activity, and determines if there is an abnormality. Recordings from opposite sides of the brain can also be compared to see if the patterns match.

An EEG is done to test for epilepsy, brain tumors, encephalitis (inflammation of the brain), and other brain disorders.

LUMBAR PUNCTURE OR SPINAL TAP

A lumbar puncture, also known as a spinal tap, is the method used to obtain a sample of cerebrospinal fluid for testing. Cerebrospinal fluid is a clear liquid that surrounds the brain and the spinal cord. In a lumbar puncture, which is usually done in the hospital, a needle is used to penetrate into the spine at the lower end, between two spinal bones called lumbar vertebrae, and draw out the fluid. The pressure in the spinal column can be measured at the same time. The fluid is examined to see if it is clear or cloudy and to see if it contains any blood. It is then tested for viruses, bacteria, and other signs of infection.

A lumbar puncture may be done to test for meningitis, encephalitis, brain hemmorrhage (bleeding in the brain), polio, and other nervous system disorders. Under the usual circumstances, there is no risk from a lumbar puncture. If the spinal fluid is under extreme pressure, however, the procedure carries some risk of complications; a different technique is then used to minimize risk.

CAT SCAN

A CAT scan is a sophisticated type of X ray. The initials stand for Computerized Axial Tomography. In a CAT scan, a series of special X rays are made of a part of the body such as the head or the torso. The patient is placed in a tunnel-like opening in the machine, and does not have to be repositioned for each picture as is done for ordinary X rays. This way, pictures can easily be taken from many different angles. A computer then assembles those X rays into a single picture which shows a cross-section of that part of the body. The whole process takes only a few seconds. CAT scans are used to find abnormal growths or other problems in areas that are inside the body and therefore difficult to see without time-consuming and potentially dangerous exploratory surgery. For example, the brain can be examined for an abnormal growth without opening up the skull.

CAT scans are usually done in a hospital. The equipment for the procedure is expensive, and a limited number of scanners is available. Sometimes a patient must be transported to another hospital, or even to another town, for this test, because a scanner is not available in his or her home town.

The normal newborn baby

Every baby is different. Although this section is especially intended for first-time parents, anyone who has a new baby may need to be reminded of things they think they know about parenthood. If you expect your second baby to be just like your first, you may be in for a surprise.

One thing that is easy to forget is how tiny even the healthiest, heftiest baby really is. A newborn usually is only 18 to 21 inches long, stretched out. And very young babies often keep their legs in the pre-birth, folded-up position for several months, which makes the baby seem even smaller. The baby was in that position for many months before birth, and it takes a while to get used to an un-cramped environment.

Remember that at birth the baby has left a warm, dark, still, safe environment, been pushed through a narrow birth canal, and been suddenly thrust into light, noise, and a new degree of independence. It's a difficult adjustment to make, even more difficult than the adjustment you must make as new parents.

There are some other things about a new baby's appearance that may worry you if you're not prepared. It is perfectly normal for a newborn baby to be:
- born with a bluish tinge to the skin, which soon turns to pinkish-red;
- born with a slightly lopsided head;
- born with soft spots, called "fontanelles," above the forehead and at the top of the head.

It is also quite common for a new baby to have jaundice, which gives a yellowish color to the skin and the whites of the eyes. Also, at birth the baby still has a lot of growing and developing to do. Many bones are still unformed; they are made of tough, elastic tissue called cartilage that will gradually harden into bone. The legs are often bowed, and shorter than you'd expect when you compare them to the arms. The head may seem too big for the body. The baby's face may seem abnormally plump in the cheeks and flat in the nose. The eyes will not move together well and may seem to be crossed. The genitals, especially on a baby boy, may seem abnormally large.

In a few months, the baby will begin to look more like an individual. Movements of limbs, eyes, and neck will become more controlled as muscles develop, and the face will become more alert and expressive.

ROUTINE TESTS FOR A NEWBORN BABY

Certain tests are done on each new baby to check for abnormalities. Many minor problems can be taken care of before the baby leaves the hospital. Others can be treated by the parents at home. Some other problems that appear at birth must be detected early so that they can be corrected before they become serious.

One test that is required in most states is a screening test on samples of the baby's blood and urine to check for PKU, or phenyl-ketonuria. This rare disorder can cause brain damage and mental retardation. But, if it is detected right away, changes can be made in the baby's diet to prevent such damage. Other routine tests may be done as well, depending on where you live. Your doctor may recommend additional tests.

SPECIAL SUPPLIES AND EQUIPMENT

Before you bring your baby home, you will want to have everything you need on hand.

Clothes. A newborn baby usually needs only diapers and soft nightgowns for sleeping and extra sheets or blankets. Overdressing a baby can cause heat rash. Babies spit up on and otherwise dirty their clothes, sometimes many times a day, so be sure you have plenty. You don't want to spend all your time washing.

Diapers. Diapers can be made of reusable cloth or disposable paper. The initial cost of new diapers may be high, but cloth diapers can be used for many years. Paper diapers cost more in the long run. Many parents use paper diapers for the first few weeks, for convenience in the initial adjustment period, then switch to cloth when a routine is established.

Skin cleaner. Many doctors recommend using just a mild soap and water to keep your baby clean. Do not use oils, lotions, or powders; clear water is best. A baby's skin can be very sensitive, and scented products can be irritating. Some babies are allergic to certain lotions and creams.

Bed. You can use a cradle or bassinet for a new baby, but a crib will work just as well and save the investment in a smaller bed that the baby will soon outgrow. Choose a crib with one side that drops, so that you can easily reach the baby. Make sure the catch is out of the baby's reach; it won't be long before the child is standing up in bed. Also, be sure the rails are close enough together so that the baby's head won't fit through them.

Mattress. The mattress should be firm, and covered with a plastic sheet. Put a regular fitted sheet over the plastic cover. Make sure the mattress is no more than half an inch from the sides of the crib, so the baby can't get wedged into the crack.

Toys. Babies like toys that are brightly colored. Soft toys are safest in the early months. Avoid sharp edges. Remember that soon everything will go into the baby's mouth, so be sure toys are safe *and* washable. Mobiles and music boxes are interesting and stimulating, but be sure they are either out of reach or safe for the baby to touch.

COMING HOME

When you come home from the hospital with a new baby, a brand-new period of your life begins. It may take several weeks, or even several months, for the mother to recover from the physical stress of labor and delivery. At the same time, the new baby is completely dependent on the parents for food, shelter, and comfort. To accommodate the mother's physical tiredness and the baby's constant needs, you may have to review what is most important to you as a family. For example, keeping the house spotless may have to take second place to caring for the baby and allowing the mother to get the extra rest she needs. Household jobs may have to be reassigned so that the mother can devote more time to the baby. Your social schedule may have to change as well. You may find that your preferences have changed, and you would rather stay home with the baby than go to a party or a movie. This certainly does not mean you must—or should—give up going

out or never do the things you enjoy. It only means that your priorities will probably change when you have an infant in your household.

FEEDING

In the first months of life, eating is a major concern of your baby. This activity will take up a lot of your time and a lot of your energy. But whether you breast-feed or bottle-feed your baby, feeding time is a time of closeness. You are giving the baby nourishment and thus meeting the child's most basic need. At the same time you are holding and cuddling the baby, and he or she is getting to know your touch and your voice.

BURPING THE BABY

As the baby nurses, from the bottle or the breast, air is swallowed along with the milk. Burping the baby helps to expel excess air and prevent discomfort. Interrupt the feeding once in the middle for a burp, and also burp the baby after a feeding. Expelling extra air in the middle of the meal ensures that the baby's stomach will fill up with food, not air.

To burp an infant, put the baby over your shoulder, sit the baby up on your lap, or place face down across your lap. Pat or rub the baby's back gently until you hear a good, solid burp. Some babies prefer one position while others need to be moved around until they burp. If burping is difficult, experiment with different positions and combinations of patting and rubbing. Some babies will protest the interruption of the meal, but burp them anyway at midmeal. They will get more nourishment and your life will be easier.

SPITTING UP

Many babies spit up either as they are being burped or a little while after a feeding. This is normal. Check with your doctor if the baby is spitting up large amounts, is having projectile vomiting (forceful, explosive vomiting), or does not appear to be gaining weight. Consult your doctor if the baby is spitting up and also seems hungry all the time, or becomes limp and not alert.

To reduce spitting up, try burping the baby more often during a feeding, or changing the feeding position slightly so that the baby is more upright. It may help to have the baby rest quietly in an infant seat for a few minutes after feeding, rather than laying the baby down or encouraging active playing.

THE PACIFIER

Babies need to suck a certain amount each day. If your baby acts hungry but only takes a small amount of food, he or she probably only needed to suck. If this happens consistently, a pacifier is a great help. It meets the baby's need to suck but spares you the inconvenience of trying to feed a baby who really isn't hungry. After about six months (remember, all babies are different and this may vary), the baby will no longer need extra sucking. Then you can take away the pacifier.

BREAST-FEEDING

Many doctors today recommend breast-feeding, if it is possible, for a number of reasons. First, breast milk passes on to the baby some of the mother's own resistance to infections. Second, many babies develop allergies to infant formulas, but it is rare for a baby to be allergic to the mother's milk. Third, breast-feeding is much more convenient than bottle-feeding, because it is always available and needs no sterilizing, mixing, or refrigeration. Fourth, the experience of breast-feeding is emotionally satisfying for both mother and baby.

Even if you breast-feed, you can give the baby an occasional bottle or give one feeding a day by bottle. This can give you a chance to be away from the baby sometimes or to sleep through the night while the baby's father gives a feeding. The breasts can be emptied with a breast pump if they become uncomfortably full.

BOTTLE-FEEDING

If you are bottle-feeding, you must have clean water and refrigeration available. Be sure to clean the top of the can before you open it, and follow the directions carefully when you're preparing the formula. Some formulas are concentrated, so you must add water. Others are "ready to feed," and if you dilute this type the baby will not get enough to eat.

Bottles and nipples must be cleaned and sterilized through the baby's fourth month. After that, only the nipples must be sterile. To sterilize, clean the nipples with soap and water, making sure the hole in the top is not clogged with dried formula. Then boil them in water for 15 minutes. Bottles should be cleaned first and then sterilized. After four months, the bottles can be washed in hot water or in a dishwasher.

Hold and rock the baby when you're bottle-feeding. Do not prop the bottle up and leave the baby alone to eat. Human contact is important to the baby's development, so don't rush the feeding time. However, try not to spend more than a half-hour to 45 minutes on each feeding.

Whether you are breast-feeding or bottle-feeding, remember that your baby's appetite is generally a reliable measure of how much he or she needs to eat. A characteristic, demanding cry will let you know when the baby is hungry. After a few weeks or months you'll probably be able to identify that hunger cry.

WHY BABIES CRY

It's normal for babies to cry. It is, after all, their only way of letting you know they need something. At first it may be difficult to figure out what the baby needs. In a newborn, though, there are only a few things a cry will signify: hunger, needing a diaper change, and needing to be held and comforted. As the baby grows up, he or she will find more reasons to complain: boredom, frustration, loneliness, fear, overstimulation, or maybe being too tired to go to sleep.

Sometimes you and your baby can get into a crying cycle. When the baby cries, you get anxious and nervous. The more the baby cries, the worse you feel, and nothing you do seems to help quiet the baby. The baby senses your feelings, your anxiety in turn makes the baby anxious and uncomfortable, and the child expresses these feelings by crying even more. If you find yourself getting into these cycles, talk about it with an experienced parent or your doctor. They may be able to suggest a solution.

Occasionally, a baby will cry because he or she is in pain. Check to see if you can figure out what is causing the pain. A sick baby may cry but will usually also have other symptoms of illness such as a fever, diarrhea, pulling on an ear, or a runny nose. Generally, a healthy baby will have a strong, loud cry. If your baby's cry becomes weak, contact your doctor right away.

WHAT TO EXPECT FROM YOUR BABY

For about the first month of life, or longer if the baby is born prematurely and is catching up, the baby will do little besides eat, sleep, and dirty diapers. An infant has a small stomach and can't eat very much at a time, but he or she is busy growing and developing and needs his or her meals. Feeding the baby the usual six to ten times a day is likely to be the biggest demand the baby makes on you. The rest of the time, the baby will probably sleep, and you may be able to catch up on your sleep too.

Every baby develops at a different rate, so the following description of a baby's development is only a guide. It will give you a general idea of what changes to expect in your baby over the first year or so of life. Many parents keep a baby book in which they note these events. But whether you record the baby's progress or not, it's fun to see a tiny infant that does nothing but eat and sleep develop into a person. Beware, though, of making comparisons between your child and your relatives' or neighbors' babies. Remember that each baby is unique. If a child is slow to say words or stand up, it doesn't mean that child is less intelligent than a cousin or a neighbor's child. But if your child lags far behind other children of the same age, check with your doctor. Basically here is what you can expect from your baby:

- At six weeks, the baby may be awake and playful, without crying, for half an hour after each feeding. This is about the time when you can expect those first spontaneous smiles.

- At three months, the baby also will follow the movement of a favorite toy dangled in front of his or her eyes.

- At four months, the baby will learn to roll over from front to back and at five months from back to front.

- Between the age of four and six months, the baby will learn to lift his or her head and shoulders, and by about six months will have enough muscle control to balance in a sitting position without support.

- Most babies begin to make simple, recognizable sounds such as "Da-da" or "Mama" at about eight months of age. This is the stage when they may try to use a spoon for the first time, and may or may not get the food into their mouths.

- At nine months, most babies can get to a sitting position from lying down and can pull up to a stand and walk holding onto furniture and walls. The baby may begin to crawl at any time now, but some babies skip crawling altogether. This is the time to "child-proof" your home and put harmful items out of reach.

- At about a year old, the baby may be able to stand up for a few seconds and may be taking a few steps alone. Luckily, 12 months is also when a baby begins to understand a few simple commands, like "NO!" In most cases, it will be a few more months before the baby is walking. By this time, your child will be eating only three to four times a day.

As your baby develops, his or her attention span and interests will also broaden gradually. A very small baby may watch a mobile for a few minutes, but then fall asleep or cry. As the child learns how to use arms and legs, he or she discovers the ability to make things move. The baby learns to grab for things, too. The eyes begin to focus better, so the baby can see more things. Still, a toy may hold a baby's interest for only five minutes before he or she needs to look at something different. As you play with your baby, you can see how long a game is satisfying. The complexities of the game and the time it holds the child's attention will slowly increase.

Using this medical guide

Each of the following articles is self-contained on two facing pages. On the right-hand page, the article begins with a clear description on what the particular disease or condition is, what causes it, and—in some cases—when or where it's more likely to occur. Some diseases, for instance, occur primarily in the first few years of the child's life; others are particularly common among adolescents; yet others tend to afflict people of a particular ethnic background.

Then, under the heading "Signs and Symptoms," are listed the clues that alert you to the fact that the child may have the condition, along with brief details about how the doctor will reach a firm diagnosis—by examining the child, for instance, or by having X rays or tests done.

Next, under "Home Care," are the measures you can take to make the child more comfortable, such as giving aspirin or acetaminophen to ease aches and pains, or performing simple first aid for a minor cut or scrape. You'll also learn when home treatment should not be attempted because the child should be seen by a doctor immediately. This section, in fact, will help you answer the question that tends to make every parent feel insecure: "Should I call the doctor, or should I be able to deal with this at home?"

Following this useful advice on home care, there's a list of definite do's and don'ts. They come under the heading of "Precautions" and include both measures to prevent your child from getting the disease in question (for example, by keeping vaccinations up to date) and suggestions about how to take care of the child if he or she does get sick. You'll also find practical information such as whether or not the child should be isolated, or should use separate towels and linens to avoid spreading an infection to other family members, or whether other family members should be treated at the same time even if they do not have definite symptoms of the condition.

This section also alerts you to possible complications that require medical attention, and points out any situations or developments that are normal and don't need a doctor's care—a useful way of finding out when it is *not* necessary to worry.

The final section of each article deals with medical treatment and tells you how a doctor goes about treating the condition. This section is designed to help you understand the doctor's orders and carry them out accurately so that your child gets well again as fast as possible. Here you'll also learn if any follow-up care or testing is going to be necessary once the child is well.

Perhaps of most importance to you as a parent is the left-hand page of each article. On this "Quick Reference" page appears a summary of the important facts about the symptoms, home care, and precautions for each condition. You can see at a glance what you need to know about the illness. Furthermore, a large "E," which stands for emergency, is in the upper left corner on those articles that deal with life-threatening conditions. An example of this would be the article on choking—a situation in which minutes count.

Acne

SYMPTOMS
Blackheads
Whiteheads
Pimples

HOME CARE
Wash with mild soap twice a day.

Apply acne preparations that contain sulfur, resorcin, salicylic acid, or mild benzoyl peroxide.

PRECAUTIONS

☐ Never allow X-ray treatment of acne.

☐ Avoid cosmetics that contain oil.

☐ Do not squeeze or pick pimples.

☐ See doctor if acne does not improve or if cysts develop.

☐ Do not treat acne in young infants.

Wash the affected skin area twice a day with a mild soap to control acne.

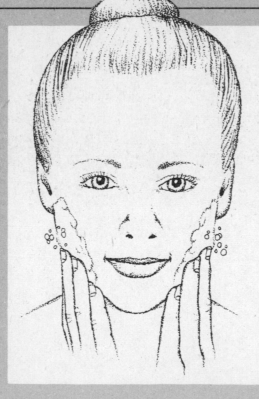

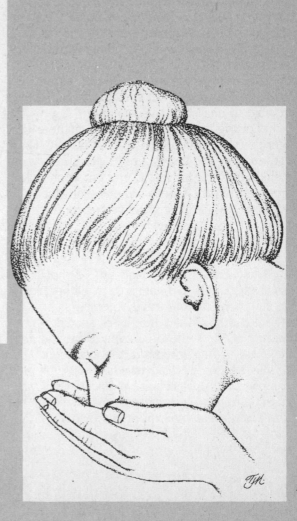

Acne is a condition of the skin that occurs most commonly during adolescence. Acne usually appears on the face, but it may also appear on the chest and back. In its mildest form, acne appears as large blackheads and whiteheads (blind blackheads). The formation of pimples occurs in a more severe case. The worst cases form cysts and scars.

For generations it was mistakenly thought that acne was caused by a lack of cleanliness and a diet of junk foods. Now it is believed that acne is caused by the action of hormones during the adolescent years. Pimples are caused by normal skin germs breaking down the oil in the blackheads and forming irritating substances. The pus that results is not an infection.

SIGNS AND SYMPTOMS

The skin breaks out in red bumps which may or may not be open. Lumps under the skin indicate that the acne has formed cysts.

HOME CARE

Wash the affected area with mild soap twice a day. After washing, apply acne preparations containing sulfur, resorcin, salicylic acid, or mild benzoyl peroxide. Large, unsightly blackheads can be gently removed with a blackhead spoon, available at your pharmacy. Changes in the teenager's diet are probably unnecessary.

PRECAUTIONS

• To avoid making a case of acne worse, adolescents should stay away from products that can irritate the skin, such as motor oil, gasoline, and oil-containing cosmetics. • Do not squeeze or pick pimples since scarring may result. • Do not treat acne in young infants. • If acne does not improve, or if cysts develop, see your doctor.

MEDICAL TREATMENT

Acne treatment has vastly improved in the past five years. Doctors now prescribe new vitamin A ointment or liquid and prescription-strength benzoyl peroxide that are applied to the skin. There is also a new medication taken by mouth for severe acne that forms cysts. Long-term treatment using tetracycline or other antibiotics taken by mouth is safe and effective. Applying antibiotics on the skin is still experimental, but promising. Disfiguring scars can be removed by a dermatologist or plastic surgeon without hospitalization once the acne is under control. **Never allow X-ray treatment of acne.**

Related topic:

Boils

Anemia

SYMPTOMS

Paleness of nailbeds
Paleness inside of eyelids
Paleness of membranes inside mouth
Tiredness
Shortness of breath
Rapid pulse

HOME CARE None. See your doctor.

PRECAUTIONS

☐ Never attempt to treat anemia without your doctor's advice.

☐ Give your children a balanced diet including proper nutrients.

☐ Keep iron supplements out of the reach of children. An overdose of iron can be serious.

☐ Detecting anemia early is important. See your doctor if you suspect your child is anemic. Be sure children have regular physical examinations.

A balanced diet with foods from each of the four food groups can prevent some forms of anemia.

Milk group

Protein group— meat, eggs, beans, nuts

Bread-cereals group

Vegetable-fruit group

34

Anemia occurs when there is too little hemoglobin in the blood. Hemoglobin is the substance that carries oxygen in the blood and gives the blood its red color. Normally, hemoglobin is contained within the red blood cells (RBCs). A child can be anemic because there are too few RBCs, because each RBC contains too little hemoglobin, or as a result of both conditions.

There are more than 30 types of anemia, each with its own cause and treatment. The most common is iron deficiency anemia. Anemia can occur at any age. Some forms run in families; others are acquired.

Among the most common causes of anemia are a poor diet that does not include enough of the nutrients needed to manufacture hemoglobin (iron, protein, folic acid, vitamin B_{12}, and copper); the loss of blood by internal or external bleeding; a failure to absorb nutrients, even though they are eaten; the formation of abnormal (short-lived) RBCs; an inability of the bone marrow to produce RBCs fast enough; and the too-rapid destruction of normal RBCs within the body. In addition to the many diseases that are forms of anemia, many other illnesses can produce anemia.

SIGNS AND SYMPTOMS

Most cases of anemia produce no symptoms. However, tiredness, shortness of breath, rapid pulse, and jaundice (yellowing of the skin and the whites of the eyes) may be clues. If a child looks pale, check the nailbeds, the inside of the eyelids, and the membranes inside the mouth for additional colorlessness. Also watch for these possible causes of anemia: vomiting of blood; blood in the stools (red or tarry-black bowel movements); excessive menstruation; a grossly inadequate diet; chronic diarrhea; and exposure to poisonous substances.

If you think your child might have anemia, see your doctor. The presence and type of anemia can only be determined by laboratory tests. Periodic examinations and a medical history taken by a doctor can help detect anemia early, an important factor in treatment. If one family member has anemia, watch for symptoms in other family members.

HOME CARE

Never attempt to treat anemia yourself. The wrong treatment can be harmful and will make a proper medical diagnosis difficult. All children should receive a balanced diet to prevent anemia caused by lack of proper nutrition.

PRECAUTION

● Iron overdosing is the second most common poisoning among children in this country. If iron supplements are prescribed by your doctor, keep them out of the reach of children. Some iron medicines are sweet, and children might mistake them for candy.

MEDICAL TREATMENT

To evaluate your child for anemia, the doctor will give your child a physical examination, take a medical history, and test for simple total blood count. Your doctor may also need to take a reticulocyte (young RBC) count, platelet (a blood element that aids in clotting) count, and measurements of iron and of the iron-binding capacity in the blood. More extensive testing, if necessary, will include hemoglobin electrophoresis, sickle cell test, urinalysis, test of stools for hidden blood, examination of bone marrow, test for poisons, examination of the child's parents' blood, X ray of the intestinal tract, and blood chemistries. These tests will determine the type of anemia.

The treatment prescribed may include adding supplemental iron and vitamins to the diet, a change in diet, and—though rarely—a blood transfusion. Iron or vitamin injections also are rarely called for and, if given, are administered for the first one or two doses only.

As treatment proceeds, be sure additional tests are scheduled to check on the effectiveness of the treatment. The proof of proper treatment is in the cure.

Related topics:

G6PD deficiency
Sickle cell anemia

Animal bites

SYMPTOMS
Bite marks
Claw marks
Bruises

HOME CARE
Scrub wound with soap and water for five to ten minutes and flush with water.

Apply antiseptic to minor wounds.

Report the wound to your doctor immediately.

Call police or health authorities to deal with the animal.

PRECAUTIONS

☐ If redness spreads out from the wound, or if the wound becomes tender, call your doctor.

☐ Make sure your children keep current on tetanus boosters.

☐ Teach children to be careful around domestic pets and to stay away from wild animals.

☐ Be sure your own pets are vaccinated for rabies.

IMPORTANT
Animal bites that break the skin may cause infection, tetanus, or rabies. Report all animal bites or claw wounds to your doctor immediately.

Be sure your child is current on tetanus boosters and that your pets are vaccinated against rabies.

Animal bites that break the skin are cuts, puncture wounds, or scrapes. However, animal bites may result in serious complications. First, animal bites often become infected by the bacteria in the animal's mouth. Second, animal bites may cause tetanus (lockjaw) or rabies.

Tetanus (lockjaw) is a serious disease caused by a germ that lives in soil, dust, and the intestines and intestinal wastes of animals and humans. It can easily enter the body through puncture wounds or scratches caused by animal bites and claw wounds. A vaccine to prevent tetanus is available.

Rabies is a fatal disease of the central nervous system that may affect any mammal. It is caused by a virus that can be identified within the brain of an affected animal. Rabies is transmitted through the saliva of the sick animal. It is most commonly found in the United States among skunks, foxes, cattle, dogs, bats, cats, and raccoons.

SIGNS AND SYMPTOMS

Even in younger children, an animal bite is usually obvious from its appearance. It is sometimes difficult to tell a bite from a claw wound; however, claw wounds should be treated in the same way as bites because a claw wound can also contain bacteria from the animal's saliva.

If the bite has caused a bruise, but there is no break in the skin, you do not need to worry about rabies or tetanus.

HOME CARE

Scrub the wound with soap and water for five to ten minutes and flush with water. Apply antiseptic to minor wounds. Report the wound to your doctor immediately for advice concerning rabies, tetanus, and repair of the wound. Let your doctor know when your child was most recently vaccinated for tetanus.

The chance of an animal bite becoming infected is very high. If redness begins spreading out from the wound, or if the wound becomes more tender, call your doctor.

If at all possible, the animal that bit the child should be inspected for rabies. Because catching an animal can be extremely dangerous, call the local police or health authorities and allow them to deal with the animal. If the animal is a pet, find out if it was vaccinated against rabies. In some states, all animal bites must be reported to the police.

PRECAUTIONS

● Keep children current on tetanus boosters. ● Always contact your doctor about treatment in the case of animal bites. ● Be sure that your own pets (dogs and cats) receive regular rabies shots.

MEDICAL TREATMENT

Because of the high possibility of infection, your doctor may decide not to stitch the wound. However, if the wound is located where scarring is not desirable (such as on the face), the doctor may choose to stitch the wound. Before stitching, treatment first includes removing the injured tissue and a thorough cleansing. Antibiotics taken by mouth may be prescribed. If necessary, your doctor may give the child a tetanus booster or antitoxin (a substance that counteracts the poisonous effects of the tetanus germ).

The decision whether or not to give anti-rabies vaccine, with or without antiserum, is difficult. There's a good possibility of serious reactions. However, with new anti-rabies vaccines now being tested, the likelihood of serious reactions may be lessened. Your doctor will arrange for examination of the animal for rabies. If the animal is not caught, the decision depends upon the likelihood of rabies in your area, the circumstances of the bite (provoked or unprovoked), and the species of the animal. Local or state health departments can provide information to help you make this decision. If you're still in doubt, contact the Center for Disease Control, Rabies Investigations Unit, Atlanta, Georgia, (404) 329-3696.

Related topics:

Bruises
Cat scratch fever
Cuts
Puncture wounds
Scrapes
Tetanus

Anorexia nervosa

SYMPTOMS
Aversion to food
Excessive dieting
Excessive exercise
Obsession with subject of food
Distorted body image
Overeating followed by self-induced
   vomiting
Absence of menstruation
Downy hair on body

HOME CARE Anorexia nervosa requires medical care.

PRECAUTIONS

☐ If her condition is not treated, the anorexic may starve herself to death.

☐ Obedient and successful children who try hard to fulfill the expectations of others are at higher risk of becoming anorexic.

Anorexia nervosa means literally "nervous loss of appetite." Actually, however, persons with this condition—almost always female from upper- and upper-middle-class homes—do not lose their appetites. Rather, they willfully suppress the urge to eat in an unhealthy desire to lose more and more weight. In short, they starve themselves because they mistakenly believe that they are fat and need to diet.

After a certain point, anorexia nervosa leads to the cessation of menstruation. It also causes the destruction of healthy muscle and organ tissue that the body must use as an energy source in the absence of food. Ultimately, anorexic patients may starve themselves to death.

Anorexia nervosa is considered to be principally caused by serious psychological problems. Anorexic youngsters are usually obedient, successful children who try to do everything expected of them by parents, teachers, and friends. As a result, the anorexic's strenuous dieting and exercising may represent a desire to gain absolute control over at least one part of her life.

Anorexics may also try to deny the onset of adulthood by dieting away all the signs of mature femininity: breasts, curved hips, and rounded thighs. The lack of menstrual periods, too, is a reminder of childhood. In addition, the current preoccupation with thinness as the ideal of attractiveness fuels the anorexic's desire to starve herself to the "perfect" weight. Frequently, the condition arises after a casual remark that the girl is slightly overweight.

The anorexic's fear of becoming fat is accompanied by a distorted body image that makes it impossible for her to realize how unattractively thin she has become. Often when an anorexic looks in the mirror, she perceives herself as fat when in reality she is exceedingly thin.

SIGNS AND SYMPTOMS

The anorexic develops an aversion to eating which cannot be overcome by threats or appeals to reason. The dieting is accompanied by overly vigorous exercise to burn off the few calories that she does consume. Although she refuses to eat more than tiny amounts of certain foods, she is often obsessed with the subject of food and will prepare elaborate meals for others.

Often the anorexic may go on an eating binge after which she forces herself to vomit. Excessive use of laxatives is also common.

After a certain percentage of body fat is lost, menstruation will automatically cease. Fine, downy hair may begin to grow all over the patient's body.

HOME CARE

An anorexic child should be under a doctor's care. The doctor will tell you how to take care of the child at home.

PRECAUTION

● If the condition is not controlled, the anorexic may starve herself to death.

MEDICAL TREATMENT

The doctor will first attempt to rule out any physical cause of the child's extreme weight loss, such as cancer, infectious disease, disorders in the digestive organs, or problems in absorbing the nutrients from food. If the patient has lost more than 25 percent of her original body weight, if she displays the classic behavior, and if the onset of symptoms occurs before the age of 25, a diagnosis of anorexia is usually warranted.

An anorexic may require hospitalization and forced feeding if her disease has led to severe malnutrition. However, most anorexics can be treated on an outpatient basis by a family physician, a psychiatrist, or a specialist in eating disorders.

The psychological problems that underlie the anorexic behavior should be exposed and resolved. In the meantime, however, the youngster must be convinced that she must gain weight and reassured that her doctor and parents will not allow her to become overweight. Healthy attitudes toward body weight and normal eating patterns must be restored.

Appendicitis

KEY SYMPTOM — Persistent pain in the abdomen, usually in the lower right quarter

POSSIBLE SYMPTOMS — Tenderness in the abdomen
Nausea and vomiting
Fever

HOME CARE — Allow only clear liquids by mouth. If you strongly suspect appendicitis, do not give the child any food or drink until you consult your doctor.

Do not apply cold to the abdomen. Gentle heat may ease a stomachache. If pain continues or gets worse, despite home treatment, call your doctor.

PRECAUTIONS

☐ Do not give pain killers such as paregoric or codeine.

☐ Do not give a laxative or enema.

☐ Do not give aspirin.

IMPORTANT — Call your doctor as soon as you suspect appendicitis. The condition can worsen rapidly and can be fatal if not treated by a doctor.

The key symptom of appendicitis is abdominal pain in the lower right quarter of the abdomen.

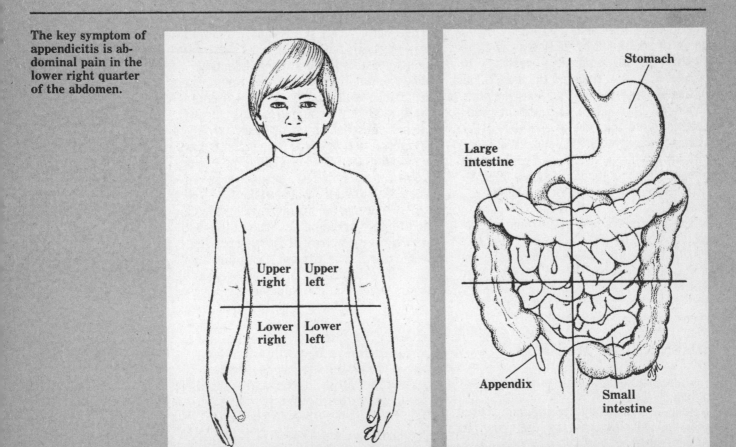

Upper right · Upper left · Lower right · Lower left

Stomach · Large intestine · Appendix · Small intestine

40

Appendicitis is an inflammation (infection) of the appendix. The appendix is a hollow tube about the size of your little finger that forms a blind pouch where the small intestine joins the large intestine. In 99 percent of all children, the appendix lies in the lower right quarter of the child's abdomen.

Appendicitis can occur at any age. If the appendix is not surgically removed, the infection worsens until the appendix bursts. Then the infection spreads throughout the abdomen. An infected appendix may perforate (rupture) within hours of the initial pain or may not rupture for a day or two. A ruptured appendix can lead to death.

SIGNS AND SYMPTOMS

Persistent abdominal pain in your child should be considered a symptom of appendicitis until proven otherwise. Typically, the pain of appendicitis is constant; it does not come and go as does the pain from cramps. Once it starts, it grows continually worse. The pain may start in the pit of the stomach, but it usually soon moves to the lower right quarter of the abdomen. The pain is made worse by walking or just moving about. The abdomen is tender to a gentle pressure in the lower right quarter, more tender than in other areas. There may be nausea and vomiting, but these symptoms usually start only after the pain has started.

Generally, there is a low-grade fever (100°F, oral; 101°F, rectal), but the temperature may range anywhere from normal to 104°F. Bowel movements are usually normal, but there may be diarrhea. Diagnosis is difficult because all of these signs may not be present. Because diagnosis is so difficult and the condition is so serious, call your doctor if you have any reason to suspect appendicitis.

HOME CARE

Try applying gentle heat, as with a heating pad turned to "low." If pain gets worse, it is probably appendicitis. **Never apply cold**; this can mask the symptoms of appendicitis.

Do not give pain killers such as paregoric or codeine. Acetaminophen is safe but useless. Aspirin can affect the blood's ability to clot, so it should not be given in case the child needs surgery. Allow only clear liquids by mouth. However, once you suspect that there is a strong possibility of appendicitis, do not give your child any food or drink until you consult your physician. Never give a laxative or enema.

PRECAUTION

● If pain persists in the lower right quarter of the abdomen, despite home treatment measures, call your doctor.

MEDICAL TREATMENT

The only acceptable treatment for appendicitis is surgical removal of the appendix (an appendectomy). Therefore, your doctor must be reasonably sure of the diagnosis. In addition to the abdomen, your child's chest and throat will be examined because a throat infection and pneumonia can cause symptoms of appendicitis. A rectal examination will also be performed and a blood count and a urinalysis done. (These last two tests do not prove or disprove appendicitis, however.) An X ray may be called for.

Once tests are complete, your doctor may operate or admit your child to a hospital to watch the child for a few hours until the diagnosis becomes more certain. Unnecessary surgery is to be avoided, but the rule of safety is to operate on a child who may have appendicitis rather than postpone surgery until the appendix ruptures.

Related topics:

Stomachache, acute
Stomachache, chronic

41

Arthritis

KEY SYMPTOMS
Swelling of joints
Stiffness or difficulty moving joints

SYMPTOMS
Pain or tenderness in joints
Warmth in joints

POSSIBLE SYMPTOMS

Redness of joints
Fever

HOME CARE
Do not treat at home until a doctor has diagnosed the cause.

If a doctor is not immediately available, give aspirin or acetaminophen and rest the affected joints.

PRECAUTIONS

☐ Infectious arthritis is an emergency; see doctor within 24 hours or permanent damage may occur.

☐ Rheumatoid arthritis and rheumatic fever require prompt treatment but are not considered emergencies.

☐ If a child has prolonged unexplained fever and stiffness in joints and neck, consider rheumatoid arthritis.

Arthritis is an inflammation of any joint or joints. Arthritis most often affects joints in the fingers, toes, wrists, ankles, elbows, knees, shoulders, hips, jaw, and spine. Six types of arthritis are common to childhood: rheumatoid arthritis; acute rheumatic fever; infectious arthritis; allergic arthritis; arthritis following a viral infection; and arthritis of rubella.

Rheumatoid arthritis can occur at any age past one year old. So far the cause is unknown. It may affect one or several joints. The joints become swollen, warm, stiff, and mildly to moderately painful, but not usually red. The neck is affected in 50 percent of the cases. Arthritis may appear months before or after other signs of illness, such as fever, irritability, loss of appetite, and a fine pink rash.

Arthritis associated with *acute rheumatic fever*, usually affects many joints, which become red, swollen, and extremely tender. Other symptoms of general illness (including fever) are also present.

Infectious (purulent) *arthritis* is an inflammation within a joint caused by various bacterial diseases (including staphylococcal, streptococcal, pneumococcal, and salmonella infections). This type of arthritis most often occurs in infants less than one year old. In older children and adults, it can be caused by puncture wounds near the joints. In this type of arthritis, the joint is tender, swollen, and red. The child usually has a fever.

In *allergic arthritis* the joints are stiff, swollen, and red, but pain is slight. The disease is caused by an allergic reaction to insect stings, medications, foods, or small particles inhaled from the air. It is generally accompanied by hives.

Post-viral arthritis occurs after an illness caused by a virus. The symptoms are similar to those from other causes of arthritis, especially rheumatoid arthritis. Post-viral arthritis corrects itself without treatment.

Arthritis of rubella occurs as a complication of rubella (German measles) or as a reaction to a rubella vaccine, especially in older children. Arthritis of rubella usually corrects itself without treatment and usually causes no permanent damage.

SIGNS AND SYMPTOMS

Arthritis should be considered whenever there is pain and a limited ability to move any joint, unless there has been a physical injury to the joint. Deciding if a child has arthritis is best left to the doctor.

HOME CARE

No home treatment is safe until after a doctor's diagnosis has been made. Trying to treat the condition at home may only delay proper treatment. Also, home treatment may make diagnosis more difficult for the doctor. If your doctor is not immediately available, pain relievers containing aspirin or acetaminophen will temporarily reduce the discomfort. Rest or immobilize the affected joints.

PRECAUTIONS

● Infectious arthritis is an acute emergency, and delay of treatment for 24 hours may result in permanent damage to a joint. ● Rheumatoid arthritis and rheumatic fever require prompt treatment to minimize damage but are not considered emergencies. ● Rheumatoid arthritis can begin with only a prolonged unexplained fever, and no outward signs of arthritis (redness, tenderness, swelling).

MEDICAL TREATMENT

For the evaluation of arthritis, several tests are required. These tests may include X rays; a wide variety of blood tests; blood culture; drawing fluid out of the joint for testing; electrocardiogram; and a stool culture. Treatment may include antibiotics, drainage of the joints, large doses of aspirin (aspirin substitutes do not have the same effect), or oral steroids. If large doses of aspirin are prescribed and taken over a period of time, aspirin blood levels should be tested regularly.

If the condition is diagnosed as allergic arthritis, the doctor may suggest using oral antihistamines to relieve the symptoms. If it is diagnosed as arthritis from rubella, no treatment is necessary.

Related topics:

Growing pains
Hip problems
Knee pains
Puncture wounds
Sprains and
  dislocations

Asthma

KEY SYMPTOMS

Wheezing
Difficulty breathing *out*

SYMPTOMS

Shortness of breath
Cough
Sensation of air hunger

HOME CARE

For the first attack, do not treat at home. See your doctor.

If further attacks occur, follow your doctor's prescribed home treatment.

Remove any identified causes of the child's asthma allergy from your home.

PRECAUTIONS

☐ Not all wheezes are asthma; have your doctor diagnose the cause.

☐ Do not use aerosol asthma medications on young children.

☐ Avoid rectal medications for asthma.

☐ Do not let any asthma attack go untreated.

☐ Avoid exposing the child to irritants like smoke, insecticides, or paint fumes.

Asthma is often caused by an allergic reaction to animal dander, including that of cats.

Asthma is an allergic reaction of the bronchial tree (the air passages leading into the lungs). It is a major and potentially dangerous form of allergy because it causes breathing difficulty. During an asthma attack, there are spasms in the smooth muscles of the bronchial tubes, and thick mucus collects in these tubes.

Asthma is often caused by an allergy to small particles breathed in from the air (animal dander, pollens, dust, feathers, molds). Less commonly, asthma is caused by an allergy to certain foods, medicines, and insect stings. Attacks may be brought on by physical exertion, upper respiratory infections, emotions, or irritants such as smoke or chlorine. The tendency to have allergies runs in families.

SIGNS AND SYMPTOMS

The major symptoms of asthma are shortness of breath, cough, sensations of air hunger, and wheezing. Wheezing is a high-pitched whistling sound heard more when the child is breathing out than when breathing in. This sound lets you know that the child is having more trouble breathing *out* than breathing in—a key symptom of asthma. The child usually does not have a fever.

Carefully noting when asthma attacks occur may help you and your doctor find the causes of asthma allergy. Do attacks begin after the child has been around a cat, dog, horse, or other animal with fur? Do attacks come in certain seasons (such as during tree, grass, or ragweed pollination)? Be alert to these and other possible causes of allergies.

HOME CARE

The first time your child has an attack that might be asthma, do not try to care for the child at home. See your doctor. The doctor will determine if the child has asthma and will select a specific treatment.

After a doctor diagnoses asthma, home care is important and effective. Prescribed medications should be given as soon as an attack begins. Medicines are less effective after an attack is under way. Rid your home of any identified causes of asthma allergy—pets, feather pillows and comforters, house dust, and sources of mold. Avoid exposing your child to airborne irritants such as insecticides, smoke, and paint fumes.

PRECAUTIONS

● Do not use aerosol anti-asthma medications on children. They can be dangerous and make other medications less effective. ● Do not use aminophylline or theophylline given in the form of rectal suppositories. Rectal medications are not reliably absorbed, and the child may receive an improper dose (either too little or too much). ● Do not let an attack go untreated. Improperly treated frequent attacks of asthma can cause permanent damage to the lungs and bronchial tubes. ● Not all wheezes are caused by asthma. Have your doctor check your child if you suspect asthma.

MEDICAL TREATMENT

The treatment for asthma should produce good results. Your doctor will begin treatment by taking a complete and detailed medical history. The doctor will conduct a general physical examination (perhaps including a chest X ray). Diagnosis can be confirmed if asthma medicines relieve the symptoms.

Medicines to treat asthma may be taken by mouth during an attack or may be inhaled. The same drugs may be recommended for daily use to prevent attacks.

The doctor may also run a series of several skin tests of suspected materials to which the child may be allergic. The substances identified as causes must be removed from the child's surroundings wherever possible. Children also may be desensitized to substances that cause allergic reactions. Desensitizing means giving weekly to monthly injections of increasing amounts of the irritating substances over a period of one to ten years.

Severe attacks may require hospitalization for intravenous medications and fluids and for oxygen.

Related topics:

Bronchiolitis
Bronchitis
Croup
Hay fever
Hives
Hyperventilation

Athlete's foot

SYMPTOMS Itching
Scaling and cracking skin

HOME CARE Apply fungicidal ointment once or twice a day (half strength for delicate skin), or use ointments containing undecylenic acid or tolnaftate.

Avoid rubber-soled or plastic-soled shoes. Wear cotton socks, preferably white. If treatment for athlete's foot does not promptly relieve the symptoms, or if symptoms reappear, see your doctor.

PRECAUTIONS

☐ Continue treatment until the skin is completely clear, or the condition may flare up again.

☐ Many medications for athlete's foot may cause skin irritation in some people.

☐ Do not scratch athlete's foot; scratching can cause additional infections.

To control and prevent athlete's foot, have your child wear only cotton socks, preferably white.

46

Athlete's foot is an infection of the skin of the feet. It is caused by one of several funguses that grow best in moisture. The mildest cases cause itching, scaling, and cracking between the toes, particularly between the fourth and fifth toes. Athlete's foot may spread to the sole of the feet as small blisters and scaling. In severe cases it may spread to the ankles and legs. It may invade and deform the toenails. Scratching may cause additional (secondary) infections. The condition is most common during adolescence, but it may occur at any age—even occasionally in infants.

SIGNS AND SYMPTOMS

The scaling and cracking appearance of the feet and the itching that accompanies it are symptoms that may indicate athlete's foot.

HOME CARE

Apply fungicidal ointment, such as Whitfield's ointment, once or twice a day (half strength for delicate skin). Or you may use ointments containing undecylenic acid or tolnaftate (available without a prescription). To decrease sweating of the feet, avoid rubber-soled or plastic-soled shoes. Use cotton socks to absorb moisture. White socks may be best since some dyes can irritate the skin.

Caution: Many "incurable" cases of athlete's foot are not athlete's foot itself but contact dermatitis caused by the treatment. Contact dermatitis is a skin rash or inflammation caused by some irritating substance. In some people, the ointments used to treat athlete's foot may cause such irritation; the athlete's foot fungus is actually cleared up, but the skin remains irritated. If treatment for athlete's foot does not relieve the symptoms, check with your doctor to determine if the skin irritation is contact dermatitis.

PRECAUTIONS

● Continue treatment until the skin is completely clear; funguses not completely treated flare up again. ● If improvement is not prompt and lasting, see your doctor; you may have a skin condition that is not athlete's foot. Many athlete's foot medications can cause contact dermatitis in some people.

MEDICAL TREATMENT

Diagnosis is confirmed by scraping the skin and then culturing the fungus or identifying the fungus under a microscope. Your doctor may prescribe other fungicidal ointments or lotions or a fungicide taken by mouth. If a secondary infection has developed, your doctor may prescribe oral antibiotics and soaking in a solution of potassium permanganate or aluminum sulfate and calcium acetate.

Related topics:

Eczema
Rash

Backaches

SYMPTOMS   Back pain
Tender or sore muscles
Stiffness

HOME CARE   Have the child rest in bed, or limit the
child's physical activities.

Give aspirin or acetaminophen for pain.

Give lukewarm baths, or apply gentle heat
with a heating pad.

Use an extra-firm mattress, or place a
bedboard or piece of plywood under the
mattress.

Do not allow strenuous physical activity
until the pain has been gone at least
a week.

PRECAUTIONS

☐ If the back pain is accompanied by
fever, problems in urination, severe
pain, or a sharp pain in one spot, see
your doctor.

☐ Do not use muscle relaxant medications on children unless your doctor
has prescribed them.

☐ If there is a visible curve in the spine,
see your doctor.

Backache is pain, soreness, or stiffness occurring anywhere in the back. Backache is almost as common in children as in adults. Almost as soon as children are old enough to complain of pain and to explain where the pain is, they complain of occasional backaches. Backache may occur more frequently during adolescence.

Most back pains are the result of strenuous activities that cause stress to the muscles and ligaments of the back. These back problems are usually minor and often correct themselves without treatment.

More serious causes of back pain are infections and abnormalities of the kidneys; malformations and abnormal curvatures of the spine; a defect of the growth plates of the vertebrae (bones of the spine), called Scheuermann's disease; compression fractures (usually caused by injuries); and arthritis.

SIGNS AND SYMPTOMS

Backache caused by *stress* causes pain and slight tenderness in the muscles that run up and down either side of the spine. The pain is aggravated by bending and twisting, but it is less noticeable when resting. If physical activities are limited, the condition improves slowly day by day.

Backache caused by kidney problems often occurs only on one side. There may be other symptoms of urinary problems, such as burning during urination, frequent urination, or discoloration of the urine.

Backache caused by a sprain is limited to one spot near the spine or to a longer area along the spine.

Backache caused by a disease of the vertebrae or by curves in the spine (scoliosis) may also be limited to one spot near the spine or to a longer area along the spine. Some abnormal curves in the spine can be seen. Minor curves to one side or the other can best be seen with the child undressed and bending forward to touch the floor with both hands. Even a slight curve causes the back to appear lopsided in this position.

HOME CARE

If there is no visible deformity, no fever, and no sharp pain in one location, home care is safe. The pain can be relieved with aspirin or acetaminophen, mild heat from an electric pad or a lukewarm bath, and bed rest. If the mattress is not extra firm, a bedboard under the mattress (a piece of plywood will do) helps relieve the discomfort. Have your child avoid any strenuous physical activity until the pain has been gone at least a week.

PRECAUTIONS

● If the child has a fever, urinary symptoms, severe pain, or a sharp pain in one area, see your doctor. ● Do not use muscle relaxant medications on children unless your doctor has prescribed them.

MEDICAL TREATMENT

In addition to a careful medical history and physical examination, urinalysis, X rays, blood count, and sedimentation rate may be required. Specific treatment depends upon the cause of the back pain. In some cases, the doctor's treatment may be the same as home care. Treatment might also include antibiotics, orthopedic exercises, a back brace, or even hospitalization and traction.

Related topics:

Arthritis
Scoliosis
Urinary tract
   infection

Baldness

SYMPTOMS

Bare spots on head
Total baldness
Scaliness of skin on scalp
Broken-off stubbles of hair

HOME CARE

Alopecia areata cannot be treated at home, except with patience until hair grows back in.

Hereditary and congenital baldness can be treated only with understanding. A hairpiece may be helpful.

PRECAUTIONS

☐ Do not use OTC preparations that promise hair growth.

☐ Do not consult cosmetologists for baldness. See a qualified dermatologist.

Baldness is a loss of hair either in one spot or over the entire scalp. Some infants are born bald or nearly so and develop a full head of hair during their first two years. Rarely do babies born bald remain bald for life. Other babies are born with a full head of hair. They may remain that way, or their original hair may be replaced by a second and permanent growth. Rarely is hair lost during infancy and never replaced.

Infants commonly rub off a band of hair in the back against the crib or playpen mat. Hair that is rubbed off in this way will grow back. Drawing the hair tightly into pigtails, braids, or ponytails also may result in temporary bald spots. Children with the habit of twisting and playing with strands of hair may also lose hair. Emotionally disturbed children may pull out their hair by the handfuls (trichotillomania); this condition requires treatment of the child's emotional problems.

Alopecia areata is a condition which results in the sudden appearance of round or oval areas that are totally bare. The bald scalp may be completely normal in appearance or slightly pink. Although temporary, the condition may last for months or years. Rarely is the entire head involved. The cause is unknown.

Ringworm of the scalp produces scattered bald spots. The scalp is scaly, and the bald spots are studded with broken-off stubbles of hair.

Hereditary baldness occurs primarily in males. It causes baldness at the temples or the top of the scalp. Occasionally this type of baldness starts during adolescence.

Teenagers often complain that they are "going bald" when they see loose hair after combing. Usually this condition is merely a normal thinning of the hair that does not worsen.

Malfunction of the parathyroid glands (hyperparathyroidism) may result in scattered baldness. The disease is accompanied by other signs of illness.

Impetigo and other infections of the scalp produce temporary bald spots.

SIGNS AND SYMPTOMS

Inspect the scalp closely for signs of ringworm or infection. Look for broken or regrowing hairs. Watch to see if the child is rubbing the head against the playpen or crib, or if the child has a habit of twisting or pulling the hair.

HOME CARE

Alopecia areata is treated with patience and time. Hereditary and congenital baldness (baldness present at birth) are treated with understanding and love; a hairpiece may be helpful.

PRECAUTIONS

● Do not treat baldness with over-the-counter (OTC) preparations that promise growth of hair. ● Do not consult cosmetologists. See a qualified dermatologist.

MEDICAL TREATMENT

Alopecia areata is sometimes successfully treated with steroids either applied to the skin or locally injected. Hyperparathyroidism must be diagnosed by blood tests; it is treated with prescribed doses of vitamin D and a special diet.

Related topics:

Impetigo
Ringworm

Bedwetting

SYMPTOM   Frequent bedwetting after age five

HOME CARE   First see your doctor to find out if the cause is physical disease.

If there is no physical cause, the best home care is patience, calmness, and understanding. Try to avoid or ignore the problem as much as possible.

Rubber sheets and plastic pants will help until the child stops bedwetting.

PRECAUTIONS

☐ If a trained child suddenly begins bedwetting, suspect a physical illness.

☐ Do not take a child out of night diapers until the child consistently remains dry.

☐ Do not make a big fuss over daytime training.

☐ Do not try to shame children into remaining dry at night.

☐ Do not use devices called enuratones.

☐ Do not let bedwetting bring anger and frustration into your relationship with your child.

☐ Do not let other children taunt a bedwetter.

Many children cannot remain dry through the night before they are four or five. About 10 percent of all children over the age of five are bedwetters. Children of any age may have occasional accidents at night, especially if ill or in exhausted sleep—conditions that do not represent true bedwetting.

Five to 10 percent of children who bedwet have a physical disease, such as an infection or abnormality of the urinary tract, diabetes, or a neurological (nervous system) disorder. If a trained child suddenly begins bedwetting, the cause may be physical. If bedwetting develops a year or more after night training has been established, or if a child wets himself both day and night, a physical disease is likely.

However, most cases of bedwetting are not caused by an identified physical disorder. Some cases seem to be hereditary, with brothers, sisters, and parents also having been bedwetters. Some are caused by overemphasis by the family on toilet training. Others are caused by taking children out of their night diapers too soon or by waking children to urinate in an effort to train at night. Some children have emotional problems that cause bedwetting. Still, the cause of many cases of bedwetting remains unknown.

SIGNS AND SYMPTOMS

A child who frequently and consistently wets the bed after age five has a bedwetting problem.

HOME CARE

Before beginning any home treatment of bedwetting, see your doctor. The doctor can perform tests to determine whether bedwetting is being caused by a physical disease, such as a urinary infection or diabetes.

If the doctor finds no physical cause, then the best home treatment is to ignore bedwetting as much as possible and to try to avoid it. Do not take a child out of night diapers until the child consistently remains dry. Do not make a big fuss about daytime training. Do not try to shame a child into remaining dry at night.

Do not use devices called enuratones, which awaken the child as urination starts.

Withholding liquids during late afternoon and evening hours is not usually successful and may seem like punishment to the child. Behavior modification techniques (rewarding success and reacting neutrally toward failure) rarely work. Rubber sheets and plastic pants are helpful until the child stops bedwetting. Until then, patience, calmness, and understanding may be the best treatment.

PRECAUTIONS

● Do not let a minor problem like bedwetting become a major destructive factor in your relationship with your child. Anger and frustration between parent and child are more costly than extra laundry. ● Do not allow other children to taunt a bedwetter.

MEDICAL TREATMENT

Your doctor will insist first upon conducting a physical examination and urinalysis. The doctor may suggest X rays of the urinary tract or consultation with a urologist; imipramine (an antidepressant) by mouth at bedtime for a trial period; dextroamphetamine, phenytoin, or caffeine also on a temporary basis; or a program of behavior modification. Although many of these treatments are not always effective, they may be worth a try.

Related topics:

Diabetes mellitus
Urinary tract
  infections

53

Birthmarks

Quick Reference

SYMPTOMS   Red, purple, or salmon-colored marks
Blue-black marks on back or buttocks
Brown or black moles

HOME CARE   In most cases, birthmarks need no treatment.

Protect strawberry marks from rubbing or scratching. If a strawberry mark bleeds, press lightly with gauze to stop bleeding.

PRECAUTIONS

☐ If there is discharge, odor, or redness of the skin around a strawberry mark, call your doctor.

☐ In rare cases, strawberry marks may cause anemia or bleeding that needs a doctor's attention.

If a strawberry birthmark bleeds, press the mark lightly with gauze.

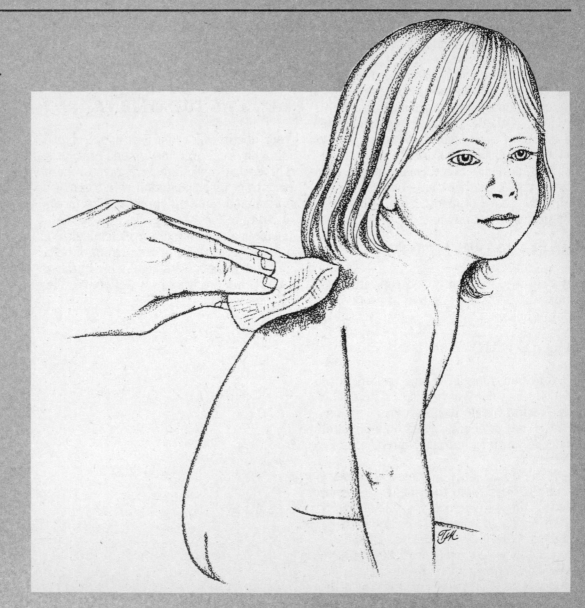

Birthmarks are any unusual marks or blemishes present on an infant's skin at birth. Almost 50 percent of all infants are born with red or salmon-colored marks on the mid-forehead, upper eyelids, upper lip, or back of the scalp and neck. These marks, which are sometimes quite extensive, fade and disappear during the first years of life.

Many black, Oriental, and Caucasian babies who are destined to become brunettes have smooth, blue-black marks on their backs and buttocks. These birthmarks are called "Mongolian spots." They are often mistaken for large bruises. They gradually disappear and are almost always gone by adolescence.

One in ten babies develops one or more strawberry marks during the first month of life. These are usually not visible at birth, or they may look like slightly pale spots on the skin. As the child grows, the marks become brilliant red. They are often raised, and vary in size from one-quarter inch to two inches across. They may appear on any part of the body and increase in size for weeks or months. The strawberry marks then gradually fade and shrink. In almost all instances, they are gone by age five or six years.

Two uncommon but permanent birthmarks are port wine marks and pigmented moles. Both may be tiny or large and may appear anywhere on the skin. They grow in proportion to the growth of the child's body. Port wine marks are smooth, flat, and purplish. Pigmented moles are brown to black, are often slightly raised, and may have dark hairs.

SIGNS AND SYMPTOMS

Each type of birthmark is recognized by its typical appearance and behavior. Mongolian spots are often mistaken for bruises, until it becomes obvious that the spots are not fading, as bruises would fade.

HOME CARE

In most cases, no treatment is necessary. Strawberry marks are made up of countless, closely packed capillaries (tiny blood vessels). They should be protected from scratching or rubbing, which can cause bleeding. If bleeding occurs, it can be controlled by pressing lightly with gauze directly on the bleeding point. If desired, port wine marks can be hidden by covering cosmetics when the child is older.

PRECAUTIONS

● Strawberry marks occasionally become infected if the overlying skin is broken. If there is any discharge, odor, or redness of the skin surrounding a strawberry mark, call your doctor. ● Strawberry marks rarely require treatment; in almost all instances, it is best to allow them to disappear by themselves. In rare situations, they may cause anemia or bleeding that requires correction.

MEDICAL TREATMENT

The doctor may decide to surgically remove some pigmented moles. Strawberry marks rarely require surgical removal, irradiation, or oral steroids. Port wine marks cannot be treated satisfactorily at present, but laser treatment is in the experimental stage and appears promising.

Related topics:

Anemia
Moles

Blisters

SYMPTOM A raised bubble of skin containing clear liquid

HOME CARE Protect blisters with gauze or bandages.

If accidentally opened, trim away loose skin, clean with soap and water, and bandage.

If a blister becomes infected (red or tender), soak it in Epsom salts or Burow's solution. Have infected blisters checked by a doctor.

PRECAUTIONS

☐ Do not break open blisters caused by rubbing or burns.

☐ If red streaks start spreading out from a blister, see your doctor.

☐ If Epsom salts solution is too weak, the soaking makes blisters larger. Use at least four ounces Epsom salts to a quart of water.

Blisters are a buildup of clear or almost clear fluid between layers of the skin. They may be caused by heat burns; chemical burns; rubbing (friction); infection by bacteria; viruses; hand, foot, and mouth disease; funguses; allergy to insect bites; or allergy to certain plants. Blisters range from the size of a pinhead to several inches across.

SIGNS AND SYMPTOMS

Blisters are obvious from their typical appearance—a raised bubble of skin containing clear fluid. The cause of blisters is sometimes determined by their location. When blisters appear on the palms or heels, they are usually due to rubbing; most blisters of the feet are caused by ill-fitting shoes or by not wearing socks. Blisters on the soles and toes may be caused by a fungus. Blisters on the cuticles or backs of fingers almost always mean an infection.

HOME CARE

Do not break open blisters caused by rubbing or by burns. Protect them with gauze and bandages. If a blister is accidentally opened, trim away the major portion of loose skin, cleanse with soap and water, and bandage. If the blister becomes infected (redness and increasing tenderness are signs of infection), it should be soaked in an Epsom salts or Burow's solution (available over the counter). An infected blister should be checked by a doctor.

PRECAUTIONS

● Red streaks spreading from a blister indicate spreading infection. If red streaks appear, see your doctor. ● Soaking unbroken blisters in too weak a solution causes marked enlargement of the blisters (suggested Epsom salts solution is at least four ounces salts to a quart of water).

MEDICAL TREATMENT

Your doctor will determine the cause of the blister and look for signs of possible infection. Infected blisters are opened and the fluid cultured to determine the type of infection. Soaks or oral antibiotics may be prescribed individually or in combination.

Related topics:

Athlete's foot
Blood poisoning
Burns
Chicken pox
Hand, foot, and
   mouth disease
Herpes simplex
Impetigo
Poison ivy

Blood poisoning

SYMPTOMS   Wavy pink or red streaks under the skin
Sudden, quickly rising high fever
Swollen or tender lymph nodes

HOME CARE   Call your doctor. Elevate the affected part of the body.

Apply warm soaks of Epsom salts (one-half cup of salts in a quart of water). If there is an infected blister, include it in the soaks. Give aspirin or acetaminophen for pain and fever.

PRECAUTIONS

☐ Always contact your doctor, since blood poisoning should usually be treated with antibiotics.

☐ If a child has a high fever or is prostrate (in a state of collapse), **call a medical facility immediately.**

Apply warm soaks of Epsom salts to an infected wound or blister with red streaks extending from it.

Blood poisoning is the spread of an infection into the bloodstream. The infection may be caused either by bacteria or by viruses. Blood poisoning can occur during early infancy, when natural resistance to infection is low. Beyond infancy, blood poisoning results in high fever, chills, and prostration (extreme exhaustion or collapse).

In popular usage, blood poisoning refers to the red streaks that may develop from an infected wound or blister. These red streaks resemble broad, wobbly, red-pencil marks. The streaks quickly (within hours) extend in the direction of the heart. They are signs of the infection traveling along the lymph vessels of the affected part of the body. If ignored, the spreading germs can—within hours or days—reach the bloodstream.

In their trip along the lymph channels, the germs enter the lymph nodes. The nodes swell, become tender, and sometimes redden as their cells fight and kill the germs. If the lymph nodes succeed in fighting off the poisonous germs, the infection is halted. No fever, or a fever below 100°F, indicates that the germs have not reached the bloodstream. A sudden, quickly rising high fever (over 101°F) generally means they have entered the bloodstream.

SIGNS AND SYMPTOMS

The pink or red, slightly wavy lines just under the skin are easily seen in a good light. These lines may be one-inch to several feet long. The lymph nodes toward which these red streaks lead are often swollen and tender.

HOME CARE

If blood poisoning occurs, call your doctor. Elevate the affected part of the body. Apply warm soaks of Epsom salts (one-half cup in a quart of water) to the entire area. If there is an unopened infected blister at the source, include the blister in the soaks. Give aspirin or acetaminophen for pain and fever, following the dose recommended on the label.

PRECAUTIONS

● Always contact your doctor. Blood poisoning is best treated with antibiotics.
● If a child with blood poisoning has a high fever or is prostrate (in a state of collapse), **contact a medical facility promptly.**

MEDICAL TREATMENT

Your doctor will give your child antibiotics by mouth or by injection. The doctor may open and drain the point of infection. Culture of the blood or from the site of the original infection may be necessary. Laboratory tests, including a blood count and urinalysis, may be required. Hospitalization may be necessary if the blood poisoning is severe.

Related topics:

Blisters
Cuts
Fever
Glands, swollen
Puncture wounds

Boils

SYMPTOMS   Redness
Pain
Pus

HOME CARE   Soak with warm Epsom salts solution
(one-half cup salts per quart of water).

When a boil drains, catch the drainage on
a sterile bandage to avoid spreading
infection.

Frequently clean surrounding skin with
soap and water.

PRECAUTIONS

☐ If boils develop on the face, see your
doctor.

☐ Do not let drainage from a boil come
in contact with the eyes.

☐ Do not squeeze boils.

☐ Treat all minor wounds and insect
bites properly to avoid boils or other
infections.

Boils are local infections that occur beneath the skin. They are almost always caused by a bacterium called *hemolytic Staphylococcus aureus*—called "staph," for short. Boils are identified by redness, pain, and the formation of pus in the center, which tends to "point" (come to a head) and drain through the skin. Pus is a mixture of live and dead white blood cells, liquified dead tissue, and live and dead staph germs. Pus is therefore infectious; it can spread boils to other areas and to other persons.

A small superficial boil is a pimple or pustule. (An acne pimple is not a true boil.) A large boil with several heads is a carbuncle. A boil on the edge of the eyelid is a sty. When many boils are present at one time the condition is called furunculosis. Abscesses are collections of pus in parts of the body other than the skin, as in muscles, brain, bone, and internal organs. Abscesses are like boils, but often they are caused by germs other than staph.

Staph germs are often harmlessly present in the nose and throat or on the skin of well persons. Staph germs on the skin cause no problems unless there is a cut or break in the skin. If the germs enter the body through a break in the skin, they cause infections.

SIGNS AND SYMPTOMS

Boils are easily recognized by their redness, pain, and the formation of pus in the center.

HOME CARE

Boils are treated with frequent or constant soaks with warm Epsom salts solutions (one-half cup per quart of water). When a boil comes to a head and drains, the drainage must be caught on a sterile bandage to avoid spreading the infection. The surrounding skin should be cleansed frequently with soap and water to avoid additional boils.

PRECAUTIONS

● Be careful with boils on the face and forehead, including the nose and lips. The lymph and blood vessel drainage from these areas is partly internal. Be especially careful that drainage from a boil does not come in contact with the eyes. See your doctor if boils develop on the face. ● Never squeeze a boil. Squeezing breaks down the wall surrounding the boil. When this wall is broken down, the infection rapidly spreads outward. ● Treat all minor wounds and insect bites properly to lessen the likelihood of infections and the forming of boils.

MEDICAL TREATMENT

Your doctor may open and drain the boil, culture pus, and order sensitivity studies on the staph germs found. These studies will help your doctor identify the antibiotic that will most effectively fight the infection. The doctor may prescribe antibiotics to be taken by mouth. Many staph infections have become resistant to penicillin. Other antibiotics that may be used include erythromycin, oxacillin, cloxacillin, methicillin, and cephalosporin.

For repeated attacks of boils, your doctor may recommend nose and throat cultures of the patient and the entire family to identify carriers of the staph germs. Antibiotic ointments applied in the nose and antiseptic baths may be prescribed.

Related topics:

Acne
Cuts
Insect bites and
    stings
Puncture wounds
Scrapes
Styes

Botulism

SYMPTOMS
Nausea
Vomiting
Diarrhea
Abdominal pain
Double vision (12 to 48 hours after start
    of pain)
Dilated pupils
Difficulty speaking, swallowing, and
    breathing
Paralysis

HOME CARE None. Call your doctor immediately.

PRECAUTIONS

☐ Do not give infants unwashed,
   unpeeled raw foods or improperly
   cooked foods or honey.

☐ Do not use food from damaged or
   dented store-bought cans.

☐ Adequately heat canned foods before
   eating. Heating for ten minutes at
   180°F or more will kill botulism toxin.

☐ Remember that foods contaminated
   with botulism look, taste, and smell
   normal.

☐ When canning and preserving food at
   home, follow directions for preparing
   and sterilizing exactly.

IMPORTANT Botulism poisoning can be fatal. If you
suspect botulism, **get medical help
immediately.**

Botulism is a specific type of food poisoning. Botulism is caused by the toxin (poison) produced by *Clostridium botulinum,* a germ which is related to the tetanus germ and prevalent everywhere. The botulism germ grows in anaerobic (no oxygen) environments (such as in tightly closed jars that were not properly sterilized). Its toxin can be destroyed if it is heated for ten minutes at 180°F. Botulism poisoning is primarily caused by improperly prepared canned or preserved foods that have not been adequately heated before they've been eaten. The foods most likely to cause poisoning are seafood, mushrooms, meat, and vegetables. The toxin and germs are undetectable. Foods contaminated with botulism look, smell, and taste normal.

With improvements in commercial food preparation and the decline in home canning in the first half of the 20th century, botulism had become a rare illness in the United States. With the increased interest in home canning and "natural" foods (those without preservatives), botulism is threatening a comeback.

Adults and children past infancy can be poisoned by botulism only if they eat food in which the botulism germ has already formed the toxin. Recent cases of fatal botulism among infants, however, suggest that the botulism germ can grow in an infant's immature intestines to form the dangerous toxin within the infant's body. The only natural food so far identified as a source of botulism germs for infants is honey. Therefore, you should not give honey to an infant. However, other raw or improperly cooked foods may eventually be identified as potential sources of the germ. Furthermore, indications that the Food and Drug Administration may outlaw nitrites as meat preservatives may make meats such as frankfurters and salami potential sources of botulism.

SIGNS AND SYMPTOMS

Symptoms of botulism are nausea; vomiting; diarrhea; abdominal pain followed in 12 to 48 hours by double vision; dilated pupils; and difficulty speaking, swallowing, and breathing. There is no fever and no loss of awareness or alertness. **Death may result.**

Suspect botulism if your infant develops symptoms within a week of eating raw or home-prepared foods. Suspect the disease if more than one member of your family develops similar symptoms after eating the same prepared food. If symptoms of stomach or intestinal upset are followed by paralysis that starts at the eyes and moves downward, botulism may be the cause. Home diagnosis, however, is totally unreliable. Consult your doctor immediately if possible symptoms of botulism occur.

HOME CARE

None. Call your doctor immediately if you suspect botulism.

PRECAUTIONS

• Do not give babies unwashed, unpeeled raw foods or improperly cooked foods.
• Do not give honey to infants. • Do not use foods in damaged or dented store-bought cans. Damaged cans may have developed leaks through which the botulism germ can enter the food. • When canning or preserving foods at home, follow preparation and sterilization directions carefully.

MEDICAL TREATMENT

Diagnosis is made by cultures of the food eaten, stomach contents, and stools and by identifying the toxin in the patient's blood. Treatment includes injection of the antitoxin (a substance that counteracts the effects of the poison). Stomach washing, laxatives and enemas, possibly antibiotics, and hospitalization may be necessary. Immunization to prevent botulism is available, but only for persons at high risk.

Bowlegs and knock-knees

Quick Reference

SYMPTOMS   Legs bent outward at knees
Legs bent inward at knees

HOME CARE   Usually no home care is needed.

If you think your child has bowlegs or knock-knees, consult your doctor.

PRECAUTIONS

- ☐ Do not use orthopedic shoes unless prescribed by your doctor.

- ☐ To prevent rickets, all children should receive recommended amounts of vitamin D.

- ☐ Milk is a good source of vitamin D.

- ☐ Do not give your child supplements of vitamin D unless your doctor has prescribed them. Overdoses of vitamin D are harmful.

Very young children often appear bowlegged as shown on the left. Preschoolers may stand knock-kneed as shown on the right. Both conditions correct themselves as the child grows older.

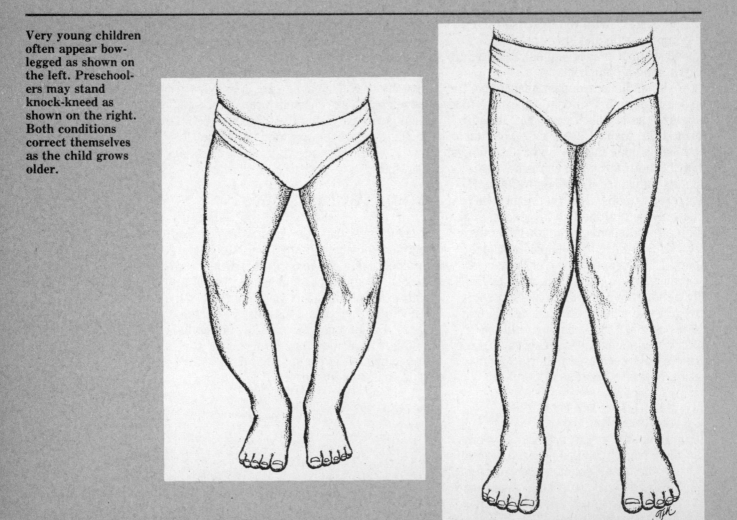

Bowlegs and knock-knees are two conditions in which the legs are not as straight as they are in most persons. In bowlegs, the legs bend outward so that the knees are farther apart than usual. In knock-knees, the legs bend inward so that the knees are closer together.

Theoretically, when a child stands straight, the ankle bones should touch or almost touch each other, and the knee bones should touch or almost touch each other. With an infant lying on the stomach or back, the legs can be pulled straight with the toes and knees pointed straight ahead to determine whether the bones of the knees and ankles come together. If ankles touch but the knees do not, the child can be said to be bowlegged. If the knees touch but the ankles do not, the child is knock-kneed.

By these standards, however, all infants, children, and adults are bowlegged or knock-kneed to some degree, so you should not become alarmed. Most infants appear bowlegged until they walk. Then when they start to walk, they walk "cowboy" style. This condition usually corrects itself by age two. Most preschoolers stand knock-kneed, especially if they are plump. This condition also corrects itself.

True bowlegs and knock-knees either are due to rickets (vitamin D deficiency) or are inherited. Once common 50 and more years ago, rickets is now rare in the United States. An unusual form of bowlegs, often occurring only on one side, is Blount's disease, in which the top of the tibia (shin bone) becomes deformed.

SIGNS AND SYMPTOMS

Have the child stand with the legs straight and the toes pointed forward. Then observe if there is any distance between the knees or ankles. Remember that any distance between the ankles or the knees varies from person to person and that these differences are usually normal. If you think that there might be a problem, ask your doctor.

HOME CARE

In most cases, no home care is needed. To prevent rickets, all children should receive about 400 international units of vitamin D daily. This amount is found in many commercial infant formulas and in most commercial milk. Some vitamin D is present in breast milk, but the amount varies. If your child is being breast-fed, ask your doctor whether the child is receiving enough vitamin D.

PRECAUTIONS

• If you think your infant or child is bow-legged or knock-kneed, watch to see if, after several months, the condition worsens. If it does, consult your doctor. • Do not use orthopedic shoes without your doctor's prescription. • Do not give your child vitamin D supplements unless your doctor has prescribed them. Overdoses of vitamin D can be harmful.

MEDICAL TREATMENT

In most instances, your doctor will examine your child and then prescribe no treatment—except to wait and watch. X rays of the knees may be required as well as blood tests for rickets. Use of orthopedic shoes or night splints is rarely necessary. For Blount's disease, braces or corrective operations on bones may be required.

Bronchiolitis

SYMPTOMS
Nasal congestion
Fever
Loss of appetite
Cough (mild to severe)
Rapid, sometimes difficult breathing
Wheezing
Irritability
Bluish skin

HOME CARE   None. See your doctor.

PRECAUTIONS

☐ Bronchiolitis can be a serious illness. See your doctor.

☐ Do not give cough medicines to a child who is having difficulty breathing.

☐ Give the child extra liquids to prevent dehydration (serious loss of body fluids).

☐ Dehydration in infants can be dangerous.

☐ If your infant has a frequent cough, see your doctor.

☐ If your infant has breathing difficulty, see your doctor.

Bronchiolitis is an inflammation in the lungs. Bronchiolitis occurs during the first two years of life, most often at about age six months. It is almost always caused by a respiratory virus.

Early symptoms are similar to symptoms of bronchitis. An infant may develop bronchiolitis after being exposed to an older child or adult with a cold. The illness may last for several days. As with bronchitis, infants who tend to develop bronchiolitis may develop asthma in later years.

SIGNS AND SYMPTOMS

The first symptoms of bronchiolitis are nasal congestion, fever, loss of appetite, and a mild cough. These symptoms may then progress to frequent, severe coughing; rapid and difficult breathing; wheezing (a whistling sound heard when the child breathes out); irritability; and cyanosis (a bluish discoloration of the skin). The child's extra efforts to breathe may cause flaring of the nostrils, as well as drawing in of the flesh in the spaces between the ribs and of the abdomen just below the ribs.

HOME CARE

Do not attempt to treat bronchiolitis on your own. Diagnosis and treatment should be handled by your doctor. See your doctor if your infant has a frequent cough, even if only for short periods. See your doctor if your child has difficulty in breathing other than that caused by nasal congestion. If your doctor recommends home treatment for bronchiolitis, it may be similar to treatment for bronchitis.

PRECAUTIONS

● Bronchiolitis can be a serious illness. See your doctor. ● Do not give cough medicine to a child with bronchiolitis. Cough medicines may be dangerous to a child who is already having difficulty breathing. ● An infant with rapid breathing can become dehydrated (a serious loss of body fluids) because the child is losing vapor from the breath. Dehydration in infants can be dangerous. Give the child extra fluids by mouth.

MEDICAL TREATMENT

In some areas, bronchiolitis is the most common reason for hospitalizing infants. An infant with bronchiolitis may require oxygen or intravenous fluids. A chest X ray, nose and throat cultures, and a blood count may be ordered. Antibiotics are of no use since they are not effective in treating viruses. If a child has repeated attacks of bronchiolitis, one injection of epinephrine may be given to determine if the child may have an allergy. If the epinephrine relieves the symptoms, it is likely the attacks are caused by an allergy, not a virus.

Related topics:

Asthma
Bronchitis
Common cold
Coughs
Dehydration
Frequent illnesses
Pneumonia
Shortness of
  breath
Viruses

Bronchitis

SYMPTOMS
Dry, hacking cough
Fever
Tightness and pain in center of chest
Loss of appetite
General weakness and discomfort
Rattling sound to breathing

HOME CARE
The child should rest during the fever stage and the worst of the cough.

Give aspirin or acetaminophen for aches and fever.

Phenylephrine or oxymetazoline nose drops may be used.

A humidifier or vaporizer helps breathing.

Give your child extra liquids.

PRECAUTIONS

☐ If there is pain on the side of the chest, see your doctor.

☐ If there is blood in the discharge coughed up, see your doctor.

☐ If bronchitis occurs more than once a year, see your doctor.

☐ If the condition worsens instead of improves after three or four days, see your doctor.

☐ Do not give oral decongestants to a child with bronchitis.

Bronchitis may be thought of as a cold that spreads to the windpipe (trachea) and to the air passages leading into the lungs (bronchial tubes). It may start with signs of a common cold, with nasal congestion and discharge, sneezing, watery eyes, and scratchy throat. Bronchitis may also develop without any cold symptoms appearing first.

Most cases of bronchitis are caused by viruses. These viruses cannot be cured by antibiotics. Bronchitis is contagious and is passed on in the same manner as a cold. If the disease occurs frequently, the child may have an underlying allergy. (Sometimes children with asthma tend to have repeated attacks of bronchitis.)

SIGNS AND SYMPTOMS

The major symptoms of bronchitis are a dry, hacking cough; a low-grade fever (100°F, oral; 101°F, rectal) or no fever; and tightness and pain in the center of the chest. Often the child experiences a loss of appetite and feels generally weak and uncomfortable. After a few days the cough loosens. Occasionally, a rattling sound can be heard in the chest when the child takes a breath, but there is never any real difficulty in breathing (except that caused by nasal congestion). The entire illness may last more than a week.

There is rarely high fever or prostration (extreme exhaustion or collapse). There is never pain on the side of the chest. No blood appears in the sputum (discharge coughed up out of the lungs).

HOME CARE

Treatment for bronchitis is similar to treatment for the common cold. Limited activity is recommended during the fever stage and the worst of the cough. Give aspirin or acetaminophen for fever and body aches. Phenylephrine or oxymetazoline nose drops may be used. A humidifier or vaporizer aids breathing. If the cough is exhausting or keeps the child from sleeping, cough medicine might help. Encourage your child to drink liquids to avoid dehydration (loss of body fluids).

PRECAUTIONS

● See your doctor if any unusual symptoms occur, such as pain on the side of the chest or blood in the sputum. ● See your doctor if bronchitis occurs more than once a year. ● See your doctor if the condition worsens instead of improves after three to four days. ● Do not use oral decongestants, which may tighten the chest and aggravate a dry cough.

MEDICAL TREATMENT

Your child's physical examination should include a careful examination of the chest. Throat or sputum cultures, a chest X ray, and a blood count may be taken. If bronchitis occurs frequently, your doctor will investigate the possibility of an allergy, a foreign body in the bronchial tubes, or a lowered resistance to infection. The use of antibiotics and some types of cough medicines is debatable. Antibiotics usually are not helpful for most types of bronchitis (those caused by virus), and some cough medicines can aggravate more than relieve the condition. If a child has repeated attacks of bronchitis, your doctor may give epinephrine by injection to determine if the child has an allergy. If epinephrine relieves the symptoms, it is likely the attacks are caused by an allergy.

Related topics:

Bronchiolitis
Chest pain
Common cold
Coughs
Cystic fibrosis
Dehydration
Frequent illnesses
Viruses

Bruises

SYMPTOM Discolored areas of the skin (black, blue, purple, red, yellow, or green)

HOME CARE Immediately after an injury, apply *cold* to decrease bleeding and bruising.

Twenty-four hours or more after an injury, apply *warmth* to help the body absorb the bruise.

PRECAUTIONS

☐ If bruises suddenly appear without injury, see your doctor.

☐ Petechiae scattered over the body may indicate an emergency. If there is also fever or collapse, **get medical treatment immediately.**

Bruises are made up of blood that has escaped from capillaries (tiny blood vessels) or larger blood vessels and can be seen through the skin. They vary from pinhead-size to several inches across. Bruises usually are black and blue in color. If they are near the skin's surface, they appear maroon or purple. Bruises of the whites of the eyeballs are always blood-red. As blood in a bruise moves back into the bloodstream, a bruise often becomes yellow or green.

If the escape of blood has been deep in the tissues—as with torn ligaments or broken bones—it may take days to reach the skin's surface as a visible bruise. Escaped blood often travels to other parts of the body. For example, a bruise of the forehead may travel to form black eyes.

Most bruises are caused by physical injuries. Most normally active children always seem to have one or more bruises. Children with fair complexions bruise more easily than children with darker complexions. Areas most likely to bruise are the shins, knees, arms, and thighs. Bruises may take days or weeks to disappear, depending upon their size.

A different type of bruises, called *spontaneous bruises*, may be a cause for concern. Spontaneous bruises suddenly appear on their own even though no injury or blow to the skin has occurred. Spontaneous bruises may be caused by abnormally fragile capillaries (sometimes due to scurvy, or a lack of vitamin C); capillaries injured by infections or by allergic reactions; or a lack of proper clotting of the blood.

Remember, however, that bruises often are caused by injuries that were simply not noticed. But if bruises appear in areas not likely to be injured, or if a great many bruises appear, it is less likely that they were caused by unnoticed injuries; these may be spontaneous bruises.

There is another type of bruise known as a *petechia*. Petechiae are pinhead to one-eighth inch in size. They are dark red or maroon in color and often appear by the hundreds. Forceful vomiting or coughing can sometimes cause many petechiae to appear on the body from the neck up.

Petechiae may also appear in one smaller area when caused by a blow to the skin.

SIGNS AND SYMPTOMS

Bruises are easily recognized when an area of the skin is discolored (black, blue, purple, red, green, or yellow). Bruises can be distinguished from other skin marks or rashes by a simple test. A bruise of any size does not blanch (turn white or lighter color) when pressed; all other red or purple marks or skin rashes will blanch when pressed.

HOME CARE

Cold applications soon after an injury has occurred help decrease bleeding and lessen bruising. Warm applications 24 or more hours after the injury can help the body reabsorb the blood in the bruise.

PRECAUTIONS

● Spontaneous bruising should always be examined by a doctor. Spontaneous bruising may be a sign of illness. ● Petechiae scattered over the body can indicate an urgent situation. If there is also fever or prostration (extreme exhaustion or collapse), a true emergency exists. Don't waste any time: **See your doctor at once.**

MEDICAL TREATMENT

For bruises caused by injuries, a doctor's treatment is the same as home care. For spontaneous bruises, including petechiae that are scattered over the body, your doctor will give a complete physical examination. The examination may include a blood count; platelet count; blood coagulation studies; nose, throat, and blood cultures; spinal tap; and bone marrow studies. The patient may be hospitalized to be given intravenous fluids and antibiotics.

Burns

SYMPTOMS
Pain
Reddened skin
Blisters
Scorched or blackened skin
Dead white skin

HOME CARE

Burns that are blistered, charred, or scorched:
Do not treat at home. Cover with a clean, wet cloth (do not apply ointments); keep the child warm; and see your doctor at once.

Burns with reddened skin only:
Immediately apply cold water compresses or cold running water until the pain lessens.
Generously apply petroleum jelly or silver sulfadiazine cream.
Cover with several layers of gauze.
Change the dressing every 24 to 48 hours until completely healed.

Sunburn:
Apply over-the-counter sunburn products, if needed, and leave uncovered.

PRECAUTIONS

☐ A severely burned child may go into a state of shock. See Signs and Treatment of Shock on this page.

☐ Never leave children home alone—not even for a moment.

☐ Keep the water heater turned low, and watch children around stove.

☐ Keep matches and cigarette lighters out of children's reach.

☐ Keep gasoline and other inflammables under lock and key outside of the house.

☐ Keep child-proof plugs in electrical outlets; keep children away from electrical wires and extension cords.

☐ Keep children current on tetanus boosters.

SIGNS OF SHOCK

Feeling faint
Weak pulse
Paleness in face
Cold sweat
Chills

Rapid breathing
Restlessness
Confusion
Cold, clammy limbs

TREATMENT OF SHOCK

☐ The child should lie flat, with the head lower than the rest of the body.

☐ Keep the child warm.

☐ Do not give food or drink.

☐ **Get medical help immediately.**

Burns are injuries of the skin caused by excessive heat, by chemicals (acids and alkalis), or by electricity. The seriousness of a burn depends on the size, the location, and the depth of the skin burned. Burns are classified as first-degree (the least serious), second-degree, or third-degree (the most serious).

First-degree burns cause reddening of the skin and pain; they may blister after one or two days. (Sunburn is a good example of a first-degree burn.) *Second-degree burns* redden and blister immediately. *Third-degree burns* are deepest and cause the death of a full depth of skin; the skin blisters or appears scorched (blackened) or dead white. If more than 10 percent of the skin surface has suffered second-degree or third-degree burns, a serious emergency exists. In fact, any second-degree or third-degree burn should be treated immediately by a doctor. A person with severe burns may go into a state of shock, which is life-threatening and requires immediate medical treatment. Burns of the fingers, joints, and face may be serious because burns in these locations may cause scarring and deformity.

SIGNS AND SYMPTOMS

Redness, blistering, or scorching of the skin are the obvious signs of a burn.

HOME CARE

Do not try to treat second-degree or third-degree burns at home; they must be treated by a doctor. If a burn is blistered, charred, or scorched, cover it with a clean, wet cloth; keep your child warm; and see your doctor at once. Do not apply ointments or other treatments to burns that will need a doctor's care.

First-degree burns (reddened skin only) can usually be cared for at home. Immediately apply cold water compresses to the burn, or place the burned area under cold running water. Continue applying cold until the pain lessens, or up to one-half hour.

First-degree burns treated at home must be covered to prevent infections.

The covering should not stick to the burn, but it should keep out air and germs until the burn has healed. (Once air is kept from the burn, there should be no further pain).

Generously apply petroleum jelly or a cream containing silver sulfadiazine to the burn. (Silver sulfadiazine requires a prescription, but your doctor may prescribe it over the telephone.) Then cover the area with several thicknesses of sterile gauze. Change the dressing every 24 to 48 hours until the burn completely heals.

Simple sunburn does not need to be dressed and covered in this manner.

PRECAUTIONS

• If a severely burned child becomes weak, pale, cold and clammy, or shows any other signs of shock, keep the child warm and get medical help immediately.
• **Prevention is extremely important.**
• Water over 115°F can scald. If there are young children in the home, turn the thermostat on the water heater down low.
• When cooking, keep your eyes on young children. • Keep matches and cigarette lighters out of your child's reach. • Do not keep gasoline or other inflammables in the home. Keep them under lock and key outside. • Avoid inflammable garments. • Keep child-proof plugs in electrical outlets. • Serious electrical burns commonly occur when young children chew live electrical wires and extension cords. • Second-degree and third-degree burns require up-to-date tetanus boosters. • Do not leave children home alone—not even for a moment.

MEDICAL TREATMENT

Your doctor will usually hospitalize your child for any third-degree burns; for second-degree burns that cover more than 10 percent of the skin; and for second-degree burns of the face, fingers, or joints. Hospital treatment involves proper dressings, close attention to the need for intravenous fluids, attention to kidney and stomach complications, and sometimes antibiotics and plastic surgery.

Related topics:

Blisters
Shock
Sunburn
Tetanus

Cat scratch fever

SYMPTOMS   Cat scratch or bite that doesn't heal
Redness
Pus
Swollen, tender, or red lymph glands
Low-grade fever

HOME CARE   Immediately scrub cat scratches or bites with soap and water for ten minutes.

Apply an antiseptic.

If the wound becomes infected, see your doctor.

PRECAUTIONS

☐ Do not allow young children to play with cats without supervision.

☐ Warn children not to tease cats or any other animals.

Scrub all cat scratches and bites immediately with soap and water for ten minutes.

74

Cat scratch fever is caused by a minor scratch or bite from a kitten or young cat. It is caused by a germ—probably a virus—although the cat is not ill. The puncture wound or scratch does not heal in the time expected. One to two weeks later, the wound is still red, sometimes with a small amount of pus. One to six weeks after the incident, the lymph nodes near the wound become swollen, tender, and red. The child has a low-grade fever (100°F, oral; 101°F, rectal). Eventually the lymph glands may break down and discharge pus through the skin.

SIGNS AND SYMPTOMS

The signs of cat scratch fever are a minor cat scratch or bite that hasn't healed; large, tender lymph nodes; and a low-grade fever. There may be pus in the wound. If you don't know that your child has been scratched by a cat, it may be difficult to tell cat scratch fever from a wound infected with staph or tuberculosis germs.

HOME CARE

Scrub all cat scratches and bites immediately with soap and water for ten minutes. Then apply an antiseptic. If the wound becomes infected, see your doctor.

PRECAUTIONS

● Unsupervised play between cats and young children is dangerous to both the child and the cat. ● Do not allow children to tease or torment cats or any other animals.

MEDICAL TREATMENT

Your doctor will rule out other illnesses by blood tests and cultures. Treatment with broad-spectrum antibiotics is occasionally helpful. Cat scratch fever may require surgical incision and drainage or the complete removal of a lymph gland.

Related topics:

Animal bites
Glands, swollen
Puncture wounds

Chest pain

SYMPTOM   Pain anywhere in the chest

HOME CARE   Give aspirin or acetaminophen.

Apply gentle heat with a heating pad.

If chest pain or soreness is caused by hard or frequent coughing, cough medicine may help.

PRECAUTIONS

☐ If chest pain is accompanied by shortness of breath, high fever, a cough producing blood flecks, or prostration (collapse), **get medical help immediately.**

☐ If there is persistent pain beneath either armpit that is made worse by breathing, see your doctor.

☐ Do not give cough medicine if the child is having difficulty breathing.

Chest pain is common during childhood. Although chest pain in adults can be serious, it is rarely a symptom of serious disease in children.

A very common form of chest pain in children is the so-called stitch in the side—a stabbing pain in the lower chest, more often on the left side than the right. This pain occurs with exercise and will stop after a minute or two of rest. This type of pain may be caused by gas pains in the large intestine, contraction of the spleen, or spasm of the diaphragm. Regardless of the cause, it is harmless.

Pain in the area of the sternum (breastbone) is common when a child has bronchitis or a head cold combined with a cough. A frequent, hard cough often makes the diaphragm sore, causing a pain just below the ribs. Pain on one side of the chest may be caused by pleurodynia (inflammation of the lining of the chest cavity) or by shingles.

Injuries (including muscle strains, bruises, and fractured ribs) cause pain that is worsened by deep breathing and movements of the chest. All of these types of chest pain are relatively minor and usually can be cared for at home.

There are a few causes of chest pain in children that are more serious, but these are also uncommon. Pleurisy that develops as a complication of pneumonia may cause chest pain; the pain is accompanied by other signs of pleurisy (fever, difficult breathing, cough).

Another more serious cause of chest pain is spontaneous pneumothorax, which is a bursting of a small bubble on the surface of the lung. When the bubble bursts, air escapes into the chest cavity, causing gradual collapse of the lung. This condition comes on suddenly, often with sharp pain, and causes increasing shortness of breath. A hernia of the diaphragm causes chest pain that is usually worse when lying down, and less or absent when sitting and standing. Heart pain in children, even those with serious heart conditions, is so rare that it is practically unknown.

SIGNS AND SYMPTOMS

Chest pain may occur alone or along with other symptoms. The exact location of the pain and the circumstances that bring on the pain or make it worse are clues to the type and cause of chest pain. Other symptoms (cough, fever, rash at the site of the pain, and shortness of breath) are also clues to the cause.

HOME CARE

Most cases of minor chest pain can be treated at home with aspirin or acetaminophen, mild heat, and reassurance. If chest pain is caused by a hard cough, cough medicines may help.

Pleurisy, spontaneous pneumothorax, and hernia of the diaphragm should be treated by a doctor.

PRECAUTIONS

● If chest pain is accompanied by shortness of breath, high fever, a cough producing blood flecks, or prostration (collapse), **get medical help immediately.**
● If there is persistent pain beneath either armpit that is made worse by breathing, see your doctor. ● Do not give cough medicines if the child is having difficulty breathing.

MEDICAL TREATMENT

Your doctor may recommend X rays and blood tests. Pneumothorax is treated by hospitalization, close observation, and possibly a puncture of the chest wall to remove trapped air.

Related topics:

Bronchitis
Pneumonia
Shingles
Viruses

Chicken pox

SYMPTOMS
Rash with blisters
Fever
Mild cold symptoms

HOME CARE
Isolate the child.

Cut the child's fingernails to lessen scratching.

Bathe the child in lukewarm water with cornstarch added.

Apply calamine lotion to the skin with a soft cloth.

Give acetaminophen, **not aspirin,** for fever or pain.

PRECAUTIONS

☐ Do not give aspirin to a child with chicken pox.

☐ If a child with chicken pox develops a high fever, prostration (collapse), headache, vomiting, or convulsions, see your doctor immediately.

☐ If an infant is exposed to chicken pox or develops it, call your doctor.

☐ If a child who is taking steroids or similar drugs is exposed to or develops chicken pox, call your doctor.

☐ If a child with unusually low resistance to disease is exposed to or develops chicken pox, call your doctor.

☐ If the pox become infected (show increasing redness, soreness, and pus), call your doctor.

☐ If lymph glands become red and tender, call your doctor.

☐ Do not apply calamine with phenol.

☐ If bruises or broken blood vessels appear under the skin (but there has been no injury), see your doctor.

☐ Avoid breaking the blisters or disturbing the scabs, since scarring can occur.

Chicken pox is caused by a specific virus which is highly contagious. Chicken pox is contracted through the air from a person who has the disease. Symptoms may appear within 12 to 21 days after being exposed to a person with chicken pox.

One attack of chicken pox makes a person immune for life, unless the attack is extremely mild. There is no vaccine available to prevent chicken pox.

SIGNS AND SYMPTOMS

Chicken pox may start with the symptoms of a mild cold, but often a rash is the first sign. The rash worsens for three to four days and then heals in three to four days. The child is contagious from 24 hours before the rash appears until all blisters of the rash have dried. Fever can be low or as high as 105°F; fever is the worst on the third or fourth day after the rash appears.

The key symptom of chicken pox is the rash. Each new spot resembles an insect bite. Within hours the spot develops a small clear blister in the center, which may be hard to see without good light. Most blisters break and are replaced by a brown scab. The rash usually begins on the trunk and moves outward to the limbs and face. However, the rash may appear anywhere on the skin, including the scalp and the mucous membranes of the mouth, genitals, anus, and eyelids. It becomes quite itchy. The spots never appear in bunches or groups. New pox continue to appear hourly for three to four days.

HOME CARE

Bed rest is not required, but your child should be isolated from other people. Cut the child's fingernails to lessen scratching. To reduce the itching, bathe your child in lukewarm water with cornstarch added, or apply calamine lotion to the skin. Give acetaminophen, **not aspirin,** for fever or pain.

PRECAUTIONS

● **Do not** give aspirin to a child with chicken pox. Aspirin use during chicken pox *may* be a factor causing Reye's syndrome, which is a life-threatening illness. ● Encephalitis (inflammation of the brain) is a rare complication of chicken pox. If high fever, prostration (collapse), headache, vomiting, and convulsions occur, see your doctor immediately. ● Chicken pox can be dangerous to newborns. If a young infant is exposed to chicken pox or develops chicken pox, call your doctor. ● Chicken pox is also dangerous to persons taking steroids or other immunosuppressant drugs and to children with immune mechanism deficiencies, which hinder the child's ability to fight infectious diseases. If such a child develops chicken pox or is exposed to it, call your doctor. ● Even if a child has already been exposed to someone with chicken pox, prevent any further exposure. The longer the exposure is, the more severe the attack of chicken pox will be. ● If the pox become infected, (showing an increasing redness, soreness, and formation of pus), call your doctor. ● The lymph glands of the neck, armpits, groin, and back of the skull ordinarily swell with chicken pox; however, if they become red and tender, they may be infected. Report this to your doctor. ● **Do not** apply calamine with phenol. ● When your child is bathed, pat the skin dry without breaking the blisters or disturbing the scabs to avoid scarring. ● If spontaneous bruises (bruises not caused by injuries) appear, or if ruptured blood vessels appear under the skin, see your doctor.

MEDICAL TREATMENT

If pox have become infected, your doctor will usually culture the infected pox and will treat your child with oral antibiotics for five to ten days. (Antibiotics do not influence the course of the chicken pox, however; they work only against the secondary infection.) If a child at high risk is exposed to chicken pox, your doctor will probably give a zoster immune globulin or a gamma globulin shot. If there are signs of encephalitis, your child will probably be hospitalized for tests and treatment. Spontaneous bleeding under the skin may be treated with oral medications, or your doctor may order hospitalization.

Related topics:

Bruises
Encephalitis
Rash
Reye's syndrome

Choking

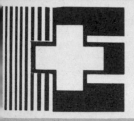

EMERGENCY SYMPTOMS

Apply emergency treatment immediately.

IMPORTANT

If an object completely blocks the air passage, you have only a few minutes to reestablish an airway before brain damage or death can occur.

SYMPTOMS

Unable to breathe
Unable to cry out or speak
Skin turns blue

EMERGENCY TREATMENT

1. Immediately call police or paramedic squad for help.

2. Give the child **one minute** to cough up the object by his own efforts. If unsuccessful . . .

3. Place the child head down over your lap. Support the head and neck to avoid neck fracture. Pound hard on the back four times. If unsuccessful . . .

4. Stand the child up. Stand behind the child with your arms around him and your hands joined in front, just below the ribs. Thrust inward and upward against the child's abdomen, which may force the object to pop out.

5. If the child is not breathing after the object is removed, give mouth-to-mouth resuscitation until trained help arrives.

PRECAUTIONS

☐ **Do not** try to reach into the throat with your fingers or tweezers to remove the object unless all other safer methods fail.

☐ Never give mouth-to-mouth resuscitation until *after* the object is removed.

☐ Support the child's head and neck before pounding on the child's back.

☐ Prevent choking. Examine all toys for loose eyes, beads, or small parts. Keep tablets under lock and key.

☐ **Do not** give peanuts, popcorn, or hard candies to toddlers. Keep such foods out of their reach.

☐ Place a vomiting baby on his or her stomach to lessen the chance of choking on the vomit.

Left: Place the child head down over your lap. Support head and neck and pound hard on back four times.

Right: Stand child up. Stand behind child with your arms around child and your hands joined in front just below child's ribs. Thrust inward and upward against child's abdomen.

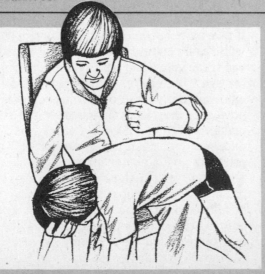

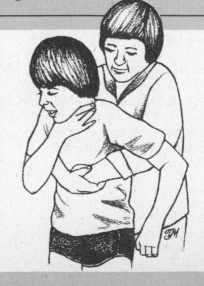

Choking is one of the few true emergencies of childhood in which minutes may determine life or death. A swallowed object is the most common and serious cause of choking. Choking is caused by the obstruction of the airway resulting in an inability to breathe. It is easily identified by two key signs: the child frantically tries to breathe, and the child is not able to cry out or to speak.

If choking continues, the child quickly becomes blue, convulsive, limp, and unconscious. If the object completely blocks the air passage, you have only a few minutes to reestablish an airway before brain damage or death can occur.

The objects that choke children are usually of a shape and size to plug the opening into the throat like a cork. Frequent and especially dangerous causes of choking are peanuts, tablets, glass eyes of toy animals, hard or hard-coated candies, beads, popcorn, and tiny toys or small parts from toys. Solid particles of food from the stomach may choke a child who breathes in during vomiting. A vomiting baby is safest from choking when lying on his or her stomach.

Choking may also occur in a child who has croup. But choking caused by croup is slightly different and is treated differently. A child choking from croup frantically tries to breathe, but the child is still able to speak or cry. See the article on Croup for treatment of that form of choking.

SIGNS AND SYMPTOMS

Choking on an object is easily identified by the two major symptoms. There are frantic, unsuccessful efforts to breathe. The child cannot talk or cry.

HOME CARE

Seconds count! Scream for help. A second adult on the scene should phone the police or paramedic squad for help. (Police are usually more quickly available in most communities than an ambulance, the fire department, or a doctor.)

First, give your child one minute to clear the obstruction by his or her own efforts. If this doesn't work, place your child's head down over a chair, table, or your lap and pound hard on his back four times. Broken ribs heal; death does not. Support the child's head and neck before pounding to avoid fracturing the neck.

If this is unsuccessful, try the Heimlich maneuver. Stand the child up. While standing to the child's back, reach around the child and thrust inward and upward with your locked hands just below the ribs below the breastbone. You are trying to squeeze the upper abdomen and lower chest. This will swiftly force up the diaphragm (a band of muscle separating the chest and abdominal cavities) so that air is pushed out of the lungs. The rush of air out of the lungs will pop the object out of the airway. Only if these safer measures fail should you consider reaching into the child's throat with a hooked finger or tweezer in an effort to remove or dislodge the foreign body: there's a good chance of pushing the object more tightly into the windpipe in your desperation to remove it. If your child is not breathing after the object is removed, give mouth-to-mouth resuscitation until trained help arrives.

PRECAUTIONS

● Never give mouth-to-mouth resuscitation until the obstructing object is removed; to do so may force the object further down the throat. ● Prevention of choking is most important. Examine all toys for loose eyes or other small parts. Keep tablets under lock and key. **Do not give peanuts, popcorn, or hard candies to toddlers.** (Clean up after adult parties before children can wander unattended into a room.)

MEDICAL TREATMENT

When the object completely blocks the air passage, the child seldom reaches a doctor in time. However, the object may only partially block the airway, even though you may not think so. Your doctor will operate, on the spot, to open the windpipe through the neck (tracheotomy). Then oxygen, artificial respiration, and intravenous fluids will be given.

Related topics:

Convulsions
Croup
Swallowed objects

Circumcision

PHYSICAL CONDITIONS REQUIRING CIRCUMCISION

No opening in the foreskin
Opening too small to allow urine through
Pulled back foreskin cannot be drawn
  forward

HOME CARE

Cover a circumcision with gauze coated with petroleum jelly and a nonstick bandage until it is healed.

Do not submerge the circumcision in bath water until it is healed.

PRECAUTIONS

☐ If a circumcision bleeds more than a few drops, call your doctor.

☐ If there are signs of infection (pus, spreading redness, swelling of the penis), see your doctor.

☐ During bathing, pull back any part of the foreskin left after circumcision in order to cleanse the base of the glans.

☐ If the foreskin is not circumcised, pull the foreskin back during bathing to thoroughly clean the glans.

☐ Boy babies born with any malformations of the penis should usually not be circumcised.

Circumcision is the removal of the foreskin of the penis. Most boy babies have a cuff of skin (foreskin) that covers the end of the penis (the glans). The natural opening in the foreskin is usually large enough to allow urine through (rarely is there no opening at all). But in a condition called phimosis, the opening is not large enough to allow the foreskin to be pulled back to uncover the glans. It is important to be able to pull back the foreskin so that the normal, waxy material that forms under the foreskin (smegma) can be removed during bathing. When the opening in the foreskin is too small to allow the foreskin to be pulled back, the foreskin can be stretched by a doctor. However, if the penis is uncircumcised, there is some possibility that the pulled back foreskin cannot be drawn forward again and may act as a tourniquet, cutting off the blood supply to the glans (paraphimosis).

Circumcision has been practiced on all continents for centuries, both for religious reasons and as a ritual to reaching manhood. In the United States, it has been commonly performed since World War II. Its advantages are easier cleansing and lessened possibility of paraphimosis. However, contrary to what many people believe, circumcision does not protect the male against cancer of the penis. The disadvantages of circumcision are a slight chance of infection or bleeding after the operation (less than 1 percent); the brief pain of the operation; and rare, accidental injury to the glans during the operation.

In recent years many doctors have declared that circumcision is unnecessary surgery. On the other hand, many other doctors feel that the advantages outweigh the disadvantages. The decision whether or not to circumcise male infants remains with the parents. Parents should ask questions and gather as much information as possible to help them make the decision.

SIGNS AND SYMPTOMS

Circumcision is required only when boys are born with no opening in the foreskin, when the opening is too small to allow passage of urine, or when paraphimosis has developed and must be immediately corrected.

HOME CARE

A circumcision should be covered, until healed (two to five days), with a nonstick bandage and gauze coated with petroleum jelly. The area should not be submerged in bath water until the wound has healed.

PRECAUTIONS

• Any bleeding of the circumcised penis beyond a few drops should be reported to your doctor. • If there are any signs of infection (pus, spreading redness, swelling of the shaft of the penis), see your doctor. • Any part of the foreskin left after circumcision should be pulled back to expose the base of the glans, and this area should be cleansed during bathing. • Boy babies born with malformations of the penis should not be circumcised because the foreskin may be used later during surgery to correct the malformation.

MEDICAL TREATMENT

Your doctor or religious leader will perform the circumcision, using one of a variety of approved techniques. Ask for specific directions for care of the circumcision. In a rare instance of postoperative infection, the doctor will culture the circumcision and blood, and start antibiotics.

Colic

SYMPTOMS

Cramps in the digestive tract
Crying for hours at a time
No other obvious cause of crying
Child does not take a complete feeding

HOME CARE

Look for other possible causes of crying and discomfort.

Look for possible signs of illness.

Offer a feeding to check if the baby is simply hungry.

If colic seems to be the problem, apply gentle heat to the baby's abdomen.

A pacifier may calm the child.

Try inserting a glycerine suppository or lubricated thermometer to help the child pass a bowel movement.

PRECAUTIONS

☐ If bottle-feeding, make sure the formula is prepared properly.

☐ Keep the bottle nipple full to keep the baby from swallowing too much air.

☐ Make sure the bottle's nipple hole is large enough so the baby can finish feeding in less than 20 to 25 minutes.

☐ After each feeding, carefully burp the baby in different positions.

☐ If breast-feeding, be sure the mother's nipples are not bleeding. Swallowed blood causes cramps.

☐ Between feedings, try keeping the baby partly upright in an infant carrier to be sure the child is not regurgitating food into the esophagus.

Colic is any cramp-like, recurring abdominal pain. Colic has a variety of causes and may occur at any age. Most often, however, people use the term to refer to colic that occurs in infants.

Infantile colic, or "three-month" colic, is a specific problem that bothers 10 to 20 percent of babies in the United States. Colic is far more common in bottle-fed babies than in breast-fed babies. Colic starts during the first few weeks of life and lasts one to six months (an average of three months).

SIGNS AND SYMPTOMS

The signs of colic are seen in the typical behavior of colicky infants. A baby with colic cries for hours a day, particularly in the late afternoon and evening. The child pulls the legs up, clenches the fists, screams, and turns red. The child may feed briefly but soon stops feeding and returns to crying. Rocking and cuddling also stop the cries only briefly. In other respects, the infant is normal; the baby gains weight well, has normal bowel movements, and doesn't spit up any more than most infants do.

A variation of this classical form of colic is the infant past two weeks of age who wakes frequently (every two hours or so), cries fretfully, takes one to two ounces of formula or a few minutes at the mother's breast, falls into a fitful sleep, and wakens later to repeat this pattern.

HOME CARE

First check for obvious causes of crying and discomfort other than colic. Look for diarrhea or constipation; loose diaper pins; severe diaper rash; a trapped arm or leg; whether the baby is too hot or too cold; or signs of illness—fever, nasal discharge, cough, reddened eyes, vomiting, hernia (a lump in the groin), or sores on the body. See whether your baby responds promptly to talking and cuddling and remains comfortable. A baby in pain can be distracted, but only temporarily. If breast-feeding, check that the mother's nipples are not bleeding. Swallowed blood causes cramps. If a breast-feeding mother drinks too much cow's milk, this can also cause cramps in the infant.

Offer your baby a feeding. If your baby drinks generously and falls asleep comfortably for several hours, the child was hungry, not colicky. Keep the baby partially upright in an infant carrier between feedings to be sure the baby is not regurgitating food into the esophagus.

If colic still seems likely, applying gentle heat to the abdomen temporarily relieves the pain. First place a cloth diaper over the infant's abdomen. Then place a heating pad (turned to "low") on top of the diaper. Giving the child a pacifier may help. Also try inserting a glycerine suppository or lubricated thermometer to induce a bowel movement.

PRECAUTIONS

● Make sure the formula is properly prepared. ● When bottle-feeding your baby, be sure that the nipple is kept full; this keeps your baby from swallowing too much air. ● Make sure the bottle's nipple hole is large enough so that the baby can finish feeding in a reasonable time. ● Carefully burp the baby in different positions after each feeding.

MEDICAL TREATMENT

Your doctor will check for signs of illness, such as sores in the mouth or urinary tract problems. A urinalysis may be ordered. Your doctor also may recommend a change in formula to investigate the possibility that the child is allergic to the formula. A breast-feeding mother may need to eliminate all milk products from her diet to see if this is what is affecting her child. The doctor may also temporarily stop any solids already started to determine if the child may be allergic to certain foods.

Related topics:

Constipation
Coughs
Diaper rashes
Diarrhea in infants
Fever
Food allergies
Hernia
Vomiting

Common cold

SYMPTOMS

Nasal congestion
Sneezing
Clear nasal discharge
Scratchy sore throat
Fever
Red, watery eyes
Dry cough
Swollen, tender neck glands
Mild pain in the ears

HOME CARE

Give the child plenty of liquids.

Do not permit strenuous activities while the child has a fever.

Increase room humidity with a vaporizer or humidifier.

Give aspirin or acetaminophen for fever or pain.

Use nose drops or oral decongestants and a nasal aspirator to relieve nasal congestion.

Use cough medicine if the cough is severe.

Isolate the child, particularly from infants and the elderly.

PRECAUTIONS

☐ Do not overuse cold medications. Overuse can cause more harm than good.

☐ Do not expose young infants to anyone with a cold, even a mild one.

☐ The following are usually not cold symptoms but signs of another illness:
- fever lasting more than two or three days
- pus-like discharge from eyes, nose, or ears
- redness or tenderness of the neck glands
- breathing difficulties
- chest pain
- severe headache
- stiff neck
- vomiting
- shaking chills
- prostration (collapse)

If any of these symptoms occur, call your doctor.

A cold is an infection of the upper respiratory tract that is caused by a virus. The infection causes discomfort of the throat, nose, and sinuses. A cold sometimes also affects the eyes (connected to the nose by the tear ducts); the ears (connected to the nose by the eustachian tubes); and the lymph nodes of the neck (connected to the nose by lymph channels). A cold is transmitted from person to person through the air or by droplets on the hands or on objects (toys, drinking glasses, handkerchiefs). Symptoms may develop within two to seven days after being exposed to a cold virus. People of all ages are subject to catching colds, but younger children and infants are particularly at risk from colds.

Many fruitless years were spent trying to develop a vaccine against the cold germ. Then it was discovered that there is not just one cold germ. Colds are actually caused by many different viruses, and all respiratory viruses can cause common colds. An attack by any of the more than 185 viruses makes a person immune to only that virus and none of the others. Often this immunity lasts only for a short time.

Many cold viruses can cause complications such as croup, laryngitis, bronchitis, bronchiolitis, viral pneumonia, and encephalitis. All cold viruses can make a child more susceptible to additional bacterial infections—ear infections, sinus infections, lymph infections, or bacterial pneumonia. No child's cold should be taken lightly.

SIGNS AND SYMPTOMS

The symptoms of a cold are nasal congestion, sneezing, clear nasal discharge, scratchy sore throat, and fever up to 103°F. In general, the younger the child, the higher the fever. Symptoms may also include reddened, watery eyes; dry cough; mild swelling and tenderness of the lymph nodes in the neck; and mild pain in the ears.

It is often difficult to tell a cold from other illnesses that have similar symptoms. Usually it is assumed to be a cold if the familiar cold symptoms occur but

symptoms of other illnesses do not. Another clue is that a cold lasts only three to ten days.

HOME CARE

Increase room humidity with a vaporizer or humidifier. Have your child drink a lot of liquids. Isolate the child from others, particularly from infants and the elderly. Bed rest is not required, but the child should avoid strenuous physical activities while fever is present. Give aspirin or acetaminophen for fever or pain. Use nose drops or oral decongestants and a nasal aspirator to relieve nasal stuffiness and discharge. Use cough medicines for easing a severe cough. Remember, however, that overuse of any of these medications can cause more harm than good. Chest rubs and vitamin C treatments have *not* proven to be helpful. Your child should eat only what he or she is able to eat.

PRECAUTIONS

● The following symptoms do not usually occur with a common cold and may be signs of another illness: fever lasting more than two to three days; pus-like discharge from the eyes, nose, or ears; large, red, tender neck glands; breathing difficulties; chest pain; severe headache; stiff neck; vomiting; shaking chills; prostration (collapse). If any of these symptoms occur, call your doctor. ● Some viruses that cause common colds stay in the body for one to two weeks, so the child remains contagious for the entire time of the cold. ● Infants should not be exposed to anyone with a cold, even a mild cold. Infants are not protected against the common cold by the mother's antibodies; young infants can become seriously ill from these viruses.

MEDICAL TREATMENT

Your doctor will perform a physical examination to check for signs of other illnesses and for signs of complications. The doctor sometimes will order a blood count and throat culture. Otherwise, the doctor's treatment is the same as home care.

Concussion

SYMPTOMS

Unconsciousness at instant of injury
No memory of the accident
No memory of events before the accident
Confusion
Persistent vomiting
Inability to walk
Eyes not parallel
Pupils of different sizes
Pupils that do not become smaller when a
   bright light is shined in the eyes
Blood coming from the ear
Bloody fluid that does not clot coming
   from the nose
Increasingly severe headache
Stiff neck
Increasing drowsiness
Slow pulse
Abnormal breathing

HOME CARE

If there are any signs of concussion, see your doctor.

If there is a head injury with no signs of concussion (or while waiting to see the doctor), have the child rest in bed with the head on a pillow.

The child may sleep but **must** be wakened every hour so that you can check on the child's condition.

Continue bed rest until at least one day after the child seems fully recovered.

Give only aspirin or acetaminophen for headache.

PRECAUTIONS

☐ **Do not** try to treat the child at home if there are any signs of concussion.

☐ **Do not** give pain killers, sedatives, or any medicine stronger than aspirin or acetaminophen to a child with any head injury.

☐ If the scalp is depressed (pushed in) at the site of the injury, see your doctor.

☐ If gentle tapping of the skull produces the dull sound of a broken melon, see your doctor.

A concussion is an injury to the brain. It is caused by a fall or by a blow on the head from a blunt object. In many ways, a concussion is like a bruise of the brain. There is swelling in the brain, and sometimes blood escapes into the brain tissue. Since a concussion is an injury to the brain matter itself, it may occur even if the skull is not fractured. Concussions range from mild to serious.

Most children suffer one or more blows to the head at some time during childhood. Typical reactions to head injuries are immediate crying, headache, paleness, vomiting once or twice, a lump or cut at the site of injury, and sleepiness for one or two hours. These are *not* the signs of a concussion; they are usual reactions to a blow on the head.

SIGNS AND SYMPTOMS

Any of the following are signs of a possible concussion: unconsciousness at the instant of the injury; no memory of the accident or of events that occurred before the accident; confusion (child doesn't recognize parents or know his or her own name); persistent vomiting; inability to walk; eyes not parallel; pupils of different sizes (note: some children have unequal pupils normally); pupils that do not become smaller when a bright light is shined into the eyes; blood coming from the ear canal; bloody fluid which does not clot coming from the nose; headache that continues to become more severe; stiff neck (the chin cannot be touched to the chest with the mouth closed); increasing drowsiness; slow pulse (less than 50 to 60 beats per minute); and abnormal breathing.

There are two rare forms of concussion in which symptoms do not develop until hours after the injury (called epidural bleeding) or until days or weeks afterward (called subdural bleeding).

HOME CARE

If the child shows any of the signs of a concussion, see your doctor.

If there are no signs of a concussion, or if you are waiting to see the doctor, have the child rest in bed. Bed rest is the most essential treatment for a head injury that does not penetrate the skull. Keep the child lying quietly, with the head on a pillow. Check the child frequently. The child may sleep but **must** be wakened every hour so that you can check on the child's condition until he or she feels well. Keep the child in bed until at least one day after the child seems fully recovered. Give only aspirin or acetaminophen for headache.

PRECAUTIONS

● **Do not** attempt home treatment if there are any signs of concussion. ● **Do not** treat a head injury at home if the scalp is depressed (pushed in) at the site of injury or if a gentle tapping of the skull produces the dull sound of a broken melon. (These symptoms rarely, if ever, occur without other signs of concussion.) ● **Do not** give pain killers, sedatives, or any medication stronger than aspirin or acetaminophen to a child with a head injury.

MEDICAL TREATMENT

Your doctor may or may not order X rays of the skull. Your child may be hospitalized for observation. A CAT scan may be useful. A CAT (computerized axial tomography) scan gives three-dimensional X rays of the brain. Echoencephalogram, electroencephalogram, and spinal tap tests are sometimes helpful. If the concussion is serious, your doctor may consult a neurosurgeon (a specialist in the brain and nervous system).

Conjunctivitis

SYMPTOMS
Redness of the entire white of the eye
Yellow pus from the eye
Swollen, red eyelids
Burning sensation in the eye

HOME CARE

If you think your child has conjunctivitis, call your doctor.

Your doctor may see the child or may prescribe antibiotic eyedrops or ointment over the telephone. Place the prescribed eyedrops or ointment into the eyes as frequently as directed.

Treat both eyes, even if only one eye seems infected. Continue treatment for 24 hours after the eye seems normal.

Isolate your child from other people.

Watch other family members for symptoms.

PRECAUTIONS

☐ If eyes don't begin clearing within 24 hours after beginning the medication, call your doctor.

☐ Eye ointments will cause blurred vision for a few minutes after each application. If there are any other vision problems, call your doctor.

☐ Notify your doctor if a child with conjunctivitis shows any other signs of illness (a head cold, nasal discharge, sore throat, earache, fever, or sore glands).

To place eyedrops or ointment into the eye, gently pull down the lower lid to form a pouch. Place the prescribed amount of medication into the pouch. Do not touch the eye dropper or ointment tube to the eye. Direct the child to close the eyes, but not to rub them. Wipe away excess medication around the eye with a clean tissue.

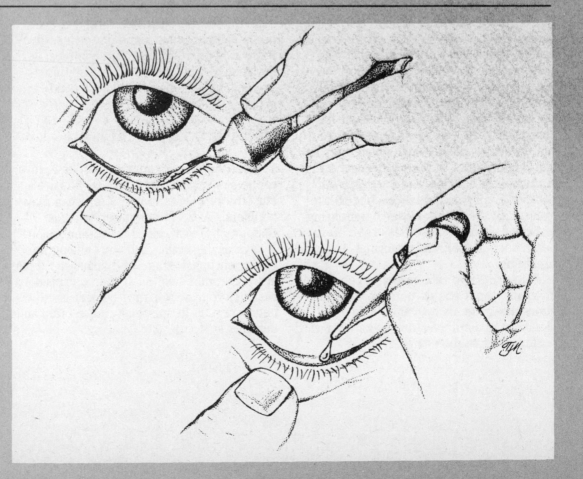

Conjunctivitis, or pinkeye, is an infection of the transparent membrane (conjunctiva) that covers the white of the eye and lines the inside of the eyelids.

Conjunctivitis is highly contagious. It is spread by contact with discharge from the eye or by contact with objects (hands, facecloths, toys, handkerchiefs) that have touched the infected eyes or that the child with conjunctivitis has handled. Symptoms of conjunctivitis may develop within one to three days after contact with the infection. Conjunctivitis usually spreads quickly to the other eye.

Conjunctivitis may exist alone. It may also develop as a complication of sore throat, tonsillitis, earache, or sinusitis.

SIGNS AND SYMPTOMS

Conjunctivitis causes redness of the entire white of the eye. There is a buildup of yellow pus. The eyelids may swell and redden. There is a burning sensation in the eye. Vision is always normal, and light rarely bothers the eye.

Conjunctivitis is different from other conditions that also cause reddened eyes. *Eye allergies* cause itching and tearing but never pain or pus. *Viruses* cause pain and tearing but no pus. *Foreign bodies* in the eye cause pain, sensitivity to light, and tearing, but no pus; redness caused by a foreign body usually appears in only one part of the white of the eye. *Glaucoma* causes pain, enlargement of the pupil, tearing, and sensitivity to light, but no pus. If your child has reddened eyes, remember to consider these other possible causes besides conjunctivitis.

HOME CARE

If you suspect that your child has conjunctivitis, call your doctor. Your doctor may wish to see the child; however, if your description of the symptoms is detailed and accurate, the doctor may decide to prescribe antibiotic eyedrops or ointment over the telephone.

Place the antibiotic eyedrops or ointment into the eyes as frequently as directed. Treat both eyes even if only one eye seems to be affected. Continue treatment for 24 hours after the eyes appear normal. Since conjunctivitis is so contagious, isolate your child from other people. Watch other members of the family for possible symptoms.

PRECAUTIONS

• With medication, the eyes should improve quickly—usually within 24 hours. If eyes don't begin clearing in that time, call your doctor. • If eye ointments are used, vision will be blurred for a few minutes after each application. Any other vision problems should be reported promptly to your doctor. • Be certain to notify your doctor of any other signs of illness, such as a head cold, nasal discharge, sore throat, earache, fever, or sore glands. Conjunctivitis may be a complication of another disease.

MEDICAL TREATMENT

The doctor will carefully examine the outside and inside of the eyeball, including looking under the eyelids for hidden foreign bodies. Your doctor may stain the eyeball with special drops to look for injuries or ulcers (scratches on the surface of the eye). The doctor may also culture any discharge from the eye, nose, or throat. Antibiotics taken by mouth might be prescribed. If necessary, your doctor may consult an ophthalmologist (a specialist in eye diseases).

Related topics:

Common cold
Earaches
Eye, blocked tear
   duct
Eye allergies
Eye injuries
Fever
Glands, swollen
Sinusitis
Sore throat
Tonsillitis

Constipation

SYMPTOMS
Hard, dry stools
Stools larger in diameter than usual
Pain during bowel movements
Red blood on or around stools
Cramps in the abdomen
Loss of appetite

HOME CARE

For immediate, temporary relief:
Use a glycerine suppository or give an enema.

For long-term cure:
Include more roughage in your child's diet (fruits, vegetables, unrefined grains, and unrefined sugars).
Give your child fewer constipating foods (such as milk and milk products).

PRECAUTIONS

☐ **Do not** give laxatives to children unless recommended by your doctor.

☐ **Do not** use enemas, suppositories, or laxatives on a regular basis. They are habit-forming.

☐ **Do not** assume a child is constipated if bowel movements do not occur daily. Constipation is hardness of the stools; it has nothing to do with the number of bowel movements. Normal, healthy children may have several bowel movements a day or only several a week.

☐ If a child becomes constipated during toilet training, stop training efforts.

Constipation is a condition in which the bowel movements are too hard. The frequency of bowel movements is not a factor of constipation. Passage of six too-firm bowel movements a day is considered constipation. Passage of one normal or soft bowel movement every third or fourth day is not constipation. Many normal, healthy children have a bowel movement only every few days and are not constipated. The hardness of a stool is judged by appearance and by diameter. A stool greater than twice the usual diameter is probably too hard.

Over 95 percent of constipation cases involve no physical abnormality. This form of constipation can always be cured by changes in the diet or by using medications that soften the stools.

Constipation occurs in the large bowel (colon). The function of the colon is to store unabsorbed food waste and to absorb and hold water from the liquid material received from the small intestine. If the colon absorbs too much water, the stools become hard.

In children, there are two common reasons for constipation. The first reason is that the diet does not include enough roughage, which holds water in the stools. Foods that prevent constipation are all fruit juices and all fruits—particularly those eaten with their skin on—except bananas and apples; all vegetables, especially if eaten raw, except peeled potatoes; unrefined grains (whole-grain cereals and breads); and unrefined sugars (brown sugar, molasses, honey). All other foods, including milk and milk products, promote constipation.

A second common reason for constipation in children is that the child resists the normal impulse to move the bowels. This allows the colon to continue absorbing water out of the retained stools; it results in stools that are too hard. A common reason why children resist the normal impulse to move the bowels is that the parents are putting too much pressure on the child during toilet training. Once the stools become too hard, bowel movements become painful. Fear of such pain makes the child even more determined to postpone bowel movements. Constipation

enlarges the colon, causing a loss of muscle tone, and the physical impulse to empty the bowel becomes weaker. This cycle can lead to chronic constipation.

SIGNS AND SYMPTOMS

The major sign of constipation is stools that are too hard, too dry, and larger in diameter than usual. Constipation can cause pain in the anus during bowel movements. Red blood may appear on and around the stools. Other symptoms are cramps in the abdomen and an eventual loss of appetite.

If constipation continues for days and weeks, paradoxical diarrhea may develop. In this condition, loose, watery stools seep around the hard stool in the colon and are passed as diarrhea. When this happens, it can be difficult to tell whether the child has constipation or diarrhea.

HOME CARE

For immediate temporary relief, use a glycerine suppository or disposable commercial enema. For a long-term cure, increase the amount of roughage and decrease the amount of constipating foods in your child's diet. If constipation occurs during toilet training, stop training efforts.

PRECAUTIONS

● Check with your doctor before using laxatives in children. Laxatives may force passage of a hard stool and cause pain that leads to further holding back by the child. ● Enemas, suppositories, and laxatives are habit-forming. They should never be used on a regular basis. ● Do not assume that a child is constipated simply because bowel movements do not occur every day.

MEDICAL TREATMENT

Your doctor will perform a rectal examination and a careful examination of the child's abdomen. X-ray studies of the bowel may be taken to look for possible physical abnormalities. Directions and follow-up by your doctor may be needed.

Convulsions with fever

SYMPTOMS
Fever
Unconsciousness
Uncontrollable jerking movements
Muscle spasms
Brief cessation of breathing
Bluish skin
Lost control of bladder or bowels

HOME CARE Protect the child from injury during the thrashing or jerking movements.

Call your doctor immediately.

Do not put your fingers into the child's mouth.

PRECAUTIONS

☐ Do not give aspirin or any other medication by mouth to an unconscious child.

☐ Do not give artificial respiration to a child having convulsions.

☐ Do not place a convulsing child in a tub of water to reduce the child's temperature.

☐ If the child cannot bend the neck forward after convulsions have ended, or if the child is collapsed or exhausted, report this to your doctor.

If a child tends to have convulsions with a fever, sponge the child's body with a damp lukewarm sponge at the first sign of fever.

Convulsions are uncontrolled contractions or spasms of the muscles. If a child who has a fever goes into convulsions, there are two possible causes. The convulsions may be caused by the fever itself or by certain diseases involving the brain that also cause fever.

Febrile convulsions are convulsions that are caused by the fever itself. Five to 10 percent of all children have febrile convulsions. How quickly the temperature rises is more important than how high the temperature is. A sudden rise of only two or three degrees may cause convulsions, but a gradual rise of five or six degrees may not.

Febrile convulsions may be thought of as shaking chills that become extreme. They are most common between the ages of three months and three years. Febrile convulsions occur less and less often from age three to age eight. After the age of eight, febrile convulsions are rare. One episode of febrile convulsions usually means the child is more likely to have them in the future. However, the tendency to have febrile convulsions does *not* mean the child will later have epilepsy.

Diseases involving the brain that cause convulsions include meningitis, encephalitis, and abscess of the brain. When convulsions occur with these diseases, the child will usually have a fever. But the disease (not the fever) causes the convulsions.

SIGNS AND SYMPTOMS

During convulsions with fever, a child will fall unconscious, become rigid, and may stop breathing briefly. The child may turn blue, lose control of the bladder and bowels, and vomit. The limbs, torso, jaws, and/or eyelids will jerk uncontrollably. The child will quickly begin normal breathing again. The seizure activity may last two minutes to 30 minutes or longer. After regaining consciousness, the child will not remember that the convulsions occurred.

Several traits of febrile convulsions can help you distinguish them from convulsions caused by diseases like encephalitis, meningitis, or brain abscess. A major sign of febrile convulsions is that the child

recovers quickly (within minutes). Immediately after a febrile convulsion, the child is alert, can respond, and is not prostrated (not collapsed or exhausted). After a febrile convulsion, the child can bend the neck forward. There is often a family history of febrile convulsions.

After convulsions caused by diseases involving the brain, the child often cannot bend the neck forward and may be in a stage of collapse or exhaustion.

HOME CARE

Do not panic! Your child is in no pain and is in more danger from improper treatment than from the convulsion. Protect the child from injury while the convulsion is occurring. Call your doctor immediately.

PRECAUTIONS

● **Do not** give aspirin or any other medication by mouth to an unconscious child. An unconscious person cannot swallow and may choke on the medicine. ● **Do not** give artificial respiration. Breathing muscles are temporarily in spasm, and forceful artificial respiration may be harmful. ● **Do not** place a convulsing child in a tub of water to reduce the child's temperature. Accidents such as scalding and injuries against the sides of the tub have occurred; this practice is *not* recommended. ● If the child cannot bend the neck forward after the convulsions have ended, or if the child is collapsed or exhausted, report this to your doctor. These may be signs of serious illness.

MEDICAL TREATMENT

Your doctor may give an injection of medication that controls convulsions—usually phenobarbital or diazepam. The doctor will perform a complete physical examination, taking blood tests and a spinal tap. If the febrile convulsion is unusual, or if convulsions occur often, your doctor may order additional tests such as an electroencephalogram and CAT (computerized axial tomography) scan. Daily medications to control convulsions are prescribed for several years under some circumstances.

Related topics:

Choking
Convulsions
  without fever
Encephalitis
Fever
Meningitis

Convulsions without fever

SYMPTOMS
Unconsciousness
Stiffened body
Jerking or thrashing movements
Muscle spasms
Lost control of bladder or bowels
Deep sleep after spasms end
Confusion and sleepiness after awakening

HOME CARE Protect the child from injury during jerking or thrashing movements.

Do not put your fingers into the child's mouth.

Call your doctor.

PRECAUTIONS

☐ Call your doctor any time a child has convulsions. The cause and treatment must be determined by a doctor.

☐ Convulsions without fever may be caused by a variety of illnesses. Epilepsy is not always the cause.

☐ If you find your child unconscious, consider the possibility that epilepsy or another illness has led to a fall and unconsciousness.

☐ If you see any symptoms of epileptic seizures without convulsions, see your doctor.

☐ Do not give artificial respiration to a child having convulsions.

Symptoms of epileptic seizures without convulsions
Staring into space
Rapid blinking or fluttering of eyes
Sitting motionless
Repeated or unusual movements
Tingling in hands and feet
Sensation of bad odors
Seeing flashing lights
Unintelligible speech

Convulsions that occur when a child has no fever may be caused by many conditions. Epilepsy is the best-known cause.

Epilepsy is a disorder of the brain that causes repeated attacks or seizures. There are several forms of epilepsy, which are identified by the type of seizure experienced. Some forms of epilepsy cause convulsions (jerking movements or spasms of the muscles). Other types, however, do not cause convulsions. Therefore the term "seizure" is more properly used to describe an attack of epilepsy. The cause of most types of epilepsy is not known.

SIGNS AND SYMPTOMS

Epilepsy must be diagnosed by a doctor. However, signs of possible epilepsy can be seen in the typical behavior that occurs in different types of seizures.

In a *generalized convulsive* seizure, the child suddenly loses consciousness and may cry out as the seizure starts. The body stiffens, and the child may fall. Muscle spasms cause jerking or wild thrashing movements. The child may lose control of the bladder and bowels. When spasms end, the child may fall into a deep sleep and will usually be confused and sleepy upon awakening. Sometimes there is a warning sensation (aura) before this type of seizure begins, including sleepiness, headache, yawning, or tingling in the arms and legs.

Generalized non-convulsive or absence seizures are so different from major convulsive seizures that they are often not recognized as epilepsy—or may not even be noticed. The child may simply stare into space. There may be rapid blinking or fluttering of the eyes. The child remains conscious yet may be totally unaware that the seizure is occurring. If it is not recognized as a seizure, it may be mistaken for a learning disability, not paying attention, or simple daydreaming.

In *complex partial* seizures the child remains conscious, but may sit motionless or may make repeated or unusual movements.

In *simple partial* seizures the child is conscious and may simply feel tingling in the hands and feet. The child may also perceive bad odors, see flashing lights, or speak unintelligibly.

HOME CARE

Call your doctor any time a child has convulsions.

Of course, you must immediately care for the child during the convulsions. The most important home care is to prevent your child from injury during the thrashing phase of convulsions. Do not put your fingers in the child's mouth.

If epilepsy is diagnosed, the doctor will give instructions for caring for the child at home. Until the seizures are controlled, discourage the child from climbing high ladders or tall trees. Do not allow the child to swim alone. Otherwise, your child can and should live a normal life with only minor changes in activities.

PRECAUTION

● If you find your child unconscious, do not assume that your child has been made unconscious by a fall. Do consider the possibility that epilepsy has led to a fall and unconsciousness.

MEDICAL TREATMENT

Your doctor will perform physical and neurological (nervous system) examinations. The doctor may order a variety of laboratory or diagnostic tests. A number of prescription medications that control seizures are available. The doctor may order blood tests to determine the amount and type of drug to be used. In difficult cases, your doctor may recommend consultation with a neurologist (a specialist in diseases of the nervous system).

Related topics:

Choking
Convulsions with fever

97

Coughs

SYMPTOM Coughing is itself a symptom of illness or irritation

---

HOME CARE Give the child plenty of liquids.

Use a vaporizer or humidifier to add moisture to the air.

Ask your doctor if cough medicine should be given for the illness your child has. If so, ask what type of cough medicine should be used.

Treat the whole illness, not just the cough.

PRECAUTIONS

☐ Do not give cough medicine if the child has croup.

☐ Do not give cough medicine if the child has any breathing difficulty (unless you know you are treating asthma and are using only anti-asthma drugs).

☐ Do not give cough medicine if the child may have inhaled a foreign body.

☐ For some illnesses (especially asthma and pneumonia), coughing is useful and should not always be suppressed.

Coughs may be a symptom of
Asthma
Bronchiolitis
Bronchitis
Common cold
Croup
Inhaling irritating particles
  from the air
Pneumonia
Sinusitis
Whooping cough

Coughing is a valuable defense mechanism of the body. It is the body's way of removing any foreign material that enters the respiratory tree (the organs used for breathing). The respiratory tree includes the throat, larynx, trachea, bronchial tubes, and lungs. Coughing is not a disease itself. It is an automatic reflex that is set off by any foreign matter that enters the respiratory tree or by any irritation of the lining of the tree.

In most cases, coughing helps remove unwanted materials from the body, although sometimes coughing does not succeed. The only harm in a cough is that it may keep a person from sleeping, or it may cause sore muscles and exhaustion if the cough is hard and frequent. Coughing may also lead to vomiting.

A cough is only as serious as the disease or condition that causes it. As with a fever, a child with a cough is no less ill if you lessen or stop the cough. A child with a mild illness and a cough is still only mildly ill. To correct the cough, cure the disease.

SIGNS AND SYMPTOMS

Coughing is itself a symptom of a disease or of an irritating substance in the respiratory tree. Most coughs are caused by viruses (common colds, croup, bronchitis, bronchiolitis). Some are caused by bacteria (sinusitis, epiglottitis, bacterial pneumonia, whooping cough). Other coughs are caused by allergies (asthma) or by inhaling irritating particles from the air.

HOME CARE

Since coughing is only one symptom of an illness, you must treat the whole illness—not just the cough. When the illness is cured, coughing and other symptoms will be relieved. There are, however, steps you can take to help relieve coughing.

Give the child plenty of liquids. Use a vaporizer or humidifier to add moisture to the air. Cough medicines are sometimes useful. There are, however, different types of cough medicines, which are used for different types of coughs or for different types of illness.

Cough suppressants are used to reduce the frequency of the cough by suppressing the cough reflex; they may contain a narcotic (codeine, dihydrocodeinone, or hydromorphine) or a nonnarcotic (dextromethorphan or benzonatate). Consult your doctor before using a narcotic cough suppressant.

Cough looseners are used to loosen a tight cough; they contain an expectorant (glyceryl-guaiacolate, guaifenesin, ammonium chloride, or antimony potassium tartate), which may help the person cough mucus out of the lungs.

Cough tighteners are used to dry up a loose cough; they contain a decongestant (ephedrine, pseudoephedrine, phenyl-propanolamine, or homatropine).

Anti-allergy drugs are used to fight the allergy causing the cough; they contain ephedrine or an antihistamine. Some cough medicines contain a combination of ingredients and are intended to serve more than one purpose at the same time. Many different combinations of drugs are on the market in liquid form or as tablets or capsules. Before purchasing a cough medicine for home use, consult your doctor about the type of cough medicine (if any) that should be used.

Remember also that sometimes it is better not to try to suppress the cough. In some illnesses (especially asthma and pneumonia), coughing helps the child get rid of excess mucus in the lungs or air passages.

PRECAUTIONS

● Do not give cough medicine to a child with croup. ● Do not give cough medicine to a child with any breathing difficulty unless you know you are treating asthma, and then give only anti-asthma drugs. ● Do not give cough medicine to a child who may have inhaled a foreign body.

MEDICAL TREATMENT

Your doctor will concentrate on treating the condition causing the cough, not on the cough itself. Narcotic cough medicines and some with antihistamines require a doctor's prescription.

Related topics:

Asthma
Bronchiolitis
Bronchitis
Common cold
Croup
Pneumonia
Sinusitis
Viruses
Whooping cough

Cradle cap

SYMPTOMS   Yellow, scaly, or crusty patches on
the scalp
Loss of hair in patches

HOME CARE   Mild cases can be cleared by daily,
vigorous shampooing. Use soap on a
wet, rough facecloth wrapped around
your hand.

If regular shampooing doesn't work, try
special shampoos that contain coal tar or
salicylic acid.

If necessary, apply ointments that contain
sulfur, salicylic acid, or coal tar to the
scalp daily.

PRECAUTIONS

☐ Keep medicated shampoos and ointments out of the child's eyes.

☐ Stop using medicated shampoos or
ointments if the scalp or skin
becomes irritated or red.

**Mild cases of cradle
cap can be cleared
up by daily sham-
pooing. Lather a
mild soap on a
facecloth and, sup-
porting the baby's
head and back over
a basin, rub scalp
vigorously. Rinse
thoroughly and
pat dry.**

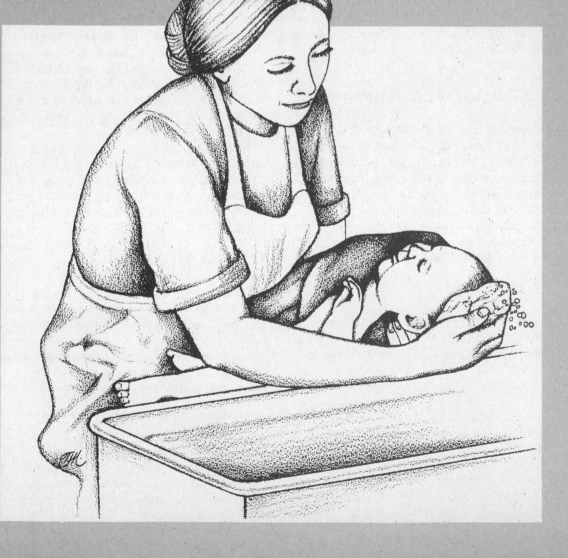

Cradle cap (seborrheic dermatitis) is a skin condition in which yellowish, scaly, or crusty patches appear on the scalp. The crusty patches are made up largely of oil and dead skin cells. Cradle cap is most common in infants, but it is seen in children through age five. Temporary loss of hair is common.

SIGNS AND SYMPTOMS

The key sign of cradle cap is the yellowish, scaly, crusty appearance of the patches. A greasy scalp film can be scraped off. The patches most often appear on the scalp, but may extend onto the forehead. Patches may also appear in the skin fold behind the ears, on the ears, and in the diaper area. The most typical location in infants is over the soft spot in the scalp (the anterior fontanelle).

HOME CARE

Mild cases of cradle cap on the scalp can be cleared by daily, vigorous shampooing. Use soap on a wet, rough facecloth wrapped around the palm of your hand. If regular soap or shampoos do not clear the condition, special shampoos that contain coal tar or salicylic acid are useful. If necessary, apply ointments containing sulfur, salicylic acid, or coal tar to the scalp daily.

PRECAUTIONS

● Be sure that medicated shampoos and ointments do not get into your child's eyes. ● Stop using medicated shampoos or ointments if the scalp or skin becomes irritated or red.

MEDICAL TREATMENT

Your doctor will determine whether the condition is cradle cap or some other skin condition, such as a yeast infection or an allergic skin reaction. The doctor's treatment will be the same as home care. In addition, a steroid cream or ointment may be prescribed.

Related topic:

Eczema

Crossed eyes

SYMPTOMS   One or both eyes turned abnormally inward toward the nose

HOME CARE   None. See your doctor.

PRECAUTIONS

☐ If the pupils of the child's eyes are not equally black, smoothly round, and the same size, see your doctor.

☐ If your child's eyes are not parallel, see your doctor to avoid development of a lazy eye.

☐ All children should have their vision checked annually, from age four or five on.

To judge the straightness of a child's eyes, shine a light into the eyes while the child is looking straight ahead. The highlight should be on the same spot in each eye as shown at the top. If the highlight is on different spots, as shown at the bottom, one eye may be crossed.

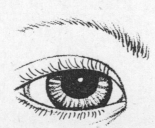
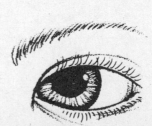

Crossed eyes is a condition in which one or both eyes turn inward toward the nose. In many cases, it is caused by improper functioning of the eye muscles.

The eyeballs are turned in all directions by six tiny muscles that lie within the bony socket of the eye. These muscles keep the eyes parallel when the child looks at a distant object (more than 20 feet). These muscles turn the eyes slightly inward when they are focusing on closer objects.

Infants learn to focus their eyes during the first three to six months of life. The eyes may occasionally turn in (*esotropia, internal strabismus*) or out (*exotropia, external strabismus*) in relation to each other during this learning period. These conditions may briefly occur even up to age one and still be considered normal. When an infant's eyes are continuously not parallel, when they are not parallel more and more often at any age, or when they are not parallel past age one, the situation is abnormal and requires your doctor's advice.

Although most cases of crossed eyes are caused by improper muscle function, some are caused by a vision problem in one or both eyes. Anything that can cause crossed eyes can also cause the development of a "lazy eye" (*amblyopia ex anopsia*). If lazy eye is not corrected by age seven, disuse may cause a loss of sight in that eye.

SIGNS AND SYMPTOMS

Watch the relationship of the eyes to each other as the child focuses near and far, looks to either side, and looks up and down. If the eyes seem to turn inward more than usual, consult your doctor.

Be aware, however, that many young children may appear to have crossed eyes, but the child's eyes are actually straight. Many infants and young children have an extra skin fold at the side of the eyelids by the nose. This fold of skin appears because of the tininess of the bridge of the nose. This extra fold allows more white of the eye to show toward the temples than toward the nose; this creates an illusion of crossed eyes.

Straightness of the eyes is best judged by observing the position of the highlights in both eyes; the highlights are the points where light is reflected in the eyes. If the highlights are in the same position in both eyes, the eyes are parallel.

HOME CARE

There is no home treatment except under the supervision and instructions of your doctor.

PRECAUTIONS

• If the pupils of your child's eyes are not equally black, smoothly round, and the same size, see your doctor. • If your child's eyes are not parallel, see your doctor to avoid the development of a lazy eye. • All children should have their vision checked annually, from age four or five on.

MEDICAL TREATMENT

Your doctor will check the eye muscles and vision and inspect the inside of the eyeballs. This examination can be done on any child at any age. If the doctor diagnoses crossed eyes, treatment will depend upon the cause. It may include eye surgery, glasses, patching of one eye, daily use of eyedrops, or eye muscle exercises guided by a specialist. If crossed eyes are diagnosed or suspected, your doctor will probably recommend that you consult an ophthalmologist (a physician who specializes in eyes).

Related topics:

Lazy eye
Vision problems

Croup

SYMPTOMS
Barking cough
Hoarseness
Difficulty breathing in
Crowing sound when breathing in
Fever (possible)
Difficulty swallowing
Sitting with head forward, mouth open,
and tongue hanging out

HOME CARE
If a child has serious difficulty breathing, do not treat at home. Notify your doctor, and go immediately to the nearest hospital emergency room.

For mild, repeated attacks of croup (if there is no serious breathing problem), add moisture to the air to make breathing easier. Use a vaporizer or humidifier. Sit with the child in a closed bathroom with a hot shower running to build steam. If steam does not relieve symptoms, call your doctor.

The first time you suspect your child has croup (even a mild attack), call your doctor.

PRECAUTIONS

☐ If your child has a high fever, difficulty breathing and swallowing, is drooling, or sits with the head forward, mouth open, and tongue hanging out, **get medical help immediately.**

☐ **Do not** give cough medicine to a child who has croup or any difficulty breathing.

☐ **Do not** give ipecac to a child with croup.

Croup is an inflammation and swelling of the larynx (voice box), usually caused by an infection. Croup is common and is passed on in the same manner as a common cold—by airborne droplets or by direct contact with an infected person.

Croup causes a tight, dry, barking cough and hoarseness. Difficult breathing develops quickly, with more trouble breathing *in* than breathing out. Efforts to breathe in cause the crowing sound that is typical with croup. (This is the opposite of the breathing difficulty that is seen with asthma. A child with asthma has more difficulty breathing *out,* and a wheezing sound is heard when the child breathes out.) Croup can be serious, but milder cases, especially repeated ones, can usually be safely handled at home.

There is a form of croup—epiglottitis—that is a life-threatening illness, a true emergency in which minutes count. It is an infection of the epiglottis (covering of the larynx) and surrounding tissues, caused by bacteria. It is most common in children between three and nine years of age. There is a rising fever to 103°F and up to 105°F. Difficulty with breathing quickly becomes severe. The child drools and may have trouble swallowing, preferring to sit with the head forward, mouth open, and tongue partially out. The condition rapidly progresses to choking and convulsions; treat immediately.

SIGNS AND SYMPTOMS

The key symptoms of croup are a barking cough, hoarseness, difficult breathing, and a crowing sound heard when the child breathes in. There may be no fever or a low-grade fever (101°F).

It is important always to consider the possibility of epiglottitis when any of these symptoms are present.

Choking on a foreign object may resemble croup, since both share the same symptom of frantic efforts to breathe. However, it is easy to tell choking from croup by one key sign. A choking child cannot speak or cry out; a child with croup can talk or cry. Fever may be another clue, since a child with croup may have a fever but a choking child does not.

HOME CARE

If a child is having serious difficulty breathing, do not try to care for the child at home. Notify your doctor, and head for the nearest hospital emergency room.

Mild, repeated attacks of croup can often be cared for at home (if there is no serious difficulty breathing). However, it is best to call your doctor the first time you suspect your child has croup.

The basic home care for mild attacks is adding moisture to the air to relieve the cough and help the child breathe more easily.

Use steam from a vaporizer or humidifier. Steam also may be generated quickly and temporarily by running a hot shower in a closed bathroom. Sit in the room with your child for a short while. If the symptoms are not relieved, call your doctor.

PRECAUTIONS

● If your child has a high fever, difficulty breathing and swallowing, is drooling, or sits with the head forward, mouth open, and tongue hanging out, **get medical help immediately.** ● Never give any type of cough medicine to a child with croup or any difficulty breathing. ● **Do not** give ipecac as a home treatment for croup; ipecac may make breathing even more difficult.

MEDICAL TREATMENT

For croup, your doctor's treatment will be the same as your home treatment. However, the doctor may hospitalize your child and use a croup tent with high humidity. The doctor may also order X rays, cultures, and a blood count. If the condition becomes severe, your child may be intubated (have a tube inserted in the airway).

Epiglottitis is always treated as an emergency. Your child will be intubated. If necessary, the doctor may perform a tracheotomy (opening the windpipe surgically through the neck). Intravenous fluids and antibiotics will be given, and the child's condition will be carefully watched.

Related topics:

Asthma
Choking
Convulsions
Fever

Cuts

SYMPTOMS   Break in the skin
Bleeding

HOME CARE   First, stop bleeding. Apply firm pressure directly on the cut for ten minutes with sterile gauze or a clean cloth.

After bleeding stops, wash the area with soap and water. If bleeding will not stop, get medical help immediately. Examine the cut to decide if a doctor should treat the wound. If so, call your doctor.

If the cut can be cared for at home:
Apply a nonstinging antiseptic.
Draw the edges of the wound together with adhesive butterflies.
Cover the wound with sterile gauze and a bandage to prevent infection.
Inspect the wound daily for signs of infection.
Remove butterflies only after the cut is completely healed (seven to ten days).

PRECAUTIONS

☐ **Do not** use a tourniquet to stop bleeding from a cut. A tourniquet is used only if a limb is partially or completely amputated.

☐ If a cut needs stitching, it must be done within eight hours to avoid infection.

☐ If a wound shows signs of infection (tenderness, swelling, discharge of pus, or red streaks spreading out from the wound), see your doctor.

☐ Be sure children receive tetanus boosters as recommended by your doctor.

If a cut can be treated at home, draw the edges of the cut together with adhesive butterflies as shown at the top. The drawing at the bottom shows you how to make your own butterfly flap.

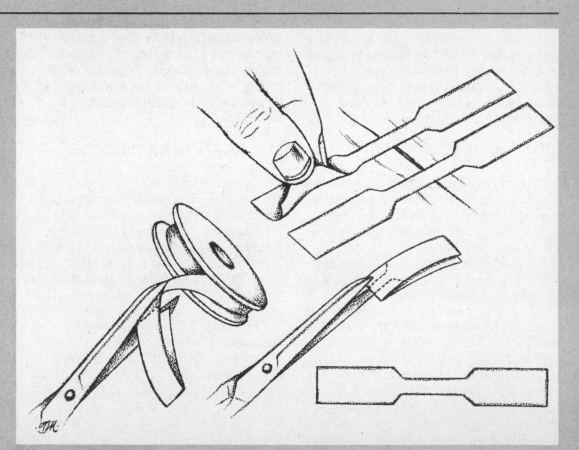

Wounds of the skin are classified as abrasions (scrapes), punctures, and lacerations. A laceration is a cut of any size and depth and can be located anywhere on the body.

SIGNS AND SYMPTOMS

A cut is obvious from its appearance and the bleeding that occurs. However, there are signs and symptoms you should look for to help you decide whether the cut needs a doctor's care or can be treated at home. Major cuts with serious bleeding obviously need a doctor's immediate attention; emergency control of bleeding is the only possible home treatment.

First, look at the depth of the cut. If a cut is more than skin deep it cannot be treated at home. Deeper structures (such as muscles, tendons, and nerves) must be repaired by sewing.

Second, look for dirtiness or raggedness in the cut. A cut with ragged edges or with deeply embedded dirt needs professional care to avoid infection and to reduce scarring.

Third, look at the width and location of the cut. A small cut rarely needs stitching to control the bleeding, but stitching may help reduce the amount of scarring. A cut heals leaving a scar the size of the opening of the skin. There is no treatment that will reduce the length of the scar. But the closer the edges of the cut are to each other during the healing process, the narrower the final scar will be. If a home-style bandage can hold the edges together for the seven to ten days required for healing, there may be no advantage to a doctor's treatment. However, if the cut is in an area that moves, such as near a joint or on some parts of the face, it is nearly impossible to keep the edges from gaping unless the wound is sewn.

HOME CARE

First, stop the bleeding. Apply firm pressure directly on the cut for ten minutes (by the clock). Use sterile gauze if it's immediately available. If not, any reasonably clean cloth—a handkerchief, towel, or shirt—will do. Even bleeding from large arteries can be controlled by pressure applied directly on the wound. You never need so-called pressure points.

Do not use a tourniquet to stop bleeding from a cut. The only time a tourniquet is necessary is if a limb is partially or completely amputated. In this severe case, the tourniquet may be placed anywhere above the wound. The new thinking is that once the tourniquet is put on, it should be left on—not released and tightened as was once suggested. Then immediately rush the person to the nearest medical facility.

Second, once the bleeding has stopped, wash the area with soap and water so that the cut is clearly visible. Look at the depth, width, dirtiness, raggedness, and location of the cut to decide if a doctor should treat the wound.

If it seems reasonable to care for the cut at home, apply a nonstinging antiseptic. Draw the wound's edges together with adhesive butterflies available at your pharmacy (or make your own). Then cover the wound with sterile gauze and a bandage to prevent infection. If the cut is near the joint of a finger, splinting the fingers can keep them from moving until the cut has healed. Cuts between the toes can sometimes be kept from moving by bandaging the toes together around the cut. Inspect the wound every day for signs of possible infection. Remove butterflies after seven to ten days.

PRECAUTIONS

● If the cut requires stitching, it must be done within eight hours to avoid infection. If a wound becomes infected (showing increased tenderness, swelling, discharge of pus, or red streaks spreading out from the wound), see your doctor. ● Be sure that your child receives tetanus boosters at the ages recommended by your doctor.

MEDICAL TREATMENT

A doctor, surgeon, or plastic surgeon has the skill and equipment to handle cuts that cannot be cared for at home. Your doctor will clean a dirty wound and decide if the wound needs stitching.

Related topics:

Animal bites
Blood poisoning
Immunizations
Puncture wounds
Scrapes
Tetanus

107

Cystic fibrosis

SYMPTOMS
Frequent respiratory infections
Frequent bronchitis or pneumonia
Chronic cough
Failure to gain weight
Frequent constipation or diarrhea with
   foul-smelling stools
Protrusion of the rectum
Broadening of fingertips and toes
Salty taste to the skin when kissed

HOME CARE
If you suspect cystic fibrosis, see your doctor. If cystic fibrosis is diagnosed, follow the doctor's instructions for home care.

PRECAUTIONS

☐ If your child shows any symptoms of cystic fibrosis, ask your doctor to perform a sweat test.

☐ If there is any history of cystic fibrosis in your family, a sweat test should be considered for all children (even if they appear healthy). The sweat test is not reliable before the age of one month and is less reliable during adolescence.

☐ The earlier cystic fibrosis is diagnosed and treated, the better the outcome.

If your child has any signs of cystic fibrosis, a sweat test—which is simple, safe, and inexpensive—should be done.

Cystic fibrosis is a chronic (lifelong), inherited disease. It affects the lungs, pancreas, sweat glands, and sometimes the liver and other organs.

Cystic fibrosis (CF) is passed from parents to child through a particular gene. Genes are the parts of the body's cells that determine inherited characteristics (such as hair color, eye color, and size, as well as inherited diseases). To have cystic fibrosis, a child must inherit the particular gene from both parents. A child who has the CF gene from only one parent will not have the disease. A person who carries the gene but does not have the disease is known as a "healthy carrier." When both parents are healthy carriers, only about 25 percent of their children receive the gene from both parents and develop the disease. Five percent of Caucasians, 2 percent of American blacks, and less than 1 percent of Orientals and native African blacks are healthy carriers. One in 2,000 Caucasian children has CF.

CF may appear at birth as an obstruction or blocking of the intestines. Symptoms may also appear during infancy or childhood and sometimes as late as adolescence.

SIGNS AND SYMPTOMS

Some common symptoms of cystic fibrosis are frequent respiratory infections, including bronchitis and pneumonia; chronic cough; failure to gain adequate weight; constipation or diarrhea with foul-smelling stools; protrusion of the rectum; and clubbing (broadening) of the fingertips and toes. Almost all persons with cystic fibrosis have unusually salty sweat. A very salty taste to a child's skin when kissed is sometimes a sign of CF.

HOME CARE

If you have any reason to suspect your child has CF, see your doctor. If CF is diagnosed, home treatment will be directed by your doctor. Treatment at home may include taking antibiotics, following a special diet, taking pancreatic enzymes by mouth, inhaling vapor and medications, and postural drainage.

(Postural drainage, conducted in a home setting, involves positioning the child over the bed with the head pillowed on the floor. The child's chest is tapped soundly to allow excess fluids to drain from the lungs. Your doctor will give specific instructions for performing postural drainage.)

PRECAUTIONS

● If your child shows any CF symptoms, a sweat test should be done. A sweat test is a painless, harmless, inexpensive, and generally reliable test for cystic fibrosis. ● If there is any history of CF in the family, a sweat test should be considered for all children, even if they appear to be healthy. ● The sweat test is not reliable before age one month and is not as reliable during adolescence.

MEDICAL TREATMENT

The doctor will perform an inexpensive test for CF called the sweat test. The doctor may also order a chest X ray. If cystic fibrosis is diagnosed, your doctor will refer you to a medical center where there are specialists in treating CF.

The outlook for prolonged life of a child with CF who is in relatively good health is better now than in the past, but a cure for CF is still being sought. The earlier the diagnosis is made and treatment started, the better the outcome.

Deafness

SYMPTOMS

Three-month-old infant ignores sounds or does not turn head toward sound

One-year-old does not speak a few words or babble

Two-year-old does not speak two-word or three-word sentences

Five-year-old does not speak so strangers understand

Learning problems in school

Child simply does not seem to hear well

HOME CARE

Home care depends on the cause and type of hearing loss. See your doctor to determine cause and treatment.

If the child has an earache, call your doctor.

PRECAUTIONS

☐ Every child should be given a professional hearing test before starting kindergarten. A deaf child should start special training as soon as possible.

☐ Do not put any object (not even cotton swabs) into your child's ear canal for any reason.

☐ Every woman of child-bearing age should consult her doctor about rubella (German measles) immunization. Rubella in a pregnant woman can cause deafness in her unborn child.

Every child should have a professional hearing test before starting school.

Deafness is a partial loss or a complete loss of the sense of hearing. A hearing loss may be slight or severe in one ear or both ears. A child may be born with a hearing loss, or it may develop at any age.

Normal hearing occurs when sound waves pass down the ear canal and cause the eardrum to vibrate. Vibrations of the eardrum in turn move the three tiny bones in the middle ear. This motion of the bones transmits the vibrations across the middle ear to the inner ear. In the inner ear, the vibrations are changed to electrical impulses which are carried to the brain through the eighth cranial nerve. The brain interprets these electrical impulses as sound. Damage, disease, or malfunction of any of these structures can result in deafness. Any of the following problems may lead to hearing difficulties.

Ear canal problems that may cause hearing loss include a buildup of earwax, a foreign object in the canal, or swimmer's ear.

Eardrum and middle ear problems may be caused by an inflammation of the middle ear or a blocked eustachian tube (the tube that connects the nose and the middle ear).

Inner ear problems may be caused by injuries or infections.

Eighth cranial nerve problems have several possible causes. A child may be born with a nerve that has not developed properly or that has been damaged before birth. (For example, if a pregnant woman develops rubella, this virus may infect the eighth cranial nerve in the unborn child.) After birth, this nerve can be damaged by an injury or by an infection with a virus (mumps, measles) or with a bacterium (meningitis). This nerve can also be affected by certain medications.

SIGNS AND SYMPTOMS

Signs of a hearing loss usually can be seen in a child's behavior. Suspect a hearing loss if any of the following behavior occurs: an infant over three months old ignores sounds or does not turn the head toward sound; a baby over one year old does not speak at least a few words; a child over two years old does not speak in at least two-word or three-word sentences; a child over five years old does not speak so that a stranger can understand; a child of any age has learning problems in school; or a child simply does not appear to hear well at home. Any of these symptoms may be caused by a hearing loss, but they also may have some other causes. Every child should be given a professional hearing test before starting kindergarten.

HOME CARE

Home care for a hearing problem depends upon the cause, as well as upon the degree of the hearing loss. If you think your child may have a hearing problem, see your doctor. A doctor can more properly determine if there is a problem and prescribe the best treatment.

PRECAUTIONS

● Every woman of child-bearing age should consult her doctor about rubella (German measles) immunization. ● Do not put any object, including cotton swabs, into your child's ear canal for any reason. You may force earwax to become packed into the canal, or you may damage the eardrum.

MEDICAL TREATMENT

Your doctor will examine the ear to determine the cause of deafness. Specialists have equipment to test hearing in children of any age past early infancy. If there is any doubt about the cause or treatment of the hearing loss, your doctor may refer you to a center that specializes in speech and hearing. A deaf child should start special education as soon as the condition is discovered, even if the child is as young as one or two years old.

Related topics:

Common cold
Draining ear
Earaches
Immunizations
Rubella
Speech problems
  and stuttering
Swimmer's ear

111

Dehydration

SYMPTOMS
Infrequent urinating
Smaller amounts of urine
Sunken eyes
Drowsiness
Rapid or slow breathing
Sunken soft spot in skull (infants)
Dryness in mouth
Skin rigid when pinched gently

HOME CARE
If there are any symptoms of dehydration, call your doctor.

If a child is vomiting, stop the vomiting first. Do not give solid foods. Give the child clear liquids only.

If a child is losing fluids, give plenty of extra liquids. Commercial mineral and electrolyte mixtures are best. Also give gelatin desserts (liquid or gelled), weak tea with sugar, carbonated drinks, and fruit juices.

Do not give the child milk or milk products.

PRECAUTIONS

☐ Do not give undiluted skim milk or boiled whole milk to a child losing fluids.

☐ The younger the child, the more serious dehydration can be.

☐ Dehydration in infants is especially serious.

☐ Infants can become dehydrated as quickly as 12 to 24 hours after the start of diarrhea, vomiting, or breathing problems.

☐ The amount of urine output is *not* a clue to dehydration in a diabetic child.

Common causes of dehydration
Diarrhea
Vomiting
Excessive sweating
Rapid breathing from an illness
Diabetes mellitus

Dehydration is a serious loss of body fluids. It occurs when the body is losing more fluids than it is taking in. When an excessive amount of body fluid is lost, the body loses the water, minerals, and salts contained in the fluid. Proper amounts of water, minerals, and salts are essential to health and to life.

Several conditions may cause the body to lose an excessive amount of water, minerals, and salts. Diarrhea, vomiting, and excessive sweating are common causes of dehydration. Illnesses that cause excessive breathing (such as bronchiolitis and asthma) may cause the child to lose water vapor from the lungs. Illnesses that cause excessive urination (such as diabetes) may also cause dehydration.

The smaller the child, the more quickly dehydration can develop. In young infants, dehydration occurs as rapidly as 12 to 24 hours after the start of any cause of dehydration (such as diarrhea or vomiting). A child who is not losing extra fluids will rarely become dehydrated simply by taking in fewer liquids. Except in young infants and in children with diabetes, the kidneys can compensate for a smaller intake of liquids. However, a small intake of liquids in a child who is also losing fluids causes dehydration to occur even more rapidly.

SIGNS AND SYMPTOMS

Except in a child with diabetes, a sign of dehydration is a smaller output of urine. A young child who goes six to eight hours without urinating, or an older child who does not urinate for ten to 12 hours, may be dehydrated. Other signs of dehydration include sunken eyes; drowsiness; rapid or slow breathing; and depression (sinking in) of the soft spot in an infant's skull. The membranes inside the mouth may feel dry when touched by a finger. The skin may feel less flexible than usual when pinched between the thumb and forefinger.

HOME CARE

If a child shows any symptoms of dehydration, call your doctor. If the child is vomiting, stop the vomiting first. With any condition that causes fluid loss (including prolonged high fever), you should encourage your child to drink extra fluids. The best liquids to give a child with increased fluid loss are commercial fluids that contain proper salts and sugar. Other good liquids are gelatin desserts (liquid or gelled); weak tea with sugar; ginger ale, colas, and other carbonated drinks. Plain water is less helpful. Milk products should be avoided.

PRECAUTIONS

● Do not give undiluted skim milk and boiled whole milk to a child who is losing fluids. Their salt and mineral content is too great for the child to tolerate. ● If symptoms of dehydration develop, contact your doctor. The younger the child, the more urgent the situation. Diarrhea in infants can be very serious. ● The amount of urine output cannot help detect dehydration in a diabetic child.

MEDICAL TREATMENT

Your doctor will diagnose and treat the condition that is causing dehydration. Your child may be admitted to a hospital to be given intravenous fluids and salts. The child may be tested for the amounts of salts and minerals in the body.

Related topics:

Asthma
Bronchiolitis
Diabetes mellitus
Diarrhea in
   children
Diarrhea in infants
Fever
Vomiting

Diabetes mellitus

SYMPTOMS
Increased hunger
Increased thirst
Frequent urinating
Greater amounts of urine than usual
Sudden onset of bedwetting
Weight loss
Fatigue
Irritability
Deep rapid breathing and unconsciousness
  (diabetic coma)

HOME CARE
Do not try to treat on your own. See your doctor for proper diagnosis and instructions for home care.

PRECAUTIONS

☐ See your doctor if a toilet-trained child suddenly begins regular bedwetting.

☐ If there is diabetes in your family background, your child should be regularly screened for diabetes.

☐ Untreated or uncontrolled diabetes can lead to dehydration.

Most diabetic children require insulin injections and can be taught, from as early as four years of age, how to give themselves injections.

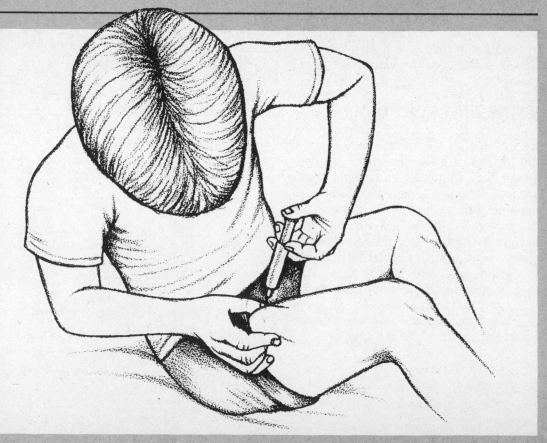

Diabetes mellitus is a condition in which the body does not properly process carbohydrates (sugars and starches). In children, it occurs when the pancreas does not produce enough insulin. Sugars and starches are the body's main sources of energy. When the body cannot properly turn sugars and starches into energy, unusually high amounts of unused sugars are found in the blood and urine. The body then burns more fats for energy in place of sugars. The process of breaking down fats into energy produces an end product called ketones. Thus higher amounts of ketones are also found in the urine.

Diabetes can occur at any age. It appears in one in 2,500 children by the age of 15. The disease usually runs in families. The parents may or may not be diabetic. There may be other family members who are diabetic, or there may have been diabetes in the family in the past.

SIGNS AND SYMPTOMS

The earliest signs of diabetes are increased hunger, increased thirst, and increased urination. The child will both urinate more often and produce greater amounts of urine. Other symptoms then appear, including weight loss, fatigue, and irritability. Most cases are detected by this stage. If diabetes is not detected and corrected, deep, rapid breathing followed by unconsciousness (diabetic coma) eventually develops.

If you notice any of these symptoms, see your doctor. An exact diagnosis can be made only through laboratory tests.

HOME CARE

Do not try to treat a diabetic child on your own. Your doctor must diagnose diabetes and prescribe treatment. The doctor will tailor the treatment to your child's exact needs. Then you must carefully follow the doctor's instructions for caring for the child at home.

You and your child must learn as much as possible about diabetes. The doctor will give instructions for making necessary changes in the child's diet, giving insulin, and testing the urine. You will learn how to recognize and treat insulin shock (caused by too little sugar in the blood) and diabetic coma (caused by too much sugar in the blood).

PRECAUTIONS

● Bedwetting that suddenly occurs regularly (after your child has been toilet-trained for some time) may be a sign of developing diabetes. Have the child's urine tested for diabetes (and urinary tract infection) if bedwetting continues. ● If there is diabetes in your family background, try to keep your children from becoming overweight. If a child already has an inherited tendency toward diabetes, being overweight increases the possibility of diabetes developing as the child grows older. ● Untreated and uncontrolled diabetes may lead to dehydration (a serious loss of body fluids) caused by increased urination. Complicating this situation is the fact that a decrease in urination is not a reliable sign of dehydration in a diabetic child.

MEDICAL TREATMENT

To properly diagnose diabetes, the doctor will order several laboratory tests. A urinalysis will test for extra sugar and ketones in the urine. A blood test can check for higher amounts of sugar in the blood. In a glucose tolerance test, the child drinks a known amount of glucose sugar; then the level of sugar in the blood is measured from time to time over several hours.

If diabetes is found, your doctor may hospitalize your child to regulate the diet and determine the amount of insulin the child will need to take. If the child is dehydrated or shows excess amounts of ketones, these conditions will also be treated in the hospital. Before discharging your child, your doctor will make certain that you and the child understand how insulin should be given and how the child's diet should be changed. Most diabetic children require insulin daily and are instructed—from as early as four years of age—to give themselves injections.

Related topics:

Bedwetting
Dehydration

Diaper rashes

SYMPTOMS
Reddened skin
Rough, scaly skin
Ammonia odor
Red, scaly spots

HOME CARE
Keep the baby as dry as possible. Change diapers often.

Avoid airtight outer covering over diapers.

Try changing the products used to launder diapers.

For *simple diaper rash,* apply petroleum jelly; zinc oxide; vitamin A & D ointment; or an ointment combining zinc oxide, cod liver oil, petrolatum, and lanolin.

For *ammonia rash,* avoid airtight outer covering over the diapers. Wash the diaper area frequently with clear water.

For *allergic rashes,* stop giving the child any new foods, beverages, or medicines started in the past month.

For *rash from infections,* wash the area with soap and water. Apply antibiotic ointment often.

PRECAUTIONS

☐ If the rash is spreading or severe, see your doctor.

☐ If the rash worsens after two days of home treatment, see your doctor.

☐ If the child has a fever, irritability, loss of appetite, or any other signs of illness, see your doctor.

☐ Do not use more than one type of ointment at the same time (unless both were prescribed by your doctor).

Diaper rashes are irritations of the skin in the diaper area. Almost all babies get diaper rash of one form or another. Diaper rashes may be caused by moisture, urine, or irritating chemicals in the diapers.

SIGNS AND SYMPTOMS

Rashes in the diaper area can usually be identified by their appearance, their location, and other typical symptoms of different types of rashes.

Simple diaper rashes are red, slightly rough, and scaly. The rash may appear over the whole area touched by the diaper. The skin may be irritated by chemicals used in laundering cloth diapers—detergent, bleach, whitener, water softener, or soap. Plastic or rubber pants worn over cloth diapers sometimes affect the skin. The skin may also react to chemicals used in manufacturing disposable diapers or to the plastic outer layer on disposable diapers.

Ammonia rash is a form of diaper rash caused by the urine itself. The skin is burned by ammonia that is formed when the urine is decomposed by normal bacteria on the skin. Ammonia rash is worse after the child has been asleep for long periods of time without a diaper change. It is identified by an ammonia smell that can be noticed when changing the diaper.

Besides these basic diaper rashes, a variety of other rashes may appear in the diaper area including rashes caused by an allergy to a food or drug, by a skin infection, or by contagious diseases (chicken pox or measles).

If your child develops a rash in the diaper area, look for the signs that indicate these different types of rashes. The appearance and location of the rash, an ammonia odor, or rash elsewhere on the body are all clues. Have you recently changed to different diapers or changed your way of laundering them? Has the child recently been given a new food or drug which could be causing an allergic reaction? Noting these factors can help you and your doctor find the cause of the rash.

HOME CARE

Keep your baby as dry as possible, changing diapers frequently. For simple diaper rash, apply protective ointments (petroleum jelly; zinc oxide; vitamin A & D ointment; or an ointment combining zinc oxide, cod liver oil, petrolatum, and lanolin). Try changing the brand of soap or the method of washing the diapers.

For rash from ammonia, avoid airtight outer covering over the diapers. Wash the diaper area frequently with clear water.

For *allergic rash* from foods and drugs, stop giving the child any new foods, beverages, or medicines started in the past month. Then try giving the child only one of these items each week. This may help determine which food is causing the rash.

For *rash from infections* or *contagious diseases,* wash the area with soap and water and frequently apply antibiotic ointment (bacitracin, neomycin).

If the rash is spreading or severe, or if the child has a fever, irritability, or loss of appetite, see your doctor.

PRECAUTIONS

● If the rash gets worse, even after only two days of home treatment, see your doctor. ● Do not use more than one type of ointment at the same time (such as an antibiotic and a fungicide) unless both were prescribed by your doctor. ● If your child has any other symptoms of illness, see your doctor.

MEDICAL TREATMENT

Your doctor may identify the rash by its appearance or may culture or scrape the rash to identify bacteria or funguses. The doctor may ask about methods of laundering diapers and about new foods or drugs being given to the child. The doctor may prescribe a medicated ointment.

Related topics:

Chicken pox
Cradle cap
Eczema
Food allergies
Impetigo
Measles
Rash

Diarrhea in infants

SYMPTOMS
Loose, watery stools
Mucus in stools
Red blood flecks in stools
Cramps
Fever
Loss of appetite
Vomiting
Weight loss

HOME CARE
If the child is vomiting, treat vomiting first. Restrict the child's diet to clear liquids only.

When vomiting stops, treat diarrhea. Stop all foods with roughage, vegetables, and fruits (except bananas and apples).
Do not give milk.

Stop any foods and beverages that have been recently added to the child's diet.

To avoid dehydration (serious loss of body fluids), give the child plenty of clear liquids: tea, water, flavored gelatin water, and commercial mineral and electrolyte mixtures.

Continue treating diarrhea until the child has no stools or normal stools for 24 to 48 hours.

Symptoms of dehydration
Infrequent urinating
Smaller amounts of urine
Sunken eyes
Drowsiness
Rapid or slow breathing
Sunken soft spot in infant's skull
Dryness in mouth
Skin rigid when pinched gently

PRECAUTIONS

☐ Do not give anti-diarrheal medications to infants and children.

☐ Diarrhea and vomiting can cause dehydration. Dehydration can be especially serious in infants and children under the age of five.

☐ In infants, dehydration can occur as rapidly as 12 to 24 hours after diarrhea or vomiting begins.

☐ If an infant or young child shows any symptoms of dehydration, call your doctor.

☐ Solid foods aggravate diarrhea. If the child is drinking plenty of liquids, solid foods can be avoided for several days without any danger to the child's health.

☐ Improperly prepared and improperly refrigerated formulas commonly cause serious infant diarrhea. Be careful when normal refrigeration and cooking facilities aren't available (picnics, camping, traveling).

☐ Many antibiotics can cause diarrhea in some infants. Some foods newly added to the diet can cause diarrhea in infants.

Diarrhea is a condition in which the bowel movements are loose and watery. Diarrhea is judged by the looseness of the stools, not by the frequency of bowel movements. (Frequent bowel movements with normal stools are not considered diarrhea.) Any bowel movement that is partially or completely runny is diarrhea. The frequency and amount of loose stools indicate how severe the diarrhea is.

Diarrhea in infants and young children (under the age of five) is potentially dangerous. Diarrhea can lead to dehydration (a serious loss of body fluids). The younger the child, the greater the possibility of dehydration.

Common causes of diarrhea in infants are infections of the digestive tract and reactions to certain foods and drugs. In infants, infections may be caused by respiratory viruses; intestinal viruses; bacteria (coliform, dysentery, staph); and parasites (Giardia, amoebas). Some foods tend to cause diarrhea in most infants (corn kernels or large quantities of prunes, for example). Other foods may cause diarrhea in some infants but not in others. Individual children react differently to different foods, and some infants are allergic to certain foods. Many antibiotics also may cause diarrhea in infants.

SIGNS AND SYMPTOMS

The looseness of the stools is the major symptom. The loose, watery stools often contain mucus and sometimes flecks of red blood. A child with diarrhea may have cramps and sometimes fever, loss of appetite, vomiting, and weight loss. There may be as few as one or as many as 20 loose bowel movements a day. However, if only one or two loose bowel movements are followed by a return to normal, the diarrhea is probably not serious.

In looking for the cause of diarrhea, consider whether a new food has recently been added to the child's diet or if the child has recently been given antibiotics. If other children in your family are ill, your infant may be suffering from the same illness.

HOME CARE

If an infant or young child has both diarrhea and vomiting, treat the vomiting first by restricting the child's diet to clear liquids only. Once vomiting stops, treat the diarrhea. Eliminate all newly introduced foods and beverages. If diarrhea is mild, eliminate foods with roughage. Stop all vegetables and fruits (except bananas and apples). Do not give the child milk. Encourage the child to drink clear liquids to ward off dehydration: tea, water, flavored gelatin water, and commercial mineral and electrolyte mixtures. Continue treatment for diarrhea until the child has no stools or normal stools for 24 to 48 hours.

PRECAUTIONS

● Do not give anti-diarrheal medications to infants. These are of no use and can cause severe problems. ● Solid foods aggravate diarrhea and can be avoided for many days without any danger to the child's general health. It is most important that the child drink plenty of liquids. ● Watch for symptoms of dehydration (infrequent urinating, dryness in the mouth, sunken eyes, drowsiness, rapid or slow breathing, sunken soft spot). If any symptoms of dehydration appear, call your doctor. ● Improperly prepared and improperly refrigerated formulas are a common cause of serious infant diarrhea. Be especially careful when normal refrigeration and cooking facilities aren't available (picnics, camping, traveling).

MEDICAL TREATMENT

Your doctor's treatment of diarrhea will be the same as your home treatment. If there are signs of dehydration, your doctor will determine if it is serious. (The loss of 5 percent of a baby's weight indicates serious dehydration.) Stools may be cultured for bacteria. If necessary, your child may be placed in the hospital to be given intravenous fluids or to determine if the intestines are functioning properly.

Related topics:

Botulism
Constipation
Dehydration
Diarrhea in
  children
Dysentery
Food allergies
Food poisoning
Viruses
Vomiting

Diarrhea in children

SYMPTOMS
Loose, watery stools
Mucus in stools
Red blood flecks in stools
Cramps
Fever
Loss of appetite
Vomiting
Weight loss

HOME CARE
If the child is also vomiting, stop the vomiting first. Restrict the child's diet to clear liquids only.

When vomiting stops, treat diarrhea. Limit or do not reintroduce solid foods. Avoid foods with roughage, fruits (except bananas and apples), vegetables, butter, fatty meats, and peanut butter.

Do not give milk.

Give the child extra liquids: tea, water, flavored gelatin water, and commercial mineral and electrolyte mixtures.

PRECAUTIONS

☐ Do not give anti-diarrheal medications to children.

☐ Isolate infants from children who are ill with vomiting and diarrhea.

☐ If there is blood in the stools, high fever, extreme weakness, or severe or prolonged diarrhea (more than two to three days), call your doctor.

☐ Call your doctor if your child has frequent diarrhea (especially if the child is losing weight).

☐ A child with diarrhea needs extra liquids to avoid dehydration (serious loss of body fluids).

Diet treatment of diarrhea
Commercial mineral and electrolyte mixtures
Sweetened tea
Flavored gelatin water
Diluted beef bouillon
Flavored gelatin
Lean beef or lamb
Boiled chicken
Cooked rice
Dry baked or boiled potato
Fresh banana
Fresh apple
Toast or crackers and jelly
Soft- or hard-boiled egg

Diarrhea refers to looseness of the stools, not to the frequency of bowel movements. (Frequent bowel movements with normal stools is not diarrhea.) The number of loose bowel movements per day measures the seriousness of the diarrhea.

Diarrhea in children over the age of five differs in several ways from diarrhea in infants and younger children. Diarrhea is less likely to cause dehydration (a serious loss of body fluids) in older children. The older and larger the child becomes, the smaller the chances of dehydration. Serious dehydration is unlikely past six years of age—unless diarrhea is combined with vomiting, which keeps the child from drinking enough liquids.

Viruses in the intestine are the most common cause of diarrhea in older children. Dysentery bacteria and parasites in the intestine are the next most common causes. Respiratory viruses and reactions to certain foods are the least likely cause of diarrhea in older children.

Other diseases may cause long-term, frequent diarrhea in older children (though they are rare or unknown in infants). *Ulcerative colitis* is a condition in which ulcers frequently appear in the colon (large intestine). *Regional enteritis* (Crohn's disease) is a recurring inflammation in the small intestine. The cause of these two diseases is not known. *Cystic fibrosis* is an inherited disease that affects the lungs, pancreas, sweat glands, and sometimes the liver and other organs. It often causes frequent diarrhea with foul-smelling stools.

SIGNS AND SYMPTOMS

Loose, watery stools is the major symptom. There may be mucus or flecks of red blood in the stools. The child may have cramps. There may also be fever, loss of appetite, vomiting, and weight loss, depending on the cause of the diarrhea.

HOME CARE

If the child has both diarrhea and vomiting, treat vomiting first by restricting the child's diet to clear liquids only. Once the vomiting stops, treat the diarrhea by limiting or not reintroducing solid foods—especially those with roughage, fruits (except bananas and apples), vegetables, butter, fatty meats, and peanut butter. Do not give the child milk, since milk may further aggravate diarrhea.

Encourage the child to drink plenty of clear liquids: tea, water, flavored gelatin water, and commercial mineral and electrolyte mixtures.

PRECAUTIONS

● Do not give anti-diarrheal medications to children, since side effects are common and can be dangerous. ● Isolate an infant from children who are ill with vomiting and diarrhea. ● If there is blood in the stools, high fever, prostration (extreme weakness or collapse), or severe or prolonged diarrhea (more than two to three days), call your doctor. Dysentery may be the cause. ● Report frequent, repeated diarrhea to your doctor. Frequent diarrhea may be a symptom of colitis, enteritis, or cystic fibrosis, especially if there is weight loss.

MEDICAL TREATMENT

Your doctor's treatment will be the same as home treatment. If necessary, the doctor may request blood tests, X rays of the large and small intestines, and sigmoidoscopy (an examination of the large intestine). In severe cases, hospitalization may be ordered.

Diphtheria

SYMPTOMS   Persistent, severe sore throat
Pus in throat
Gray membrane in throat
Fever
Cough
Difficulty breathing

HOME CARE   None. Diagnosis and treatment must be handled by a doctor.

If your child has a severe sore throat, see your doctor.

If a child with a sore throat is not immunized or has not had diphtheria boosters, tell your doctor. Otherwise, the doctor may not look for diphtheria.

PRECAUTIONS

☐ Diphtheria is a serious (possibly fatal) illness.

☐ Prevent diphtheria by getting your children immunized and by getting required booster shots.

☐ If your child is not immunized, every cough, sore throat, or case of croup could be diphtheria.

☐ If a child is having any trouble breathing, **do not** attempt to look in the child's throat.

☐ Do not give cough medicine to a child who is having any trouble breathing.

☐ Throat cultures to detect strep throat do not show diphtheria bacteria. A separate culture for diphtheria must be taken.

☐ A child may have both strep throat *and* diphtheria at the same time.

☐ A child who is not immunized can catch diphtheria from a healthy person who carries the diphtheria bacteria.

☐ Do not travel to an underdeveloped country where diphtheria is common without proper immunization and booster shots.

Diphtheria is a frequently fatal disease caused by a specific bacterium *(Corynebacterium diphtheriae)*. Diphtheria is caught by exposure to a person with the disease or to a carrier of the disease. (A carrier is a person who has the bacteria in the body but is healthy.) Symptoms of diphtheria may develop within two to four days after exposure to the bacteria.

The diphtheria germ causes infection of the nose, throat, tonsils, and lymph nodes of the neck. The germ kills, sometimes by destroying tissue, and sometimes by producing a toxin (poison) that causes heart damage and paralysis. Croup and pneumonia are common complications of diphtheria.

The protective immunization against diphtheria has been available for over 40 years. It is among the safest, cheapest, and most effective of all known vaccines. Even though this safe vaccine is available, diphtheria still exists throughout the world because many persons are not immunized.

SIGNS AND SYMPTOMS

The major symptom of diphtheria is a persistent, severe sore throat. The infected throat develops pus and a gray membrane that looks similar to strep throat and mononucleosis. Other symptoms include fever, cough, and troubled breathing.

If these symptoms appear in a child who is not immunized, diagnosis of diphtheria must be done by a doctor. The only way to detect diphtheria is by taking a nose and throat culture that looks specifically for diphtheria bacteria.

Diphtheria is difficult to diagnose for several reasons. First, many American doctors have never seen a case of diphtheria. Second, diphtheria closely resembles mononucleosis, strep throat, and various forms of croup. And finally, the doctor may not suspect diphtheria and therefore will not test for it. A doctor may assume your child is immunized against diphtheria. Routine throat cultures taken in a doctor's office to detect strep do not show diphtheria bacteria. Even if a throat culture finds strep, it is possible that the throat is infected by both strep and diphtheria.

HOME CARE

There is no home treatment for diphtheria. It is a serious (possibly fatal) disease, and treatment must be handled by a doctor. If your child has a severe sore throat, see your doctor. If your child is not immunized or has not had boosters, you must report this so that the doctor knows to look for diphtheria as well as strep throat.

The best step parents can take is to prevent diphtheria through proper immunization. It is essential that infants be routinely immunized for diphtheria. Three shots are required during the first six months of life. Routine boosters are required at 18 to 24 months of age and again at five years of age. Boosters are further required every ten years thereafter for a lifetime. If your child has not been immunized, every cough, sore throat, or case of croup could be the beginning of diphtheria.

PRECAUTIONS

● If your child is not up-to-date on immunization against diphtheria, be sure to inform the doctor treating your child. Diphtheria may be the furthest thought from your doctor's mind. ● If a child is having any trouble breathing, **do not** attempt to look in the child's throat. ● Do not give cough medicine to a child who is having any trouble breathing. ● Remember that a child who is not immunized can contract diphtheria from a well child or adult who is a carrier. ● Never travel to an underdeveloped country where diphtheria is common without proper immunization or booster shots.

MEDICAL TREATMENT

If your doctor suspects diphtheria, the disease can be diagnosed and treated. Diphtheria antitoxin and large doses of penicillin or erythromycin are effective if started early enough. A tracheotomy (opening the windpipe surgically through the neck) may be required if the condition is severe.

123

Dislocated elbow

SYMPTOMS

Pain in the arm (anywhere from the elbow
to the wrist)
Holding arm against the side with the
palm facing back
Pain when trying to turn the palm forward
Swelling of wrist and hand
Arm has been yanked or pulled

HOME CARE

The first time you suspect a dislocated
elbow, see your doctor for proper
treatment.

If the elbow becomes dislocated often,
your doctor may teach you how to correct
a dislocated elbow at home.

PRECAUTIONS

☐ Do not try to correct a dislocated
elbow unless you have been taught
the correct procedure by a doctor.

☐ Do not use the procedure for correcting a dislocated elbow unless the
symptoms exactly match the description *and* you are sure the arm has
been yanked. A fracture of a forearm
bone can cause similar symptoms.

☐ A dislocated elbow should be
treated as soon as possible (within a
few hours).

☐ Be especially careful for three to four
weeks after dislocation. The joint can
easily become dislocated again during
the healing period.

☐ Do not lift children by pulling on their
hands, wrists, or forearms. Lift children by their upper arms or under
the armpits.

A dislocated elbow
can occur when
there is a sudden
yank on the child's
hand or wrist, such
as often happens
when a parent tries
to prevent the child's
falling.

A child with a dis-
located elbow will
hold the arm to the
side with the palm
facing backward.

A dislocated elbow (Malgaigne's subluxation) is a condition in which the bones are out of their proper place in the joint. Actually, a dislocated elbow is not completely out of place. Therefore, it is more properly called a "subluxation" (partial dislocation). It is also known as "nursemaid's elbow." It is the only common dislocation in young children. It frequently occurs between one and three years of age; it is rare beyond age four.

The elbow contains two separate joints. The larger is a hinge joint that allows the forearm to bend and to straighten in relation to the upper arm. The smaller, less obvious joint of the elbow is between the upper ends of the two bones of the forearm (radius and ulna). This smaller joint allows the forearm to rotate, to turn the palm up and down. It is this smaller joint (radioulnar joint) that is partially dislocated when there is a sudden yank on the child's hand or wrist. It may occur when a parent tries to save the child from a stumble or fall. It may also occur when a child is swung around by the wrists in a game or when the child tries to grab a handhold to prevent falling.

SIGNS AND SYMPTOMS

When an accident causes a dislocated elbow, there is immediate pain. The pain may be felt anywhere from the elbow to the wrist. The child refuses to use the affected arm, clutching it against the side with the good arm. The child holds the affected arm with the palm of the hand facing back. Attempts to turn the palm forward cause pain. Swelling of the wrist and hand develops several hours later.

If you know that the arm has been yanked and the child holds the arm with palm facing back, a dislocated elbow is a likely cause. However, if you do not know that the arm has been pulled, you may not realize the cause of the problem. A dislocated elbow is commonly mistaken to be an injured wrist.

HOME CARE

The first time you suspect your child has a dislocated elbow, have a doctor treat it.

A dislocated elbow tends to occur again, however. There is a simple procedure for correcting a dislocated elbow, which parents can frequently do themselves. Your doctor may teach you the procedure if the elbow becomes dislocated often. If this maneuver is done within a few hours of the accident, a sharp snap or click is heard and actually felt near the elbow. The child is immediately relieved of pain and can use the arm freely. **Caution:** Do not attempt to correct a dislocated elbow unless you have been taught the correct procedure by a doctor.

PRECAUTIONS

● **Do not** use the procedure for correcting a dislocated elbow unless the symptoms exactly fit the description and you are sure the arm has been yanked. A fracture (break) of a forearm bone can produce similar symptoms. ● A dislocated elbow should be treated as soon as possible. If the elbow is dislocated for more than a few hours, correcting it may be more difficult because of the swelling; then for one to two days after correction, the arm may still be sore and not fully usable. ● After an elbow is dislocated, the joint remains susceptible to another dislocation for three to four weeks. Be careful. ● Make a habit of lifting your child by the upper arms or under the armpits. Do not lift a child by pulling on hands, wrists, or forearms.

MEDICAL TREATMENT

Your doctor will determine if the elbow is dislocated and may request an X ray to be sure there are no broken bones. (Sometimes, positioning the arm for the X ray returns the dislocated bone to its proper place.) After the diagnosis is certain, your doctor will correct the dislocation using the standard procedure mentioned.

Related topics:

Fractures
Sprains and
    dislocations

Dislocated hips

SYMPTOMS   Dislocation present at birth
Child moves one leg more than the other
Folds of the buttocks do not match
Creases on sides of groin do not match
Child limps
Child waddles

HOME CARE   None. See your doctor.

PRECAUTIONS

☐ Dislocation of the hip(s) is a disabling condition if not treated early and properly.

☐ Be sure your baby's hips are examined during regular visits to the doctor until the child is older than one year.

☐ If your child's legs are not the same (in length, size, shape, position, or movement), tell your doctor.

A baby's hips should be examined at birth and again at regular intervals so that a possible dislocated hip can be detected early.

A dislocated hip occurs when the thigh bone is out of its proper place in the hip socket. Before or after birth, a baby's hip socket may develop too shallowly. Eventually, the thigh bone (femur) dislocates from the socket, either before or at the time the child begins to stand and walk. The condition may occur on one side or on both sides. The cause is not certain, although some cases seem to be inherited. Other cases seem to be caused by an abnormal position of the infant's legs in the uterus before birth.

If the hip condition is not diagnosed until after dislocation has occurred, correcting it is more difficult. If it is not corrected before the child walks, the child will limp if the dislocation is in only one hip. The child will waddle if the dislocation is on both sides.

SIGNS AND SYMPTOMS

If the condition is in only one hip, parents may notice that the infant moves one leg more than the other. The folds of the buttocks or the creases on the sides of the groin may not match. A child who is already walking may limp or waddle.

HOME CARE

There is no home treatment until the condition is identified by a doctor. Dislocation of the hip(s) is a disabling condition if not treated early and properly. If you see any signs of hip problems, see your doctor as soon as possible.

PRECAUTIONS

● Be sure that your baby is thoroughly examined (while completely undressed) at regular "well-baby" visits to the doctor. Your doctor should examine the hips at each visit until the baby is older than one year. ● If the child's legs are not the same (in size, shape, position, or movement), tell your doctor.

MEDICAL TREATMENT

Your baby should be carefully examined for dislocated hips during each checkup. A doctor will suspect dislocation if any of the early signs and symptoms appear. The doctor will then check the ability of the thighs to be rotated outward. The doctor will also listen for a "clunking" sound which a dislocated hip makes when put through a certain series of movements. Your doctor will order X rays of both hips if the disorder is suspected.

The diagnosis is not usually made at birth, but the condition becomes more obvious with passing months. As soon as the diagnosis is made, you should consult an orthopedic specialist. If the hip is not yet dislocated, the doctor will treat the child with a special pillow positioned to keep the thighs spread or with a body splint or cast. If the hip is already dislocated, surgery may be required.

If both you and your doctor are alert, the problem can be noticed early. Early diagnosis is the key to easier treatment and perfect, permanent results.

Related topic:

Sprains and
    dislocations

Dizziness

SYMPTOMS
Spinning sensation
Loss of balance
Jerking movements of the eyes
Nausea
Vomiting

HOME CARE
Have the child lie down to rest. Put the legs up with the feet higher than the head. This relieves symptoms of faintness.

If rest does not relieve dizziness, see your doctor.

Have the child sit with the head between the knees. Place your hand on the back of the child's head, and have the child push up slightly against your hand.

PRECAUTIONS

☐ See your doctor if dizziness occurs often.

☐ See your doctor if dizziness lasts more than one or two hours.

☐ Before calling your doctor, be sure the child is describing a sense of rotating.

☐ Children sometimes confuse dizziness with faintness, light-headedness, nausea, or vision problems.

Simple dizziness may be helped by having the child sit down and lower head to knees.

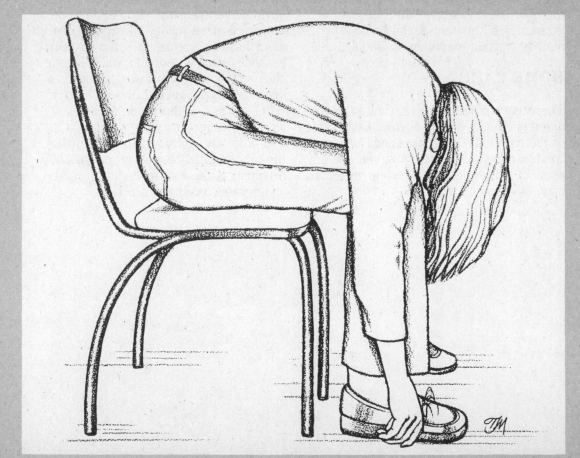

Dizziness (vertigo) is the sensation that the person is spinning around *or* that the environment is turning around the person. It is a sense of rotating and can be experienced normally by twirling rapidly in one spot until the room reels. Dizziness makes it difficult for a person to keep balanced. If dizziness continues, it may cause nausea and vomiting.

If possible, it is important to find out exactly what a child means when complaining of dizziness. Children often use the word "dizzy" to describe faintness, light-headedness, nausea, and vision problems. Any of these problems can have many causes.

True dizziness has few causes. The most common cause is infection of the inner ear (semicircular canals), sometimes from a virus (Meniere's syndrome). This disease usually is harmless and clears up without treatment, but it may last for weeks.

Dizziness may also accompany middle ear infections, concussions, and fractures of the base of the skull. Dizziness occurs with tumors that involve the eighth cranial nerve or the cerebellum of the brain. It may also occur in cases of meningitis and encephalitis.

SIGNS AND SYMPTOMS

If your child complains about feeling dizzy, ask the child to try to describe the feeling as clearly as possible. Be sure the child is describing a spinning sensation and not some other sensation (faintness, light-headedness, nausea, or vision problems). Look at the child to see if there is a loss of balance. Also look for jerking motions of the eyes when they are turned to one side or the other; this is another sign of dizziness. A long period of dizziness may cause nausea and vomiting.

HOME CARE

Have a dizzy child sit or lie down to rest. Raise the feet higher than the head to relieve symptoms of faintness or light-headedness. If the dizziness was caused simply by turning or spinning during play, the dizziness will quickly disappear. If rest does not relieve the dizziness, the cause must be determined by a doctor for proper treatment.

PRECAUTIONS

● Try to be sure the child is describing a sense of rotation before reporting the condition to your doctor. ● See your doctor if dizziness occurs often or if dizziness lasts more than a short period (one or two hours).

MEDICAL TREATMENT

The doctor will perform careful physical and neurological (nervous system) examinations. X rays of the skull and a blood count may be required. An ear, nose, and throat specialist may be asked to test the functioning of the inner ear, as well as the child's hearing. Your doctor may also consult a neurologist (a specialist in diseases of the nervous system). A CAT (computerized axial tomography) scan and an electroencephalogram may be necessary.

Related topics:

Concussion
Earaches
Encephalitis
Fainting
Meningitis
Vomiting

Draining ear

SYMPTOM Any discharge from the ear (except normal earwax)

HOME CARE Do not treat at home. See your doctor promptly.

While waiting to see the doctor, give aspirin or acetaminophen if there is pain.

PRECAUTIONS

☐ A doctor should examine a draining ear within 12 to 24 hours.

☐ Do not pack cotton into a draining ear.

☐ Do not use a cotton swab or any other instrument to remove material still in the ear canal.

☐ Do not wash out a draining ear, since the eardrum may be broken.

A draining ear should be examined by a doctor within 12 to 24 hours.

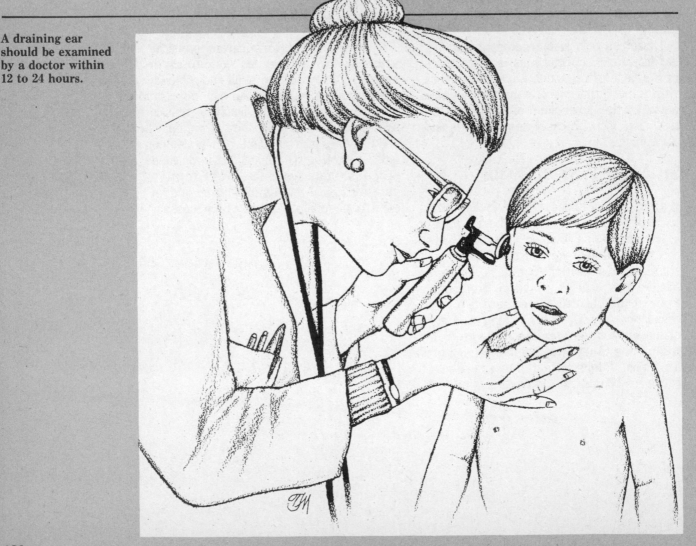

130

A draining ear occurs when any abnormal discharge or fluid comes out of the ear canal. The only material that normally comes from the ear canal is wax (cerumen). Earwax is ordinarily brown, though it may be beige or even yellowish if mixed with water when bathing, showering, or swimming. Normally, earwax has only a mild odor, contains no blood, and never flows out in large amounts.

Any other material discharging from the ear canal signals a potentially serious condition. It may be a symptom of a middle ear infection; a boil in the ear canal; swimmer's ear (infection of the ear canal); rupture (break or tear) of the eardrum by injury or infection; a foreign object in the ear canal; tumor of the middle ear (cholesteatoma); or fracture of the base of the skull.

SIGNS AND SYMPTOMS

Abnormal discharge from the ear may be thin and watery, bloody, odorous, cheesy, green, yellow, or white.

HOME CARE

Any drainage from the ear canal (except typical earwax) should be considered abnormal. Do not try to treat a draining ear at home. It should be promptly seen by a physician.

While waiting to see the doctor, pain accompanying a draining ear may be temporarily treated with aspirin or acetaminophen pain relievers.

PRECAUTIONS

● A draining ear should be examined by a doctor within 12 to 24 hours. ● Do not pack cotton into a draining ear. Packing the canal may force the discharge back into the middle ear. ● Do not use a cotton swab or any other instrument to remove material still in the canal. ● Do not attempt to wash out a draining ear since the eardrum may be broken or torn.

MEDICAL TREATMENT

Your doctor will gently clean your child's ear, inspect it, and diagnose the cause. Depending on what is found in the ear canal, treatment may require oral antibiotics, medicated ear drops, removing a foreign body, an X ray of the child's skull or mastoid bone, or surgery for cholesteatoma (tumor of the middle ear). In the case of a ruptured eardrum, antibiotics may be required for a long time, until the eardrum is healed and hearing returns to normal.

Related topics:

Deafness
Earaches
Swimmer's ear

131

Dysentery

SYMPTOMS Severe, bloody diarrhea
Prolonged high fever
Extreme weakness

HOME CARE Do not treat on your own. Whenever diarrhea is severe and bloody, see a doctor.

While waiting to see the doctor, give the child plenty of clear liquids: tea, water, flavored gelatin water, and commercial mineral and electrolyte mixtures.

Limit or stop giving solid foods. Avoid giving the child foods with roughage, fruits (except bananas and apples), vegetables, butter, fatty meats, and peanut butter.

Do not give the child milk.

PRECAUTIONS

☐ Always report severe or bloody diarrhea to your doctor.

☐ If any diarrhea lasts more than two or three days, call your doctor.

☐ A child with diarrhea needs extra liquids to avoid dehydration (a serious loss of body fluids).

☐ Dehydration is more likely in younger children. Infants can become dehydrated rapidly (within 12 to 24 hours after diarrhea begins).

☐ Do not give anti-diarrheal medications to children.

☐ When traveling, beware of unsanitary sources of food and water.

☐ If you suspect dysentery, isolate the child and dispose of stools carefully.

☐ Practice good hygiene at home.

In popular usage, dysentery is taken to mean any severe form of diarrhea. More accurately, dysentery is an infection of the intestinal tract caused by one of several specific bacteria. Dysentery causes diarrhea, but dysentery is a distinct disease.

The germs that cause dysentery are salmonella and shigella bacteria. (Typhoid bacteria are a type of salmonella.) Dysentery may also be caused by amoebas (amoebic dysentery). Some doctors consider cholera to be a form of dysentery.

Dysentery is the result of eating or drinking food, milk, or water that is contaminated with these specific bacteria or amoebas. It also may be contracted from someone who has the disease or is a carrier of dysentery. (A carrier is a person who has the germ in the body but is healthy.) Complications that may develop from dysentery include arthritis, meningitis, and perforation (ulcers) in the intestines.

SIGNS AND SYMPTOMS

The major symptom of dysentery is diarrhea. The diarrhea is often severe and is commonly bloody. The child may have a prolonged high fever (103°F to 105°F). The child may also be extremely weak and exhausted. Any persistent diarrhea should be suspected of being dysentery, especially if it is severe or bloody.

HOME CARE

Do not attempt to treat dysentery on your own. Whenever diarrhea is severe and bloody, see your doctor. Dysentery must be diagnosed by a doctor and often requires treatment with specific medications.

While waiting to see the doctor, give the child plenty of clear liquids. Liquids are needed to replace those being lost from the diarrhea. Extra liquids will help prevent dehydration (a serious loss of body fluids). Clear liquids that are the most helpful include tea, water, flavored gelatin water, and commercial mineral and electrolyte mixtures.

Limit or eliminate solid foods from the child's diet. Especially avoid foods with roughage, fruits (except bananas and apples), vegetables, butter, fatty meats, and peanut butter. Do not give the child milk, since milk may further aggravate diarrhea.

PRECAUTIONS

● Always report severe or bloody diarrhea to your doctor. ● If any diarrhea lasts more than two or three days, call your doctor. ● The younger the child, the more easily dehydration can occur with diarrhea. Infants can become dehydrated rapidly (within 12 to 24 hours after diarrhea begins). ● Do not give anti-diarrheal medications to children, since side effects are common and can be dangerous. ● When traveling, carefully choose sources of food and water. Avoid sources where sanitation may be poor. ● If you suspect dysentery, isolate the child and dispose of stools carefully. ● Practice good hygiene in your own home. Wash hands after treating an ill member of the family. Wash hands carefully before cooking and eating.

MEDICAL TREATMENT

A culture of the stools (with microscopic examination for amoebas and other parasites) confirms the diagnosis. Cultures of the blood and urine are sometimes performed, as well as tests for specific antibodies in the blood.

If dysentery is diagnosed, your doctor may hospitalize your child for treatment and isolation. Specific antibiotics for treating dysentery are available, although they are not always necessary. Diagnosed cases of dysentery must be reported to health authorities.

Related topics:

Arthritis
Dehydration
Diarrhea in children
Diarrhea in infants
Meningitis

Dyslexia

SYMPTOMS Confusion about being right- or
left-handed
Difficulty telling time or remembering
sequences
Hyperactivity
Language problems
Lack of coordination
Poor memory
Lack of balance
Seeing letters or numbers reversed

HOME CARE The dyslexic child needs to be encouraged
and supported, but not overprotected by
the family.

Work with the child's doctor and teachers
to help the child.

Be sensitive to the effect the child's dyslexia may have on other family members.

PRECAUTIONS

☐ Professional help for the dyslexic
child should be sought as soon as
possible.

☐ Be aware that an intelligent child who
experiences unexpected reading problems may have dyslexia.

☐ The brothers and sisters of a dyslexic
child may need special attention or
professional counseling. Parents also
may find counseling helpful in meeting
the dyslexic child's needs.

☐ Remember that dyslexia is not caused
by, or a sign of, mental retardation,
nor is it related to low intelligence,
physical disability, cultural disadvantages, social or economic position, or
brain damage.

☐ The possibility of a physical or psychological cause for the child's problems must be ruled out before a
diagnosis of dyslexia is made.

Dyslexia, also known as "developmental dyslexia" or "specific developmental dyslexia," is a type of learning disability that affects a child's ability to learn to read. It is more common in boys than in girls. It's not known exactly what causes the problem. Dyslexia often runs in families, but no specific genetic defect has been found to account for it. Some children with dyslexia may have had an accident that caused an undetected brain injury, but others have no such history. It is known, however, that dyslexia is not a form of mental retardation. And dyslexia is *not* related to low intelligence, physical handicaps, cultural disadvantages, low social or economic status, or brain damage.

A child with dyslexia often has no difficulties until entering school. Then the child finds that he or she cannot do things that other children can do easily. This experience can be embarrassing and painful. The child often finds it impossible to explain the problem and may become so frustrated that he or she either disrupts classes or becomes overly quiet and withdrawn. Other children may brand the dyslexic child as "stupid"; teachers and parents may consider the child lazy or unmotivated. The dyslexic child may, in fact, be very intelligent and may be trying extremely hard to learn to read. Pressure from teachers and parents to "work harder" can be confusing and frustrating and can lead to anger and rebellion. Some children with dyslexia find other activities that they can do well, such as sports or music. This may help them to adjust and feel more comfortable.

SIGNS AND SYMPTOMS

Dyslexia varies in severity. Some of the problems dyslexics may have include: confusion about whether they are right-handed or left-handed; difficulty learning to tell time or remembering the order of days, months, or seasons; hyperactivity; problems with language; difficulty telling left from right and up from down; coordination and balance problems; problems with memory; and seeing letters and numbers reversed.

Dyslexia is diagnosed by a series of tests of visual perception, memory, and space and time perception, and by medical and psychological evaluations. A child who has the symptoms of dyslexia may have a disorder or disease of the central nervous system, problems with hearing or vision, or emotional problems, rather than a learning disability. The possibility of a physical or psychological cause for the problem must be ruled out before a diagnosis can be made.

HOME CARE

A child with dyslexia needs special support and help from the family. However, the child does not need to be over-protected. The child should be challenged as well as encouraged. Finding a balance is not an easy job. The child's teachers and doctor may be able to help parents work with a dyslexic child. The situation can be hard on the whole family, so a parent needs to be sensitive to how the problem may affect the dyslexic child's brothers or sisters. They may need extra attention or professional help.

PRECAUTIONS

● If your child sems to be intelligent but has unexpected problems with reading, the child may have dyslexia. The sooner the problem is identified, the easier it will be for the child, so get professional help as soon as possible. ● Rather than consider the child a failure, encourage him or her to develop new skills.

MEDICAL TREATMENT

There is no cure for dyslexia. If the child has physical or emotional problems as well as dyslexia, these will probably be treated first. Then a treatment plan will be made to work on the reading problem. The plan may be developed by a team of educational professionals, in consultation with the child and the child's parents, doctor, and teachers. The plan will include special education and training for the child based on his or her particular problems and strengths.

Related topic:

Hyperactivity

Earaches

SYMPTOM   Mild to severe pain in the ear

POSSIBLE SYMPTOMS
Fever
Nasal congestion
Hearing problems

HOME CARE

Give aspirin or acetaminophen to relieve pain.

Applying gentle heat to the ear may relieve pain but sometimes worsens pain.

Check with your doctor before using anesthetic ear drops.

If earache may be caused by nasal congestion, use nose drops and oral decongestants to relieve congestion.

PRECAUTIONS

☐ If an earache is severe, see your doctor.

☐ If an earache lasts more than a few hours, see your doctor.

☐ Never put any object (not even cotton swabs) in your child's ear canal for any reason.

☐ Children with congested noses should not go swimming or fly in an airplane unless absolutely necessary.

☐ Babies and children under two years old should not submerge their heads under water.

☐ Early treatment of nasal congestion with nose drops and oral decongestants may prevent some ear problems.

☐ Children who tend to get swimmer's ear should have their ear canals cleaned by a doctor at the start of each swimming season and then use preventive ear drops at the end of each swimming day.

An earache is any pain or ache in the ear. Earaches may occur at any age from infancy on. However, they usually occur less and less often after the age of eight.

The most common cause of an earache is blockage of the eustachian tube (which connects the nose with the middle ear). This tube may become blocked as a result of a nasal allergy, a head cold, infected adenoids (lymph glands in the passage between the nose and throat), swimming in fresh or chlorinated water, or flying in an airplane. This blockage causes a vacuum in the middle ear, changes in the pressure on the eardrum, and secretion of fluid into the airspace of the middle ear. If obstruction of the eustachian tube continues, it may rapidly develop into an infection of the middle ear with pus (*otitis media*). If the eardrum ruptures (breaks), discharge begins to drain out of the ear.

An earache may also result from foreign objects in the ear canal, a buildup of earwax, pain in the jaw or molar teeth, or boils in the ear canal. Boils can be caused by scratching or digging in the ear with bobby pins, hairpins, fingernails, or cotton swabs.

Complications of untreated middle ear infections include mastoiditis (infection of the bone behind the ear), meningitis, perforated eardrum, and draining ear. Both middle and outer ear infections can cause swollen, tender lymph nodes.

SIGNS AND SYMPTOMS

Earaches may be mild or extremely painful. The pain may be constant, may come and go, or may occur only with chewing, burping, or nose blowing. Earaches may or may not be accompanied by fever or signs of a cold. They may or may not affect hearing. Progression to an infected middle ear (*otitis media*) usually causes intense, often throbbing pain. If the eardrum ruptures, pain quickly lessens. If there is a boil, a foreign body, a buildup of earwax, or an infection in the ear canal, the pain is mild at first and gradually builds. Gentle pressure on the earlobe aggravates the pain.

If your child is too young to tell you where the pain is, prolonged crying should be considered a possible sign of an earache. An earache is especially likely if the crying infant also has a head cold or congested nose, pulls on his or her ear, has recently gone swimming, or has flown in an airplane.

HOME CARE

Any ear pain can be temporarily relieved by aspirin or acetaminophen. Gentle heat applied to the ear may relieve pain but occasionally worsens it. Anesthetic ear drops must penetrate to the eardrum, and some ear, nose, and throat doctors prefer that these drops not be used. Nose drops and oral decongestants may unblock the eustachian tube to relieve an earache accompanied by nasal congestion or allergy.

PRECAUTIONS

● Severe earaches and earaches that last more than a few hours should be seen by your doctor. ● Children with congested noses should not go swimming. ● Babies and children under two years old should not submerge their heads underwater. ● When flying in an airplane, give your child something to drink as the plane ascends and descends. ● Early treatment of head colds and nasal allergies with nose drops and oral decongestants may prevent some ear problems. ● Children who tend to get swimmer's ear (infection of the ear canal) should have their ear canals cleaned by a doctor at the start of each swimming season. Then preventive ear drops should be used at the end of each swimming day. ● Never put any object (not even cotton swabs) in your child's ear canal for any reason.

MEDICAL TREATMENT

To determine the cause of pain, the doctor will carefully inspect your child's ears, nose, throat, and neck. For *otitis media,* your doctor will prescribe antibiotics by mouth for five to ten days or until the ear is normal. Nose drops, oral decongestants, and anti-allergy medications also may be prescribed.

Related topics:

Boils
Common cold
Deafness
Draining ear
Glands, swollen
Hay fever
Meningitis
Swimmer's ear

137

Earring problems

Quick Reference

SYMPTOMS
Redness of the earlobe
Itchy, scaly skin on earlobe
Swelling of earlobe
Lumps in earlobe
Tenderness of earlobe
Discharge from earlobe
Rawness around pierced openings
Tear in earlobe from injury

HOME CARE At the first sign of an earlobe problem, remove pierced earrings and leave them out until the condition is healed.

Apply antibiotic ointment to the front and back of earlobe.

Soak earlobe in warm water.

One common cause of an earlobe infection is an earring guard that is pushed in too far along the posts. This creates pressure on the earlobes and injury to the skin, inviting infection.

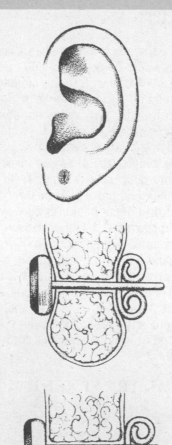

PRECAUTIONS

☐ If the irritation is severe, see your doctor. If the irritation does not clear up with home treatment, see your doctor.

☐ If there are any signs of infection (swelling, redness, lumps, tenderness, discharge, rawness), see your doctor.

☐ Leave training earrings in place for one month after piercing. Turn them daily, and splash fronts and backs with alcohol.

☐ Do not use earrings with posts that are too short for the earlobes.

☐ Do not push guards in too far along the posts so that earrings are too tight.

☐ Do not pull down on the earlobe when inserting earrings.

☐ Do not permit your child to wear earrings containing metals to which her skin is sensitive.

☐ Do not permit your child to wear large earrings or hoop earrings during athletics or dancing.

Pierced ears frequently cause problems involving the earlobes. These problems not only are annoying but are occasionally serious. Three common earring problems are infection, eczema, and injury. Problems may occur if the ear piercer does not give proper instructions for care of the ears, or if the instructions are not properly followed.

Infection of the earlobes immediately after the operation may be caused by lack of proper sterile technique during the piercing. Infection occurring weeks later is usually from failure to leave "training" (post) earrings in place or to care for the pierced earlobes adequately.

Infections that occur after the first month are the result of improperly inserting the earrings. One common error is inserting earrings with posts that are too short for the earlobes. Another common error is pushing the guards in too far along the posts. Both of these mistakes cause pressure on the earlobes and injury to the skin; infection quickly sets in. Pulling down the lobe to to insert the post can also cause infections. Pulling the lobe curves the straight channel the piercer has made and results in scratching the inside of the channel with the end of the post; the scratches then become infected. Sometimes infection is caused simply by inserting unclean earrings.

Eczema is a skin irritation. Eczema may develop on the earlobe if a person is sensitive or allergic to the metals used in inexpensive earrings. The skin of the earlobe becomes red, scaly, itchy, and sometimes infected.

The most common injury occurs when wearing hoop earrings during athletics and dancing. If a hoop is accidentally pulled or gets caught on something, the hoop can tear the earlobe neatly in half.

SIGNS AND SYMPTOMS

Signs of eczema are redness, irritation, itching, and scaliness of the skin of the earlobe. Signs of infection are swelling, redness, lumps in the earlobes, tenderness, discharge, and rawness around the pierced openings.

HOME CARE

At the first sign of any earlobe problem, remove the earrings. Then leave them out until the condition is corrected. Infection often is impossible to cure with earrings in place. If the infection is severe, the opening may heal closed and require repiercing.

After removing the earrings, apply antibiotic ointment to the front and back of the lobes. Soak the earlobes in warm water.

If the irritation is severe, if the irritation does not clear up with treatment, or if there are signs of infection, see your doctor.

PRECAUTIONS

● Ask the ear piercer for detailed instructions for care of newly pierced ears. ● Inquire whether the piercer will treat problems if they should occur. ● Leave training earrings in for one month after piercing. Turn them daily, and splash the fronts and backs with alcohol.

MEDICAL TREATMENT

Oral antibiotics may be required to cure infection. If the earlobe is badly cut or torn, plastic surgery may be necessary. The doctor may prescribe a steroid ointment if there is eczema but no infection.

Related topics:

Eczema
Rash

Eczema

SYMPTOMS Dry, scaly, pink rash
Itching skin

HOME CARE Stop giving the child any new foods, beverages, and medications that were added to the child's diet in the month before the rash broke out.

If stopping these new items does not improve the rash within four to seven days, stop giving the child all foods and beverages most likely to cause eczema. (See lists of foods on this page.)

Look for and remove irritating substances that may be coming in contact with the child's skin. (See list of substances likely to cause eczema on this page.)

To avoid further drying of the skin, use a humidifier to moisten dry air.

Bathe the child sparingly, using mild dermatologic soaps.

If eczema clears up, try gradually returning stopped foods to the child's diet.

Reintroducing one food per week should help detect foods that cause a reaction. Then avoid those foods.

PRECAUTIONS

☐ If the rash is severe or infected, see your doctor.

☐ If the rash does not improve after one week of home treatment, see your doctor.

☐ As you add new foods to your infant's diet, watch for signs of rash.

☐ If your infant is allergic to both cow's milk and soy formula, your doctor can recommend a nonsoy, nonmilk formula.

☐ Keep a child using coal-tar ointments out of the sun as much as possible. Coal-tar ointments increase sensitivity to sunburn.

Foods likely to cause eczema (in infants under one year)
Cow's milk
Milk products
Wheat flour
Eggs
Citrus fruits and juices
Chocolate
Nuts
Peanut butter
Fish
Shellfish
Tomatoes and tomato juice
Tropical fruit drinks and desserts

Foods likely to cause eczema (in children over one year)
Citrus fruits and juices
Chocolate
Nuts
Peanut butter
Fish
Shellfish
Tomatoes and tomato juice
Tropical fruit drinks and desserts
Candies
Ice cream
Spices (except salt)
Corn
Berries

Substances likely to cause eczema
Soaps
Detergents
Fabric softeners (especially sheets for the dryer)
Wool
Synthetic fabrics
Stretch-cotton fabrics
Fabric dyes (particularly red and blue)
Water softeners
Cosmetics
Metals
Plastics

Eczema is a common, noncontagious rash in children. Generally, it starts between one month and two years of age, but sometimes it begins later. Eczema may disappear after two years of age, or it may appear off and on throughout childhood.

The cause of eczema is questionable but the condition is usually inherited. Eczema is a form of atopic dermatitis (any inflammation of the skin due to allergy). Children who have eczema often later develop other allergies, such as hay fever, asthma, and eye allergies.

Eczema sometimes is an allergic reaction to foods, beverages, and medications (including vitamin supplements). It also may be an allergic reaction to substances that come in contact with the skin. In some children, conditions such as heat or cold or emotions such as anger may cause itching and scaly skin all over the body.

Skin affected by eczema can easily become infected, especially if the skin is scratched. Common complications of eczema include infections with herpes simplex virus, vaccinia virus, and impetigo.

SIGNS AND SYMPTOMS

The eczema rash is dry, slightly scaly, pink, and itchy. The rash becomes red from rubbing and scratching. There is no fever or other symptoms, except when scratching causes an infection.

Eczema often begins on the cheeks ("clown" eczema) and around the mouth. It may also crop up on the buttocks or elsewhere. The most common location is behind the knees and in the folds of the elbows. Eczema rarely covers the entire body. It sometimes takes the form of round coin-like patches scattered on the body (nummular eczema). When it appears in this round patchy form, eczema may be confused with ringworm and pityriasis rosea. Often eczema occurs in combination with seborrhea (cradle cap).

HOME CARE

Home treatment of eczema is often successful, except in severe or infected cases.

First stop any new foods, beverages, and medications that were added to the child's diet within a month of the appearance of the rash.

If stopping these new items does not improve the rash in four to seven days in a child under one year, stop all foods and beverages most likely to cause eczema. Look for and remove possible irritating substances coming in contact with the child's skin. (See Quick Reference for a list of these foods and substances.)

Ointments that contain coal-tar derivatives are safe to use, but their use can obscure the physician's initial evaluation of the condition. To avoid further drying of the skin, use a humidifier to moisten dry air. Bathe the child sparingly, using mild dermatologic soaps.

If following this procedure clears up the eczema, try gradually returning the stopped foods to the child's diet—one at a time. Reintroducing one food each week should help detect the foods that cause a reaction. Those foods should then be avoided. If the condition is not better in one week, see your doctor.

PRECAUTIONS

● As new foods are added to your infant's diet, watch carefully for any sign of rash.
● If your infant is allergic to soy formula as well as cow's milk, your doctor will recommend a nonsoy, nonmilk formula.
● Coal-tar ointments increase sensitivity to sunburn. When using these ointments, keep the child out of the sun as much as possible.

MEDICAL TREATMENT

Help your doctor find the cause of eczema by trying home treatment first and noting what doesn't work and what seems to help. Inform your doctor, too, of any similar cases that have occurred in your older children. Your doctor may prescribe steroid creams, ointments, or lotions to ease the rash. Oral steroids will not be prescribed unless eczema is severe, and then they they will be given for only a brief period. Oral antibiotics may be prescribed if eczema is infected.

Encephalitis

KEY SYMPTOMS
Stiff neck
Inability to sit up unassisted

IMPORTANT

Encephalitis is a life-threatening disease. See your doctor immediately if key symptoms appear.

OTHER SYMPTOMS
Headache
Vomiting
Sleepiness
Disorientation (confusion)
High fever or no fever
Convulsions or loss of consciousness

HOME CARE None. See your doctor immediately.

PRECAUTIONS

☐ If there are symptoms of encephalitis, let your doctor know if the child has been exposed to any poisons (including lead and mercury).

☐ If your child has had a severe reaction to any vaccines, tell your doctor before the child gets booster shots.

One of the symptoms of encephalitis is an inability to sit up unassisted without supporting the trunk with both hands braced behind.

Encephalitis is an inflammation of the brain. The causes are many, including poisons, bacteria, vaccines, and parasites. Most cases are caused by viruses, many of which cause familiar diseases such as mumps, measles, rubella, chicken pox, herpes, mononucleosis, hepatitis, and influenza. The whooping cough bacterium can cause encephalitis, as can the vaccines used to prevent whooping cough, measles, influenza, rabies, yellow fever, and typhoid. The vaccines are far less likely to cause encephalitis, however, than are the illnesses they prevent. Lead, mercury, and other poisons also may cause encephalitis.

SIGNS AND SYMPTOMS

Encephalitis may start with the symptoms of a common cold. The child may have no fever or a high fever (105°F). The child usually has a headache, vomits, and is disoriented (confused) and sleepy. Occasionally, convulsions and unconsciousness may occur.

A child with encephalitis will usually be unable to flex his or her neck forward to touch the chin to the chest while the mouth is closed. Sometimes the child cannot sit up without supporting the trunk with both hands braced behind (in a tripod fashion). **This is a life-threatening situation.**

HOME CARE

None. See your doctor immediately if your child shows any symptoms of encephalitis.

PRECAUTION

● If your child has had a severe reaction to any of the vaccines listed, be sure to tell your doctor before a booster of the vaccine is given.

MEDICAL TREATMENT

Since encephalitis may be a complication of another disease (such as measles, mumps, whooping cough), a child with such a disease and encephalitis symptoms will probably be examined for encephalitis. Knowing that the child has been exposed to poisons may also lead the doctor to suspect encephalitis.

A definite diagnosis is based on the child's medical history; a blood count; a spinal tap; identification of the infecting organism in the spinal fluid, nose, throat, or stools; and the presence of antibodies (protective substances made by the body to fight the infecting organism) in the patient's blood.

If encephalitis is diagnosed, hospitalization may be required. There is specific treatment for only a few types of encephalitis, since most viral infections are hard to treat. There is no medication that can kill the invading virus after it has caused the infection. Usually, however, treatment to ease the symptoms and to help the patient withstand the disease until it runs its course leads to recovery.

Related topics:

Chicken pox
Common cold
Convulsions
  with fever
Hepatitis
Herpes simplex
Immunizations
Infectious
  mononucleosis
Influenza
Lead poisoning
Measles
Mumps
Poisoning
Rubella
Whooping cough

143

Eye allergies

KEY SYMPTOMS
Red, itchy eyes
Watering eyes
Swollen whites of eyes

OTHER SYMPTOMS
Swollen, red eyelids
Rough, scaly skin on eyelids
Swollen, bluish pouches beneath eyes

HOME CARE
Give the child antihistamines by mouth.

Apply cold compresses to the eyes.

Try to identify and avoid substances that cause allergic reactions.

PRECAUTIONS

☐ If there is pus or pain in the eyes, the condition is probably not an allergy.

☐ If the pupils of the eyes are enlarged and slow to respond to light, see your doctor.

☐ If home treatment does not improve the eyes within 24 hours, see your doctor.

☐ If vision is affected, see your doctor.

☐ Check with your doctor before using any eyedrops in the child's eyes.

Allergic reactions of the eyes are often caused by substances, such as finger paints, carried to the eyes by the hands.

Eye allergies are allergic reactions of the eyes. They may affect the conjunctiva (the transparent covering over the whites of the eyes and the insides of the eyelids). They may also affect the skin on the eyelids and around the eyes.

Eye allergies are caused by a wide variety of substances carried to the eyes by the air or by the hands. Seasonal, airborne materials are pollens from trees, grass, ragweed, and other plants. Non-seasonal airborne materials include house dust, feathers, molds, and animal dander (tiny scales from the skin of an animal). Many irritants may be carried to the eyes by the hands, including nail polish, household cleaning products, materials from stuffed toys, and finger paints.

SIGNS AND SYMPTOMS

The whites of the eyes become red and itchy. The eyes water, but no pus is formed. Occasionally, the whites become visibly swollen with clear jelly-like material. The eyelids become swollen and red. The skin of the eyelids may be smooth or rough and scaly. Pouches beneath the eyes may become swollen and bluish and resemble shiners.

Certain clues can distinguish eye allergies from several other conditions that also cause reddened eyes (conditions such as conjunctivitis, viruses, foreign bodies in the eyes, styes, glaucoma). Eye allergies cause itching and tearing but never cause pain or pus. Swelling of the whites of the eyes is a key sign of an eye allergy.

HOME CARE

Oral antihistamines usually help. With your doctor's permission, use of eyedrops containing phenylephrine or ephedrine brings temporary relief. Applying cold compresses to the eyes may also ease the discomfort. Whenever possible, identifying and avoiding the irritating substance is clearly the best solution.

PRECAUTIONS

● If there is pus or pain in the eyes, the condition is probably not an allergy. ● If the pupils of the eyes are dilated (enlarged) and slow to respond to light, see your doctor. ● If home treatment is not effective in 24 hours, see your doctor. ● If vision is affected, see your doctor.

MEDICAL TREATMENT

Your doctor will examine the outsides and insides of your child's eyes. Medicated eyedrops are effective but are safe only after a doctor's examination. Skin tests may be suggested to help identify the substances causing the allergic reaction. Desensitization shots over an extended period are rarely recommended.

Related topics:

Conjunctivitis
Eye, blocked
   tear duct
Eye injuries
Styes
Viruses

Eye, blocked tear duct

SYMPTOMS
Watering eyes
Green or yellow pus in eyes
Red, raw skin at outer corners of eyelids
Swollen tear sac at side of nose

HOME CARE
Simple tearing needs no treatment. Wipe away tears and clean eyelids with sterile water on a cotton ball.

If skin is red at outer corners of eyes, if eyes themselves are red, or if there is pus, call your doctor. The doctor may prescribe antibiotic eyedrops by telephone.

If the tear sac at the side of the nose is swollen, see your doctor.

PRECAUTIONS

☐ With home treatment, the eyes should improve within 24 hours. If there is no improvement, call your doctor.

☐ If improvement is prompt, continue home treatment until the eye is clear for at least two days.

☐ Repeated problems of eye tearing from obstructed tear ducts are common in infants.

Tears form in the tear glands that lie above the eyeballs within the bony eye sockets. These tear glands continuously produce fluid that flows across the eyeballs and down the slender tear ducts that connect each eye with the nose (nasolacrimal ducts). The two openings into each tear duct are pinpoint in size and can be seen at the edge of the upper and lower eyelids, near the corner of the eye next to the nose.

In newborns, the openings into the tear ducts are often too small. These openings may be further blocked by the silver nitrate or other drops placed in the eyes at birth to prevent eye infections. Blockage of these openings may cause tears to flow out of the outer corner of the baby's eye, even when the infant is not crying. Occasionally, instead of normal eye fluid, green or yellow pus will collect in the eye. This discharge will further block the tiny tear ducts.

If the nasolacrimal duct becomes blocked at the end inside the nose, tearing and possible infection will occur. Blockage at the nose end of the duct can be present at birth, or it may be caused by congestion from a cold or an allergy. When the nose end of the duct is blocked, the nasolacrimal sac between the eye and the side of the nose may swell with fluid and be visible as a distinct lump the size of a green pea.

SIGNS AND SYMPTOMS

In infants, simple tearing of one or both eyes is so common as to be considered normal; it is harmless. However, if there is pus in the eye, redness and rawness at the outer corners of the eyelids, or swelling of the tear sac (with or without redness), treatment may be needed.

HOME CARE

Simple tearing needs no treatment. The tears can be wiped away and the eyelids cleaned by wiping with a cotton ball dipped in sterile water. Call the doctor if the eye is red, pus is present, or the tear duct is swollen. Redness of the skin at the outer corner of the eye, redness of the eye itself, or the presence of pus may be treated with antibiotic eyedrops prescribed by the doctor, often over the telephone. If the tear sac at the side of the nose is swollen, your doctor may teach you how to gently massage the tear sac. (Do not attempt to massage the tear sac without a doctor's instructions.)

PRECAUTIONS

● With home treatment, the eyes should improve within 24 hours. If there is no improvement, notify your doctor. ● If improvement is prompt, continue treatment until the eye is clear for at least two days. ● Repeated problems of eye tearing are common in infants; save the eyedrops for possible future use, but check the expiration date on the label before reusing.

MEDICAL TREATMENT

Your doctor's treatment is the same as home treatment. Your doctor can demonstrate the proper method of massaging the tear sac, if needed. If the condition continues past the age of eight months to one year, your doctor may refer your child to an ophthalmologist (an eye specialist) who may surgically enlarge the nasolacrimal duct under general anesthesia.

Related topics:

Conjunctivitis
Eye allergies

Eye injuries

SYMPTOMS
Pain in eye
Inability to open eye
Bleeding from or in eyeball
Differences in size or color of pupils
Differences in color or position of irises
Collapse of eyeball

Blurring of vision
Visible foreign object on eye surface or
  under eyelid
Harmful liquid or powder in contact with
  the eye

HOME CARE

If a harmful liquid or powder enters the eye:
Act immediately! Seconds count! Hold the eye open, and flush it with several pints of cool water. If possible, put the child into a cool shower, clothes and all, and wash out the eye. Then immediately take the child to a doctor.

If an object has penetrated the eye:
Do not try to remove the object. See a doctor immediately.

*If the child **cannot** easily open the eye:*
Do not try to force the eye open. Do not try to treat the injury at home. Place a soft bandage over the eye, and see a doctor promptly.

*If the child **can** easily open the eye:*
Look for the following signs of damage:
  bleeding from or in the eyeball;
    differences in the size or color of the
      pupils;
    differences in the color or position of
      the irises;
  any collapse of the eyeball;
  blurring of vision.

If any of these symptoms appear, do not try to treat at home. Place a soft bandage over the eye, and see your doctor promptly.

*If the child **can** easily open the eye and none of the above signs appears:*
Look for a speck on the eyeball or under the eyelid. If the child is cooperative, you may try to remove a speck with gentle strokes with a cotton swab. If the speck does not immediately come off, **stop.** The object may be embedded. See a doctor.

PRECAUTIONS

☐ Be cautious about treating eye injuries yourself.

☐ Do not let young children play with golf balls. Do not let anyone unwind a golf ball. If unwound, some golf balls explode and cause eye injuries.

☐ Aerosol spray cans and carbon dioxide cartridges explode violently in fires. Be sure your child knows this.

☐ Keep children far away from areas where machine sanders, paint removers, and grindstones are being used. These machines throw off particles that can injure the eyes. Anyone around these machines should wear protective glasses.

The eyeball is a fragile, hollow sphere whose wall is less than one-eighth-inch thick. Within the eyeball, there are many complex and delicate structures. Fortunately, the eyeball is well protected by its bony socket and the eyelids.

The eye can be injured by small objects like sand or metallic splinters which land on or become embedded in the surface or which penetrate to the inside of the eye. Sharp objects such as fingernails, knives, and fishhooks can scratch the surface and penetrate the eye. Dull objects such as balls and baseball bats can jar the eye and dislodge its internal structures. A tiny speck in the eye may lodge on the surface or hide under the eyelid. The eye may also be injured by harmful liquids or powders (acids, alkalis, caustics, gasoline) that come in contact with the eye.

SIGNS AND SYMPTOMS

If the child cannot easily open the eye, *do not* try to force it open to look in the eye. See your doctor promptly.

If the child can easily open the eye, then you can examine the eye to look for signs of damage. Look carefully for all of the following signs of injury. Is there any free blood coming from the eyeball? (Do not be misled by blood from a cut near the eye that may have run into the eye.) Are there any differences in the pupil of the affected eye compared to the good eye (larger? smaller? different color?)? Is there any difference in the color or position of the iris (colored part of the eye)? Is there any sign of collapse of the eyeball? Is there any puddling of red blood in front of the iris? Is there any blurring of vision? If none of these symptoms is present, you may safely look for foreign objects on the surface of the eyeball or lodged under the eyelid.

HOME CARE

Do not attempt to treat an eye injury at home if the child cannot easily open the eye. Place a soft bandage over the eye, and see your doctor promptly.

Do not attempt to treat at home if the child has any of the following symptoms:

bleeding from or in the eyeball; differences in the size or color of the pupils; differences in the color or position of the irises; any collapse of the eyeball; or blurring of vision. If any of these symptoms appear, place a soft bandage over the eye, and see your doctor promptly.

Do not attempt to remove a fishhook or any other object that has penetrated the eye. See a doctor immediately.

If a harmful liquid or powder enters the eye (acids, alkalis, caustics, gasoline), **immediate action is essential.** Seconds count! Hold the eye open, and flush it with several pints of cool water. If possible, put your child into a cool shower, clothes and all, and wash out the eye. Then immediately take the child to your doctor for further care.

If none of the above signs is present and you see a speck on the eyeball or under the lid (and the child is cooperative), you may try to remove the speck by gentle strokes with a cotton swab. If the speck does not immediately come off, stop. The object may be embedded. See a doctor.

PRECAUTIONS

● Be cautious about treating eye injuries yourself. ● Some golf balls explode if they are unwound and can cause eye injuries. Do not let young children play with golf balls, and do not allow anyone to unwind them. ● Beware! Aerosol spray cans and carbon dioxide cartridges explode violently in fires or in extreme heat. Be sure your child knows this. ● Machine sanders, paint removers, and grindstones throw off particles that can injure the eyes. Anyone around these machines should wear protective glasses. Keep children far away from such machines.

MEDICAL TREATMENT

A doctor can easily anesthetize the eye and examine it internally and externally without pain or damage. Your doctor may stain the eyeball with drops to make small injuries and foreign objects readily visible. Areas inside and outside of the eye can be examined with a special microscope.

Related topics:

Eye allergies
Vision problems

Fainting

SYMPTOMS

Light-headedness
Dizziness
Blurred vision
Cold, moist skin
Mild nausea
Pale or greenish skin
Glazed look in eyes
Loss of consciousness
Rapid, complete recovery

HOME CARE

Protect a fainting child from being injured from a fall. Try to catch the child.

Place the child flat on the back with legs raised higher than the head.

Cool air from a window or air conditioner may help.

Keep the child lying down for five to ten minutes after regaining consciousness.

If the child feels faint but is still conscious, have the child sit with the head between the knees. Place your hand on the back of the child's head, and have the child push up slightly against your hand.

PRECAUTIONS

☐ If fainting occurs often, or if there are any signs of epilepsy, see your doctor.

☐ If the child's skin turns bluish during an apparent faint, or if the child is not completely well before and after fainting, see your doctor.

☐ Smelling salts are not necessary and are not always helpful. If you use smelling salts to revive the child, be careful not to burn the membranes inside the nose.

Place a child who has fainted flat on the back with feet raised higher than the head.

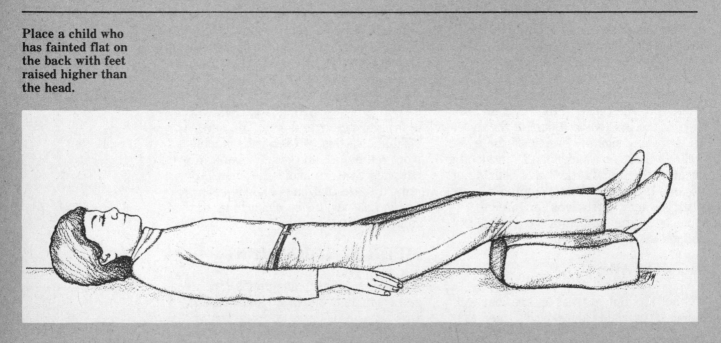

Fainting is a temporary loss of consciousness caused by the involuntary (autonomic) nervous system. It is usually due to a temporarily insufficient amount of blood in the brain. Fainting can be brought on by pain, physical fatigue, low blood sugar, a disturbing scene, sudden fright, and other strong emotions.

Fainting is common in pre-adolescent and adolescent children. It often occurs after the child has gone without eating for an extended period of time. A partial faint (light-headedness and dizziness) or a complete faint is also common when a teenager abruptly changes position (for example, after jumping up from a reclining or sitting position). It also can occur in a dentist's chair caused by a combination of pain, anxiety, and turning the head sharply to one side (which places pressure on the carotid artery in the neck).

SIGNS AND SYMPTOMS

Just before unconsciousness, the child experiences light-headedness, blurred vision, cold and moist skin (clamminess), and sometimes mild nausea. An observer may notice a paleness or greenish color of the skin and a glazed look in the eyes before the child loses consciousness. Rarely will the child lose control of the urine or stools. Consciousness will be recovered within a few minutes and the child will probably not remember fainting.

The pulse at the wrist may be characteristically feeble and slow or not present at all. The heart beat (place your ear against child's chest) is slow, usually 50 beats per minute or slower.

Consider the circumstances under which the child fainted. If they were circumstances that typically can cause fainting, and if the child rapidly and completely recovers, this suggests nothing more serious than an isolated spell.

HOME CARE

The only danger in fainting is possible injury from falling. Try to catch the child before the fall or as the child goes down. Place the child flat on the back, raising the legs to return blood to the head. Although not required, the coolness from an open window or air conditioner may help. Keep your child lying down for five to ten minutes after consciousness returns.

If your child is not yet unconscious, but feels a faint coming on, have the child sit with his or her head between the knees. Place your hand on the back of the child's head, and have the child push the head up slightly against your hand. This maneuver forces extra blood into the head.

PRECAUTIONS

• Sometimes a first convulsion is mistaken for fainting. If fainting occurs often, or if there are any signs of epilepsy, see your doctor. • If the child's skin turns bluish during an apparent faint, or if your child is not completely well before and after fainting, consult your doctor. Extremely rare heart conditions might resemble fainting. • Smelling salts are not necessary and are not always helpful. If you use smelling salts to revive your child, be careful not to burn the membranes inside the nose.

MEDICAL TREATMENT

If there is any question about the cause of your child's fainting, the doctor will examine your child for various causes of unconsciousness. Your doctor may order an electrocardiogram, electroencephalogram, blood chemistries, or a chest X ray.

Related topics:

Convulsions
    without fever
Dizziness

151

Fifth disease

KEY SYMPTOMS
Bright red rash on cheeks
Pink rash (forming lace-like pattern) on trunk and limbs
Slight fever or no fever
Itching

POSSIBLE SYMPTOMS (older children only)
Headache
Sore throat
Runny nose
Loss of appetite
Nausea

HOME CARE
No treatment is required.

Itching may be treated with anti-histamines.

PRECAUTIONS
☐ None.

A child with fifth disease can attend school or daycare if the child feels well enough and if there is no fever.

Fifth disease (*erythema infectiosum*) is a moderately contagious childhood disease. It is caused by a virus that has not yet been identified. Symptoms may appear an average of two weeks after being exposed to a person with the disease (although they may appear anywhere from one week to four weeks after exposure). Some epidemics of fifth disease occur in a school or a neighborhood.

SIGNS AND SYMPTOMS

Usually the child has little or no fever and feels only slightly or not at all ill. The disease is identified by the sudden appearance of a bright red rash on the cheeks, making it look as though the child has been slapped. A pink rash forming a pattern like a lace tablecloth appears on the trunk and limbs. The condition can last two to 40 days and may itch. In older children and young adults, headache, sore throat, runny nose, loss of appetite, and nausea may occur.

Fifth disease usually is obvious from the typical appearance of the rash, especially if an epidemic is occurring in the neighborhood or school. Fifth disease is occasionally confused with rubella, rashes from medications, and other viral rashes. The condition is rarely confused with scarlet fever.

HOME CARE

No treatment is required. The child need not be isolated. Public health authorities have stated that a child with fifth disease can attend school if there is no fever and the child feels well enough. Itching can be treated with antihistamines.

PRECAUTIONS

● None.

MEDICAL TREATMENT

There are no laboratory tests to diagnose the disease. There is no work for the doctor beyond confirming the diagnosis from the appearance of the rash.

Related topics:

Rash
Rubella

Flat feet

SYMPTOMS
No arches in feet
Entire soles of feet rest on the ground
Walking on inner edges of feet
Tops of shoes broken down from the
  inside
Worn inner edges of heels and soles
  on shoes
Pain in feet after brief exercise

HOME CARE
If a child past age three years seems flat-footed, have the child tiptoe barefoot for five to ten minutes a day.

If a child over six to eight years old seems flat-footed, have the child walk barefooted on the outer edges of the feet with the toes clenched for ten minutes a day.

PRECAUTIONS

☐ Don't be concerned if your young child has flat feet. All infants and toddlers have flat feet to some degree. Arches are not fully developed until children are three or four years old.

☐ Toddlers should not wear walking shoes until they can walk unaided on hard surfaces.

☐ If a child under three or four years old wears out the inner edges or the upper portions of shoes before the shoes are outgrown, buy shoes with stronger counters.

☐ Do not use orthopedic shoes or devices without competent professional advice.

☐ Orthopedic shoes and devices may actually harm normal feet.

☐ Pain in the feet after excessive use and exercise is normal.

Flat feet is a condition in which the arches of the feet are flattened out so that the entire sole of the foot touches the ground.

A normal, newborn baby does not have arches of the feet. (The normal condition of a child's feet before arches develop is sometimes called "physiological flat feet.") Arches don't start to develop until the child begins to walk unaided. They are not fully formed until the child is three to four years old. Arches are formed by the developing strength of the leg muscles exerted on the normal bones and ligaments of the feet.

SIGNS AND SYMPTOMS

With true flat feet, there are no arches when a child stands. The child walks on the inner edges of the feet. This practice breaks down the tops of the shoes from the inside and wears down the inner edges of the heels and soles on the shoes. The child may complain of painful feet after brief exercise.

The presence or absence of an arch at any age can best be judged when a child stands on the tips of the toes. After age three or four, your child should no longer wear out the inner edges of the shoes.

HOME CARE

To encourage development of the feet, children should not wear walking shoes until they start to walk unaided on hard surfaces. If a child under three or four years of age breaks down the upper portions of the shoes or wears out the inner edges of the heels before the shoes are outgrown, buy shoes with stronger counters (the inner part of the back third section of the upper shoe). If your child past age three appears flat-footed, have the child tiptoe barefoot five to ten minutes per day. A child over six to eight years of age should walk barefooted on the outer edges of the feet with the toes clenched for ten minutes daily.

PRECAUTIONS

● Do not use orthopedic shoes or devices without competent professional advice. Thomas heels, scaphoid pads ("cookies"), and orthopedic shoes are expensive if not needed, and they actually may harm normal feet. ● Painful feet after excessive use and exercise do not indicate abnormal feet.

MEDICAL TREATMENT

Your doctor will examine your child's feet carefully while the child stands, sits, stands on tiptoes, and walks. The doctor will conduct tests for the movement of the joints of the feet, the strength of the foot muscles, and the strength of the tendons. Your doctor will examine worn shoes. Rarely will the doctor X-ray your child's feet. Considering all these factors along with the child's age, the doctor may prescribe exercises or orthopedic shoes.

Food allergies

SYMPTOMS
Abdominal cramps
Vomiting
Diarrhea
Blood in stool
Hives
Eczema
Runny nose
Asthma

HOME CARE

If you suspect that an unfamiliar food is causing stomach cramps, diarrhea, or vomiting, withdraw that food from your child's diet.

Introduce new foods slowly, one at a time. If a child continues to have symptoms, or seems generally unwell, call the doctor.

PRECAUTIONS

☐ An enzyme deficiency (malabsorption syndrome) can cause symptoms similar to those of a food allergy. A child who is generally not doing well should be seen by a doctor.

☐ Persistent diarrhea may indicate an allergic or malabsorption problem.

☐ When you introduce new foods into a child's diet, watch for reactions that may indicate an allergy or other problem.

Food allergies—unusual reactions or increased sensitivities to food or drink—are more likely to occur in infants than in older children. The condition involves vomiting, diarrhea, and abdominal cramps and occurs from minutes to hours after the child has had certain foods, beverages, or medications. Nonpasteurized cow's milk is the most common cause of food allergy, but eggs, wheat, soybean formulas, orange juice, tomatoes, chocolate, fish, berries, and melons may also be responsible.

A malabsorption syndrome, which occurs when the digestive system lacks certain natural chemicals to digest food, may produce symptoms similar to those of a food allergy. Normally, the body produces natural chemicals called enzymes that break down starches, fats, proteins, and sugars into forms that the body can use. In a malabsorption syndrome an enzyme is missing, which means that the child cannot digest certain foods. For example, a condition called celiac disease may interfere with the digestion of gluten (starch found in wheat and rye), and the disease cystic fibrosis may hamper the digestion of fats and proteins.

SIGNS AND SYMPTOMS

Hives, eczema, runny nose, and asthma can all be signs of food allergy. Sometimes blood appears in the baby's stool. If a particular food brings on abdominal cramps and diarrhea (with or without vomiting), a food allergy can be suspected. By changing the diet and observing your child's reactions, you may be able to identify the problem. Often, however, specific and complex tests are required to diagnose a food allergy. If the child does not seem to tolerate several kinds of foods and is not doing well generally, the cause may be a malabsorption syndrome.

HOME CARE

If your infant vomits or has cramps or diarrhea after you have introduced a new food into the child's diet, withdraw the food promptly. This does not necessarily indicate a food allergy, but you should wait (two to four weeks) before reintroducing the food. Add new foods to the child's diet one at a time, and allow several days between each introduction so that you can be sure that no problems are occurring.

PRECAUTIONS

● Persistent diarrhea is a clue to a malabsorption or an allergic problem. ● If diarrhea persists, temporarily cut milk and milk products out of the child's diet and substitute clear liquids. ● Certain antibiotic drugs and digestive tract viruses may cause a temporary loss of digestive enzymes, particularly lactase (the enzyme that aids digestion of milk sugar). This enzyme deficiency can last up to six weeks after viral gastroenteritis. ● Symptoms of malabsorption call for a sweat test to rule out cystic fibrosis.

MEDICAL TREATMENT

The doctor diagnoses a food allergy or malabsorption syndrome on the basis of the following: changes in the child's diet; culture and examination of stools for blood, fat, and starch; analysis of digestive enzymes; biopsy of the intestinal lining; sugar tolerance tests; sweat test; chest X rays; and other factors. Treatment involves a controlled diet and, sometimes, a prescription of digestive enzyme supplements.

Related topics:

Asthma
Cystic fibrosis
Diarrhea in infants
Eczema
Gastroenteritis, acute
G6PD deficiency
Hives

Food poisoning

SYMPTOMS   Vomiting
Abdominal cramps
Diarrhea
Fever or no fever

HOME CARE   Treat vomiting first by restricting the child's diet to clear liquids only.

Once vomiting stops, treat diarrhea by limiting or not reintroducing solid foods. Especially avoid foods with roughage, fruits (except bananas and apples), vegetables, butter, fatty meats, and peanut butter.

Do not give the child milk.

Give the child plenty of clear liquids: tea, water, and commercial mineral and electrolyte mixtures.

PRECAUTIONS

☐ Do not prepare food that needs refrigeration for a child's lunchbox or for a picnic if refrigeration will not be available.

☐ A child with diarrhea and vomiting needs plenty of clear liquids to avoid dehydration (a serious loss of body fluids).

☐ Do not give anti-diarrheal medications to children.

☐ Isolate an infant from children who are ill with vomiting and diarrhea.

☐ If there is blood in the stools, high fever, extreme weakness, or severe or prolonged diarrhea (more than two to three days), call your doctor.

Do not prepare food that requires refrigeration for your child's lunchbox if refrigeration is unavailable.

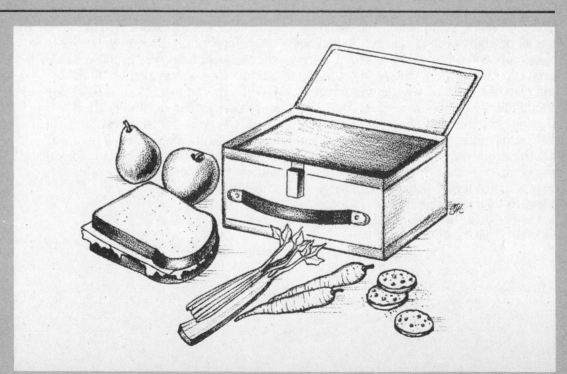

Food poisoning is a disorder of the stomach and intestines caused by bacteria or chemicals in foods. The classical form of food poisoning is caused by staphylococci (called "staph"), the same germs that cause boils and impetigo. The germs enter the food during its preparation. If the food is not properly refrigerated, the germs multiply hourly, contaminating the food with a toxin (poison) given off by the germs. The foods in which staph germs grow best are pastries and other starchy foods ordinarily served cold; salads; cold chicken; ham and beef in gelatin; whipped cream; and custards. Since staph germs and their toxins are odorless and tasteless, the contaminated food smells and tastes normal.

A variety of germs other than staph also can cause food poisoning of a milder nature. Two more serious conditions that are sometimes classified as food poisoning are botulism and dysentery.

SIGNS AND SYMPTOMS

Eating contaminated food causes vomiting, abdominal cramps, and diarrhea within one to six hours. The child may or may not have a fever. Symptoms last 12 to 24 hours.

Food poisoning is usually considered when a number of people who have eaten the same food become ill within hours of one another. Food poisoning can occur after picnics, parties, or eating out in a cafeteria or restaurant where foods have been prepared in advance and improperly stored.

HOME CARE

Home treatment is the same as for any vomiting and diarrhea. When a child has both diarrhea and vomiting, treat vomiting first by restricting the child's diet to clear liquids only. Once the vomiting stops, treat the diarrhea by limiting or not reintroducing solid foods—especially those with roughage, fruits (except bananas and apples), vegetables, butter, fatty meats, and peanut butter. Do not give the child milk, since milk may further aggravate diarrhea.

Encourage the child to drink plenty of clear liquids: tea, water, flavored gelatin water, and commercial mineral and electrolyte mixtures.

PRECAUTIONS

● Do not prepare food that requires refrigeration for your child's lunchbox or for a picnic if refrigeration will not be available. ● A child with diarrhea and vomiting needs plenty of clear liquids to avoid dehydration (a serious loss of body fluids). ● Do not give anti-diarrheal medications to children, since side effects are common and can be dangerous. ● Isolate an infant from children who are ill with vomiting and diarrhea. ● If there is blood in the stools, high fever, prostration (extreme weakness or collapse), or severe or prolonged diarrhea (more than two to three days), call your doctor.

MEDICAL TREATMENT

In severe cases, hospitalization may be required so that the child can be given intravenous fluids. Local health departments can investigate food poisoning outbreaks and trace the source of food poisoning by testing suspected foods.

Related topics:

Botulism
Dehydration
Diarrhea in
  children
Diarrhea in
  infants
Dysentery
Stomachache,
  acute
Vomiting

Fractures

SYMPTOMS
Deformity of a bone that can be seen
  or felt
Pain that is worsened by moving the bone
Tenderness to pressure
Inability to move a bone normally
Swelling
Bruising

HOME CARE
Whenever you suspect a broken bone, see your doctor.

When a possible fracture occurs, protect the injured part of the body.

Keep the injured bone from moving.

Use a thick newspaper to splint a fractured arm or leg.

Keep the child from putting weight on a possibly fractured leg, foot, or toe.

Once the injured area is immobilized in a comfortable position, take the child to a doctor.

PRECAUTIONS

☐ Have a doctor treat all possibly fractured bones. A fractured bone that is not properly positioned during healing can affect growth or cause bone deformity in children.

☐ Do not move an injured limb when applying a splint. Splint a possible fracture in the position you found it in.

IMPORTANT
Do not move the child if there is any possibility of a spine or neck fracture. Call an ambulance to take the child to a doctor or emergency room.

A fracture, a broken bone, and a fractured bone are all terms for the same condition. Since children's bones are still growing, their fractures are different in some ways from adult fractures—especially in very young children. For example, broken bones heal more quickly in children than in adults. Also, any fracture that heals in a poor position can cause deformity of the fractured bone, but in children, such deformity is sometimes corrected as the bone continues to grow. However, if the poor position of the bone during healing shortens or rotates the bone, further growth of the bone will not correct the deformity. Also certain types of fractures in children (such as fractures through the growing areas called cartilage near both ends of long bones) may stop growth of the bone and cause major deformities.

SIGNS AND SYMPTOMS

Deformity of the bone that can be seen or felt is the most obvious sign of a fracture. In many fractures, however, there is no visible deformity. Then you must look for other symptoms of a fracture. There is pain in the area of the fracture, which is aggravated by attempts to move the broken bone. There is tenderness to pressure, which is most severe at the point of the fracture. The fractured part does not function or move normally. There is swelling at the fracture site. Bruising often develops, but sometimes not until days later and often in areas many inches from the fracture.

HOME CARE

If you think your child may have a fractured bone, see your doctor. The doctor will properly diagnose and treat the fracture and will give you instructions for caring for the child at home.

Of course, you must take certain precautions immediately after the injury occurs. Protect the injured part of the body and keep it from moving. If the arm or shoulder is fractured, the child will usually hold the arm in the most comfortable position with the other arm. If a leg fracture is suspected, prevent your child from putting weight on the leg. If splinting is required for your child's arm or leg, a thick newspaper tied around or under the affected area is often the best splint. Once you have immobilized the fractured area in a comfortable position, take the child to your doctor.

If there is any possibility that the spine or neck may be fractured, do not move the child. Call for an ambulance and allow professionals to take the child to a doctor or emergency room.

PRECAUTIONS

• Do not move an injured limb when applying a splint. Splint a possible fracture in the position you found it in; do *not* try to straighten it out to make it conform to the splint. • Have a doctor treat possible fractures.

MEDICAL TREATMENT

Your doctor will examine the injury and order X rays. Treatment will depend largely upon what bone is fractured and what the X rays show. If necessary, the doctor will return the fractured bone to its normal position for proper healing. A cast or mechanical pins may be used.

Related topics:

Dislocated elbow
Sprains and
dislocations

Frequent illnesses

SYMPTOMS

Frequent attacks of the same illness
Frequent different minor illnesses
Frequent complications of minor illnesses
Frequent major illnesses

HOME CARE

Consider whether your child is actually ill more often than most other children.

Keep older children who are ill away from infants.

Keep an ill child away from your other children as much as is practical.

Isolating your healthy child from other children in an attempt to prevent illness can do more harm than good.

PRECAUTIONS

☐ Frequent illnesses are not necessarily a sign of an underlying medical problem.

☐ The average, normal child between one and 12 years of age may have as many as eight illnesses per year.

☐ If a child has frequent attacks of the same illness, discuss this with your doctor.

☐ Frequent illnesses that could interfere with normal growth must be investigated.

☐ Repeated pneumonia in the same part of a lung must be evaluated by your doctor.

☐ In children who have frequent lower respiratory infections with a prolonged cough, cystic fibrosis and asthma should be considered.

Parents often become concerned that their children are ill too frequently. Sometimes the parents are right, and the child does have some underlying medical problem. But, normally, having many illnesses is not due to any particular problem in the child. Usually, how often a child becomes ill depends on the number of children in the family and the number of diseases each child is exposed to.

Except for accidents and allergies, 95 percent of all illnesses are caused by germs that live exclusively in humans. Most children's illnesses are caught from other children. Whether a child will catch a disease depends on two factors: whether the child is exposed to the germ and how strong the child's resistance is.

If your child is frequently ill with different minor illnesses, the illnesses are usually due simply to exposure to many people. As soon as a child begins going to daycare or school, the child is exposed to other children with illnesses. The number of children in a household also is a factor. Mathematically, a four-child family could have 16 times as many childhood illnesses as a one-child family.

A child frequently ill with the same illness may have a defect of local resistance (a lowered resistance to disease in one area of the body). For example, repeated pneumonia in the same part of a lung suggests an abnormality in that area.

A child with frequent major illnesses or frequent complications of minor sicknesses may have a general lack of resistance. This occurs with immune mechanism defects, which hinder the child's ability to fight infectious diseases. For instance, colds that always end up as croup, bronchiolitis, bronchitis, or pneumonia may indicate an underlying allergy.

SIGNS AND SYMPTOMS

The first step is to decide whether a child is actually ill more often than most other children. Some reports show that the average, normal child between one and 12 years of age may have as many as eight illnesses per year. Other figures show that a first child will seldom be ill during the first year; then the child will have increasingly frequent sicknesses as he or she begins to play with other children and attend school. An infant with older brothers or sisters will be sick the first year as often as the other children are. To decide if your child is ill too frequently, compare the number and seriousness of the illnesses with those of the child's brothers, sisters, and friends.

HOME CARE

How much your child is exposed to illnesses depends somewhat on you and your circumstances. Overprotectiveness and isolation from other children can lead to emotional problems that could be harder to treat than physical problems. On the other hand, overexposure to other children who may be ill can lead to almost constant minor illnesses, especially in very young children. Keep older children who are ill—yours and the neighbor's—away from infants. Isolate any ill child from your other children as much as is practical.

PRECAUTIONS

• Frequent illnesses that could interfere with normal growth must be investigated. If the child stops gaining height or weight or begins to lose weight, see your doctor.
• Repeated pneumonia in the same part of a lung must be evaluated by your doctor.
• Frequent lower respiratory infections with a prolonged cough can be a sign of cystic fibrosis or asthma.

MEDICAL TREATMENT

Your doctor will help you decide whether your child is ill more often than others of the same age and under similar circumstances. If so, your doctor will seek the cause through a variety of tests. These tests may include a sweat test, measurement of immune globulins, blood count, sedimentation rate, chest X ray, sinus X rays, nose and throat cultures, and allergy tests. You and your child may be referred to an ear, nose, and throat specialist, to an allergist, or to a medical center for thorough investigation of all immune mechanisms.

Related topics:

Asthma
Common cold
Cystic fibrosis
Pneumonia

Frostbite

SYMPTOMS

First-degree
White or yellowish color to skin
Burning or itching sensation

Second-degree
Loss of sensation
Reddening and swelling of tissues
Rewarmed skin may blister and peel

Third-degree
Waxy white, hard skin
Swelling

HOME CARE

Prevent frostbite by having your child wear adequate and appropriate clothing.

If frostbite does occur, warm the affected area by immersing in lukewarm (not hot or cold) water, then carefully pat the skin dry.

Or, have the child warm the frostbitten areas by placing them in contact with warm parts of the body.

Give warm drinks and keep the affected areas clean.

After thawing, raise the affected part to improve circulation and keep the skin at room temperature.

Call the doctor.

PRECAUTIONS

☐ In administering first aid for frostbite **do not** rub the affected areas.

☐ Do not let the child walk on frostbitten feet or exercise frostbitten parts of the body.

☐ Do not expose frostbitten areas to the heat of a radiator, stove, or fire.

☐ Loss of sensation in the affected areas is a danger signal.

☐ Frostbite can have serious consequences, including gangrene which may necessitate amputation of the affected part.

Frostbite is the freezing of skin tissue caused by exposure to the cold. It can occur anywhere on the body but most often appears on the toes, feet, fingers, ears, nose, and cheeks—areas that are frequently exposed to the cold and that have the lowest degree of circulation. The very young and the very old are particularly susceptible to frostbite.

Frostbite can have serious consequences. If the frostbite is severe enough to cause the death of skin tissue, surgery may be necessary to remove the dead tissue. Muscles, tendons, and nerves may be damaged. Severe frostbite can also cause blood clots to form in small blood vessels in the area affected by the frostbite. This in turn causes death of deeper tissues because their blood supply is reduced. Gangrene can result, necessitating the amputation of the affected parts.

Prolonged exposure to the cold is the most frequent cause of frostbite, but even a short exposure can freeze skin tissue if the cold is severe enough. Obviously, inadequate or inappropriate clothing can increase the child's chances for developing frostbite, and strong winds can intensify the effect of cold air on the skin.

SIGNS AND SYMPTOMS

Frostbite occurs in stages. As with burns, there are three stages of frostbite. In first-degree frostbite the skin becomes whitish or slightly yellow and this discoloration is accompanied by a burning or itching sensation. If the affected areas are warmed promptly, the child will recover completely. If exposure to the cold continues, the child will lose sensation in the affected area and will feel no pain. This loss of sensation is a danger signal and should be heeded.

Second-degree frostbite is characterized by a reddening and swelling of the tissues involved. Rewarming the area may produce blisters and peeling of the skin. In third-degree frostbite the skin becomes waxy white and hard throughout. This indicates that skin tissue has died, and the affected parts may swell up with edema (collection of fluid in the tissues).

HOME CARE

The best treatment is prevention. Be sure your child is adequately dressed on cold days, and be aware of the warning signs of frostbite. If the child does get frostbitten, first aid is important. However, it's just as important to know what *not* to do. Do not rub the affected part with snow. In fact, do not rub the area at all, since this can cause further damage to the frozen tissue. Do not let the child exercise the frostbitten part or walk on frostbitten feet. Take the child indoors as soon as possible, and rewarm the frostbitten area. Rapid rewarming produces pain, redness, and perhaps blisters, but it also reduces tissue loss and helps prevent complications.

Do not expose the affected area to the heat of a radiator, stove, or fire. Instead, immerse the frostbitten area in water at a temperature of 100° to 110°F. Be sure that the temperature does not exceed 110°F, since higher temperatures can cause a burn in skin that lacks sensation. If you do not have a thermometer try to make the water lukewarm, neither hot nor cold. Pat the skin dry carefully.

If the child is outdoors, the affected areas can be warmed by placing them in contact with warm areas of the body, for instance, under the arms or between the thighs. Frostbitten toes can be wrapped in a warm, dry blanket. Warm drinks (not alcohol) may be helpful, and the affected areas should be kept clean.

After the frozen areas have thawed, elevate the extremity to improve blood circulation. Keep the frostbitten skin at room temperature and do not rub it. Then, call the doctor.

PRECAUTIONS

● Even brief exposure to extreme cold can cause frostbite. ● Strong winds can intensify the effect of cold air on the skin.

MEDICAL TREATMENT

The doctor may prescribe medications to ward off infection, or drugs to prevent the formation of clots in the blood vessels.

Related topic:

Blisters

Funnel chest

SYMPTOMS　Breastbone sinks in when child
　　　　　　　　breathes out
　　　　　　　Hollow appears in center of chest

HOME CARE　True funnel chest need not be treated at home. Bring it to your doctor's attention at a routine checkup.

If the breastbone retracts (pulls in) in a child who has shown no earlier signs of funnel chest, this may be a sign of breathing difficulty. Treat the disease that is causing breathing problems.

PRECAUTIONS

☐　Don't be alarmed if the breastbone is only mildly sunken in an infant or young child.

☐　A mild funnel chest usually causes no harm and will gradually correct itself as the child's ribs grow heavier and stronger.

☐　Do not restrict your child's activities.

When a child with funnel chest breathes out, the lower half of the breastbone is pulled in, causing a hollow in the center of the chest.

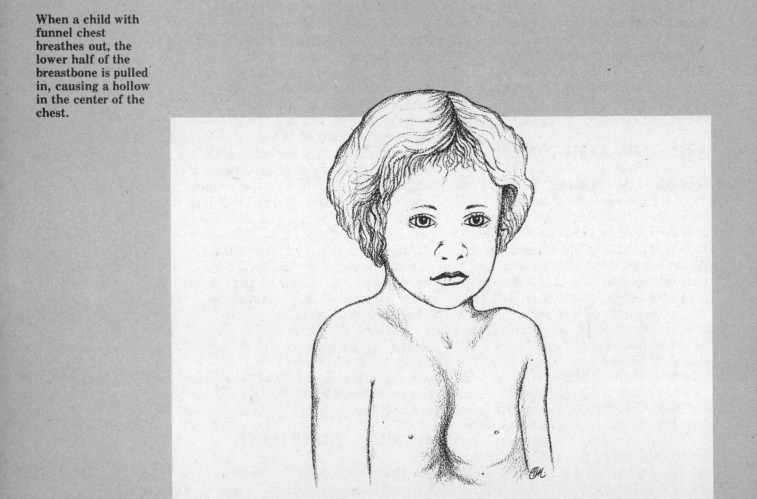

Funnel chest is a condition in which the breastbone is depressed or sunken in. The breastbone (sternum) connects the front end of the ribs. The diaphragm (a band of muscle separating the chest and abdominal cavities) attaches in front to the lower ribs and to the bottom of the breastbone. In children, the ribs are made of tough elastic tissue called cartilage; this cartilage gradually hardens into bone as the child grows. Since cartilage is not as strong as bone, the ribs of a baby are delicate, but the diaphragm is relatively strong. When some babies breathe in, the diaphragm pulls in the lower half of the breastbone, causing a hollow in the center of the chest. This hollow is exaggerated when the child makes a greater effort to breathe, as with bronchitis, bronchiolitis, pneumonia, and choking. This condition, called *retracting,* is a sign of breathing difficulty. If retracting occurs only when the child has difficulty breathing, it is not considered to be a true funnel chest.

A true funnel chest exists if the breastbone is depressed when the child breathes out, even while the child is at rest and is having no difficulty breathing. If mild or moderate, a funnel chest will cause no harm and will gradually correct itself over the years as the child's ribs grow heavier and stronger. If funnel chest is severe, it may not correct itself and may interfere with breathing. Rarely is it severe enough to affect the position or functioning of the heart.

SIGNS AND SYMPTOMS

A funnel chest can be seen by observing the chest of a well child. The breastbone appears to be sunken in, forming a hollow in the center of the chest. If this hollow appears whenever the child breathes out, this may be a sign of true funnel chest.

If a child has not previously shown signs of a funnel chest, retractions of the lower breastbone are an important sign of breathing difficulty.

HOME CARE

A fixed deformity (true funnel chest) cannot be treated at home. Bring it to the attention of your doctor.

If retractions of the breastbone begin in a child with no earlier signs of funnel chest, look for other signs of breathing difficulty. Then treat the disease that is causing the breathing problems.

PRECAUTIONS

● Don't be alarmed by persistent mild to moderate depression of the breastbone in an infant or young child. ● Do not restrict your child's activities.

MEDICAL TREATMENT

The doctor will determine if the child has a true funnel chest or if the child is having temporary difficulty breathing. In marked cases of funnel chest, the severity and effect on heart and lungs is judged by X-ray and other test results.

If funnel chest is severe and persists without gradual improvement, the condition may require surgery. Surgery may be performed if there are signs of limited heart or lung function or for cosmetic reasons. Your doctor may order X rays, an electrocardiogram, and measurements of the lung capacity.

Related topics:

Bronchiolitis
Bronchitis
Choking
Hyperventilation
Pneumonia
Shortness of
    breath

Gastroenteritis, acute

SYMPTOMS
Sudden vomiting
Sudden diarrhea
Abdominal cramps
High fever, low fever, or no fever
Small amounts of blood in the vomit

HOME CARE

Treat both vomiting and diarrhea by limiting the child's diet to clear liquids until the illness subsides.

To avoid dehydration (a serious loss of body fluids), give the child plenty of clear liquids: tea, water, flavored gelatin water, and commercial mineral and electrolyte mixtures.

Do not give the child milk.

Give acetaminophen rather than aspirin for fever, since aspirin sometimes aggravates vomiting.

PRECAUTIONS

☐ Wash hands carefully after contact with the child to avoid spreading the disease.

☐ The disease is usually not serious except in young babies, who may become dehydrated.

☐ If a young child develops the disease, watch for signs of dehydration (infrequent urinating, dryness in the mouth, sunken eyes, drowsiness, rapid or slow breathing, sunken soft spot in the scalp). If any of these symptoms appear, call your doctor.

☐ Do not give anti-diarrheal medications to children.

☐ If there is blood in the stools, high fever, extreme weakness, or severe or prolonged diarrhea (more than two to three days), call your doctor.

Acute gastroenteritis is a highly contagious infection of the digestive tract. It is probably caused by viruses, only a few of which have been identified. There is evidence that the disease may also be caused by some types of *Escherichia coli* bacteria. These bacteria are normally found in the human intestines, and most types of the bacteria are known to be harmless and even beneficial.

This disease is readily transmitted from person to person. Symptoms may begin within one to four days after being exposed to the germ. The disease is not generally serious except in young babies, who may become dehydrated (a serious loss of body fluids). Acute gastroenteritis has no relationship to true influenza (a disease of the respiratory tract).

SIGNS AND SYMPTOMS

Acute gastroenteritis causes sudden vomiting or diarrhea and cramps. The disease may last one to three days or as long as a week. Fever may be high (104°F), low (101°F), or absent. Blood in diarrhea is rare. Occasionally, if vomiting is severe, there are small amounts of blood in the vomit, and petechiae (red spots) may appear on the face.

Acute gastroenteritis is more easily identified if there are other cases in the family or neighborhood. It occasionally may be confused with dysentery and food poisoning.

HOME CARE

Treat both vomiting and diarrhea by limiting food intake to clear liquids until the illness subsides. To avoid dehydration, give the child plenty of the following clear liquids: tea, water, flavored gelatin water, and commercial mineral and electrolyte mixtures. Do not give the child milk.

Acetaminophen is better for relief of fever than aspirin because aspirin occasionally aggravates vomiting in some children.

PRECAUTIONS

● Practice good hygiene. Be sure to wash your hands before going from the patient to other children in the house. Wash hands carefully before preparing food. ● If a young child develops the disease, watch carefully for signs of dehydration (infrequent urinating, dryness in the mouth, sunken eyes, drowsiness, rapid or slow breathing, sunken soft spot in the scalp). If any symptoms of dehydration appear, call your doctor. ● Do not give antidiarrheal medications to children, since side effects are common and can be dangerous. ● If there is blood in the stools, high fever, prostration (extreme weakness or collapse), or severe or prolonged diarrhea (more than two to three days), call your doctor. Dysentery may be the cause.

MEDICAL TREATMENT

Your doctor will confirm the diagnosis by knowledge of what illnesses are occurring in the community, by the circumstances of the child's illness, and by absence of other physical findings on examination. Blood count and a stool culture might be required if diagnosis is in doubt. Otherwise, your doctor's treatment will be the same as home treatment. If there is evidence of dehydration in an infant, hospitalization will be necessary in order to give the child intravenous fluids.

Geographic tongue

SYMPTOM Smooth, bright red patches on the tongue
that change size, shape, and location

HOME CARE No treatment is necessary.

PRECAUTIONS

☐ Geographic tongue is harmless.

☐ Geographic tongue does not indicate a
vitamin deficiency, a reaction to
toothpaste, or any other problem.

☐ Do not try any home treatment.

☐ Reassure your child that there is
no need to be concerned about a
geographic tongue.

**Be sure your child
knows that geo-
graphic tongue is no
cause for concern.**

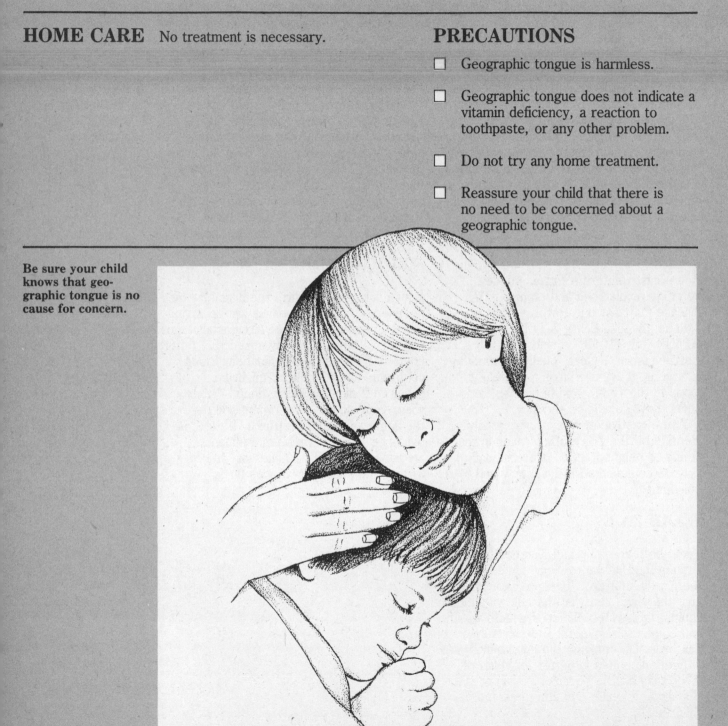

Geographic tongue is a common, harmless patterning of the tongue. It is seen in 5 to 10 percent of all infants and children. The cause is unknown. There are no other symptoms and no discomfort of any sort.

The usual velvety-and-rough, whitish-pink surface of the tongue is made up of closely packed papillae (taste buds). The smooth, red areas of changing shape on a geographic tongue are made up of papillae that have shrunk or temporarily disappeared (atrophied).

SIGNS AND SYMPTOMS

Geographic tongue is easily identified by the typical appearance of the tongue. No other condition resembles geographic tongue.

One or more smooth, bright red patches appear on the surface of the tongue. In the course of several days, these patches change size, shape, and location. The general appearance is that of a slowly changing map (hence the name). The condition lasts for months to years, and may recur during upper respiratory infections.

Although the condition involves changes in the taste buds, there are no noticeable changes in the sense of taste, and there is no pain.

HOME CARE

No treatment is necessary.

PRECAUTIONS

● Geographic tongue does not indicate a vitamin deficiency, a reaction to toothpaste, or any other problem. ● Do not try any home treatment. ● Reassure your child that there is no need to be concerned about a geographic tongue.

MEDICAL TREATMENT

Your doctor will identify the condition and reassure you and your child that geographic tongue is not a cause for concern. No other treatment is necessary.

Glands, swollen

SYMPTOMS   Swelling and tenderness of lymph glands
(a sign of illness)

Unusual swelling, pain, and redness of the
skin (a sign of infected glands)

HOME CARE   In the case of mild swelling, identify and
treat the disease or infection responsible.

Infected glands require medical attention.

PRECAUTIONS

☐ Infants have limited immunity to disease; swollen glands in an infant should be examined by a doctor.

☐ Consult the doctor if a lymph node continues to increase in size and tenderness, or if the overlying skin becomes red.

☐ When your child turns his or her head, you may notice lymph nodes the size of a pea or smaller in the sides of the neck; these nodes are normal.

☐ Swollen lymph nodes in many areas of the body usually indicate a general illness or widespread infection.

The term *swollen glands* is often used to refer to swelling of the lymph nodes. Lymph nodes are sometimes called lymph glands, although they are not true glands. Lymph nodes are widely distributed throughout the body, and in their normal state are an eighth-inch to a quarter-inch in size.

Many lymph nodes lie just beneath the skin. These lymph nodes are located in front of the ears, behind the ears, at the base of the skull, under the chin, down the sides of the neck, in the armpits, in the folds of the elbows, and above and below the creases in the groin. Lymph nodes are also found within the chest and abdomen, but these lie too deeply within the body to be felt.

All lymph nodes lie along thin-walled tubes called lymphatic vessels. These vessels resemble and roughly follow the course of the veins in the body. They do not contain blood, however. These vessels carry a thin, clear, slightly sticky liquid called lymph, which resembles the clear, watery fluid that oozes from a scrape or that forms within a blister caused by rubbing.

Lymph nodes are important in helping the body fight infections and disease. When lymph nodes become swollen and mildly tender, it is a sign that they are fighting an illness or infection. The lymph nodes of the entire body may be swollen, or nodes may be swollen only in one area of the body.

When all the lymph nodes or the nodes in many areas are swollen, this usually indicates a general illness or widespread infection affecting the body.

When nodes are swollen only in one location, this is a sign of an infection in the area of the body guarded by those nodes. Swollen glands in one area might be caused by a variety of local infections. The appearance of red streaks under the skin (which typically precede blood poisoning) is caused by infection traveling along the lymphatic vessels in that area.

In some cases an infection may become too severe for the lymph nodes to handle. In such a case, the lymph node itself may become infected.

SIGNS AND SYMPTOMS

Swollen, slightly tender lymph glands are a symptom of illness or infection. If glands continue to swell, become painful and more tender, and redden the overlying skin, the glands themselves may have become infected. If the node is killed by the infection, it breaks down into pus, which may erupt through the skin as would a deep-seated boil.

HOME CARE

Mildly swollen glands usually require treatment only for the disease or infection causing the swelling. Note which lymph nodes are swollen, look for the cause, and treat that disease or infection.

If lymph nodes are greatly enlarged, very tender, and red, see your doctor.

PRECAUTIONS

• In infants, swollen glands in the neck (and sometimes other locations) usually require a doctor's treatment because infants have a limited resistance to diseases. • Any lymph node that continues to increase in size and tenderness or that becomes reddened needs a doctor's attention. • Healthy children have visible lymph nodes the size of fresh peas or smaller in the sides of the neck. These may become especially noticeable when the child turns the head; they are normal.

MEDICAL TREATMENT

Your doctor will seek the cause of swollen glands by conducting a complete examination of all sites of glands as well as the spleen and liver. The doctor may also order a blood count, mononucleosis test, and, in severe cases, chest and kidney X rays, bone marrow examination, and test of sedimentation rate. Your doctor will treat the disease causing the swollen glands and may treat the glands themselves by prescribing antibiotics. An infected gland may be opened and drained or removed either as treatment or for a biopsy (culture and examination).

Related topics:

Blood poisoning
Boils
Burns
Cat scratch fever
Chicken pox
Common cold
Cuts
Impetigo
Infectious
    mononucleosis
Insect bites and
    stings
Leukemia
Rubella
Scabies
Scrapes
Sinusitis
Tonsillitis
Toothache

Goiter

SYMPTOM　　Swelling in the front of the neck

HOME CARE　Do not attempt to treat at home. Treatment depends on the cause, which must be diagnosed by a doctor.

PRECAUTIONS

☐ During pregnancy, do not take medications (even over-the-counter drugs) without your doctor's approval.

☐ Since not all thyroid glands are in exactly the same position, a lump in the neck should never be removed without first testing to be sure it is not the thyroid gland.

A goiter is a swelling in the neck due to an enlarged thyroid gland.

A goiter is an enlargement of the thyroid gland which causes a swelling in the front of the neck. The thyroid gland lies just below and to either side of the larynx (Adam's apple). The thyroid gland produces hormones that control the body's metabolism rate—the rate at which foods are used for energy and growth. A normal thyroid is barely if at all visible and can barely be felt.

A goiter may be present in a newborn infant, especially if the pregnant mother was on certain medications (including iodides in anti-asthma or cough medicines). Insufficient iodine in your child's diet also can cause a goiter. Once common, this disease is now rare because of general use of iodized table salt and more widespread eating of seafood. (Seafood is naturally high in iodine content.)

A goiter is most common between the ages of six and 16 years. It occurs in girls nine times as often as it does in boys. It is most often due to an autoimmune (self-destructive) disease—Hashimoto's thyroiditis—of unknown cause. Enlargement of the thyroid is rarely due to malignancy. A goiter may be hyperactive (producing too much hormone) or hypoactive (producing too little hormone), but usually it is neither.

SIGNS AND SYMPTOMS

A goiter can be seen and felt as a swelling in the front of the neck. This swelling usually appears just below and to either side of the Adam's apple. Often the swelling is noticed when a shirt collar or neck jewelry no longer fits. Generally, there are no other symptoms.

HOME CARE

No home treatment should be attempted until the cause of goiter is diagnosed by your doctor. The cause cannot be diagnosed without laboratory tests.

PRECAUTIONS

● During pregnancy, do not take medications (even over-the-counter drugs) without your doctor's approval. ● Not all thyroid glands are in exactly the same position in the neck. Any lump in the midline of the neck may be a goiter of an unusually positioned thyroid. A lump should never be removed from this area without first testing to be sure it is not the thyroid gland.

MEDICAL TREATMENT

Blood tests, often requiring complicated laboratory work, are used to find the cause of a goiter. The treatment for a goiter depends on the cause and can include giving oral thyroxine (thyroid hormone) or desiccated thyroid for months or years. Surgery is rarely necessary except in rare cases of malignancy or when the goiter obstructs breathing in infants.

Related topic:

Thyroid disorders

Gonorrhea

SYMPTOMS
In boys
Burning during urination
Discharge from penis

In girls
Vaginal discharge
Abdominal pain
*Gonorrhea in girls often shows no
symptoms*

HOME CARE
Gonorrhea must be diagnosed and treated by a doctor.

The best preventive measure is to provide your children with appropriate and adequate sex education.

PRECAUTIONS

☐ Be aware that venereal (sexually transmitted) gonorrhea is being seen with increasing frequency among sexually active teenagers and younger children.

☐ Sexually abused children may contract this disease.

☐ A mother who has gonorrhea can transmit the disease to her baby as the child passes through the birth canal during delivery.

☐ A girl with gonorrhea may show no symptoms and the infection may go undetected and untreated, with serious consequences including sterility (inability to bear children).

☐ Some doctors recommend that sexually active girls be tested for gonorrhea at the time of routine school or annual medical checkups.

Gonorrhea is an infection caused by a specific gonococcus germ, which is usually sexually transmitted.

In the days before antibiotics, infants born to mothers who had gonorrhea commonly developed gonorrhea infections of the eyes, which caused blindness. Now antibiotics and the required Credé's treatment (placing silver nitrate solution into the eyes of all newborns) have almost eliminated this previously common cause of blindness.

Today, venereal (sexually transmitted) gonorrhea in adolescent and younger boys and girls is being seen with increasing and alarming frequency. One of the dangers of genital gonorrhea is that often a girl who has gonorrhea will show no symptoms; therefore, the infection may not be detected and treated. Serious consequences, including sterility, may result from untreated gonorrhea in females.

Another disease, caused by gonococcus bacteria, is now being recognized in adolescents and even in younger children who have been sexually abused. It causes sore throat and anal infection, with or without fever. Ordinary throat cultures done for sore throats do not grow the gonococcus germ, which leads to the false conclusion that this infection is viral and that no antibiotic need be prescribed.

SIGNS AND SYMPTOMS

Gonorrhea of the genitals in boys causes burning during urination and a discharge from the penis. In girls, gonorrhea may cause vaginal discharge and abdominal pain, but frequently there are no symptoms at all. In cases with no symptoms, diagnosis can be made only by alertness and awareness of the possibility of the disease.

HOME CARE

There is no home treatment. Gonorrhea must be diagnosed and treated by a doctor. Diagnosis requires special culture techniques with microscopic examination of discharges from the vagina or penis.

PRECAUTIONS

● Be aware that the disease still exists and that it exists in children of all ages.
● Provide sex education for your children.
● Many physicians advocate the practice of taking periodic vaginal cultures at the time of routine school and annual examinations of sexually active girls.

MEDICAL TREATMENT

Your doctor will diagnose gonorrhea by smear and special culture techniques. If gonorrhea is diagnosed, antibiotics will be prescribed. Although some gonococci germs are now resistant to penicillin (that is, not destroyed by it), other new antibiotics are reliably effective. By law, cases of gonorrhea must be reported to health departments. Most cases are diagnosed by tracing the sexual contacts of the individuals with known cases of gonorrhea. Treatment of minors is confidential; parental consent is not required.

Related topics:

Sore throat
Vaginal discharge

Growing pains

SYMPTOM   Pain in legs or feet occurring only while the child is resting or sleeping

HOME CARE   Massage or apply heat to painful muscles.

Give aspirin or acetaminophen for pain.

Having the child wear sturdier shoes may reduce the frequency or severity of the pains.

Growing pains can be quite severe and it's important to reassure and comfort the child.

PRECAUTION

☐ If your child complains of frequent pain that occurs at night in the same part of the body, take the child to a doctor.

The term *growing pains* is half truth and half myth. Growing children do have normal pains, particularly in their legs and feet. These pains, however, are not caused by growing but by excessive use of young muscles and joints that are not yet completely developed. Young children are extremely active, and this extra activity places stress on their still developing muscles and joints.

SIGNS AND SYMPTOMS

Growing pains generally occur in different parts of the thighs, calves, and feet. The pains can be severe enough to awaken a child from sleep.

A key symptom of growing pains is that they occur only when the child is at rest—usually at night or during naps. They never occur when the child is active. This fact distinguishes growing pains from pains caused by diseases or abnormalities, which are typically worse when the child is active. Growing pains do not interfere with or interrupt a child's daily play or routine, and are never accompanied by fever or other symptoms of general illness.

HOME CARE

Apply heat to painful muscles. Massaging the muscles also helps. Giving the child aspirin or acetaminophen may relieve pain. Sometimes sturdier shoes reduce the frequency and severity of growing pains. Since the pain can be quite severe, sympathy and understanding are important in comforting the child.

PRECAUTION

● One rare bone disease, osteoid osteoma, causes severe bone pain that occurs almost exclusively at nighttime. If your child complains of frequent pain *in the same spot* at night, the cause must be checked by your doctor.

MEDICAL TREATMENT

Your doctor will perform a careful examination to rule out other diseases. X rays may be necessary on more than one occasion to check for osteoid osteoma.

Related topic:

Arthritis

G6PD deficiency

SYMPTOMS   Paleness
Jaundice
Dark-colored urine
Back pain

HOME CARE   Consult your doctor if your child shows signs of having this condition, particularly if the child has an infection or has been taking medication.

PRECAUTIONS

☐ A child with G6PD deficiency should not be given aspirin.

☐ Before a child is given medication, the prescribing doctor should be told that the child has G6PD deficiency.

☐ The mother of a breast-fed baby who has this condition needs to be careful about what kinds of foods and medications she takes.

☐ Keep fava beans out of the child's diet if they cause a reaction.

Glucose-6-Phosphate Dehydrogenase, known as G6PD, is an enzyme. An enzyme is a type of protein produced by the body that participates in digestion and other chemical functions in the body. G6PD deficiency is an inherited disorder in which there is not enough of this enzyme in the body.

It is possible for a person from any ethnic or racial group to have G6PD deficiency. However, it is most common in ethnic groups from around the Mediterranean Sea, and in Orientals and blacks.

G6PD deficiency is less common in females, because a female who inherits the gene for G6PD will often have a second, normal gene that causes the body to produce normal G6PD, and in fact she may never have symptoms of the disorder. However, a female may inherit two defective genes, in which case the disorder is the same as it would be in a male.

When a person with the deficiency has an infection, takes certain drugs, or eats certain foods, his or her red blood cells separate from the blood and break up. This causes anemia, a shortage of red blood cells. Some of the substances that can cause a G6PD reaction are: drugs for malaria; sulfa drugs and nitrofuran drugs, which are antibacterial drugs; aspirin and other pain relievers; poison antidotes such as methylene blue and dimercaprol; and fava beans. Infections that can cause a reaction include viruses such as colds and flu, hepatitis, infectious mononucleosis, and bacterial pneumonia.

SIGNS AND SYMPTOMS

The symptoms of G6PD deficiency include paleness, jaundice (yellowing of the skin and the whites of the eyes), dark-colored urine, and back pain. In extreme cases, anemia can become severe enough to cause shock and even death. Between attacks, there are usually no symptoms, but occasionally a person with G6PD deficiency will have long-term anemia and jaundice and also an enlarged spleen. Infants with the disorder may be born with jaundice. This is most common in Orientals, families of Mediterranean ancestry, and premature black babies.

G6PD deficiency is diagnosed through blood tests. The enzymes in the red blood cells are analyzed to see if normal amounts of G6PD are present. The problem may be difficult to detect in blacks during an attack, because in the form of the disorder that blacks usually have the red cells are affected suddenly and are quickly replaced with normal cells. In other forms of the disorder, defective red cells remain in the blood for a longer period. Screening tests for the deficiency may be given to members of families that have a history of the disorder. Many doctors routinely screen all Oriental and black male children for G6PD deficiency. Otherwise, the problem may not be discovered until a child who is not known to have G6PD deficiency has a sudden attack of anemia.

HOME CARE

If your child has the symptoms of G6PD deficiency, especially during an infection or after taking a drug, consult your doctor.

PRECAUTIONS

● If your child has G6PD deficiency, avoid giving aspirin to the child. ● Be sure that any doctor who is prescribing drugs for the child knows he or she has this disorder. ● If fava beans cause a reaction in your child, do not include them in the child's diet. ● If you are breast-feeding a baby who has this disorder, be careful about what you eat and what drugs you take. Some drugs and foods are retained in the milk and can cause a reaction in the baby.

MEDICAL TREATMENT

There is no cure for G6PD deficiency. The only treatment is to try to avoid the foods and drugs that cause the problem. In mild cases, no other treatment is necessary, even during an attack. In severe cases, a child may have to be hospitalized during an attack, and treated for severe anemia and possibly shock.

Gumboils

SYMPTOMS
Inflammation, swelling, or pain at the base of a decayed tooth
Injury or discoloration of associated tooth

HOME CARE
Aspirin or acetaminophen will help relieve pain.

Have the child rinse the mouth with warm salt water or apply warm soaks to the affected area.

If the tooth is about to come out naturally, the loss of the tooth will allow the pus to drain and the gumboil to heal without treatment.

If the tooth is not loose, or is a permanent one, consult a dentist.

PRECAUTIONS

☐ Do not confuse a gumboil with a canker sore, which does not protrude in the same way as a gumboil.

☐ If the child loses baby molar teeth prematurely, the spacing and positioning of the permanent teeth can be affected.

☐ Some dentists believe that a gumboil on a baby tooth can endanger the permanent tooth before it emerges. If your young child has a gumboil, see the dentist.

Warm salt water rinses will help relieve inflammation and promote drainage of gumboils.

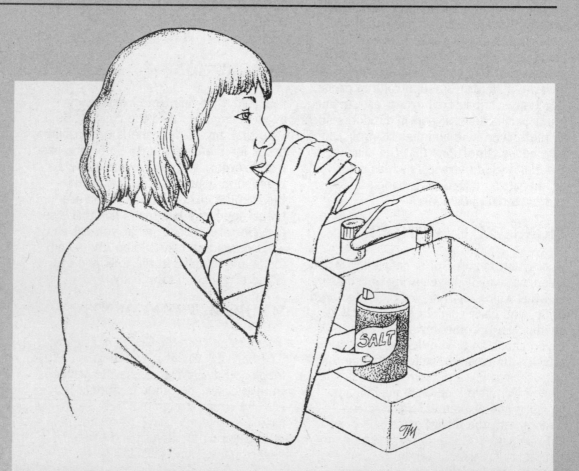

182

A gumboil is an abscess (a collection of pus in inflamed tissue) in the gum at the base of a decayed tooth. It is caused by infection reaching the root canal and traveling to the tip of the tooth's root. Gumboils usually occur only with baby teeth, rarely with permanent teeth. Gumboils are common after a cavity in a tooth has been repaired and filled. They are also common in untreated decayed or injured teeth.

SIGNS AND SYMPTOMS

Gumboils can be recognized by their typical appearance. Inflammation or swelling that comes to a point, like a tender pimple, appears where the lip meets the gum at the base of a decayed tooth. The area is sometimes painful. Eventually, the gumboil discharges yellow pus. Usually the associated tooth is obviously injured (fractured or discolored) or has an untreated or recently filled cavity. The tooth may be tender when tapped or may be slightly loose. A gumboil is not usually accompanied by fever.

A gumboil may be confused with a canker sore. However, a canker sore is ulcerated (dug out); it does not protrude like a gumboil.

HOME CARE

Give aspirin or acetaminophen for pain. Warm soaks or warm salt water rinses will help the inflammation and promote drainage of the boil. (Use one-half teaspoon of table salt in one-half glass of warm water.) If the associated tooth is about to fall out naturally, a gumboil can be left untreated. The loss of the tooth will allow the pus to drain and the gumboil to heal.

PRECAUTIONS

● If a young child has a gumboil, consult the dentist. ● Some dentists feel that a gumboil on a baby tooth endangers the permanent tooth that has not yet emerged. ● Premature loss of first-year or second-year molars (or permanent six-year molars) can cause later problems in spacing and positioning of the permanent teeth.

MEDICAL TREATMENT

Your dentist will decide whether to leave the tooth in, pull it, replace it with a space retainer, or save the tooth by performing root-canal work. It's seldom necessary to give the child antibiotics, or to open and drain the gumboil.

Related topics:

Herpes simplex
Toothache

Gynecomastia

SYMPTOM   Development of breasts in a boy

HOME CARE   Reassure the child that the condition will disappear.

Try to spare the child embarrassing situations, such as undressing or showering in front of other children.

Be sure that the child is not subjected to teasing or taunting by other children.

PRECAUTIONS

☐ Normal adolescent boys commonly develop small breasts that may persist for up to two years. It's only necessary to consult a doctor if the condition persists for an unusually long time.

☐ Parents should be aware of, and sympathetic towards, the embarrassment gynecomastia can cause a boy.

☐ Overweight boys may develop accumulations of fat that resemble breasts but contain no true breast tissue.

☐ If the boy tries to conceal breast development because he's embarrassed, parents may not be aware of the condition.

Gynecomastia is the name given to development of breasts in a boy. Normal males have undeveloped breast tissue that can become enlarged by estrogens (female hormones) and, rarely, by androgens (male hormones). A boy with tumors of the testes or adrenal glands may develop breasts. Rarely, the breasts develop from mistakenly taking a medication that contains sex hormones or from eating poultry fattened by hormones.

Normal adolescent boys commonly develop small breasts on one or both sides. These persist for two to 24 months. They may be tender and are often an embarrassment. The breasts may become quite pronounced and remain so for years, but this is very rare. Overweight boys may develop large accumulations of fat that resemble breasts but contain no true breast tissue. This condition is known as pseudogynecomastia.

SIGNS AND SYMPTOMS

The development of breasts is obvious except when the boy tries to hide gynecomastia out of embarrassment. If this happens, the parents may not be aware of the problem.

HOME CARE

It is very important to be understanding and to reassure the child that the condition will disappear. In more obvious cases, the boy may need to be excused from activities in physical education that require undressing or showering with other boys.

PRECAUTIONS

● Ninety-eight percent of all cases of gynecomastia are normal and will disappear on their own. ● Your doctor should examine your boy if the condition persists. ● Take steps to insure that the boy is not subjected to taunting by other children.

MEDICAL TREATMENT

Your doctor will examine your boy carefully. The doctor will check for the presence or absence of true breast tissue; check the coloration of areolae (nipples); and examine the boy's abdomen, testes, and body hair. The doctor will consider whether any drugs or foods could be causing the problem. If other causes of the condition are ruled out, the doctor can usually only recommend that you patiently support and counsel the child. Hormonal studies or chromosome studies are rarely needed. In severe or prolonged cases, plastic surgery can remove the extra breast tissue without visible scarring.

Hand, foot, and mouth disease

SYMPTOMS　Blisters and sores inside the mouth, on the fingers, hands, toes, and feet
Fever

HOME CARE　Give aspirin or acetaminophen for fever or soreness of the mouth.

Do not give the child foods that will sting the mouth, such as citrus juices, ginger ale, or heavily spiced foods.

Consult the doctor before giving antihistamines to relieve itching.

PRECAUTIONS

☐　Keep the child away from babies, in whom this disease can be dangerous.

☐　If your infant contracts hand, foot, and mouth disease, call the doctor.

☐　Children may become dehydrated if they refuse liquids because of mouth pain.

Give a child aspirin or acetaminophen for the fever and soreness of the mouth caused by hand, foot, and mouth disease.

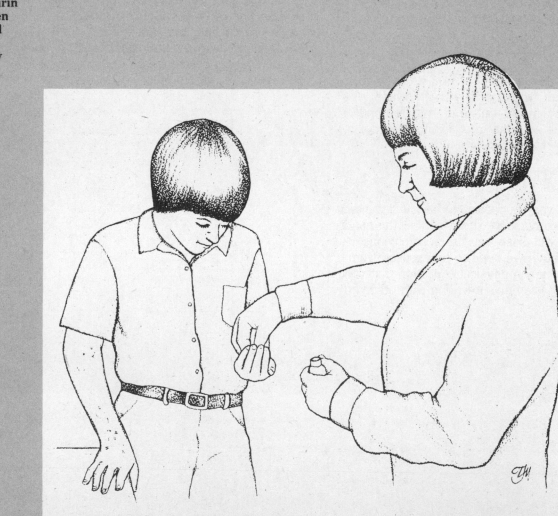

Hand, foot, and mouth disease is a common contagious illness caused by the Coxsackie viruses. The disease is common during warm weather. It is transmitted by mouth-to-mouth contact with someone who has the disease or by eating something that has been contaminated with feces. Symptoms of the disease may appear within three to five days after exposure to the virus.

SIGNS AND SYMPTOMS

The disease is easily identified. Blisters and sores (resembling canker sores) appear inside the mouth, on the tongue and inside the cheeks, lips, and throat. Small clear blisters (one-sixteenth to one-eighth inch round) appear on the fingers, hands, toes, and feet. The child may have a low fever (101°F), a high fever (104°F), or no fever. The illness lasts three to seven days. Other types of Coxsackie illnesses in the family or among your child's friends are another clue to the disease.

HOME CARE

Give the child aspirin or acetaminophen for fever and soreness of the mouth. Avoid giving the child foods that sting the mouth, such as citrus juices, ginger ale, and spices. Popsicles are soothing and a good source of fluids. Check with your doctor before giving the child antihistamines for the itchiness of blisters and rash.

PRECAUTIONS

● Occasionally this disease can be dangerous for young infants. Isolate babies from older children who are ill with this disease. ● If your infant contracts this disease, call your doctor. ● Children occasionally become dehydrated if they refuse all fluids because of the pain in the mouth.

MEDICAL TREATMENT

Your doctor's treatment is the same as home treatment. In rare cases a seriously ill infant may need to be hospitalized.

Related topics:

Dehydration
Rash
Viruses

Hay fever

SYMPTOMS

Nasal congestion
Sneezing
Clear nasal discharge
Itchy nose
Pale membranes inside nose
Headache
Slight hearing loss
Blue bags under eyes
Fatigue

HOME CARE

Try to keep the child away from the substances responsible for the allergic reaction.

Have the child sleep on a nonallergenic pillow.

The use of air conditioners or dehumidifiers can help remove allergy-causing substances from your home, as can filters on hot air ducts.

Consult your doctor before giving the child medications for hay fever.

PRECAUTIONS

☐ Antihistamines and decongestants can help relieve the child's allergic reaction but should only be given on a doctor's recommendation.

☐ Repeated use of decongestant nasal drops or sprays can have a rebound effect and cause even worse congestion.

☐ Nonallergenic rubber pillows may breed molds as they age.

☐ The dander of a cat or dog allowed into the house only once can remain for weeks.

☐ Hay fever rarely occurs as a reaction to foods, drinks, or medications.

☐ Dander from guinea pigs, hamsters, gerbils, or mice does not usually cause hay fever.

☐ Hay fever can be followed by bacterial infection indicated by fever, earache, swollen neck glands, or thick nasal discharge.

☐ A child with severe hay fever may need a series of injections to make him or her less sensitive to the allergy-causing substances.

Hay fever is an allergic reaction of the membranes of the nose and sinuses to substances inhaled out of the air. When it occurs only during a particular time of the year (seasonal allergies), hay fever is usually due to pollens of trees, grasses, or weeds. (Pollens of flowers are usually too heavy to be airborne or inhaled.)

When hay fever occurs year-round (perennial allergies), it may be due to animal dander (tiny scales from the skin of an animal). The reaction may be to dander from a cat, dog, horse, or cow. Horse or cow dander may be present in some felt underpaddings of carpeting that contain horse or cow hair. Hay fever is not usually caused by a reaction to dander from guinea pigs, hamsters, gerbils, or mice. It can, however, be caused by house dust, molds, and feathers from pillows, comforters, or pet birds. Hay fever is rarely a reaction to foods, beverages, or medications.

SIGNS AND SYMPTOMS

The major symptoms are nasal congestion, sneezing, clear nasal discharge, and itching of the nose. This runny, itchy nose leads to the frequent rubbing of the nose referred to as an "allergic salute." Membranes inside the nose are pale and white instead of the normal pink.

The eyes may also be affected. Congestion in the sinuses may cause a headache. The ears feel blocked and are sometimes painful. The child may not hear as well as usual if there is congestion in the eustachian tubes (which connect the nose with the ears). The child may have bluish bags under the eyes, called "allergic shiners." The child may snore and complain of fatigue (allergic fatigue syndrome). If oral antihistamines quickly relieve the symptoms, this is often a clue that the congestion is due to an allergy rather than to some other illness.

Secondary (additional) bacterial infections are common complications of hay fever. Symptoms of an additional bacterial infection include fever, moderate to severe earache, swollen glands in the neck, or opaque (green, yellow, or milky) nasal discharge.

HOME CARE

Consult your doctor before giving a child medications for hay fever. The most common medications for hay fever are oral antihistamines. Decongestants containing ephedrine, pseudoephedrine, or phenylpropanolamine may provide added relief.

Whenever possible, try to avoid exposing the child to substances that seem to cause hay fever reactions. (The dander of a cat or dog allowed in the house only once can remain in the home for four to six weeks.) Keep the windows closed against pollens, and use an air conditioner if possible. Hot air ducts should have filters at room inlets to reduce the amount of dust in the air. Use nonallergenic (non-allergy-causing) pillows and keep the house as dry and free from humidity as possible.

PRECAUTIONS

● Rubber pillows, which are considered nonallergenic, may breed molds as they age. ● Avoid repeated use of decongestant nose drops and nasal sprays. These can cause worse congestion following the initial, brief relief.

MEDICAL TREATMENT

The doctor will confirm the diagnosis by examining the child's nose and by testing nasal secretions for allergic white blood cells (called eosinophiles). As well as confirming the diagnosis, your doctor can help identify the offending substances by investigating the child's medical history and, if necessary, conducting allergy skin tests. Your doctor may recommend desensitization shots for severe cases. These shots decrease the child's sensitivity to the allergy-causing substances.

·Related topics:

Asthma
Common cold
Earaches
Eye allergies
Glands, swollen
Headaches
Sinusitis

Headaches

SYMPTOM   Pain, ache, or throbbing in any area of the head

HOME CARE

Give aspirin or acetaminophen to relieve pain.

Apply cold compresses to the forehead.

Have the child lie down in a dark room.

If the headache is accompanied by nasal congestion, antihistamines or nose drops may ease both conditions. Warm compresses may also help.

Try to identify any source of stress that may be causing headaches. Comfort and cuddle the child whose headache may be due to emotional factors.

See the doctor if the headaches persist.

PRECAUTIONS

☐ **Get medical help immediately** if the child has a sudden, severe headache, especially if it is accompanied by any of the following: fever, extreme weakness or collapse, severe vomiting, stiff neck, or confusion.

☐ If the child has recurring headaches that become more frequent or severe, consult the doctor.

☐ Your information about the child's headaches will be important to the doctor. Note where the pain is located, when it occurs, what circumstances seem to provoke it, how long it lasts, if there are also other symptoms, and whether or not the headache responds to pain-relieving medication.

Headaches are probably as common in children as in adults and have as many or more causes. Fever and strong emotions (anxiety, fear, excitement, sadness, and worry) account for about 95 percent of all headaches in children. Less common causes of childhood headaches are high blood pressure, head injuries and concussions, tumors and inflammation of the brain (such as meningitis, encephalitis), bleeding inside the skull, sinusitis, eye strain, and psychiatric problems.

SIGNS AND SYMPTOMS

Pain, ache, or throbbing in any area of the head are obvious signs of a headache. The type of headache experienced depends somewhat on the cause of the headache. Some clues to the cause are the location of the pain, how long pain lasts, the time of day at which it occurs, the circumstances leading to the pain, other accompanying symptoms, and the effect medications have on the pain. In general, a headache is not serious if it can be relieved by aspirin or acetaminophen, rest, or comforting attention to the child.

Migraine. A child that has migraine headaches usually has a strong family history of the condition. A migraine headache is often on one side of the head. It is generally accompanied by nausea and vomiting ("sick headache"). Sometimes it is preceded by an aura (seeing light flashes or having double vision). A migraine lasts for hours and usually cannot be relieved by aspirin or acetaminophen.

High blood pressure. A throbbing pain occurs with a headache caused by high blood pressure. The child may sweat and turn pale or become flushed. Heart and pulse pound. Aspirin or acetaminophen do not relieve this type of headache.

Concussions. A headache caused by concussion follows an injury to the head.

Tumors, infections, bleeding within the head. Headaches associated with these conditions gradually become more severe and more frequent. The child starts to vomit and to show other signs of disorders of the nervous system such as stiff neck, vision problems, confusion, loss of balance, and sometimes fever.

Sinusitis. When headache is caused by sinusitis, the nose is congested or runny.

Eye strain. A headache from eye strain follows reading or watching television.

Psychiatric problems. Behavior problems also occur along with a headache that is caused by psychiatric problems. The headache is frequently at the top of the head, or it may affect the entire head, which is unusual with other forms of headache.

HOME CARE

Try aspirin or acetaminophen to relieve the pain. Cold compresses on the forehead may offer relief. If the child has nasal congestion, warm compresses on the forehead, antihistamines, or nose drops may help both the congestion and the headache. Have the child lie down in a dark room. Comforting and cuddling the child often helps, since many headaches are caused by emotions. Do whatever you can to remove stress. If the headache persists, see your doctor.

PRECAUTIONS

● Sudden, severe headache may be a true **emergency**—especially if the child also has fever, extreme weakness or collapse, violent vomiting, disorientation (confusion), vision problems, or a stiff neck. Get medical help **immediately**. ● Repeated headaches that become more frequent and severe may be serious. See your doctor.

MEDICAL TREATMENT

Your doctor will perform a complete physical examination of your child, including measuring the blood pressure and examining the eyes. The doctor will perform a nervous system examination, and may order laboratory tests. To discover if the headache is a migraine, your doctor may prescribe the drug ergotamine for a trial period, since this drug relieves only migraine headaches.

The doctor may have you consult a neurologist (a specialist in nervous system disorders); an allergist; an ear, nose, and throat doctor; or a psychiatrist.

Related topics:

Concussion
Encephalitis
High blood
  pressure
Meningitis
Sinusitis
Vision problems

Head lice

SYMPTOMS

Itching scalp
Red scaly rash on back of neck
Sores caused by scratching
Enlarged lymph glands at base of skull
Dandruff-like eggs (nits) attached to hair

HOME CARE

You can distinguish the eggs (or nits) of head lice from dandruff because dandruff can easily be brushed away but the nits cling to the hair shafts.

Your doctor will prescribe a shampoo to kill the lice and the nits. Apply the shampoo exactly according to the instructions, taking care not to get it in the child's eyes or mouth.

If necessary, apply a vinegar rinse to loosen the nits, then fine-comb the child's hair until all the nits are removed.

Clean combs and brushes with the shampoo, launder pillowcases, and have caps or hats washed or dry-cleaned.

Check other family members for the lice.

PRECAUTIONS

☐ If one member of the family has head lice, it is often necessary to treat the rest of the family too (except infants and pregnant women).

☐ The ingredient gamma benzene hexachloride prescribed in shampoo form for head lice is poisonous if swallowed or absorbed through the skin. It can also harm the eyes. Use it exactly as directed; do not repeat the application more than twice, at the stated intervals; and do not leave the shampoo within reach of the child.

☐ Consult your doctor if head lice are accompanied by infected sores on the scalp or enlarged lymph nodes at the base of the skull.

Check your child's scalp on a regular basis for nits if your child is exposed to head lice in school or daycare.

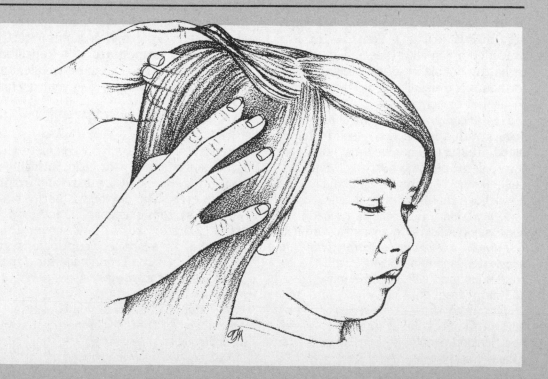

Head lice are tiny parasites (smaller than fleas) less than one-eighth inch long. They are grayish-white, almost transparent, six-legged creatures that live exclusively on humans, never on pets. The lice pass easily from one human to another. Head lice live on or close to the scalp, where they bite and suck blood. Their visible eggs (or nits), which stick to the hairs, are milk-white and about the size of a flake of dandruff. During the past few years, infestation with head lice has become common among school-age children.

SIGNS AND SYMPTOMS

Head lice cause itching of the scalp and sometimes a red, scaly rash on the back of the neck at the hairline. Scratching may cause sores on the scalp. The lymph glands at the base of the skull may be enlarged.

Unless hundreds are present, it is difficult to see lice in a child's hair. Look for the small but easily visible nits attached to the shafts of the hairs. Though nits are about the same color and size as flakes of dandruff, they can be easily distinguished from dandruff. Flakes of dandruff can be blown or brushed away; nits can be removed with the fingernails only with difficulty.

HOME CARE

Apply two tablespoonfuls of a 1-percent gamma benzene hexachloride shampoo (which your doctor will prescribe) to your child's dry hair. Work it into a lather, and leave it on four minutes. Then rinse well with water. Be very careful not to get this shampoo into the child's eyes or mouth. After rinsing, fine-comb your child's hair to remove the nits. If necessary, use a vinegar rinse to loosen the nits before combing. Repeat the shampoo and combing only once, four to seven days later. This procedure kills both the lice and the eggs. Clean combs and hairbrushes with the gamma benzene hexachloride shampoo. To kill stray lice, clean hats and pillowcases by washing and ironing or by dry cleaning.

Lice can also be killed by applying a 25-percent benzyl benzoate lotion (available over the counter) to the hair and scalp; shampoo after 12 to 24 hours. Repeat the procedure in four to seven days.

PRECAUTIONS

● Gamma benzene hexachloride is lindane, a white powder used chiefly as an insecticide. It is *poisonous* if swallowed or absorbed through the skin. It can also harm the eyes. Do not let it come in contact with the eyes or mouth. Do not leave it within your child's reach. Do not apply it more than twice. ● If one person has head lice, all family members except infants and pregnant women should be treated once with the shampoo. ● If the lice are accompanied by infected sores on the scalp or enlarged tender glands at the base of the skull, consult your doctor.

MEDICAL TREATMENT

Your doctor will ordinarily treat head lice as you would at home. If there are infected sores and infected lymph glands, your doctor may culture the sores and will usually prescribe an oral antibiotic for five to ten days.

Related topic:

Glands, swollen
Scabies

Heart murmurs, innocent

SYMPTOM Extra sounds made by the heart that are known not to indicate an abnormality

HOME CARE No home care is required for an innocent murmur.

PRECAUTIONS

☐ Believe your doctor's assurance that innocent murmurs are normal.

☐ Do not make the mistake of over-protecting a child who has an innocent murmur; it is not necessary.

☐ Try not to be alarmed by the long medical names given to innocent murmurs.

☐ Most innocent murmurs disappear by the time the child is a teenager.

At birth and at periodic checkups, a doctor listens to a child's heart to see if the heartbeat is regular and to detect heart murmurs.

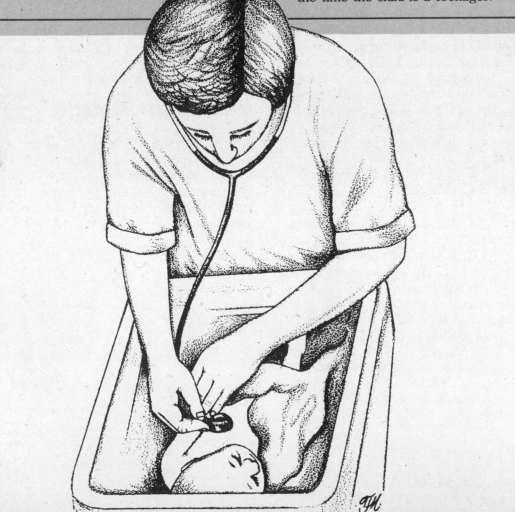

A heart murmur is an extra sound made by the heart as it pumps. A heart murmur may indicate abnormalities in the heart, or it may simply be a normal sound caused by turbulence as the blood rushes through the heart. The sounds that do *not* indicate heart disease or abnormalities are called "innocent murmurs," "insignificant murmurs," or "functional murmurs." They are perfectly normal. Some experts believe that almost every healthy child has at least one innocent murmur, and if the child will stay still long enough in a quiet room a doctor will eventually be able to hear it. Other experts put the figure lower, at half of all normal children. As the child grows, the extra sound or sounds usually become increasingly hard to hear. By the time the child is a teenager, the murmur usually disappears, or becomes so quiet it cannot be detected. Only 15 to 20 percent of innocent murmurs continues into adolescence or adulthood.

SIGNS AND SYMPTOMS

When a child is born, and also at periodic checkups, a doctor will listen to the child's heartbeat with a stethoscope. The doctor is listening to see if the heartbeat is regular and strong, and also to detect heart murmurs. Ordinarily, the doctor will hear the noise made by the lower chambers of the heart, which are called the ventricles, as the heart muscle contracts. Also, the valves that regulate the flow of blood through the heart can be heard as they shut. Most other unexpected sounds that the heart makes are called "murmurs," and the doctor can usually identify the innocent murmurs. If any murmur is found, however, the doctor may recommend a complete examination of the child's heart, to make sure that the heart and circulation are normal and healthy. This will involve taking a detailed medical history, making a complete physical examination, and possibly giving the child a series of tests including an electrocardiogram, a chest X ray, and an echocardiogram, in which sound waves bounce off the heart and form a visual image of it.

HOME CARE

An innocent murmur is completely normal and does not require any treatment or extra care. Treat the child as the normal, healthy child that he or she is.

PRECAUTIONS

● No precautions are needed. Sometimes parents are frightened by the idea of a heart murmur and overprotect a child whose heart is quite normal. This is not good for the child's health or well-being.
● If your doctor diagnoses an innocent murmur, do not be alarmed by the complicated names for innocent murmurs or by the tests your child may have.

MEDICAL TREATMENT

No medical treatment is necessary for an innocent murmur. The doctor may listen for the murmur at routine checkups to see if the sound can still be heard, but it really doesn't matter whether the murmur continues or not.

Occasionally, an innocent murmur will sound somewhat like another type of murmur. If this happens, the doctor may wish to check the child's heart again after a few years, to be sure the original diagnosis was correct.

Heat rash

SYMPTOM Tiny pink or red eruptions each surrounding a skin pore on the cheeks, neck, shoulders, in skin creases, and in diaper area

HOME CARE Keep the child as cool as possible, preferably in an air-conditioned room.

Cool baths and careful dusting with cornstarch or baby powder help relieve discomfort.

If the rash is on the face, rest the child's face on an absorbent pad placed in the crib.

Be careful not to overdress the child.

Use prickly heat powders during warm weather.

PRECAUTIONS

☐ Use powder carefully; if a baby inhales large amounts of powder, lung inflammation can occur.

☐ Overdressing a baby is a frequent cause of heat rash; the baby need be dressed no more warmly than you dress yourself.

☐ The use of detergents and bleaches on bed linens and clothing may aggravate heat rash.

☐ Avoid using bubble baths, water softeners, or oily lotions on a child with heat rash.

Keep a child with heat rash as cool as possible. Allowing the child to play or rest for short periods without clothing may help.

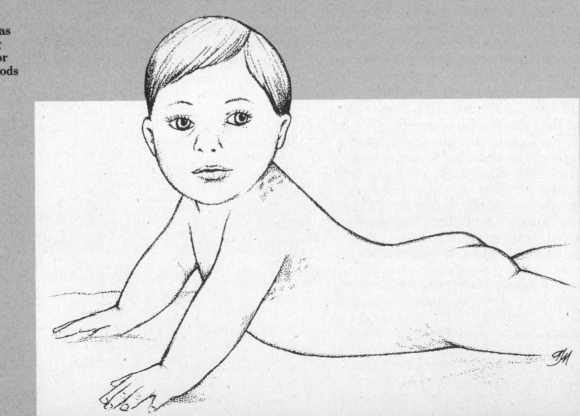

Heat rash is a mild skin condition caused by temporary blockage of the sweat gland openings on the skin. Heat rash, also known as prickly heat or miliaria, is the most common of all rashes in children of any age. Almost all babies get heat rash during hot weather. Heat rash can even occur in cold weather if your child is over-dressed either during the daytime or night-time. Fair-skinned children (redheads and blonds) get heat rash more frequently than other children, and they suffer the most from it.

SIGNS AND SYMPTOMS

Heat rash consists of hundreds of tiny pinhead eruptions, each surrounding a skin pore. These eruptions may look like small pink or red bumps or like tiny water blis-ters. They are moderately itchy and may show scratch marks. If you look at the rash with a magnifying glass in good light, each dot of heat rash can be seen at the mouth of a pore from a sweat gland.

The rash usually appears on the cheeks, neck, or shoulders, in skin creases, and in the diaper area. It fre-quently appears if the child has been wearing a wet bathing suit. Hot humid conditions, perspiration, and overdressing are further clues that the rash is heat rash.

HOME CARE

Infants and children are safest from heat rash in an air-conditioned environment. Keep a child with heat rash as cool as possible. Cool baths, or baby powder or cornstarch applied lightly with a powder puff, help ease the condition. If the heat rash is on your baby's face, rest the child's face on an absorbent pad in the crib. During warm weather, using prickly heat powders may give some relief.

PRECAUTIONS

● Be careful with powder. If a baby in-hales a large amount of powder, inflamma-tion of the lungs can occur. ● Detergents and bleaches in clothing and bed linens may aggravate heat rash. ● Bubble baths, water softeners, and oily lotions should be avoided. ● Do not overdress the child. The clothing that's appropriate to the weather for you is also appropriate for the baby.

MEDICAL TREATMENT

A doctor's treatment is not necessary. Heat rash can be adequately and safely treated at home.

Related topics:

Diaper rashes
Rash

Heatstroke

EMERGENCY SYMPTOMS

Apply emergency treatment immediately.

IMPORTANT

A child with heatstroke who does not revive within minutes after treatment is in danger and requires **immediate emergency care.**

SYMPTOMS

Feeling that lungs and muscles are "on fire"
Dry mouth
Breathing difficulty
Dizziness
Nausea
Blurred vision
Hot, dry skin
High fever
Absence of sweating

EMERGENCY TREATMENT

1. Call for emergency help and begin first aid.

2. Remove the child's clothing and lay the child down, feet higher than head, in a shady area.

3. Pour cold water over the child's body, rub the body with ice, then fan the child to promote evaporation.

4. When the child is conscious and his or her body temperature is normal, give plenty of fruit juices to replace fluids and minerals lost during dehydration.

5. Watch the child closely and repeat treatment if the symptoms recur.

PRECAUTIONS

☐ Heatstroke can be fatal if not treated immediately.

☐ Heatstroke occurs most often when both temperature and humidity are high.

☐ Strenuous exercise within one week of an attack of heatstroke increases the possibility of another attack.

☐ Susceptibility to heatstroke is increased by: lack of water; excessive sweating; vomiting or diarrhea.

☐ Salt tablets are not helpful in preventing heatstroke.

Heatstroke is a sudden, uncontrolled rise in body temperature. Heatstroke occurs when the body is exposed to excessive heat but cannot replace the body fluids lost through perspiration. If the lost fluids are not replaced, dehydration (depletion of total body fluids) occurs and leads to a decrease in blood volume.

At this point the body has to decide whether to supply the diminished amount of blood to the internal organs or to the skin; since the internal organs take priority, they will receive the blood. At the same time, the body loses its ability to sweat. The situation now becomes critical for two reasons: the body cannot now produce enough sweat, so the evaporation of sweat on the skin cannot cool the body; and the skin is now being deprived of the blood supply that insures that excess heat can be released through the skin. The lack of blood supply to the skin and the inability to sweat together cause the body to overheat.

If it is not treated quickly and correctly, heatstroke can cause permanent brain damage or death. When there is loss of blood volume, which can mean there is not enough blood to circulate through the body, the victim goes into shock. Also, at high temperatures the blood cannot clot properly, and this can result in blood leaking from the vessels into body organs.

Heatstroke most often strikes athletes or other people who do strenuous work in hot weather. People who have had heatstroke once are more likely to suffer another attack if they return to strenuous exercise within a week. Lack of water, excessive sweating, vomiting, or diarrhea all increase the body's susceptibility to heatstroke.

SIGNS AND SYMPTOMS

The onset of heatstroke is signaled by a feeling that lungs and muscles are "on fire." The child may have a dry mouth, difficulty in breathing, dizziness, nausea, and blurred vision. However, the most characteristic signs of heatstroke are extremely hot, flushed, dry skin; high fever; and the complete absence of sweating, which usually leads to unconsciousness.

HOME CARE

If you suspect that your child has heatstroke, call immediately for emergency help and then begin first aid. Remove the child's clothing and place him or her in a shady area. Place the child in a reclining position with the feet higher than the head. Pour cold water over the child, rub the body with ice, then fan the child to promote evaporation which will lower the body temperature. Continue this treatment until the child is conscious and the body temperature is back to normal. Then give fruit juices, which will replace minerals as well as fluids lost during dehydration. Watch the child carefully, and if the symptoms recur repeat the treatment process. If the child does not revive within minutes emergency care is essential.

PRECAUTIONS

● Heatstroke can cause brain damage or death if not treated correctly and promptly. A child with heatstroke who doesn't revive within minutes requires emergency care immediately. ● Heatstroke occurs most often when both temperature and humidity are high. ● Strenuous exercise within one week of an attack of heatstroke may lead to another attack. ● Lack of water, excessive sweating, vomiting, and diarrhea increase the child's susceptibility to heatstroke. ● Taking salt tablets can increase rather than lessen a person's risk of getting heatstroke.

MEDICAL TREATMENT

If a child with heatstroke does not revive in minutes injections of special intravenous fluids will be required.

Related topics:

Dehydration
Shock

Henoch-Schonlein purpura

SYMPTOMS   Purpura rash—tiny purplish spots or a
               purple bruise
               Abdominal pain
               Blood in urine
               Pain and swelling in joints

HOME CARE   A doctor should direct treatment of this
                disease.

PRECAUTIONS

☐ Contact the doctor promptly if your
child develops a rash that looks like
large bruises or tiny purple dots.

☐ A purpura rash can also indicate a
serious blood disease.

☐ If a child with Henoch-Schonlein
purpura has severe abdominal pain or
blood in the stool, consult the doctor
at once.

☐ A child who has had this disease
should have a checkup and kidney and
urine tests for up to six months after
recovery.

One way to tell if a rash is purpura is to press a glass against the skin. If the rash remains visible, it is purpura.

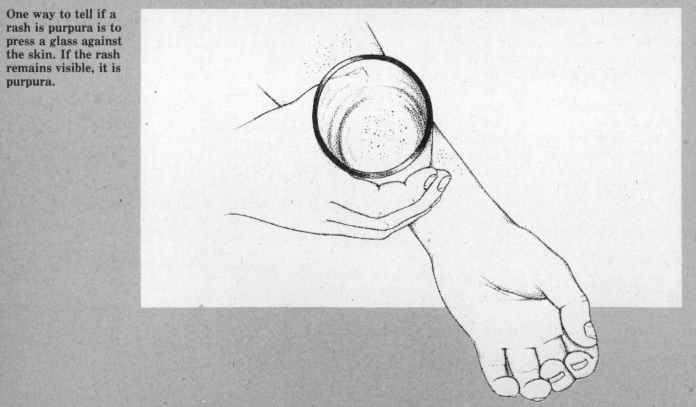

Henoch-Schonlein purpura is a combination of symptoms that includes a type of rash called purpura. This rash is caused by bleeding from tiny blood vessels just below the surface of the skin. This disease affects four body systems: the skin, the kidneys, the digestive tract, and the joints.

The cause of Henoch-Schonlein purpura is not known, but some experts believe it is an allergy-based reaction. It often appears as a child is recovering from a viral infection. The disease usually lasts about six weeks. In a few children, it reappears several times over the next few months, or even over several years. In rare cases the condition leads to complications, but usually the symptoms disappear and leave no lasting effects.

SIGNS AND SYMPTOMS

If you hold a glass pressed against the rash and the rash remains visible, it is purpura. Other types of rashes are on the skin surface and will not show under a glass. Purpura may look like tiny purplish spots or a purple bruise. The other symptoms of this disease are abdominal pain, blood in the urine, and pain and swelling in the joints. The disease can be identified from the unique combination of symptoms. The doctor may have the child's urine and bowel movements tested for blood to confirm the diagnosis and learn if the digestive tract is involved.

HOME CARE

A child with this disease should be under a doctor's care. Ask the doctor about treatment to make the child more comfortable if he or she has joint pain or abdominal pain.

PRECAUTIONS

● If you notice a rash on your child that looks like large bruises or tiny purple dots, contact the doctor at once. Purpura does not always indicate Henoch-Schonlein purpura. It can be a sign of a serious blood disease. ● Henoch-Schonlein purpura can lead to damage to the intestine. Watch a child with this disease for severe abdominal pain or a large amount of blood in the stools. These symptoms may indicate that the wall of the intestine is perforated, or that it has telescoped into itself. Report such symptoms to the doctor at once. ● It is possible, though rare, for a child who has recovered from Henoch-Schonlein purpura to later develop kidney complications, such as nephritis. To detect kidney involvement before it leads to kidney damage and possibly kidney failure, the child should have checkups and urine and kidney tests for up to six months after recovery.

MEDICAL TREATMENT

There is no specific treatment for this disease. Routine blood tests are usually done to make sure the rash is not caused by a blood disorder. The doctor will want to test the child's urine and bowel movements for blood several times, in order to detect complications early. The child will also be tested for strep throat, because strep infection can be associated with Henoch-Schonlein purpura. If a strep infection is found, the doctor will probably prescribe an antibiotic.

In some cases, to guard against complications, the child may be hospitalized when the disease is at its worst.

Related topics:

Arthritis
Nephritis
Rash
Stomachache,
   acute
Strep throat

Hepatitis

SYMPTOMS
Loss of appetite
Nausea
Vomiting
Upper abdominal pain
Jaundice (yellowed skin and whites of
    eyes, dark amber urine, and
    light-colored stools)
Fever
Headache
General discomfort

HOME CARE Isolate the child, then call the doctor.

When a diagnosis has been made the doctor will order a home care program that includes rest, liquids, and a low-fat diet.

PRECAUTIONS

☐ Hepatitis must be diagnosed and treated by a doctor.

☐ A child and other family members who have been exposed to hepatitis should be given preventive gamma globulin or hepatitis B immune globulin injections as soon as possible after exposure.

☐ Hepatitis B is contagious; isolate the child and practice good health habits to limit spread of the disease.

☐ Hepatitis A can be contracted from contaminated water or food, such as shellfish.

☐ A pregnant woman can pass hepatitis B to her unborn baby.

Hepatitis is an infection of the liver. Only recently have two viruses that cause hepatitis been identified. Hepatitis A virus causes infectious hepatitis. Hepatitis B virus causes serum hepatitis. Another form of hepatitis can occur as a complication of infectious mononucleosis. Serious, acute complications and long-term progressive (continually worsening) liver disease may occur as a result of hepatitis.

Hepatitis A is contracted from the stools or blood of a person with the disease. The virus is also present in contaminated water and food (for example, shellfish). Symptoms may appear within 15 to 45 days after being exposed to the virus. The patient is contagious from three weeks before the onset of jaundice until one week after onset.

Hepatitis B is contracted in one of two ways: either by close mouth-to-mouth contact or from the blood of a patient or carrier (someone who carries the virus without having the disease). It is usually transmitted by a blood transfusion or by an injection with a contaminated needle (as in drug addiction and tattooing). It can also be passed by a pregnant woman to her unborn baby. Symptoms may appear six weeks to six months after being exposed to the virus. Hepatitis B is contagious during the incubation period (the time between exposure to the virus and the onset of symptoms), and possibly for months and years. Symptoms are similar to those of hepatitis A, but often come on more gradually and are milder. Arthritis and rashes are common complications.

SIGNS AND SYMPTOMS

First symptoms are fever, malaise (body discomfort), headache, and sometimes signs of a common cold. The key symptoms are a marked loss of appetite (often with nausea, vomiting, and upper abdominal pain) and the onset of jaundice (yellowed skin, yellowed whites of eyes, dark amber urine, and light-colored stools).

Jaundice lasts two to four weeks, followed by one to two months of diminishing fatigue. The liver often is enlarged and tender. Specific diagnosis (A type or B type) depends upon blood tests and must be made by a doctor.

HOME CARE

If symptoms of hepatitis appear, isolate your child from friends, school, or work to lessen the chance of spreading the disease. Then call your doctor. Hepatitis must be diagnosed and treated by a doctor. Your doctor will give you specific instructions for caring for the child at home and will probably recommend rest, liquids, and a low-fat diet that is easy to digest.

PRECAUTIONS

● If your child is exposed to hepatitis, call your doctor. The child and other family members should be given preventive gamma globulin or hepatitis B immune globulin injections as soon after exposure as is practical and before symptoms appear. ● If you are caring for a child with hepatitis B, remember that this form is now known to be contagious (contrary to past beliefs). Practice good hygiene, particularly careful hand washing, to avoid spreading the disease.

MEDICAL TREATMENT

Your doctor may hospitalize your child for treatment. Tests are also available to determine when hepatitis B is no longer contagious.

203

Hernia

SYMPTOM   A bulge in one of the typical locations:
- just above or below the crease of the groin
- just above or below the navel
- at the navel

HOME CARE   If you suspect a hernia, take the child to the doctor.

PRECAUTIONS

☐ A strangulated hernia is a **medical emergency** that must be immediately corrected surgically (within hours). Signs that a hernia has become strangulated are: swelling; severe pain; nausea; vomiting; severe weakness or collapse. If these symptoms appear, take your child to the emergency room immediately. Never attempt home care for a strangulated hernia.

☐ Trusses or belts used to reduce a hernia are useless and may be harmful or dangerous.

☐ Doctors do not consider it beneficial to strap an umbilical hernia.

A hernia (or rupture) is a protrusion of tissue through the wall of the body cavity. It might be compared to the protrusion of an inner tube through a hole in an automobile tire. Several types of hernias may occur in children.

The most common hernia in a child is an *indirect inguinal hernia*, which is present at birth but may or may not be recognized immediately. In fact, this type of hernia is not usually noticed until some later age. The hernia begins as a bulge just above the midpoint of the crease of the groin. It then enlarges toward the middle of the body until it reaches and enters the scrotum (the pouch containing the testes) of a boy or the labia majora (outer folds of the external genitals) of a girl. The bulge is actually a pouch-like sac underneath the skin made of peritoneum (the membrane that lines the abdominal cavity). The sac usually contains either a portion of the veil-like apron that overlies the intestines or a loop of the small intestine. Less often, it contains a loop of the large bowel, part of the urinary bladder, or an ovary.

A rarer hernia in children is a *femoral hernia*, which appears below the crease of the groin, near where the pulse of the main artery to the leg can be felt. Occasionally, a *ventral hernia* appears in the midline of the abdomen, above or below the navel. In infants, an *umbilical hernia* often appears at the umbilicus (the navel). This is not a true hernia, however, because it contains no sac. An umbilical hernia usually disappears on its own before the child reaches five years of age.

SIGNS AND SYMPTOMS

The key sign of a hernia is a bulge in one of the typical locations: just above the crease of the groin; in the scrotum of a boy; in the labia majora of a girl; below the crease of the groin; just above or below the navel; or at the navel.

A hernia in any of these locations is called a *simple* hernia if the contents of the sac can be reduced (pushed gently back into the abdominal cavity). If a hernia cannot be reduced, it is called *incarcerated*. Simple and incarcerated hernias often produce no discomfort or pain; they may merely cause a sense of heaviness. If the blood supply to the contents of the hernia is cut off, it is said to be *strangulated*. A strangulated hernia causes intense pain and swelling.

HOME CARE

If there is any sign of a hernia, see your doctor.

A simple hernia can be temporarily reduced by gentle pressure while the child is relaxed—in a tub of warm water if necessary. Trusses and belts to keep a hernia reduced are useless and may be harmful or even dangerous. Strapping an umbilical hernia is considered of no benefit.

PRECAUTIONS

● A strangulated hernia is a **medical emergency** that requires immediate (within hours) surgical correction. Signs that a hernia has become strangulated are swelling; severe pain; and sometimes nausea, vomiting, and extreme weakness or collapse. If any signs of a strangulated hernia appear, take your child to a doctor or emergency room **immediately.** ● Never attempt to reduce a strangulated hernia.

MEDICAL TREATMENT

Surgical repair is required for all except umbilical hernias. An umbilical hernia usually cures itself. Since inguinal hernias often appear on both sides, the surgeon may correct both sides even though only one side is visibly herniated.

Related topics:

Testis, torsion of
Testis,
   undescended

Herpes simplex

SYMPTOMS

Oral herpes
Multiple painful ulcers of mouth membranes or eyeballs
Painful, red, swollen gums
Swollen lymph nodes in neck
Fever
Fever blisters near the lips

Genital herpes
Painful ulcers and blisters on genitals

HOME CARE

For oral herpes give aspirin or acetaminophen to relieve pain, and have the child eat bland foods.

An older child can rinse the mouth with a mild salt solution or be treated with triamcinolone or local anesthetic ointments.

Apply antibiotic ointment to fever blisters to prevent cracking and lessen the possibility of further infection.

For genital herpes, warm soaks help relieve inflammation and pain.

PRECAUTIONS

☐ In the case of herpes of the eyeball, consult an eye doctor promptly.

☐ If a baby contracts herpes, get prompt medical attention.

☐ Keep adults or children with herpes isolated from babies.

☐ A pregnant woman with genital herpes can infect her child as the infant passes through the birth canal during delivery.

Herpes simplex is a highly contagious disease caused by *herpesvirus hominis* types 1 and 2. It is commonly known as canker sores (when it occurs in the mouth) or fever blisters (when it appears near the mouth). The infection is transmitted by direct contact with an infected person.

The type 1 infection (oral herpes) is common before the age of four but can occur at any age. Once contracted, the virus continues to live in the body for months or years, sometimes for the person's lifetime. When the person's resistance is lowered, (for instance by fever, sunburn, exhaustion, or emotional stress), the "sleeping" virus is reactivated.

Infection with the type 2 virus is genital herpes and, like oral herpes, it is contagious and often recurrent. It is usually transmitted sexually when the lesions (blisters) are present. A baby born to a mother with genital herpes can contract the disease while passing through the birth canal during delivery. In this case there is a 50 percent chance that the infant will be severely damaged or die.

SIGNS AND SYMPTOMS

Oral herpes (type 1 infection) causes multiple ulcers of the membranes of the mouth (lips, cheeks, tongue, and palate) or the eyeballs. The ulcers are painful and are accompanied by painful, red, swollen gums and swollen lymph nodes in the neck. The child's fever may climb to 105°F. The canker sores have a distinctive appearance and are easily distinguished from other mouth sores such as gumboils. Canker sores are open, red ulcers which have a scooped-out appearance, unlike gumboils which protrude above the surface of the membranes. When oral herpes appears as fever blisters, the blisters can be mistaken for impetigo. Fever blisters, however, are usually more painful. To confuse the diagnosis, fever blisters may become further infected with impetigo.

Oral herpes lasts seven to ten days, but the virus remains in the body and may cause recurrent outbreaks. This recurrent condition is contagious each time it appears.

Genital herpes (type 2 infection) causes painful ulcers and blisters on the genitals. Like oral herpes, genital herpes is contagious when the blisters are present and often recurrent.

HOME CARE

For oral herpes, give aspirin or acetaminophen to relieve pain. Have the child eat bland, soothing foods such as ice cream, gelatin desserts, puddings, and milk. Encourage an older child to rinse the mouth with a mild table salt solution. Canker sores can be treated in older children with triamcinolone in dental ointment form, or with thick solutions of local anesthetic available from the pharmacy. Antibiotic ointment applied to fever blisters may prevent painful cracking and lessen the chances of impetigo developing.

For genital herpes, warm soaks help relieve inflammation and pain. There is a drug that has been used by adults to lessen the recurring attacks, but this drug has not been tested in children.

PRECAUTIONS

• Herpes simplex of the eyeball is serious and requires the immediate attention of an eye doctor. • Herpes can be severe in an infant. Adults or children with herpes should be kept away from the baby. If a baby contracts herpes, consult a doctor. • There is no cure for recurrent herpes.

MEDICAL TREATMENT

The doctor will probably prescribe eyedrops to treat herpes of the eyeball. An experimental drug, Cytosine arabinoside (Ara-C) is available to treat life-threatening complications of herpes, such as may occur in infants. If a child with herpes has a severely ulcerated mouth, hospitalization may be necessary for intravenous fluids to be given until the child can swallow normally again.

A Cesarean section (delivery by surgery) may be performed in the case of a pregnant woman who has genital herpes and whose baby might be exposed to the disease during a normal delivery.

Related topics:

Gumboils
Impetigo

High blood pressure

SYMPTOMS   Most often there are no symptoms

POSSIBLE SYMPTOMS
Headaches
Pounding heartbeat
Shortness of breath during exercise
Flushed face

HOME CARE   High blood pressure must be diagnosed and treated by a doctor.

PRECAUTIONS

☐ Your child should have regular check-ups, and the doctor should measure the child's blood pressure during each examination.

☐ High blood pressure can be dangerous if left untreated.

Be sure that your doctor checks your child's blood pressure during each checkup.

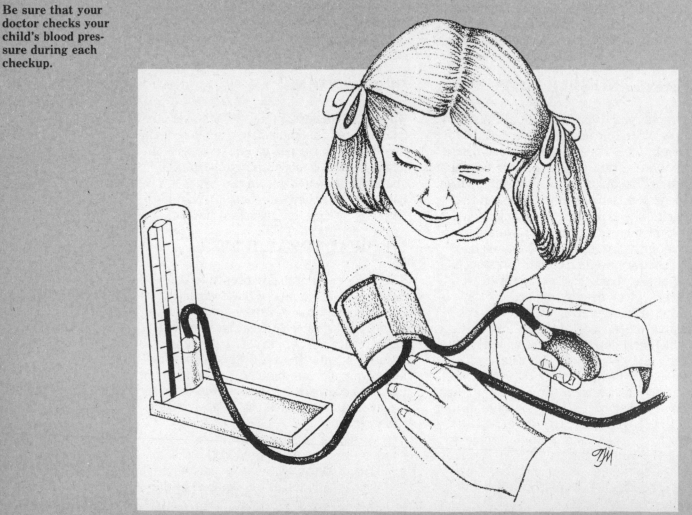

Although it has been known for decades that high blood pressure (hypertension) occurs in infants and children as well as in adults, many people are not aware of this fact. A baby's normal blood pressure at birth is about 80/40 systolic pressure over diastolic pressure. Systolic pressure is the pressure the heart pumps out with; diastolic pressure is the pressure required to fill the heart with blood. The blood pressure then rises gradually until, by the time the child is a teenager, it is about 120/80. If the blood pressure is substantially higher than that, a child is considered to have high blood pressure.

The most common cause of transient (temporary) high blood pressure in children is emotion—fear or worry, for example. Persistent high blood pressure can be caused by kidney disease (tumors, obstructions, infections, nephritis); adrenal and testicle tumors; defects of the heart or a major artery; overactive thyroid; medications such as steroids or ephedrine; extreme overweight; and, eating too much licorice. "Essential hypertension," the most common cause in adults, may be hereditary and has no known cause.

SIGNS AND SYMPTOMS

High blood pressure has been called the "silent disease," because it often has no symptoms. Symptoms, if they occur, can include headaches, pounding heartbeat, shortness of breath during exercise, and flushing of the face. Accurate diagnosis can be made only by taking careful blood pressure measurements with instruments that are the correct size for your child's size. If the blood pressure is high on the first reading, the doctor will check it several times at return visits to make sure that the first reading was accurate.

HOME CARE

There is no home treatment for high blood pressure. The condition must be diagnosed and treated by a doctor. All children should have an annual physical examination. High blood pressure in childhood is curable, but it can be dangerous if it is not treated.

PRECAUTION

● Be sure the doctor checks your child's blood pressure during each annual checkup.

MEDICAL TREATMENT

Your doctor will give the child a complete physical examination, including measuring the blood pressure, palpating the arteries in the groin, and examining the eye for changes in the blood vessels in the back of the eyes (where effects of high blood pressure may be recognized early). The doctor will also examine the child's heart, abdomen, and genitals.

It takes complicated laboratory investigation to check for all of the many possible causes of high blood pressure. Except for rare cases, all the causes of high blood pressure can be successfully treated or cured by medications, changes in diet, or surgery. However, the condition frequently requires the child to be hospitalized for tests and determination of treatment.

Related topics:

Nephritis
Thyroid disorders

Hip problems

SYMPTOMS
Pain in hip or knee
Limp
Limited movement of hip joint
Slight fever (in case of acute synovitis)

HOME CARE Keep the child off his or her feet for three or four days.

Consult the doctor if the condition does not improve.

PRECAUTIONS

☐ Pain in the knee may be a sign of a hip problem.

☐ A severe form of arthritis may be signaled by hip pain and a limp accompanied by high fever. If the child appears to have a hip problem and also has a high fever, call the doctor.

☐ Some hip problems can cause permanent deformity if left untreated.

Children are susceptible to joint pains, most of which come and go and are not serious—for example, sprains and growing pains. Occasionally children get arthritis, which may affect the hips. Dislocated hips sometimes occur in infants and toddlers. There are also three specific causes of hip pain that occur commonly in children.

Acute synovitis of the hip can be described as a bruise of the inside of the hip joint. It is usually associated with a viral illness and is nearly always a harmless condition that disappears by itself. It can occur at any age, but most frequently happens between ages two and six.

Legg-Calvé-Perthes disease is a serious condition in which the upper end of the thigh bone (femoral head) softens and becomes deformed. No one knows why it happens, but it usually begins between ages four and ten years and affects boys more often than girls. If it is not treated, Legg-Calvé-Perthes disease results in a severe and permanent deformity of the hip.

Slipped femoral epiphysis is another condition of unknown origin, but it is possible that it happens as a delayed result of an injury. It occurs most often in the teen years, usually in overweight (obese or muscular) children. It results in severe deformity if it is not treated.

SIGNS AND SYMPTOMS

All the three conditions described above cause pain in the hip accompanied by a limp. It is important to note, however, that pain in the knee can also indicate a hip problem. In rare cases, synovitis may be accompanied by a slight fever; the other two conditions do not produce fever. In all three conditions the hip joint is limited in one or more of its movements: stretching and flexing, rotating inward or outward, or movement toward and away from the midline (adduction and abduction).

HOME CARE

The child should stay off his or her legs for three or four days. (Note that crawling rather than walking does *not* keep weight off the hip). If the condition does not seem to be corrected after three to four days of rest, consult the doctor.

PRECAUTIONS

● If your child complains of pain in the knee consider the possibility of a hip disease. ● Marked pain, a limp, and high fever may be symptoms of a serious form of arthritis and require medical attention. ● Consult the doctor if the child's hip pain is accompanied by a high fever.

MEDICAL TREATMENT

The doctor will examine the child carefully and may order hip X rays. However, synovitis rarely shows at all on an X ray, and early Legg-Calvé-Perthes disease and slipped epiphysis do not always show on X rays. The doctor may suggest that the child continue bed rest, either at home or in the hospital. In the hospital traction (immobilizing the leg) may be prescribed and X rays taken at intervals so that the doctor can monitor the child's progress. Tests for arthritis may also be performed. Slipped epiphysis always requires surgery. Legg-Calvé-Perthes disease is treated by having the child keep weight off the legs and not walk for a period of months until the condition heals; sometimes surgery is necessary.

Hives

SYMPTOMS Raised, red welts
Itching
Welts change appearance rapidly

HOME CARE Use cold water compresses, calamine lotion, and cornstarch baths to help relieve itching.

If hives are caused by an allergy, medication prescribed by the doctor can be given to the child when the hives appear.

PRECAUTIONS

☐ See the doctor if hives appear on the child's tongue.

☐ See the doctor immediately if the child is coughing or has difficulty breathing or swallowing.

☐ If the child has hives accompanied by fever, the doctor will order a culture to check for strep throat.

☐ If an allergic child's medication doesn't relieve the hives, call the doctor.

Use cornstarch baths to help relieve the itching of hives.

Hives (urticaria) are an allergic reaction of the skin, and about 20 percent of children develop hives once or repeatedly. Hives can involve any area of the skin, and 95 percent of cases are caused by foods, beverages, or medications to which the child is allergic. Among the substances most likely to trigger a reaction are citrus fruits, chocolate, nuts (including peanut butter), tomatoes, berries, spices, candies, tropical fruits and fruit juices, and artificial food flavorings.

The small proportion of cases of hives not caused by a food or medication allergy is caused by one of the following: a substance that the child has touched, such as a plant, ointment, or cosmetic, or the saliva of a dog or cat; an insect bite or sting; overexposure to sunlight or cold temperatures; or something the child has inhaled, for instance, pollen, mold, an insecticide, animal dander, or feathers. One rarely seen form of hives is caused by respiratory or other viruses, by the streptococcus bacterium, or by certain medications. This form of hives is known as *erythema multiforme.*

SIGNS AND SYMPTOMS

Hives appear as itchy, red, raised welts that can range in size from a quarter-inch to several inches across. The most noticeable characteristic of hives is that they change appearance rapidly—they come and go and change in size from one hour to the next. No other type of rash has these same characteristics, so you can be pretty sure that any welts that itch and change appearance rapidly are hives.

Sometimes an insect bite looks like a hive at the point of a bite; however, it does not come and go as rapidly. Hives that are triggered by an allergic reaction to an insect bite appear at sites distant from the bite itself. Hives can also accompany allergic arthritis, which is signaled by stiff, swollen, red joints.

The form of hives known as *erythema multiforme* appears as welts that look like red targets of different sizes painted on the skin.

You can sometimes pinpoint the cause of your child's hives by considering his or her activities in the minutes or hours before the hives appeared.

HOME CARE

Unless the child has been given medication with instructions to take it when the hives recur, home treatment of hives should be confined to measures to relieve the itching. Cold water compresses, calamine lotion, and cornstarch baths may help make the child more comfortable. Frequent or repeated cases of hives require medical attention. Also, if the child has been given medication but the medication fails to relieve the symptoms, you should call the doctor.

PRECAUTIONS

● If hives appear on the tongue, make the child cough, or cause difficulty in breathing or swallowing, see your doctor immediately. ● If hives are accompanied by fever see your doctor to rule out a strep infection. ● If antihistamines don't help relieve a case of hives, telephone your doctor for advice.

MEDICAL TREATMENT

When your child has hives the doctor may administer epinephrine to reduce the intensity of the outbreak and then prescribe antihistamines to be taken by mouth. If the hives recur and it's not possible to pinpoint the cause, the doctor may order skin tests or refer the child to an allergy specialist. The doctor may also order a throat culture to check for strep infection. If the child shows symptoms of arthritis, tests are necessary to confirm or rule out that possibility. If the hives are caused by an allergy to the venom released in an insect bite, the doctor may suggest a long-term course of injections to decrease the child's sensitivity to the venom; these shots may be given over a period of years. In the case of an allergy of this type, the child may also be given medication and instructed to take it if he or she gets bitten.

Related topics:

Arthritis
Food allergies
Insect bites and
  stings
Rash
Strep throat

Hoarseness

SYMPTOMS
Speaking or crying in an unusually
   low pitch
Inability to speak above a whisper
Voice loss

HOME CARE
Have the child rest his or her voice.

Encourage the child to inhale steam and drink warm liquids.

If hoarseness is caused by an allergy, antihistamines prescribed by the doctor should help.

PRECAUTIONS

☐ Consult the doctor if the hoarseness is severe or persists longer than two to three days.

☐ Note that babies are sometimes born with soft larynxes. This may give a hoarse note to the baby's cry, but it is nothing to worry about and usually disappears after six to eight months of age.

Offer warm liquids, such as broth, to relieve hoarseness.

Anything that interferes with the normal vibrations of the vocal cords can cause the cords to swell and produce hoarseness—distortion or loss of the voice. In children, the most common cause of hoarseness is abuse of the voice by screaming. Hoarseness can also be caused by croup, laryngitis, or an allergy. More rarely, the condition can result from diphtheria, injury to the larynx (voice box), or a foreign body that the child has inhaled.

Extreme hoarseness can cause total temporary voice loss. Repeated hoarseness leads to the formation of tiny, wart-like growths on the vocal cords. In children, these growths are known as "screamer's nodes." When they occur in adults they're referred to more politely as "singer's nodes." Either way, they can cause the hoarseness to become a chronic condition.

Note that a baby may be born with a soft, underdeveloped larynx that collapses partially each time the baby takes in a breath; the baby makes a crowing sound (congenital laryngeal stridor), and there may be a hoarse note to the baby's cry. This condition should clear up without treatment, and you don't need to be concerned about it.

SIGNS AND SYMPTOMS

Hoarseness may lead your child to speak or cry in a lower pitch than usual, or to be unable to speak above a whisper. Check whether the child has other symptoms—fever, cough, difficulty with breathing, sore throat, or an obstruction of the nose—which might be responsible for the voice change. If not, and if the child has been yelling or screaming a lot, it's probably a simple case of hoarseness.

HOME CARE

A hoarse child should rest his or her voice, inhale steam, and drink warm liquids. If the hoarseness is due to an allergy and your child has been prescribed antihistamines for an allergic condition, the medication should relieve the hoarseness. Remember that hoarseness in a baby's cry, if it's happening because the larynx is still soft, is not a cause for concern and should disappear by the time the child is a year old.

PRECAUTIONS

● Hoarseness in children is not usually due to any potentially dangerous cause. If no other signs of illness are present, therefore, the home care recommended above should take care of the problem.
● If the hoarseness gets more severe or persists for longer than a few days consult your doctor.

MEDICAL TREATMENT

A doctor using a tongue blade and flashlight can see no further than the epiglottis (a "lid" that covers the voice box above the vocal cords) and cannot examine the vocal cords. However, a doctor who is concerned about the child's hoarseness may refer you to an ear, nose, and throat specialist who has the equipment necessary to perform a more complete examination. It's rarely necessary to surgically remove the "screamer's nodes."

Related topics:

Choking
Coughs
Croup
Diphtheria
Fever
Laryngitis
Sore throat

Hyperactivity

SYMPTOM Inability to sit still or be quiet for more than a very short period.

HOME CARE Hyperactivity always requires professional evaluation and treatment.

PRECAUTIONS

☐ Do not confuse a child's natural tendency to be active with true hyperkinesis.

☐ Never accept a diagnosis of hyperkinesis from anyone except a professional.

☐ Do not try to deal with hyperactivity at home; it always requires medical assessment and treatment.

☐ Note that the hyperactive child is not misbehaving; the behavior is involuntary.

☐ If a child over the age of two suddenly becomes much more active than usual, look for causes in the child's environment; true hyperkinesis is present from infancy.

☐ A child who is overactive with one family member but not others is not hyperactive.

☐ A hyperkinetic child may need to take medication for extended periods. The child may also need special schooling or counseling.

All healthy children are active—frequently more active than the adults in their lives would wish them to be. Some children are extremely lively and always on the go. Of such children, however, only a small handful (1 to 10 percent) are truly hyperactive. The term is used very freely, and in common use its true medical definition is distorted. In fact hyperactivity—or hyperkinesis—is part of the clinical picture known as Minimal Brain Dysfunction (MBD) and is a specific condition which makes a child incapable of being quiet and still for more than a few moments. Hyperactivity may be due to late or faulty development of the brain centers which filter incoming stimuli—things that the child sees, hears, smells, touches, or tastes—and enable the child to react appropriately to these stimuli.

Sometimes children who are either neglected or raised in an over-permissive environment exhibit behavior that closely mimics hyperactivity. These children may have normally developed brain centers, but may have been deprived of the social training that teaches children to control their behavior.

SIGNS AND SYMPTOMS

An extremely hyperactive child is constantly in physical motion. The child cannot sit still (for instance, to listen to a story or watch television) for more than a few seconds or minutes. The child's behavior may be annoying or destructive, but it's not motivated by malice; the child is not deliberately misbehaving—he or she cannot control the hyperactive behavior. An experienced pediatrician or neurologist (a specialist in nervous system disorders) may be able to recognize a severely overactive child at a glance. Many cases, however, are more difficult to pinpoint, and it may require a number of professionals to confirm the diagnosis.

HOME CARE

Until the hyperactive child has been professionally evaluated and diagnosed, home treatment cannot be undertaken. Once the diagnosis is confirmed, the family of the hyperactive child is given specific recommendations tailored to the child's needs. Removing from the child's diet foods that contain artificial colorings, flavorings, or preservatives is believed by some specialists to lessen the incidence of hyperactive behavior. However, others feel that the special attention given to a child whose diet is being controlled, not the diet itself, probably accounts for any improvement in behavior. Ask your doctor before you initiate any changes at home.

PRECAUTIONS

● True hyperactivity is present from infancy. If your normally active child is over two years old and suddenly becomes overactive, look for clues in the child's environment. ● Never accept a diagnosis of hyperkinesis from anyone but a trained, skilled, and experienced professional. ● Remember that an accurate diagnosis usually requires a team approach involving all those who care for the child—parents, teachers, doctors, and other professionals. ● Don't mistake ordinary misbehavior for hyperactivity; if a child is overactive with one family member but not with the others, the child is not hyperactive.

MEDICAL TREATMENT

A child suspected of hyperkinesis must have a complete medical examination, including vision and hearing tests. The doctor will take a detailed account of the child's medical background, evaluate school reports, and usually recommend a series of tests that are carried out by a psychologist. The doctor may also try various medications. Among the medications that may be given are drugs such as dextroamphetamine, methylphenidate, or permoline. Both you and the child's teachers will be asked to keep the doctor informed of changes in the child's behavior once a program of treatment is established. The hyperkinetic child may need special educational placement; also, because hyperkinetic children often have emotional problems resulting from poor social relationships at home and at school, counseling may be indicated.

Related topic:

Dyslexia

Hyperventilation

SYMPTOMS
Feeling of breathing difficulty, when the child is actually getting many full breaths of air
Tingling or numbness in hands and feet
Muscle spasms
Fainting

HOME CARE
Remain calm and reassure the child.

Have the child breathe into a paper bag placed loosely over the mouth and nose.

PRECAUTION

☐ Rapid, deep breathing that causes fainting has become a party stunt in some circles. Discourage this kind of game.

Hyperventilation is a breathing difficulty in which too-rapid or too-deep breathing causes a marked loss of carbon dioxide from the blood. There are many physical illnesses that cause difficulty in breathing, including asthma, bronchiolitis, diphtheria, colds, croup, hay fever, and pneumonia. Hyperventilation, however, is *not* a physical illness at all. It causes the sensation of difficult breathing or air hunger, but there is no physical condition preventing the person from taking in or letting out air.

Hyperventilation is common in older children, teenagers, and young adults. The person complains, often bitterly or fearfully, of being unable to "get enough air," while at the same time taking deep breaths in and out with no visible difficulty. The rate of breathing may be rapid or normal. There is no abnormal sound to the breathing as in croup, bronchitis, or asthma. Temperature and color are both normal, and there is no cough. In fact, the deep breathing can be recognized as sighing, one sigh right after another, lasting for minutes or hours. The cause is essentially the same as that of sighing: nervous tension, fear, anxiety, or depression.

If hyperventilation continues long enough, the person will experience tingling and numbness in the hands and feet, followed by spasms of the muscles that control the hands, fingers, ankles, and toes. This is caused by breathing out too much carbon dioxide. If hyperventilation continues long enough, fainting can occur. Unconsciousness temporarily cures the condition, and the person recovers.

SIGNS AND SYMPTOMS

Close observation will determine if your child is having trouble breathing or if the child is actually getting many full breaths of air in and out. Hyperventilation syndrome is never accompanied by cough or fever. There is no abnormal sound during breathing. Children who tend to hyperventilate may have repeated attacks.

HOME CARE

It is important to remain calm and to reassure the child. Have your child breathe into a large paper bag held loosely over the mouth and nose. This will allow the child to rebreathe the exhaled carbon dioxide. Look for such causes as intolerable pressures or anxieties in the child's surroundings—at home, at school, or in relationships with friends.

PRECAUTION

● Hyperventilation syndrome can develop as a result of rapid, prolonged, forced deep breathing, which has become a party stunt in some circles. Encourage other kinds of games.

MEDICAL TREATMENT

A doctor will treat an acute attack the same as you would at home. Treatment of the underlying causes of hyperventilation depends upon investigating and analyzing possible sources of stress and emotional upset in your child. Psychiatric counseling may be advised for severe cases.

Related topics:

Asthma
Bronchiolitis
Bronchitis
Common cold
Croup
Diphtheria
Fainting
Hay fever
Pneumonia
Shortness of
    breath

Impetigo

SYMPTOMS   Blisters containing thin, yellow pus
Broken blisters developing into open,
  weeping sores
Pus dries to consistency of hardened
  honey

HOME CARE   A mild case of impetigo can be treated by scrubbing the crusts of the sores with soap and water, then applying a nonprescription antibiotic ointment at intervals.

Cover the affected area with gauze; this will help keep the child from scratching and spreading the condition.

PRECAUTIONS

☐ Impetigo is highly contagious (catching).

☐ Minor scratches and scrapes on the skin may invite impetigo; to avoid infection, clean such minor wounds with soap and water and cover them with a sterile bandage.

☐ Keep an infected child's clothes and linens separate from those used by other family members; this will help prevent the disease from spreading. Launder the child's clothes frequently.

☐ If home treatment for impetigo is effective, continue it until all the sores are completely healed; it can take a long time to eliminate the condition.

☐ See the doctor if home treatment is not effective.

A mild case of impetigo can be treated by scrubbing the crusts with soap and water and then applying an antibiotic ointment several times a day.

Impetigo is a highly contagious infection of the outer layers of the skin. It's caused by staphylococcus and/or streptococcus bacteria. The germs are transmitted by direct contact when the child touches either an infected person or something that person has been using—for example, clothing, towels, or toys. The condition appears two to five days after the child has been exposed to the germs.

SIGNS AND SYMPTOMS

Impetigo typically appears as a fragile blister containing thin, yellow pus. The initial sore often occurs at a point where the skin has been injured or irritated by an insect bite, a scrape, or a skin condition. If the child picks at the nose, the blister may appear in that area. The blister breaks easily, leaving an open, weeping sore that increases in size. The discharge hardens into a yellow crust or scab that looks like hardened honey. Impetigo spreads rapidly and the child can aggravate this by scratching a sore and transferring the discharge on his or her hands to other parts of the body. The infecting bacteria can only be identified through laboratory tests. If the culprit is the streptococcus bacterium, the doctor will watch for the possible development of a kidney condition known as glomerulonephritis.

HOME CARE

If only a few small areas are involved, scrub the crusts of the sores with soap and water. (Streptococcal and staphylococcal infections thrive under the crusts.) Apply a nonprescription antibiotic ointment several times a day. Cover the sores with gauze to keep the ointment in place and to discourage the child from scratching and spreading the disease.

PRECAUTIONS

● To prevent impetigo, wash minor scratches and scrapes with soap and water and cover with a sterile bandage.
● Impetigo is highly contagious; if your child has impetigo, watch the rest of the family carefully for signs of the disease and treat cases promptly if they occur.
● Keep the washcloth, towel, and clothing used by the child separate from items used by other family members. This will reduce the chance of the disease spreading. ● Launder the infected child's clothing and linens frequently; ordinary laundering sterilizes adequately. ● If home treatment for impetigo is effective, do not discontinue the treatment until the sores are completely healed and the skin is smooth; it can take a long time to clear the condition completely. ● If home treatment doesn't seem to be working within four or five days or if the sores continue to spread or multiply, see your doctor.

MEDICAL TREATMENT

The doctor may culture the sores and, if steptococcal infection is present, prescribe a ten- to 14-day course of penicillin medication. In the case of staphylococcal infection, tests may be required to determine the most effective antibiotic medication.

Related topics:

Eczema
Insect bites
Nephritis
Poison ivy
Rash
Scrapes

Infectious mononucleosis

SYMPTOMS
General weakness and bodily discomfort
Sore throat
Pus on tonsils
Prolonged fever
Swelling of lymph glands
Prolonged fatigue
Mottled red rash

HOME CARE
Rest, aspirin or acetaminophen, and a general diet as tolerated are necessary.

If your doctor finds that the child's spleen is enlarged, the child's activities should be restricted.

PRECAUTIONS

☐ If a child who is being treated with antibiotics for a strep throat does not respond to the medication within 24 to 48 hours, inform the doctor; the child may have mono in addition.

☐ Do not allow a child who has had mono to return to school or work until weakness and fatigue disappear.

☐ Do not allow a child with an enlarged spleen to take part in contact sports or other strenuous activity until the spleen returns to its normal size.

Swollen lymph glands in the neck are one of the common symptoms of infectious mononucleosis.

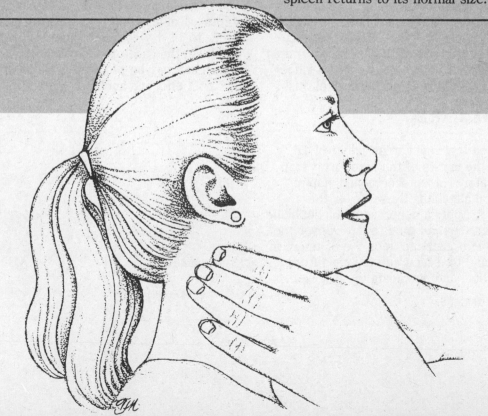

Infectious mononucleosis—often called "mono"—is a fairly common contagious disease. It's caused by the Epstein-Barr (EB) virus and is transmitted by secretions from the nose and throat—which is why it's also commonly known as the "kissing disease." Mono can occur at any age from infancy on, but is most often seen among young people of high school or college age. The disease appears one to six weeks after exposure to the virus, and one attack generally makes a person immune to (able to resist) further bouts.

SIGNS AND SYMPTOMS

The usual symptoms of mono are general weakness and bodily discomfort accompanied by sore throat (often with pus on the tonsils), prolonged fever, and swelling of the lymph glands. These glands may be slightly tender. In 10 to 20 percent of cases, mono produces a mottled red rash, especially on the trunk of the body. The spleen may be enlarged. A person with mono can be acutely ill for weeks, and fatigue and weakness can continue for months. In most teenagers, the acute illness lasts about two weeks and complete recovery occurs within four to six weeks.

Because mono symptoms are also typical of other diseases, it's rarely possible to make an accurate diagnosis without laboratory tests. Symptoms such as fever, severe sore throat, swollen lymph glands in the neck, and rash can also be signs of a strep infection, viral pharyngitis, or diphtheria. If these symptoms don't improve with time or treatment, the doctor will suspect mono. In some cases of mono a positive culture will give a diagnosis of strep throat, and mono is not diagnosed until the strep infection fails to respond to treatment.

The most common laboratory test for mono is a blood test called "mono spot test." A positive test confirms the diagnosis of mono. However, often the mono spot does not become positive until two to three weeks into the disease.

HOME CARE

A child with mono needs rest, aspirin or acetaminophen, and a general diet as tolerated. Although mono is contagious, it's not necessary to isolate the child and it's unlikely that other family members will contract the disease. The child can return to school as soon as the weakness and fatigue disappear and the child feels well enough. If the spleen is enlarged, however, the child's activity should be restricted. An enlarged spleen protrudes beneath the ribs, which normally protect it, and is susceptible to injury or rupture. In this situation, the child should not take part in contact sports or other energetic activity until the spleen returns to its normal size; this can take weeks or months.

PRECAUTIONS

● If your child is being treated with antibiotics for a strep infection but the condition does not improve within 24 to 48 hours of starting the medication, inform your doctor. The doctor will order tests for mono. ● If the child's spleen is enlarged, contact sports and other strenuous activity should be avoided.

MEDICAL TREATMENT

Your doctor will examine the child thoroughly, paying special attention to the lymph nodes, liver, and spleen. The doctor will also take a throat culture. If the throat culture reveals a strep infection, the child will be given penicillin or another antibiotic. Although most cases of mono can be treated at home with proper rest, diet, and a medication such as aspirin or acetaminophen, some severe cases require hospitalization. This would be the case where the child needed to be given fluids intravenously or other types of supportive care.

Related topics:

Diphtheria
Glands, swollen
G6PD deficiency
Hepatitis
Sore throat
Strep throat

Influenza

SYMPTOMS
Sudden chills
Sharp rise in body temperature
Flushing
Headache
Sore throat
Cough
Pain in back and limbs
Vomiting and diarrhea (in young children)

HOME CARE

Bed rest is necessary while the fever is high.

Give acetaminophen, **not aspirin**, for fever and pain.

Have the child drink plenty of fluids.

Isolate the child from other family members.

Keep the child home from school or work until he or she is completely well.

PRECAUTIONS

☐ Because influenza is one of the diseases associated with Reye's syndrome, do not give aspirin; use acetaminophen instead.

☐ Do not assume that the child is better because the fever goes away for a day; it will probably recur.

☐ Watch for complications and inform the doctor if they occur.

☐ Do not allow the child to resume everyday activities until the temperature has been normal for at least two days.

☐ Influenza vaccines are not generally recommended for children who do not fall into a "high risk" category.

A child with any upper respiratory viral infection will probably be described as having the "flu," particularly if the child also has chills, fever, cough, and muscle aches. However, true influenza is a specific, highly contagious (catching) respiratory infection that occurs in epidemics in which large numbers of persons in a community get the disease within a short period of time. It is caused by the influenza A or influenza B virus and is transmitted by droplets from nose and throat discharges of persons who have the disease. Influenza has a short incubation period—the time it takes for symptoms to develop once a person has been exposed to the virus—of one to three days and is contagious for seven days starting even before symptoms appear.

SIGNS AND SYMPTOMS

The symptoms of influenza are sudden chills, a sharp rise in body temperature to 102°F to 106°F, flushing, headache, sore throat, a hacking cough, redness of the eyes, and pains in the back and limbs. Young children may vomit and have diarrhea. Fever lasts three to four days and is followed by days of weakness and fatigue during which the child is susceptible to other illnesses.

Secondary bacterial complications are responsible for many of the serious outcomes of flu, and their presence is suggested by: the return of high fever after the child's temperature has been normal for three or four days; progressive worsening of the cough, changing from dry and hacking to loose and productive; formation of pus in the eyes; rapid breathing and shortness of breath beyond that expected from the fever; severe earache; stiff neck; confusion; and extreme weakness, exhaustion, or collapse.

In isolated cases, flu cannot be diagnosed with certainty by physical exam. During an epidemic, the disease is diagnosed by similarity to other cases.

HOME CARE

The prescription for home care is: bed rest during the height of the fever and acetaminophen, **not aspirin**, for fever and pains. You should encourage the child to drink a lot of fluids. Keep the child isolated from the rest of the family, and don't let the child return to school or work until fully recovered. This will lessen the child's chances of getting another disease while his or her resistance is lowered by the influenza.

PRECAUTIONS

● Reye's syndrome has been linked to the use of aspirin during influenza. Although a cause-and-effect relationship has not been established, aspirin should not be given if your child is suspected of having influenza. Watch for signs of complications and report them to your doctor. ● If there are no complications, the fever accompanying influenza often peaks in two cycles. The child's temperature is elevated for a day or two, normal for a day, then elevated for a day or two. Do not misinterpret 24 hours of normal temperature as a "cure," and do not allow your child to resume activities until the temperature is normal for two or more days.

MEDICAL TREATMENT

If there are no complications, the doctor will tell you to continue with the home treatment described above. If complications occur, cultures, blood tests, antibiotics, and hospitalization may be required.

Vaccines to prevent influenza are not very helpful for children. The influenza viruses have a number of different strains that change their structures from year to year. Therefore, last year's vaccine may be useless against this year's virus. Moreover, reactions to influenza vaccines in children are frequent, although these reactions are rarely serious. At the moment, medical experts advise that only children at special risk from influenza should be immunized annually. The conditions that constitute "special risks" are: rheumatic heart disease, congenital and hypertensive heart disease, cystic fibrosis, severe asthma, tuberculosis, nephrosis, chronic nephritis, chronic diseases of the nervous system, and diabetes.

Related topics:

Asthma
Common cold
Coughs
Cystic fibrosis
Diabetes mellitus
Fever
Nephritis
Reye's syndrome

Ingrown toenails

SYMPTOMS

Swollen, red, and painful area near toenail
Thin, watery pus from the infected area
Raw, red tissue covering part of the nail

HOME CARE

Soak the toe frequently in warm water.

If possible, gently cut out the ingrown part of the nail.

If the ingrown spur cannot be removed, soak the bandaged foot in a solution of Epsom salts and encase the foot, complete with bandage, in plastic wrap or a plastic bag.

In the case of an infant, do not try to remove the ingrown nail, but wipe the toe several times daily with rubbing alcohol, then soak in warm water.

Any time home treatment does not work, consult the doctor.

PRECAUTIONS

☐ Be sure your child always wears well-fitting shoes; if the shoes are too small or too pointed they can cause ingrown toenails.

☐ Show your child how to trim the toenails correctly.

In most cases, correct trimming of toenails—straight across—will prevent ingrown nails.

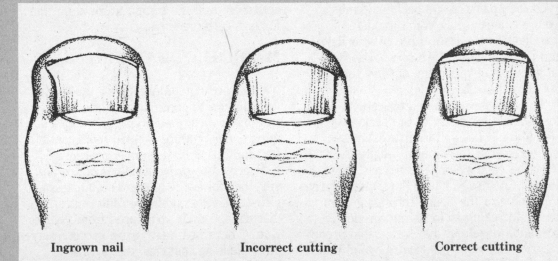

Ingrown nail   Incorrect cutting   Correct cutting

Sometimes the corners and edges of toenails break the skin surrounding the nail. Once the skin is broken, infection can set in. The infection causes the tissues to swell, forcing the corner of the nail further into the toe. This condition is known as ingrown toenail, and it cannot heal as long as the nail remains within the tissues.

The initial wound may be caused by injury to the toe as a result of being stepped on or being squeezed by ill-fitting shoes. Or the nail may have been trimmed to leave a sharp spur at the corner; this spur pierces the skin as the nail grows.

Most cases of ingrown toenails involve the big toes of older children; however, any toe can be involved, at any age. A baby can develop an ingrown toenail by digging bare toes into the crib mattress or into another surface onto which he or she has been placed face down.

SIGNS AND SYMPTOMS

The toe becomes red, painful, and tender to the touch. The wound produces a thin, watery pus that works its way under the nail. The tenderness, redness, pain, and swelling gradually get worse, eventually involving one entire side of a toenail. Often the nail becomes partly covered by raw, red tissue and a wet crust.

HOME CARE

If you catch it early, you can treat an ingrown toenail successfully by gently cutting out the spur or the ingrown corner of the nail, and then frequently soaking the toe in warm water for long periods. Even if the toe is so tender to the touch that you cannot remove the embedded nail, prolonged soaking in a strong Epsom salts solution (one cup to one quart of water) may cure the condition. Cover the lower foot and toe with a bandage or cloth and soak both foot and bandage thoroughly in the solution. Then cover the dripping foot with plastic wrap or encase the foot in a plastic bag. In this manner the nail can soak for hours with little effort on your part. Because of the delicacy of the nails

involved, the ingrown toenail of an infant can often be cured by wiping the area several times a day with rubbing alcohol, and then soaking the toe in clear warm water.

PRECAUTIONS

● If your child repeatedly develops ingrown toenails check his or her shoes; they may be too small or too pointed.
● Teach your child to trim the toenails straight across without leaving sharp spurs that may cause problems. ● An infection near the nail that lasts for more than a few days is probably an ingrown nail.

MEDICAL TREATMENT

If an ingrown toenail doesn't clear up with home treatment, your doctor can remove the embedded piece of nail. If the toe is very painful, the doctor may apply a local anesthetic before removing the ingrown area of the nail. If ingrown toenails occur frequently your doctor may suggest minor surgery to narrow the nail and make ingrowing less likely.

Insect bites and stings

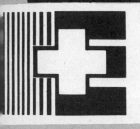

EMERGENCY SYMPTOM

Allergic reaction:
  Hives
  Difficult breathing

EMERGENCY TREATMENT

Take the child to the nearest emergency room if he or she has an allergic reaction.

SYMPTOMS

Swelling
Itching
Stinger left in wound (honeybee)
Small, dark bumps (ticks)

HOME CARE

Relieve swelling by applying ice.

Apply calamine lotion to relieve itching.

Give a nonprescription antihistamine to relieve itching and swelling.

If a tick is still attached to the skin, touch the protruding tip of the insect with the still-hot tip of a burned match; the tick will usually fall off the skin.

PRECAUTIONS

☐ Protect children with appropriate clothing and insect repellents. Use mosquito netting if necessary.

☐ If your child is allergic to certain insect bites or stings, make sure your doctor tells you what to do if the child is bitten or stung.

☐ Find out which insects are common in your neighborhood and how to protect your child against them.

☐ If your child develops hives or breathing difficulties after being bitten or stung by a scorpion, black widow spider, bee, wasp, or hornet, take the child to the nearest emergency room.

The bites and stings of most insects are minor annoyances to most children. Usually, the only common complication is impetigo, a highly contagious skin infection which tends to occur at a point where the skin is already broken—for instance, where a child has scratched the site of an insect bite.

Some insect bites, however, can cause serious conditions.
• Black widow spiders and scorpions can inject a venom (poisonous secretion) powerful enough to kill.
• The brown recluse spider bite can cause a large open ulcer and fever.
• Female wood tick bites can cause paralysis and death.

Among diseases transmitted by insect bites are: Rocky Mountain spotted fever, Colorado tick fever, and tularemia (wood ticks); rickettsialpox (mouse mites); viral encephalitis (mosquitoes); and typhus (red mites, lice, and rat fleas).

Some people are allergic to the venom contained in the stings of bees, wasps, hornets, and yellow jackets, and can suffer a severe reaction if stung. This reaction can take the form of generalized hives, asthma, or circulatory collapse (insufficient blood pressure to maintain circulation of the blood), and can even lead to death.

Some children become allergic to the bites of mosquitoes, stable flies, fleas, and lice, but an allergic reaction to the bite of one of these is usually less severe than that caused by stinging insects.

SIGNS AND SYMPTOMS

Flying insects usually bite only exposed areas of the skin. Crawling insects bite anywhere, and often in groups. Flea bites tend to be concentrated on the ankles and lower legs. Bedbugs often leave three to five bites an inch or two apart and arranged in a fairly straight line. Honeybees leave the stinger in the wound; bumblebees and other stinging insects do not. Ticks remain attached to the skin for long periods while they suck blood and, when engorged with blood, resemble small plump raisins.

HOME CARE

In most instances, insect bites can be treated by applying ice for a few minutes and then applying calamine lotion. A nonprescription antihistamine taken by mouth should relieve the itching and reduce the swelling. For a tick, the still-hot tip of a burned-out match touched to the protruding tip of the biting insect will usually cause the tick to fall off the skin without leaving the head in the wound.

PRECAUTIONS

● Protect children with proper clothing, mosquito netting, and insect repellents.
● Learn to recognize the insects in your locale and to know their characteristics.
● If your child develops hives or difficulty with breathing, speaking, or swallowing after being bitten by a scorpion or black widow spider or stung by a bee, a wasp, or a hornet, take the child immediately to the nearest emergency room.

MEDICAL TREATMENT

If the child has an allergic reaction to an insect bite or sting, the doctor will probably prescribe epinephrine, antihistamines, or steroids to inhibit the reaction. The doctor may advise that the allergic child be given a series of injections to reduce his or her sensitivity to the insect in question. The doctor may also teach you or the child how to treat a bite or sting at home.

In the case of scorpion and black widow spider bites, the doctor will give the child an antidote—or antivenom—that counteracts the effects of the poisonous venom. Steroid medications are also prescribed for these bites and the bites of the brown recluse spider.

Related topics:

Asthma
Encephalitis
Hives
Impetigo
Rocky Mountain
   spotted fever

229

Jaundice in newborns

SYMPTOM Yellow tinge to the skin and the whites of the eyes

HOME CARE Watch your newborn baby closely for signs of jaundice in the first week after the baby goes home from the hospital. Inform the doctor if you suspect jaundice.

PRECAUTIONS

☐ Many newborns develop a normal jaundice in the first week of life; however, jaundice that develops in the first 24 hours after birth is not normal.

☐ If the baby develops jaundice—or jaundice worsens—after the baby comes home, consult your doctor.

☐ Consult the doctor immediately if your jaundiced baby is nursing poorly, seems excessively drowsy, or is fevered or irritable.

☐ If your baby develops jaundice, follow your doctor's instructions exactly.

Jaundice in newborns can be treated by exposing the baby to ultraviolet light under a doctor's supervision.

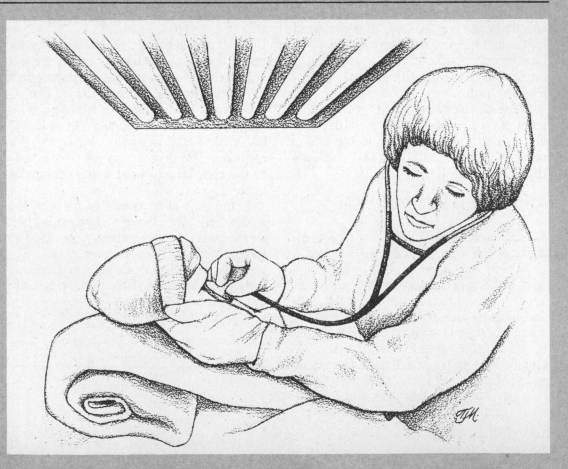

The liver transforms a substance known as bilirubin, released when old blood cells are replaced by new cells, into bile. The bile is then passed into the intestine. When damage to the liver prevents or slows down this process, bilirubin accumulates in the body and jaundice results.

Sixty percent of full-term infants and 80 percent of premature babies develop a normal jaundice during the first week of life. This occurs because of the rapid destruction of the excess number of red blood cells with which all healthy babies are born. The jaundice usually begins in the second or third day of life and disappears between the fifth and tenth day. With rare exceptions, this jaundice is harmless. Its major importance is the difficulty distinguishing it from abnormal jaundice.

The two most frequent causes of abnormal jaundice in the newborn are blood poisoning and erythroblastosis fetalis. Blood poisoning, a generalized infection caused by bacteria or viruses, causes jaundice in the newborn by destroying red blood cells and injuring the liver. Erythroblastosis fetalis is due to an incompatability between the child's blood and that of the mother. The mismatch may be in the Rh factor (for example, when the mother is Rh-negative but the infant is Rh-positive), in the ABO factors (when the mother's blood is type O but the baby's is type A or B), or in rarer blood factors. Because of the incompatability, the mother's blood forms antibodies (protective substances that form to fight off disease or anything the body interprets as an attacking organism). These antibodies rapidly destroy the infant's red blood cells.

Breast-fed newborns may also develop jaundice because a substance in the mother's milk interferes with the proper function of the baby's liver. This form of jaundice by itself usually is harmless. There are many other causes of jaundice in the newborn, including certain forms of anemia, hepatitis, and German measles, but jaundice due to these causes is rare.

Because either erythroblastosis fetalis or blood poisoning can be fatal to newborn babies if not treated immediately, a doctor's diagnosis must be made promptly. Other forms of jaundice can also be serious if the bilirubin in the blood exceeds a safe level. If jaundice is suspected, a doctor must monitor the bilirubin level closely.

SIGNS AND SYMPTOMS

The condition is recognized by a yellow tinge to the skin and the whites of the eyes. To judge the yellowness of the skin and eyes accurately, observe the baby in natural light. (Artificial light obscures the true color.) If you suspect jaundice, inform the doctor at once.

HOME CARE

The parents of a newborn should watch carefully for the development of jaundice in the first week of the child's life at home. If jaundice develops, a doctor should see the child promptly.

PRECAUTIONS

● Jaundice in the first 24 hours of life is abnormal. Because a newborn infant's nervous system is especially susceptible to permanent damage, jaundice during the first days of life has special significance. ● Jaundice that develops or worsens after a baby leaves the hospital should be reported to your doctor. ● Poor nursing, excessive drowsiness, irritability, and fever in a jaundiced baby should be reported to the doctor immediately. ● If your infant develops jaundice, follow your physician's directions exactly.

MEDICAL TREATMENT

Blood tests and cultures are used to identify the cause of the jaundice and to chart the progress of the condition. To lower the bilirubin level, your doctor may expose the baby to ultraviolet light or replace the infant's blood with that of a donor.

Related topics:

Blood poisoning
G6PD deficiency
Jaundice in children

Jaundice in children

SYMPTOM   Yellowing of skin and whites of eyes

HOME CARE   Home treatment cannot be undertaken until an accurate diagnosis has been made.

PRECAUTION

- [ ] Jaundice caused by a drug will disappear when the child is taken off the particular medication. All other types of jaundice in children are potentially serious and require prompt medical attention.

A yellow-gold-orange color to the whites of the eyes may indicate jaundice.

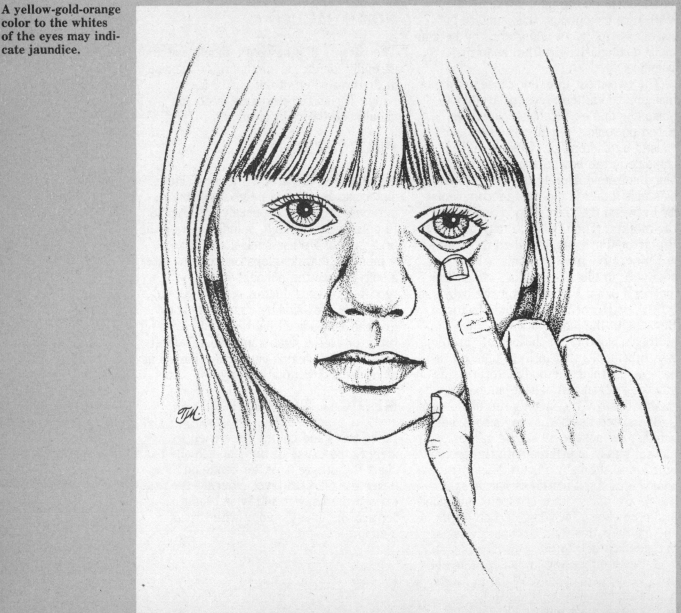

Jaundice is a yellowing of the skin and the whites of the eyes due to the accumulation in the body of a substance called bilirubin, which is released when old red blood cells are replaced by new ones. Bilirubin is excreted by the liver into the intestine as bile. Jaundice develops when the red blood cells are rapidly destroyed (as in sickle cell and other forms of anemia); when the liver cannot transform bilirubin into bile; or when bile cannot flow through the bile ducts into the intestine, for example, if the bile duct is blocked by stones, cysts, or a malformation.

Jaundice rarely occurs as a complication of a generalized infection, but it may be caused by some drugs and poisons. The usual cause of jaundice in children over one month of age is hepatitis, which damages the liver cells and interferes with the formation of bile.

SIGNS AND SYMPTOMS

The yellow-gold-orange color of the skin and whites of the eyes suggests jaundice. When a child has jaundice, all of the body fluids are stained; the tears are yellow, and the urine is dark orange. However, the diagnosis can be exceedingly complex and depends upon laboratory tests.

HOME CARE

Only after a clear diagnosis has been made can anything be done in the home.

PRECAUTION

● Jaundice caused by a certain medication will disappear when the child is taken off the medication. Other causes of jaundice in children are potentially serious and hard to diagnose. They all require a doctor's attention.

MEDICAL TREATMENT

A child suspected of having jaundice will require laboratory tests to define the reason for the jaundice. Hospitalization is sometimes required.

Related topics:

Anemia
G6PD deficiency
Hepatitis
Jaundice in
   newborns
Sickle cell anemia

Knee pains

SYMPTOMS   Tenderness or pain
Swelling
Difficulty in straightening the leg

HOME CARE   Home care for knee pain usually involves limiting the child's activity. However, the extent of the limitation depends on what is causing the pain.

PRECAUTIONS

☐ If the child's knee is swollen, or if the child cannot straighten the leg, a doctor should be consulted. The child should be careful not to put weight on the knee until the doctor has diagnosed the cause of the swelling.

☐ Treatment for most types of knee pain involves limiting the child's activities.

☐ Note that knee pain may indicate a hip problem.

Because of its complexity, the kneecap is susceptible to a wide variety of injuries.

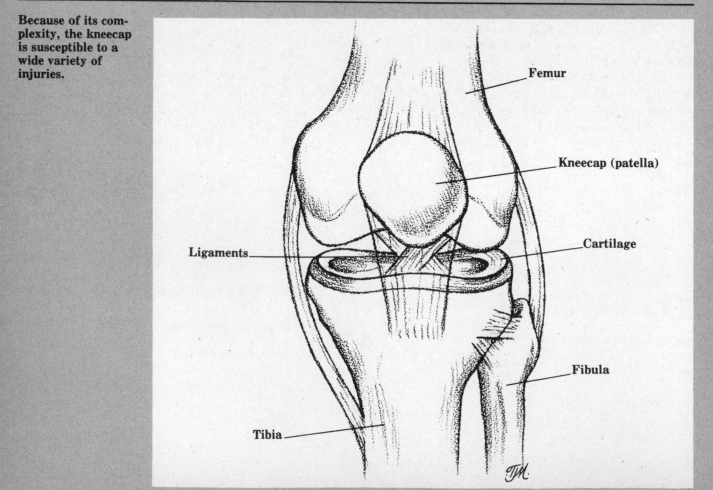

Femur

Kneecap (patella)

Ligaments

Cartilage

Fibula

Tibia

The knee is the most structurally complicated joint in the body. At the knee, four bones come together: the thigh bone (femur); the shin bone (tibia); the small outer bone of the lower leg (fibula); and the kneecap (patella). Internally, there are two crescent-shaped pieces of the soft tissue known as cartilage and two crossed ligaments, which are the tough connective tissues that hold bones together. Along with these structures the knee also contains all the cartilages and ligaments that are common to all joints. Because of this complexity, the knee is subject to a wide variety of injuries and complaints—ranging from rheumatoid arthritis (the form of arthritis that occurs most commonly in children) to puncture wounds occurring during play or sports activity. The knee can also be the seat of pain without being the site of the actual problem; a hip condition can show up as a pain in the knee.

Active adolescents are subject to Osgood-Schlatter's disease, a painful and tender swelling of the bony prominence (tibial tuberosity) at the upper end of the shin bone. When a youngster is kicking a ball or climbing, the large muscle at the front of the thigh pulls (via the kneecap) on this tuberosity; the action straightens the leg. If an injury cuts off the blood supply to it, the tuberosity becomes swollen and tender and straightening the leg causes pain.

SIGNS AND SYMPTOMS

Tenderness without swelling at the edges of the kneecap usually indicates that the cartilage on the underside of the kneecap has been bruised and softened (chondromalacia). Swelling of the knee joint—a fullness on both sides of the kneecap—indicates inflammation in the joint or an internal injury. Diagnosing the cause of knee pain depends upon the patient's history, the presence or absence of symptoms, and upon the location of pain.

HOME CARE

Treatment depends upon the problem, but usually—as in Osgood-Schlatter's dis-

ease—it involves limiting your child's activities. For two to four weeks, or until the swelling and tenderness are gone, the knee must not be bent; if the knee is not bent, it follows that it cannot be forcefully extended. From the child's point of view, this rules out two-legged stair climbing, bicycling, running, and jumping. An elastic knee support can be a helpful reminder that the knee needs rest during this period of healing. Treatment of chondromalacia involves the temporary limitation of strenuous activities like track, trampoline, football, and soccer.

PRECAUTIONS

● Swelling of the knee joint may be serious; it requires a doctor's attention. ● If one knee cannot be straightened to match the opposite knee, fluid (blood or the serum that remains after blood has formed a clot), or pus has probably accumulated at the joint; the knee should be seen by a doctor. ● The child should not put weight on a swollen knee until it has been seen by a doctor. ● Remember that knee pain may be a sign of a hip problem.

MEDICAL TREATMENT

The doctor will make a thorough, detailed examination of each part of the knee and leg and check the range of normal and abnormal movement. The doctor may order X rays of knees and hips. Sometimes, an arthrogram, which is an X ray taken after a special opaque fluid has been injected into the area, will be necessary. The opaque fluid, which can be seen on the X ray, outlines the interior of the joint. Swelling, accumulation of fluid, and distortion or injury of parts of the joint can then be seen. The doctor may also require tests of fluid drawn from the joint. Depending upon the diagnosis, treatment of knee pain may include bed rest, antibiotics, a cast, crutches, or surgery.

Related topics:

Arthritis
Hip problems
Puncture wounds
Sprains and
 dislocations

Laryngitis

SYMPTOMS Hoarseness
Dry, hacking cough
Scratchy throat
Low-grade fever

HOME CARE Use a vaporizer in the child's room.

Give the child warm drinks.

Give aspirin or acetaminophen to reduce fever and relieve pain.

A nonprescription expectorant cough remedy may relieve a troublesome cough.

A child with laryngitis should be discouraged from talking.

PRECAUTIONS

☐ If laryngitis is accompanied by breathing difficulty, the child should see a doctor.

☐ A cough along with climbing fever and breathing difficulty may indicate inflammation of the epiglottis. This is a **medical emergency**; take the child to the doctor at once.

☐ If laryngitis persists, the doctor may have the child see an ear, nose, and throat specialist.

Laryngitis can be relieved by using a vaporizer in the child's room to add moisture to the air.

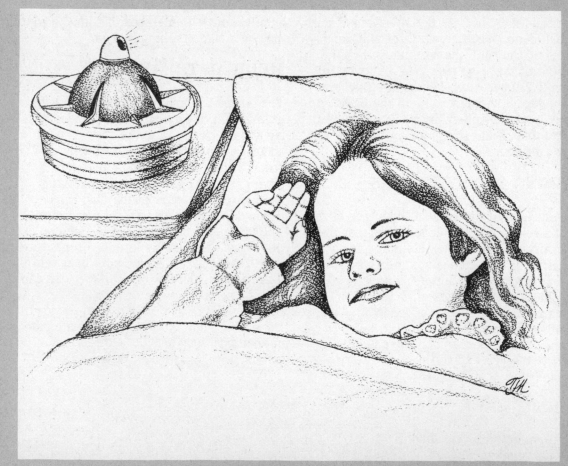

Laryngitis is an inflammation of the voice box (larynx). It is closely related to croup but, unlike croup, it isn't associated with breathing difficulties. Laryngitis is almost always due to a respiratory virus, and may last from a day to a couple of weeks.

SIGNS AND SYMPTOMS

Signs of laryngitis are hoarseness, dry hacking cough, and scratchy throat, sometimes accompanied by low-grade (101°F) fever. Diagnosis is based on the typical symptoms of hoarseness and dry cough unaccompanied by breathing difficulty.

HOME CARE

Use a vaporizer in the child's room. Give your child warm drinks. Encourage the child not to try to talk. Give aspirin or acetaminophen for fever or pain, and a nonprescription expectorant cough remedy for temporary relief of cough.

PRECAUTIONS

● If any breathing difficulty arises, notify a doctor. ● If a child has a climbing fever and difficulty breathing, he or she may have an inflammation of the epiglottis (the structure in the back of the throat that prevents food from entering the larynx and windpipe). **Inflammation of the epiglottis is a medical emergency; take your child to a doctor promptly.**

MEDICAL TREATMENT

The doctor will verify a diagnosis of laryngitis and rule out other conditions by physical examination of the child. The doctor may take a throat culture and a complete blood count. If laryngitis persists your doctor may X-ray the child's chest and neck or refer you to an ear, nose, and throat specialist.

Related topics:

Coughs
Croup
Hoarseness

Lazy eye

SYMPTOMS   Eyes are not parallel
The pupil of one eye is a different color
    from the other
Child has trouble judging distance
Child cocks head or moves face in effort
    to see clearly

HOME CARE   Home care cannot be undertaken until a
doctor has diagnosed the condition.

PRECAUTIONS

☐ A child under seven whose eyes are
   not parallel all or most of the time
   should be seen by a doctor.

☐ If lazy eye is not diagnosed and
   treated, the condition can become
   permanent.

☐ Have your child's eyes checked every
   year after the age of three or four.

Lazy eye may be corrected by patching or hindering the vision in the good eye, thus forcing the child to use the lazy eye.

238

A "lazy eye" is one in which the vision is poor because the child has suppressed the image received by that eye. Basically it's loss of vision from lack of use and is known technically as *amblyopia ex anopsia*. Most cases of lazy eye result from weakness of one or more of the six small muscles that move the eyeball. Eye muscle weaknesses can cause the eyes to turn in or out in relation to each other. This can lead to the child's seeing double. If a young child learns to ignore one of the double images, a loss of vision in the unused eye results. On the other hand, if the eye muscles are normal but the vision is poor in one eye, the young child may ignore the poor image received. This can result from marked near- or farsightedness, astigmatism, or other interference with vision in one eye. Such interference might be caused by congenital cataracts (clouding of the lens of the eye) or scars on the cornea (the transparent front part of the eye).

SIGNS AND SYMPTOMS

Lazy eye should be suspected when the eyes are not parallel all or most of the time, or are parallel less and less often in a child under seven years of age. See your doctor if: your child's eyes aren't parallel; the pupil of one eye is a different color from the other; your child is over two years old and has trouble seeing or judging distances when reaching for an object; or your child cocks his or her head to one side or turns his or her face to see better (the child may be compensating for double vision).

HOME CARE

No home treatment for lazy eye is advised until a doctor has diagnosed the condition.

PRECAUTIONS

● You should understand lazy eye so that if the condition occurs in your child you can catch it in time for treatment to be successful. ● Have your child's vision checked each year after age three or four. Lazy eye can be treated successfully in children up to age seven. If it's left untreated the condition may become permanent.

MEDICAL TREATMENT

Your doctor will inspect the insides and outsides of both eyes and test their movements in all directions. If the child is old enough to understand directions, the doctor can check the vision. Vision will be checked with a letter or picture chart. A younger child's vision should be checked by an ophthalmologist who can use a system that does not require the child to follow instructions.

Lazy eye is corrected either by patching the good eye or hindering the vision in the good eye with eyedrops or glasses. By blocking the good eye, the child is forced to use the lazy eye. As a final resort, surgery is sometimes necessary to correct the weak eye muscles.

Related topics:

Crossed eyes
Vision problems

239

Lead poisoning

SYMPTOMS
Poor appetite
Vomiting
Constipation
Irritability
Slow development
Aggressive behavior
Seizures
Personality changes
Clumsiness
Paleness
Fatigue
Weakness

HOME CARE
Discourage your child from putting non-food objects into his or her mouth and swallowing them.

If your home was built before 1950, have the paint and plaster tested for lead content.

Watch for changes in your child's behavior.

PRECAUTIONS

☐ Check your home and yard for possible sources of lead.

☐ Scraping, sanding, and other tasks involved in remodeling an older building may release lead into the air. Such a location should be avoided by infants, small children, and pregnant women until the work is completed.

☐ A person who works in an occupation that involves exposure to lead should take steps to avoid bringing lead-containing dust into his or her home on work clothes.

☐ Sources of lead poisoning can include artist's pigments, exhaust from cars, soil around buildings on which lead-based paint was used, city air, and improperly glazed pottery.

Lead is a heavy and dense metal that, in the human body, acts as a poison. Microscopic particles of lead can enter the body if a person swallows something that contains lead or inhales air contaminated with lead. The metal then accumulates in the blood and in body tissues. The most serious effects of lead poisoning are on the brain and nervous system. It can also damage the digestive system and the kidneys.

Before 1950, lead was an ingredient in paint, plaster, and putty, and most cases of lead poisoning occur when a small child eats fragments of lead-based paint that have peeled off a wall or have been left in the soil around a house. Today, house paint does not contain lead, but the metal is found in many other places. Some of the sources of lead poisoning include artist's pigments, exhaust from cars (some gasoline contains lead), soil around buildings that were once painted with lead-based paint, and the air in cities where lead may be used in industry and where the exhaust from many cars is concentrated. Also, lead is found in high-acid food and drinks (for example, orange or tomato juice) that have been stored in lead-containing pottery that was not properly glazed.

Lead poisoning can cause permanent damage to the brain, especially in cases where the symptoms are severe. Such damage may not occur if the problem is quickly identified and treated. However, a child who has had lead poisoning may take as long as a year to recover completely. Lead poisoning occurs most often in children under five. It is most dangerous if the child is under two years old.

SIGNS AND SYMPTOMS

The symptoms of lead poisoning vary with the age of the child and the amount of lead that is in the child's body, and are difficult to identify because they may build up gradually. Symptoms may include poor appetite, vomiting, constipation, extreme irritability, slow mental and/or physical development, aggressive behavior, seizures or convulsions, personality changes, clumsiness, or symptoms of anemia—

paleness, tiredness, weakness, breathlessness, and fainting. In severe cases, the child may become unconscious.

A routine blood or urine test will not detect lead poisoning. Before the problem can be diagnosed, the doctor must suspect that lead may be causing the child's symptoms. Specific laboratory tests are then done to measure lead content in the blood and urine.

HOME CARE

Parents should be alert for changes in a child's behavior. Also, watch to see if your child has a habit of putting nonfood objects in the mouth and swallowing them. This habit, which is called pica, can result in lead poisoning. Check your home and yard for sources of lead. If your house was built before 1950, the paint and plaster should be tested for lead content.

PRECAUTIONS

● If you are remodeling an older home, and especially if you are burning, scraping, or sanding paint and plaster inside the house, you may be releasing lead into the air. Pregnant women, infants, and small children should live elsewhere until the work is completed and the dust is cleaned up. ● Anyone who works in an occupation that involves exposure to lead should be especially careful about bringing home lead-containing dust on work clothes. Such occupations include lead smelting; storage battery manufacture, repair, and recycling; automobile assembly; automobile body and radiator repair; and others.

MEDICAL TREATMENT

Treatment for lead poisoning is called chelation therapy. The doctor prescribes a drug that combines with the lead in the body and draws it out of the body tissues where it is stored. The lead passes out of the body in the urine. A special diet or a change in diet may also be prescribed. Of course, this treatment will not be effective if the child is still taking in lead. The source of lead must be identified and removed first.

Related topics:

Anemia
Constipation
Convulsions
    without fever
Vomiting

Leukemia

SYMPTOMS
Paleness, weakness, or fatigue
Spontaneous bruising
Red, swollen, or bleeding gums
Persistent low-grade fever
Swollen lymph glands
Bone pain
Nosebleeds
Blood in urine or stool
Enlarged spleen or liver

HOME CARE Treatment for leukemia must always be regulated by a doctor.

PRECAUTION

☐ Many common diseases can imitate the symptoms of leukemia. Do not assume that a child has leukemia because he or she has one or more of the symptoms listed above. Have the doctor see the child to make a diagnosis.

Leukemia is cancer of the white blood cells. It can afflict children at any age, but most frequently occurs in children between three and four years old. Some 25 percent of leukemia cases are diagnosed during a routine physical examination before the child shows any symptoms of the disease. Symptoms similar to those of leukemia can also show up in a child suffering from some quite different (and often very simple) disorder. Although it's rare, leukemia is one of the four types of cancer most frequently seen in children. The disease can progress slowly or rapidly.

SIGNS AND SYMPTOMS

Typical symptoms of leukemia are: anemia, indicated by paleness, weakness, or fatigue; bruises that appear on the body for no apparent reason; swollen, red, and bleeding gums; a low-grade fever (101°F); swelling of the lymph glands (although the glands are neither red nor painful); bone pain; frequent, heavy nosebleeds; and the appearance of blood in the child's urine or stool.

Doctors may suspect leukemia when a physical examination reveals the above signs and symptoms along with an enlarged spleen or liver. Suspicion is strengthened by an abnormal blood count that reveals malignant (cancerous) white blood cells. The diagnosis is confirmed by an examination of bone marrow.

HOME CARE

No home care is advised until a doctor has diagnosed the condition. Leukemia is a serious condition that always requires close medical attention.

PRECAUTION

● Leukemia itself is fairly uncommon. However, many illnesses imitate leukemia, and these illnesses are *not* uncommon; among them are infectious mononucleosis, herpes infections of the mouth, vitamin C deficiency, rheumatic fever, rheumatoid arthritis, sickle cell anemia, and other diseases that cause spontaneous bruising. Do not jump to the conclusion that your child has leukemia because of the presence of any of the signs or symptoms described above. To ease your mind, have the doctor examine the child.

MEDICAL TREATMENT

Today, leukemia can be treated with a wide range of anti-cancer drugs. These drugs may result in long periods of remission (during which the illness gets no worse) and perhaps even cure. Pediatric cancer specialists (oncologists) decide on and supervise the treatment of leukemia. The survival rate of childhood leukemia has been rising over the last few years because of the use of new, complex, anti-cancer drugs.

Related topics:

Anemia
Arthritis
Bruises
Herpes simplex
Infectious
  mononucleosis
Sickle cell anemia

Measles

SYMPTOMS

Runny nose
Red eyes
Cough
Fever
Rash

HOME CARE

Give aspirin or acetaminophen for fever and a cough medication for severe cough.

Give the child extra liquids.

Bright light bothers (but does not injure) the eyes; keep the child out of brightly lit areas.

PRECAUTIONS

☐ A vaccine is available to prevent measles. Be sure that your child receives the proper vaccination.

☐ If your child has not been vaccinated, is under the age of three, and has been exposed to the measles virus, call the doctor.

☐ When a child has measles, the fever and cough should subside as the rash peaks. If they do not, watch for signs of complications.

☐ Earache during measles may indicate a middle ear infection. Consult the doctor.

Measles, which is also known as rubeola, is a highly contagious disease caused by a specific virus. It affects mainly the respiratory system, the eyes, and the skin, and is spread from person to person in airborne droplets of moisture from an infected person's respiratory system. The incubation period—the time it takes for symptoms to develop once the child has been exposed to the virus—is ten to 12 days. Measles can be passed to other people between the fifth day of the incubation period and the sixth day after the appearance of the rash that is characteristic of this disease.

Measles used to be one of the more dangerous of the childhood diseases, but it is relatively uncommon today because a vaccine is now available to protect against it. Most children are now vaccinated against measles by an injection given at around the age of 15 months. If a mother is immune to measles (because she has either had it or been vaccinated against it), her baby before birth will receive temporary protection against the disease. This protection lasts only three to six months after birth. The reason that vaccination is delayed until the baby is 15 months old (and not given as soon as the temporary immunity acquired from the mother wears off) is that the vaccination is not fully effective in a baby under 15 months. It's also fairly unlikely that a child under that age will be exposed to measles. It's important to note, however, that measles is dangerous in a child under three years old, and if an unvaccinated young child is exposed to the virus you should consult the doctor at once. Measles is also likely to be serious in children who have chronic (long-term) diseases.

Measles is considered dangerous mainly because of the complications it can cause, among them pneumonia (infection of the lungs), middle ear infection, and encephalitis (inflammation of the brain). Encephalitis occurs in only one or two out of every 1,000 cases of measles, and today death from measles or its complications is very rare.

SIGNS AND SYMPTOMS

The first symptoms of measles are a runny nose, reddish eyes, a cough, and fever. However, measles cannot be diagnosed during the earliest stages of the disease. After three or four days the fever rises to 104°F or 105°F, the cough worsens, and a heavy, splotchy, red rash develops on the neck and face. The rash quickly spreads over the trunk, arms, and legs. When the rash has erupted fully, the fever breaks, and the child gets better.

Just before the rash develops, spots that look like grains of salt surrounded by a red rim (Koplik's spots) appear inside the cheeks near the molars.

HOME CARE

With measles, prevention is better than cure; be sure that your child is properly vaccinated against this disease. A child with measles should be given aspirin or acetaminophen to reduce the fever and a cough suppressant to ease a severe cough. Keep the child away from bright light; light bothers the eyes but does not injure them. Have your child drink extra liquids if possible.

PRECAUTIONS

● If the fever and cough do not subside as the rash peaks, suspect complications. Watch for earaches, which signify middle ear infection. ● A newborn baby is immune to measles for three to six months only if the mother is immune. ● If a child under the age of three who has not been vaccinated against measles is exposed to the virus, call the doctor. ● Be sure your child receives the proper vaccination against measles.

MEDICAL TREATMENT

If your child has not been vaccinated and has been exposed to the virus, your doctor can give injections of gamma globulin within six or seven days of exposure to prevent or lessen the disease.

Related topics:

Earaches
Encephalitis
Immunizations
Pneumonia

Meningitis

SYMPTOMS
Fever
Stiff neck
Headache
Vomiting
Exhaustion or collapse
Convulsions

HOME CARE
Meningitis is a medical emergency. Do not attempt home care. Take the child to the doctor immediately.

PRECAUTIONS

☐ A child who is very weak, has a stiff neck, and fever should see a doctor immediately.

☐ Laboratory examination of spinal fluid is the only way to diagnose meningitis.

☐ Meningitis can follow an upper respiratory tract or middle ear infection, or certain types of skull fracture.

☐ The unnecessary use of antibiotics for an upper respiratory tract infection may mask the onset of meningitis.

☐ Meningitis is often contracted through direct contact with a carrier of the disease who appears quite healthy.

Meningitis is an infection of the meninges, the layers of tissue that cover and protect the brain and spinal cord. Most often, meningitis is caused by a viral infection. Bacterial meningitis is usually caused by one of three types of bacteria: meningococcus, pneumococcus, or *Hemophilus influenzae*. Meningitis is seldom spread by a person who has the disease. It's usually contracted by direct contact with a healthy person who is a carrier of the disease, or by inhaling airborne droplets of moisture from that person's respiratory system. (A carrier is a person who does not get sick with the disease but can pass it on to others.)

Meningitis may be a complication of a skull fracture if the fracture has extended into the nose, middle ear, or nasal sinus. Meningitis can also follow an upper respiratory tract infection or middle ear infection.

SIGNS AND SYMPTOMS

The characteristic symptoms of meningitis are moderate to high fever, headache, vomiting, exhaustion or collapse, convulsions, and a stiff neck—the child cannot touch his or her chin to the chest with the mouth closed. Purplish red spots (petechiae) scattered over the body together with fever may indicate one form of meningococcus infection. The diagnosis of meningitis can only be made with certainty by testing spinal fluid obtained by a spinal tap.

HOME CARE

Meningitis is a medical emergency in which hours, if not minutes, count. Do not attempt any home treatment. See a doctor at once.

PRECAUTIONS

● The unnecessary use of antibiotics for an upper respiratory tract infection may mask the onset of meningitis. ● A child who is suffering from exhaustion or extreme weakness, and who has fever and a stiff neck is in danger and should be taken to a medical facility immediately.

MEDICAL TREATMENT

Your doctor will take the child's complete medical history and perform a thorough examination. The doctor will then order a spinal tap. Spinal fluid will be examined for cells, bacteria, and abnormal chemical components. This is the only way to differentiate between meningitis and encephalitis (inflammation of the brain), which is also a life-threatening disease. The doctor will also require cultures of the spinal fluid, blood, and nose and throat mucus. Immediately following the spinal tap and cultures your doctor will administer intravenous fluids and antibiotics. If the infecting organism is unknown, the doctor may put the child on two antibiotics at the same time. If the meningitis turns out to be caused by a virus, no antibiotics will be used, since viruses do not respond to antibiotics.

If your child has been in contact with a person with meningococcal or *Hemophilus influenzae* meningitis, your doctor may choose to administer penicillin, sulfonamide, or rifampin by mouth to prevent your child from developing meningitis.

Vaccines against meningococci, pneumococci, and *Hemophilus influenzae* are available, but they are still in the experimental stage and not currently recommended for general use.

Related topics:

Bruises
Earaches
Encephalitis

Menstrual irregularities

SYMPTOMS
Severe abdominal pain or backache
Menstruation before age nine
Failure to menstruate by age 17
Long-term absence of menstruation
Excessive bleeding

HOME CARE
Give aspirin or acetaminophen for pain.

Encourage the girl to follow her normal schedule of activities during her period.

Consult her doctor in the situations listed above under "Symptoms."

PRECAUTIONS

☐ After a girl starts to menstruate it may take months or even years for her periods to become regular. This does not necessarily indicate a problem.

☐ Cramps and backaches may be related to tension or anxiety rather than to menstruation itself. However, these symptoms can also be caused by a hormone imbalance or an abnormal condition of the pelvis.

☐ Make sure that your daughter fully understands the process of menstruation.

Girls in the United States begin to menstruate sometime between nine and 17 years of age. The average age is 12. Following the onset of menstruation (menarche), it may take from several months to five years for the hormones to balance and produce regular menstrual periods. Menstrual irregularity during this time is to be expected and is not necessarily abnormal.

SIGNS AND SYMPTOMS

For about 5 percent of adolescent girls abdominal cramps and backaches—which last one or two days at the start of a menstrual period—may be severe enough to interfere with normal activities. In many instances cramps and backaches are related to emotional factors such as tension or anxiety. They also may be due to a hormonal imbalance or pelvic disease.

Because the range of normal is so broad, it is diffficult to judge whether a menstrual abnormality exists or not. Symptoms that warrant investigation are: menstruation before age nine or failure to menstruate by age 17; absence of menstrual periods for six months (or for one month in a sexually active teenager where the failure to menstruate may indicate pregnancy); repeated excessive bleeding; or pain severe enough to interfere with normal activity.

HOME CARE

Give aspirin or acetaminophen to relieve mild pain. Encourage your daughter to maintain her normal activities during her menstrual period.

PRECAUTIONS

● Explain the facts about menstruation to your preteen daughter; this way you can counteract any "old wives' tales" she may have heard from others, and prepare her for this important part of growing up.
● There are good books available (for both parents and teenagers) that can help explain the process of menstruation and provide accurate information.

MEDICAL TREATMENT

If a girl is having menstrual problems the doctor should conduct a complete physical examination, which includes a rectal and a limited pelvic examination. Chromosome and hormone studies may also be required. In some cases the doctor will order blood tests or tests of thyroid function. (The thyroid gland, located in front of the throat, regulates the body's temperature, energy production, growth, and fertility.) If the girl is sexually active and has missed a period, a pregnancy test will be called for.

Your doctor may well find no abnormality and no treatment will be necessary. In some cases, the doctor will prescribe hormone medications to be taken over a period of several months. In other cases an iron supplement or a thyroid medication may be prescribed.

Related topic:

Vaginal bleeding

Moles

SYMPTOM   Flat, dome-shaped, or protruding skin growths that can be up to a half-inch long and vary in color

HOME CARE   If a mole requires treatment of any kind it will be necessary to see a doctor.

PRECAUTIONS

☐ A doctor should see any mole that is bleeding or crusting, changing color, or growing rapidly. The doctor should also be consulted if a mole has been partly removed by accident, or if the color is extending into surrounding skin.

☐ Most moles are noncancerous. However, a type of mole known as pigmented nevus can become cancerous; this mole (unlike other types) is present at birth and is dark in color and very large.

☐ Moles cannot safely be burned off by the following methods: electrocautery, acids, dry ice, or liquid nitrogen. The doctor must remove them completely, if necessary, with a scalpel.

☐ No child is completely free of moles; some children develop many of them during childhood.

Moles are benign (noncancerous) growths on the skin. They can be flat, dome-shaped, or protruding. They vary in color from tan or brown to blue or black, and in size from one-sixteenth to one-half inch or larger. Moles are rarely present at birth; they develop during childhood. No child is totally free of moles, and some children develop hundreds of them.

It's very unlikely that any mole will become cancerous (malignant). However, one exception to this is a type of mole called a pigmented nevus. This mole, which is present at birth, is extremely large (several inches wide) and dark, and a mole of this type can become malignant.

SIGNS AND SYMPTOMS

Moles are easily recognizable, but if the doctor is in any doubt about a growth on the skin a laboratory examination of part of the growth may be necessary. Examination of an entire mole under the microscope may be needed.

HOME CARE

If a mole requires any kind of treatment, it will require medical, not home, care.

PRECAUTIONS

A mole should be seen by a doctor if: ● it has been partly removed by accident; ● it is bleeding or crusting; ● it is changing color or growing rapidly; ● if the pigment (color) is moving into the surrounding skin.

MEDICAL TREATMENT

If the mole shows any of the characteristics listed above under "Precautions," the doctor will remove the mole surgically. Any pigmented nevus probably should be surgically removed because of the possibility of a malignancy. Moles must be removed completely with a scalpel. The surgery will leave a scar of some sort. Moles cannot safely be burned off by a procedure called electrocautery, or by acids, dry ice, or liquid nitrogen. Moles are sometimes removed for cosmetic reasons.

Molluscum contagiosum

SYMPTOM Pimple-like skin eruptions that are plump and waxy in appearance and firm to the touch

HOME CARE Call the doctor for instructions about home care.

PRECAUTION

☐ Molluscum contagiosum spreads rapidly; to avoid spreading keep the infected child's clothing and linens separate from those of other family members. Launder the child's belongings frequently to kill the virus.

Molluscum contagiosum is a skin infection of plump, round eruptions with indentations in the centers.

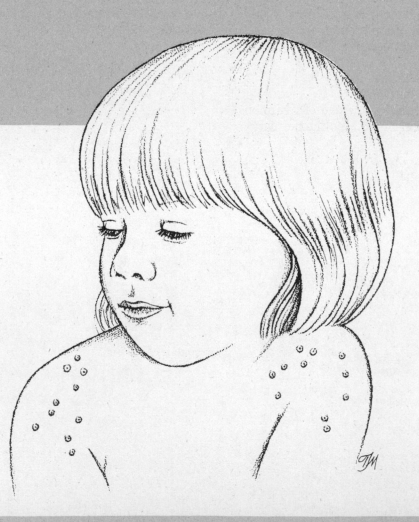

The condition known medically as molluscum contagiosum is often mistaken for an outbreak of warts or pimples. In fact, it is a common, chronic infection of the skin and it is caused by a specific virus.

The disease is spread by direct contact with an infected person, or by indirect contact with personal articles used by that person. The virus has a long incubation period (the time it takes for symptoms to develop once the child has been exposed to the virus)—two to seven weeks. Scratching can cause the eruptions, or mollusca, to become infected. Molluscum contagiosum has no other symptoms.

SIGNS AND SYMPTOMS

Each molluscum is a plump, round, slightly waxy looking "pimple" that grows to a diameter of one-quarter inch or more. It is firm to the touch. In the course of months, mollusca may spread and may number in the hundreds.

The diagnosis is based on the appearance of the pimple-like eruptions. The indentation in the center of each molluscum can easily be seen on close inspection in good light.

HOME CARE

Molluscum contagiosum requires medical treatment. Call the doctor, who will give directions for home care.

PRECAUTION

● The condition readily spreads among members of a family; keep the infected child's clothing, linen, and towels separate from those used by other family members. Ordinary laundering with soap or detergent kills the virus.

MEDICAL TREATMENT

The doctor will treat this condition by recommending a special cream to be applied to the mollusca and then buffed with a rough pad. The doctor will give specific instructions about this treatment. If this does not work, the doctor may use a pointed scalpel to open each molluscum and remove the hard, white, pearl-like center.

Motion sickness

SYMPTOMS
Nausea
Paleness or "green" tinge to skin
Excessive perspiration
Vomiting
Anxiety

HOME CARE Give the child an anti-nausea remedy recommended by the doctor. Give this medication an hour before a trip and then every four hours during the journey.

Keep the child cool.

Restrict the diet.

Have the child look out the window while traveling. Distract the child with a game during the trip.

PRECAUTIONS

☐ Some children are more susceptible than others to motion sickness.

☐ Motion sickness is not brought on by the child, and the child can't control it.

☐ Prolonged motion sickness can lead to severe vomiting and finally to dehydration, which is an emergency situation and requires hospital care.

☐ A child who is susceptible to motion sickness will have repeated attacks every time he or she travels.

Car, air, and sea sickness are all forms of motion sickness. Prolonged rhythmic motion up and down or from side to side will make most children nauseated, presumably because the movement affects the balance mechanism of the inner ears. Some children are more susceptible to motion sickness than others; young infants are apparently immune. Motion sickness is not deliberately brought on by the child, nor can the child control it. Susceptible children will have attacks over and over.

SIGNS AND SYMPTOMS

Motion sickness is fairly easy to recognize. A motion-sick child becomes nauseated, pale or "green," and anxious; the child may perspire and vomit.

HOME CARE

If your child suffers from motion sickness, ask your doctor to recommend an anti-nausea medication. Give your child an anti-nauseant by mouth one hour before the start of each trip, and then every four hours during the trip. Dimenhydrinate anti-nauseant tablets or liquid are highly effective and safe. It also helps to keep the child cool and on a light diet before and during the trip. Having the child look out the car window will often eliminate motion sickness. Distracting the child with a game can also be useful.

PRECAUTION

● Prolonged motion sickness (over hours) can eventually result in excessive vomiting and dehydration.

MEDICAL TREATMENT

Your doctor's treatment will be the same as your home treatment unless the child has become dehydrated. Dehydration requires hospital care during which the child is given fluids intravenously.

Related topics:

Dehydration
Vomiting

Mumps

SYMPTOMS
Low-grade fever
Loss of appetite
Headache
Swelling of the salivary glands

HOME CARE
The child with mumps needs rest. Give aspirin or acetaminophen for pain and fever.

Do not give the child spicy foods.

Isolate the child from other family members.

PRECAUTIONS

☐ Make sure that your child is vaccinated against mumps.

☐ One attack of mumps provides lifelong immunity. If the child has had mumps, but develops symptoms similar to those of mumps, the problem is some other disease of the salivary glands. Report the problem to the doctor.

☐ If mumps involves the ovaries or pancreas, the child will have abdominal pain. If the testes are involved, the testes will be swollen and tender.

☐ If a child who has not been vaccinated is exposed to mumps, he or she can receive the vaccine shortly after exposure to the disease to prevent becoming ill with mumps.

Mumps is caused by a virus that infects the salivary glands, particularly the parotid gland, which results in swelling of the face in front of the ear.

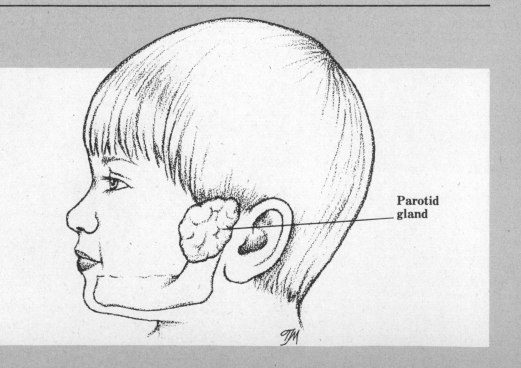

Parotid gland

Mumps is a moderately contagious infection caused by a specific virus which involves the salivary glands. It is contracted by contact with the saliva of an infected person. The incubation period—the time it takes for symptoms to develop once the child has been exposed to the virus—for mumps is 14 to 21 days, and the disease can be passed on any time from two or more days before symptoms appear until all symptoms have gone. One attack provides lifelong immunity; if a child has had mumps and subsequently develops similar symptoms, the problem is not mumps but some other disease of the salivary gland.

Complications of mumps include meningitis, encephalitis, permanent deafness, and orchitis (inflammation of the male sex glands called the testes). The disease may also involve the ovaries, the female sex glands, or cause an infection of the pancreas.

A vaccine is available to prevent mumps. It is usually given in combination with measles and rubella (German measles) vaccines during the child's second year at around 15 months of age. This vaccine is 95 percent effective in preventing mumps.

SIGNS AND SYMPTOMS

Typical symptoms include fever (low-grade—101°F—or as high as 105°F), loss of appetite, and headache. One or two days after the onset of these symptoms, one or more of the salivary glands become painfully swollen; the swelling lasts about a week.

The diagnosis of a typical case of mumps is obvious from the swelling of the parotid salivary gland that lies behind, below, and in front of the earlobe. Only a swelling of the parotid gland has the earlobe as its center. Other salivary glands, such as the salivary glands which lie under the edge of the jaw, may be swollen with or without swelling of the parotids. Swelling may occur on one or both sides of the face.

Accurately diagnosing mumps may be difficult if complications of mumps develop before, or sometimes even without, swelling of the salivary glands. If the pancreas or ovaries are involved, the child will have abdominal pain. If the testes are involved, they will be swollen and tender. Encephalitis has symptoms of stiff neck, headache, and fever. In the absence of swollen salivary glands, these other symptoms may be difficult to link with mumps.

HOME CARE

Rest and isolation are recommended until all symptoms have gone. Aspirin or acetaminophen may be given to reduce pain and fever. Avoid feeding the child spicy foods.

PRECAUTIONS

● Routine immunization against mumps is strongly advised. ● If a mother is immune to mumps (because she has had it or has been vaccinated against it), her baby acquires some temporary immunity before birth. This immunity lasts only until the infant is four to six months old. ● In an adult man, inflammation of the testes caused by mumps can result in sterility—the inability to conceive a child. That is why it is important for males to be vaccinated against mumps in childhood.
● Attacks that seem to recur are not due to mumps but to inflammation of the parotid salivary gland, a stone in the salivary duct, or a bacterial infection of the gland. These disorders should be reported to your doctor.

MEDICAL TREATMENT

If complications are suspected, your doctor may order a spinal tap to test for meningitis or encephalitis or blood tests to measure the number of mumps antibodies in the blood. (Antibodies are protective substances that the body produces to fight against disease.) Doctors do not follow any specific treatment for mumps, but may hospitalize a child if necessary to arrive at a diagnosis or to provide supportive treatment.

An unvaccinated child may receive mumps vaccine shortly after exposure to the disease to prevent mumps.

Related topics:

Encephalitis
Immunizations
Meningitis

Nephritis

SYMPTOMS   Discolored urine
Puffy eyes
Headache
High blood pressure

HOME CARE   Most cases of nephritis are mild and pass unnoticed. If the symptoms are marked enough to be recognizable, the child requires medical attention.

PRECAUTIONS

☐ If the child's eyes are puffy, or the urine is scanty and dark, the child may have nephritis.

☐ If symptoms of nephritis are pronounced enough to be noticed, take the child to the doctor.

☐ Nephritis usually follows a strep infection. Watch for the condition to follow a strep throat or impetigo, even if the infection is being treated with antibiotics.

There are many forms of nephritis, or inflammation of the kidneys, but the form that is most common in children usually follows a streptococcal infection such as strep throat, scarlet fever, or streptococcal impetigo. The first symptoms of nephritis develop one to three weeks after the onset of a strep infection, and these symptoms are usually mild. In fact, most cases of nephritis probably go unnoticed (or undiagnosed) and pass without treatment. Occasionally, however, nephritis starts abruptly and the illness is severe. Most children recover completely from nephritis, but a few develop chronic kidney disease.

SIGNS AND SYMPTOMS

In most cases, the first sign of nephritis is the child's producing urine that is a smoky color or brownish-red and tinged with blood. The child may have puffy eyes and run a fever of 101°F to 102°F for several days. In severe cases, the illness produces high fever, headache, vomiting, high blood pressure, and convulsions; urination ceases almost completely, and the urine the child does produce contains a lot of blood. An analysis of urine will confirm the diagnosis. Positive cultures of nose and throat secretions for the strep bacteria support the diagnosis.

HOME CARE

As mentioned earlier, most cases of nephritis are mild and don't attract attention or require treatment. If the symptoms are severe enough to be recognized, however, do not attempt home treatment; the child should see a doctor.

PRECAUTION

● You should be aware that nephritis most often follows strep impetigo and can follow a strep throat whether or not the strep throat has been treated with antibiotics.

MEDICAL TREATMENT

In a case of suspected nephritis the doctor will examine the child thoroughly and take the child's blood pressure. The doctor may take a throat culture to identify a strep infection, and order urine and blood tests. If the child does have nephritis the doctor will usually prescribe penicillin or erythromycin for ten days. The doctor will monitor the child's blood and urine until they are normal again. The child should stay in bed only during the acute phase of the disease. A severe case may require the child to be hospitalized for observation and treatment of high blood pressure or convulsions. In some cases the doctor will prescribe continued medication, sometimes for several months both while the child is recovering and afterward.

Related topics:

High blood
  pressure
Impetigo
Strep throat
Urinary tract
  infections

Nightmares

SYMPTOMS   Child wakes screaming
Confusion on awakening
Frantic activity on awakening
Sleepwalking

HOME CARE   Rouse the child slowly and gently.

Hold the child and speak soothingly and reassuringly.

If the child is sleepwalking, make sure he or she cannot fall or get hurt.

PRECAUTIONS

☐ Frequent nightmares indicate that the child is under excessive stress; try to identify and relieve the problem. If necessary, enlist the doctor and school personnel to help pinpoint the source of the child's distress.

☐ Be alert to the school, social, and family pressures that can cause a child to have nightmares.

☐ Be sure you know how much TV your child is watching, and that the program content is suitable.

☐ A child who sleepwalks must be protected from falls and other injury.

Some experts distinguish bad dreams from nightmares and night terrors. For practical purposes, however, all three have the same cause and treatment; they differ only in degree.

In a nightmare, the mind relives the fears and anxieties the child has experienced during his or her waking hours. Occasionally a nightmare may be the result of the usual stresses your child encounters in daily life. Frequent nightmares, however, are abnormal and indicate unreasonable pressures on the child.

High fever and illness—measles, for instance—have been known to induce nightmares. When this happens, the condition resembles delirium, and it should not recur once the child is well again. If no illness is involved, a nightmare is easily identified.

SIGNS AND SYMPTOMS

A child experiencing a terrifying dream may wake up screaming, frightened, and wild-eyed. The child may be confused or frantically active for several minutes, and may or may not immediately recall the details of the dream. Often the incident will be forgotten by the next morning. Nightmares may also cause the child to sleepwalk.

HOME CARE

Immediate treatment involves holding and hugging the distraught child and speaking calmly and soothingly. Do not try to rouse the child to full consciousness too quickly. Sleepwalkers must be protected from falls or other injuries.

The basic home treatment is to identify and relieve the stress that is causing the child to have nightmares. Most nightmares are the result of a situation such as one of the following: school problems (fear of failure or teacher-student conflicts); peer relationships (playing with older children, being bullied, sexual experimentation); or family pressures (marital friction, alcoholism, physical or emotional abuse, divorce, hospitalization, death). Watching too much TV—or the wrong type of program—can also cause enough anxiety to give a child nightmares.

PRECAUTIONS

● Be aware of school, social, and family pressures that can cause a child to have nightmares. ● Be sure you know how much TV the child is watching and what kinds of programs. ● Protect a sleepwalking child from injury.

MEDICAL TREATMENT

Your doctor will try to uncover the cause of your child's anxieties by getting the child to talk about his or her daily relationships and experiences. The doctor may ask for assistance from school personnel in order to identify the reason for the child's nightmares.

Nosebleeds

SYMPTOMS   Bleeding from one or both nostrils or from the mouth
Vomiting blood

HOME CARE   To stop a nosebleed, compress the entire soft portion of the nose, not just the nostrils, between the thumb and fingers for ten minutes.

Teach your child at an early age how to stop a nosebleed him- or herself.

To prevent nosebleeds apply petroleum jelly to the insides of the nostrils morning and evening for up to 14 days.

Use a vaporizer or humidifier in the child's room.

PRECAUTIONS

☐ A child with a nosebleed should not lie down.

☐ Stay calm and don't let the child panic.

☐ Do not use cold compresses, nose drops, or other household remedies; they are not necessary.

☐ Do not pack the child's nose with cotton or gauze.

Teach your child to control a nosebleed by pinching the entire soft portion of the nose between thumb and forefinger.

Nosebleeds are as inevitable a part of childhood as scraped knees and bruised shins. Ninety-nine percent of nosebleeds are caused by the rupture of tiny blood vessels in the septum, the midline partition of the nose located about one-quarter inch in from the nostrils. These small blood vessels are easily broken by a minor blow to the nose, and the scab that forms during healing is easily disturbed by rubbing or picking, which starts the bleeding again. This sequence of events may be further aggravated by: an allergic reaction or a head cold that causes the blood vessels in the nose to dilate; heated air that dries out the nasal membranes; sneezing, coughing, and blowing the nose; and rubbing and scratching the nose, especially during sleep (most nosebleeds start at night).

SIGNS AND SYMPTOMS

You will have no difficulty recognizing a nosebleed. Since the two sides of the nose join in the back, and also join with the throat and the esophagus (which lead to the stomach), blood may flow from both nostrils or from the mouth; the child may also vomit blood.

HOME CARE

Teach your child at an early age how to stop a nosebleed by him- or herself. Tell the child to remain calm and to sit upright with the head held high; this will decrease blood pressure in the blood vessels. Show the child how to grasp the whole lower half of the nose between his or her thumb and fingers and in this way compress both sides of the nose firmly against the septum. The child should hold the nose this way for ten minutes to allow time for the blood to clot. If bleeding recurs when the pressure is released, it probably means that a large clot in the nose is preventing the broken blood vessel from sealing. The child should blow the nose vigorously to dislodge the clot; then, after the clot has been removed, compress the nose again for ten to 12 minutes.

To prevent recurring nosebleeds, put petroleum jelly in the child's nose morning and evening for seven to 14 days. Use a vaporizer or humidifier to add moisture to the air at night.

PRECAUTIONS

● To stop a nosebleed, do not merely pinch nostrils together, but compress the entire soft portion of the nose. Otherwise, the blood will dam up and run down the throat. ● Do not lay your child down.
● Remain calm and reassure your child.
● It is not necessary to use cold compresses, pressure on the upper lip, nose drops, and other household remedies.
● Do not pack the nose with cotton or gauze.

MEDICAL TREATMENT

Generally, your doctor's treatment will be the same as your home treatment, and you only need to consult the doctor when home treatment is not effective. If the nosebleed is due to an allergy or a cold your doctor will treat that condition. Your doctor will rarely need to pack the nasal passages or cauterize (seal off) the blood vessels in order to control recurring nosebleeds.

Related topics:

Common cold
Hay fever

Perleche

SYMPTOMS
Painful red and crusted cracks in the edges of the mouth
Cracks bleed when mouth is opened wide

HOME CARE
Have your child brush the teeth with table salt or bicarbonate of soda instead of with toothpaste.

Discourage the child from using mouthwashes or other chemical-containing products.

PRECAUTIONS

☐ If home treatment does not clear up the condition, consult a doctor or dentist.

☐ It is possible for perleche to be confused with fever blisters or impetigo, or to appear simultaneously with one of these conditions.

☐ Note that it may be necessary to treat the child for a secondary infection along with the perleche.

Irritation from toothpaste is a common cause of perleche. A child with perleche should clean the teeth with table salt or bicarbonate of soda.

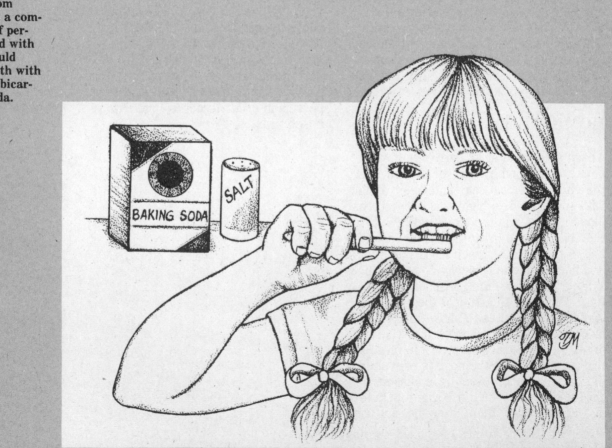

Cracks or fissures at the edges of the mouth that become red, sore, and crusted are called perleche. Classically, perleche is a sign of a vitamin B deficiency, a dietary condition common in India but almost unknown in the United States. Almost all of the cases that occur in this country are caused by an irritation from toothpastes. Chemicals in mouthwashes, orthodontic or dental materials, or plastic toys can also cause the condition.

SIGNS AND SYMPTOMS

Chronic, painful sores where the upper and lower lips meet are the telltale signs of perleche. The cracks may bleed when the mouth is opened wide. Occasionally, perleche may be confused with, or occur together with, fever blisters or impetigo.

HOME TREATMENT

Temporarily stop the child from using regular toothpaste, and have the child brush the teeth with table salt or bicarbonate of soda. If this does not relieve the condition, have the child avoid mouthwashes or other products containing chemicals. After perleche heals, try other toothpastes or ask your dentist for advice.

PRECAUTION

● If the condition does not clear up after the child has stopped using toothpaste, mouthwashes, or other substances containing chemicals, consult a dentist or doctor.

MEDICAL TREATMENT

Your doctor's treatment is basically the same as the home treatment. However, it may also be necessary for the doctor to treat a secondary staphylococcal or streptococcal infection.

Related topics:

Herpes simplex
Impetigo

Pigeon toes

SYMPTOM   Turning in of the toes

HOME CARE   Encourage your infant to sleep with the toes turned outward.

If so instructed by your doctor, massage the child's feet to correct the toeing-in.

PRECAUTIONS

☐ If your child sits on the floor a lot, encourage him or her to sit cross-legged, not on his or her haunches.

☐ Note that most cases of pigeon toes correct themselves; however, if the child is toeing in after the age of three months, consult a doctor.

☐ Never allow a shoe salesperson to recommend orthopedic or corrective shoes for your child. The prescription must always be made by a qualified professional.

If a baby usually sleeps face down with the toes directed inward, pigeon toes may develop.

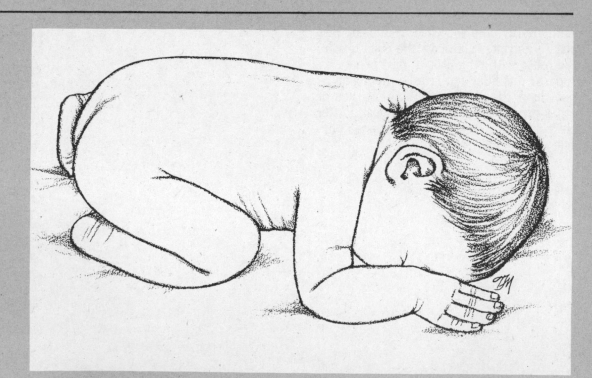

Toeing-in of the feet, particularly when standing and walking, is known as pigeon toes. After birth, the position and shape of the feet and legs reflect the position they held during the baby's last weeks in the mother's womb. By the age of three months, the child's feet and legs should have assumed a normal shape.

Throughout infancy and early childhood, however, the position of the feet and legs can be influenced by the manner in which they are held while the child is sitting and lying down. If the child habitually sleeps face down with the toes directed inward, this position encourages the development of pigeon toes.

Pigeon toes also may result from a malformation of the foot (adductovarus deformity), of the lower leg (tibial torsion), or of the thigh bone (femoral torsion or femoral anteversion). Depending on the severity of the malformation the child's toes will point inward to a greater or lesser degree. A child who has a marked malformation will tend to trip over his or her feet until he or she learns to compensate for the condition.

SIGNS AND SYMPTOMS

The turning in of the toes is easy to see; if the condition persists, it should be brought to the doctor's attention. You can do a preliminary test for an adductovarus deformity of the foot by laying a straight-edge along the outer border of the child's foot. If the outer border of the foot is not absolutely straight from the heel to the little toe, the child has adductovarus deformity. To discern tibial torsion, place the infant or child on his or her back with the legs straight out, kneecaps pointed upward, and feet at right angles to the lower legs. If the toes point toward the midline instead of straight up, the child may have tibial torsion.

Femoral torsion or anteversion usually does not appear until age four or five; from then on it gradually worsens. It can be detected by rotating the thighs at the hip joint. If the thighs make a larger arc internally than externally the child has femoral torsion.

HOME CARE

By three months of age, your infant will prefer to sleep with the toes directed outward. This position is normal and should be encouraged. When the child is old enough to sit upright, the feet should be straight or turned outward. Until 18 to 24 months, your toddler usually will walk with one or both feet turned outward; this gives the child a wider base and better balance, and is normal. A tendency to toe in after three months of age should be called to your doctor's attention.

PRECAUTIONS

● An uncorrected adductovarus deformity makes it very difficult to fit the child's shoes properly; this may eventually lead to the child developing a skewed foot and bunions in adolescence or adulthood. ● A child who sits on the floor a lot should be taught to sit cross-legged, not on his or her haunches with the toes directed outward. ● Corrective orthopedic shoes should be prescribed only by a medical professional, never by a shoe salesperson. ● Most minor cases of pigeon toes correct themselves. Nevertheless, let a doctor judge if the condition is minor or not.

MEDICAL TREATMENT

Your doctor will observe the child while he or she stands and walks both with and without shoes. The feet, the lower and upper legs, and the rotation of the hips will be examined. If necessary, your doctor will instruct you in massaging your child's feet to correct mild toeing-in. If this massage does not correct the condition by the time the child is three or four months old, your doctor will order specific kinds of shoes or plaster casts. To correct tibial torsion, the doctor may prescribe a splint that holds the feet outwardly rotated while the child sleeps. In the case of femoral anteversion the doctor may not start treatment until your child is a teenager. If the condition has not corrected itself by that time, surgery on the thigh bones may be necessary.

Pinworms

SYMPTOMS　Itching or burning in the anal or genital
areas
Bedwetting
Abdominal cramps
Inflammation of the vagina or bladder

HOME CARE　Ask the doctor to prescribe a medication
to get rid of the pinworms.

Keep the fingernails of the infected child
cut and scrubbed to avoid spreading the
pinworms.

Launder the child's clothing and linens to
kill the worms.

PRECAUTIONS

☐ If one member of the family has pinworms, all members (except infants
and pregnant women) should be
treated at the same time.

☐ Do not blame a child's case of pinworms on the family dog or cat; pinworms do not live in these animals.

☐ Worm medications should be obtained
only with a doctor's prescription.

☐ Be aware that pinworms may be the
cause of recurrent inflammation of the
vagina or bladder.

The pinworm, a distant cousin of the earthworm, lives only in humans and the higher apes. The adult pinworm is one-quarter to one-half inch in length, white in color, and about as thick as stout sewing thread. It lives in the large intestine and, moving with a caterpillar-like motion, comes out at night to lay microscopic eggs on the skin around the anus, the opening from the intestine to the outside. The eggs are transmitted from the anus to the mouth on the child's hands or by toys and food that the child has touched. The child then swallows the eggs. The eggs hatch into larvae, the immature form of the pinworm; by two to six weeks later the larvae have developed into mature, egg-laying adult pinworms and the cycle continues. Pinworms can be transmitted to other children and to adults in the same manner.

SIGNS AND SYMPTOMS

A child with pinworms has few symptoms. The child may complain at night of itching or burning around the anal or genital area. Pinworms can also be a cause of a sudden onset of bedwetting. If the infestation is heavy the child may have abdominal cramps. Pinworms can cause appendicitis (although this is rare), and they can work their way into a girl's vagina and urethra (the passageway from the bladder to the outside) causing inflammation of the vagina or bladder.

Usually the diagnosis of pinworms is easily made by examining the skin around the anus at night while the child sleeps, or just after waking. Pinworms head back into the anus if disturbed by light, so the search must be done quickly. A pinworm can be mistaken for lint on the skin; if the lint moves, it's a pinworm. Occasionally pinworms may be found in a bowel movement, but this is not a reliable way of making a diagnosis.

HOME CARE

Vermifuges (worm medicines) must be obtained by prescription, but many doctors will prescribe them over the telephone. When one member of a family has pinworms, all members (except infants and pregnant women) should be treated at the same time.

PRECAUTIONS

● Suspect that pinworms may be the cause of recurrent inflammation of the vagina or bladder. ● If one member of a family has pinworms, launder that person's underclothes, bed linens, and towels to destroy the worms' eggs. Also, cut and scrub his or her fingernails to remove any eggs. ● Do not mistake lint or thread for pinworms; look for movement. ● Do not blame household cats and dogs for a child's having pinworms. These worms live only in humans.

MEDICAL TREATMENT

Your doctor investigates for pinworms using clear tape that will pick up any eggs that are on the skin. The tape is then examined under the microscope. If the test is positive, the doctor will prescribe worm medication for the entire family.

Pityriasis rosea

SYMPTOMS
Round or oval scaly patch followed by
  rash
Itching
Headache
Lethargy
Joint pain
Sore throat

HOME CARE
No treatment is necessary.

If the rash causes itching, give the child
antihistamines.

Bathing with soft soap and exposure to
sunlight may help clear the rash faster.

PRECAUTIONS

☐ The first or "herald" patch may look
like ringworm, eczema, or impetigo.
The subsequent rash may be confused with ringworm.

☐ The condition may last for up to eight
weeks but is harmless.

**Exposure to sunlight
seems to shorten the
duration of the rash
of pityriasis rosea.**

Pityriasis rosea is a common, harmless, long-lasting disease that goes unrecognized by most parents. Generally it affects teenagers and young adults, but it may occur at any age. The disease is almost certainly caused by a virus, but the specific germ has not been identified. Pityriasis rosea is mildly contagious but isolation is not considered necessary. One attack gives lifelong immunity.

SIGNS AND SYMPTOMS

In most cases of pityriasis rosea the first sign is a single patch (herald patch) the size of a nickel or a quarter on the skin of the trunk or extremities. The patch is round or oval, salmon-colored (pink or reddish), and slightly crinkled in the center; the edges are slightly scaly. The patch is not tender but may itch. Occasionally it is accompanied by headache, lethargy, pain in the joints, and a sore throat. Five to 14 days after the appearance of the herald patch, spots break out on the body; each is similar in appearance to the original patch, but smaller. The rash does not affect the face, forearms, and lower legs of an older child, although in a younger child these areas may also be involved. The rash lasts for three to eight weeks, during which time the child feels fine.

The diagnosis is based on the characteristic appearance of the rash, which includes both round and oval spots.

HOME CARE

No treatment is necessary. Itching, if present, can be relieved by giving the child nonprescription antihistamines by mouth. Bathing with a soft soap and exposure to sunlight both apparently shorten the duration of the rash.

PRECAUTION

● The appearance of the herald patch may suggest ringworm, eczema, or impetigo; if the patch does not respond to treatment for any of these conditions, consider pityriasis.

MEDICAL TREATMENT

No medical treatment is required.

Related topics:

Eczema
Impetigo
Rash
Ringworm

Pneumonia

SYMPTOMS

Bacterial pneumonia
Mild upper respiratory tract infection
High fever
Chills
Cough
Rapid breathing
Chest pain

Viral pneumonia
Headache
Fatigue
Fever
Sore throat
Severe, dry cough

HOME CARE

Viral pneumonia usually clears up on its own.

Bacterial pneumonia requires medical attention.

PRECAUTIONS

☐ Watch for signs of pneumonia in a child whose resistance is lowered by a cold or infection.

☐ If a cold suddenly gets worse and is accompanied by high fever, cough, chills, chest pain, or rapid breathing, suspect pneumonia.

☐ Flaring of the nostrils, grunting breathing, and pulling in of the chest in an infant are serious and require immediate medical attention.

☐ If a child coughs up a discharge tinged with blood, consult a doctor.

Pneumonia is an infection of one or more areas of the lungs. It's caused by bacteria or viruses. The common bacterial cause of pneumonia is pneumococcus or, less often, streptococcus or staphylococcus. The viral causes include the influenza and parainfluenza viruses, the respiratory syncytial virus, and adenoviruses. Pneumonia also may be caused by mycoplasma organisms.

In order to contract bacterial pneumonia, the child must be exposed to it at a time when he or she is particularly susceptible. Pneumococci, streptococci, and staphylococci bacteria frequently are present in the nose and throat of a healthy child. Before these organisms can invade the lungs, however, the child's resistance must be lowered by a cold or some other upper respiratory tract infection. Therefore bacterial pneumonia is not considered to be contagious in the usual sense.

The types of pneumonia that are caused by viruses are known as "walking pneumonias" and are contagious. The incubation period—the time it takes for the symptoms to develop once the child is exposed to the disease—for mycoplasma is one to three weeks; for most viruses it is two to five days.

SIGNS AND SYMPTOMS

The symptoms of bacterial pneumonia include a mild upper respiratory tract infection, followed by the sudden onset of high fever (105°F), chills, cough, rapid breathing, and sometimes pain on either or both sides of the chest. In infants the respiratory distress may cause flaring of the nostrils, retractions (pulling in) of the soft spaces of the chest, and grunting sounds when the child breathes out.

The onset of viral pneumonia is gradual, creating symptoms of headache, fatigue, fever of variable degrees (100°F–105°F), a sore throat, and a severe, dry cough.

The diagnosis requires careful examination of the chest, X rays, a complete blood count, and sometimes cultures of the blood and, in older children, the sputum (the coughed-up discharge).

HOME CARE

Many cases of viral pneumonia are mild and are not recognized as pneumonia at all. You may assume that the child has a cold and give cold remedies. The pneumonia then clears up on its own after ten to 14 days.

If signs of respiratory distress as listed above are present, the child should be seen by a doctor.

PRECAUTIONS

• Sudden worsening of a cold accompanied by high fever, cough, chills, chest pain, or rapid breathing suggest pneumonia. • In infants, flaring of the nostrils, pulling in of the chest, and grunting breathing are serious symptoms and require immediate medical care. • In children, sputum tinged with blood may or may not be serious, but it indicates the need for a doctor's attention.

MEDICAL TREATMENT

Your doctor will diagnose pneumonia by means of a physical examination and laboratory tests. In the past a child with pneumonia was always hospitalized. Now, only the youngest and the most severely ill are hospitalized.

Most pneumonias respond to antibiotics. A patient with pneumococcal pneumonia will recover rapidly once antibiotics are begun. Another, with a streptococcal or staphylococcal infection, may require in-hospital administration of the antibiotics. Mycoplasma pneumonia responds to some antibiotics, but viral pneumonias do not. For viral pneumonias, your doctor will recommend rest, plenty of fluids, and time for the condition to run its course.

Related topics:

Chest pain
Common cold
Coughs
Fever
G6PD deficiency
Sore throat

Poisoning

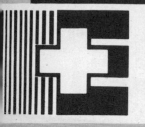

EMERGENCY SYMPTOMS

Apply emergency treatment immediately.

EMERGENCY TREATMENT

1. Try to find out what the child has taken, how much the child took, and when the incident occurred.

2. Call the doctor or local poison control center for instructions.

3. Be prepared to read the label of the substance over the telephone.

4. Always keep syrup of ipecac in your home.

SYMPTOMS

Depending on type of poison taken, symptoms may include a number of the following:
Rapid breathing
Ringing in the ears
Nausea

Overexcitement
Unconsciousness
Burns on lips, mouth, and tongue
Abdominal pain
Vomiting
Blood in vomit

PRECAUTIONS

☐ Keep the phone numbers of the doctor, poison control center, and other emergency services next to your telephone.

☐ Keep all poisonous substances out of the reach of children, preferably in a locked cupboard to which only you have the key.

☐ Never store a dangerous substance in anything but its original container.

☐ Do not keep medication in an unlabeled container.

☐ Make sure *all* medications, not just those intended for children's use, have child-proof caps.

☐ Make sure that your children do not come into contact with dangerous substances in other people's homes.

☐ Be aware that treatment for poisoning depends on the substance taken, and that in the case of some poisons vomiting can worsen the child's condition.

☐ Never induce vomiting in a child who is not fully conscious.

☐ Remember that the most common cause of poisoning in children is aspirin overdose.

In a large enough quantity, any substance, even water, can be poisonous. But some substances are more apt to be swallowed in harmful amounts, either accidentally or deliberately, than others. In the United States the most common cause of poisoning among children between the ages of one and five years is an overdose of aspirin. Then come soaps, detergents, cleansers, bleaches, vitamins, iron tonics, insecticides, plants, polishes and waxes, hormones, and tranquilizers. Less common but more toxic poisons include boric acid, oil of wintergreen, volatile hydrocarbons (gasoline, kerosene, turpentine, naphtha, cleaning fluids), strong acids, alkalis (drain and oven cleaners), and many prescription and over-the-counter medications (including aspirin substitutes and acetaminophen).

SIGNS AND SYMPTOMS

The diagnosis of poisoning depends primarily upon knowing what the child has eaten or drunk. Otherwise, the diagnosis relies on suspicion, a careful physical examination for telltale clues, and laboratory tests. Usually, the telltale signs of aspirin overdose are rapid breathing, ringing in the ears, nausea, overexcitement, and unconsciousness. Poisoning from acids and alkalis causes burns on the lips, mouth, and tongue. An overdose of an iron tonic produces abdominal pain and severe vomiting, often with blood in the vomited material, followed by collapse.

HOME CARE

Two steps are vital. *First,* try to determine quickly what the substance is that your child has taken, how much of the substance your child has taken, and when the incident happened. *Second,* call your doctor or local poison control center for instructions. Read the label of the drug or other preparation over the phone. You will be told whether or not to induce vomiting.

If your child has not vomited, if the poison was *neither* a strong acid *nor* an alkali, and if your child is conscious, induce vomiting by giving two to three teaspoonsful of syrup of ipecac followed by a half to a full glass of water. Do not give milk. If the child does not vomit within 20 to 30 minutes, repeat the syrup of ipecac liquid dose. *It is not safe to induce vomiting after the child has swallowed volatile hydrocarbons* (gasoline, turpentine, and so on).

In general, if your child has taken a normally edible substance (medications, for example), induce vomiting. If your child has taken a substance that is not normally edible (gasoline or furniture polish, for instance), do not induce vomiting. If your child is not fully conscious, do not induce vomiting.

PRECAUTIONS

● The most important precaution is prevention: see that all poisonous substances are stored out of reach of children—under lock and key if necessary. ● Keep the telephone numbers of police and fire departments, your doctor, and the local poison control center near the telephone. ● Always have syrup of ipecac in the house. ● Do not transfer any poisonous substance to an ordinary glass or bottle and do not keep any medication in an unlabeled container. ● Insist upon childproof tops on all medicines, not just those intended for children. ● More children are fatally poisoned by adult aspirin than by children's flavored aspirin. ● Be careful with iron tablets. They taste sweet, look like candy, and can be deadly. ● When visiting other people's homes, do not let your children explore until you are sure there are no poisons within reach. ● When guests visit you, be certain their medications are out of reach of any children.

MEDICAL TREATMENT

Your doctor may induce vomiting with syrup of ipecac or wash out the stomach by means of a tube. Further treatment varies with the substance taken and your child's condition.

Poison ivy

SYMPTOMS   Blistered rash
Itching

HOME CARE   To remove the irritant from the skin, bathe the child immediately with soap and water and scrub the fingernails.

Calamine lotion on the rash and antihistamines by mouth may help relieve itching.

Contaminated clothing should be laundered.

PRECAUTIONS

☐   If the child scratches the rash, the skin may become susceptible to impetigo. Watch for signs of infection.

☐   Teach your child to recognize and avoid the poison ivy vine.

☐   Dress your child in long pants and socks when he or she is in the woods or other areas where poison ivy grows.

☐   If the rash continues to spread after several days, it means the child is still coming in contact with the plant. Try to locate the source of the contact.

Rashes among children in the two- to 12-year-old age group are generally due to contact with certain agents, one of the most common of which is poison ivy vine. Other plants such as poison oak and poison sumac can also cause a rash.

Poison ivy rash develops in sensitive children after direct contact with any part of the vine. It can also occur after the child has been exposed to smoke from the burning vine or to pets that have rolled in the plant. Poison ivy rash can be spread to any part of the body by the hands, the fingernails, and contaminated clothing.

SIGNS AND SYMPTOMS

Itching develops within two to 24 hours after contact with poison ivy. It is followed by reddening and swelling (edema) of the skin. Pin-sized, clear blisters develop and may merge to create blisters as large as one-half inch across. The rash often appears in straight lines where the plant has brushed against the skin or where the child has scratched. Poison ivy is often carried to a boy's penis by his hands.

Basically, a blistered, itching rash that appears in straight lines is indicative of poison ivy. However, the rash may appear generally over the skin and look similar to rashes caused by other agents.

HOME CARE

Bathe the child promptly with soap and water, and cut and scrub the child's fingernails; this will remove much of the poison ivy from the skin and hands. To relieve itching, apply calamine lotion to the rash or give the child nonprescription antihistamines. Launder contaminated clothing to remove the irritant.

PRECAUTIONS

● Scratching can make the skin susceptible to impetigo, so watch for signs of infection. ● If poison ivy continues to spread after four to seven days your child is still coming into contact with the plant, directly or indirectly. Try to find the source. ● Teach your child to recognize and avoid the poison ivy vine. ● Make sure your child is dressed appropriately (in long pants and socks) when in the woods or around campsites.

MEDICAL TREATMENT

Your doctor will confirm the diagnosis, treat any secondary infection, and sometimes prescribe steroid medication if the rash is severe. Vaccines are available to lessen sensitivity to poison ivy, but they are not very effective. Preparations taken by mouth are even less helpful.

Related topics:

Impetigo
Rash

277

Polio

SYMPTOMS   General bodily discomfort
Fever
Sore throat
Nausea
Sore, stiff muscles
Stiff neck or spine

HOME CARE   The best home care is prevention; be sure your child is adequately protected against polio by immunization.

PRECAUTIONS

☐ The child needs the full series of immunizations to receive long-lasting immunity.

☐ If the child originally received the Salk polio vaccine, he or she must have boosters or receive two full series of the Sabin vaccine in order to be fully protected.

☐ Polio is caused by one of three different viruses, and attack by any one of the three confers immunity against that virus only. It is, therefore, technically possible to have three separate attacks of polio.

Polio—poliomyelitis or infantile paralysis—is an infection of the spinal cord. It is due to one of three related but different viruses. Attack by one of these three viruses confers lifelong immunity against that type only. Therefore, it is possible to have three separate attacks of the disease.

The polio virus is found in the saliva and the stool of the infected person. It is transmitted by direct contact or through contact with something that has been contaminated by the virus carried in an infected stool—for example, foods, toys, or the water in a swimming pool. The incubation period—the time it takes for the symptoms to appear once the person is exposed to the virus—for polio is three to 14 days.

SIGNS AND SYMPTOMS

Of those children who develop polio, 93 to 95 percent of them have no symptoms, but develop immunity. Four to 5 percent of those infected develop a minor illness, with fever, general bodily discomfort, sore throat, and nausea for three to four days. One to 2 percent develop clinically recognizable polio, with symptoms of a minor illness plus sore, stiff muscles and a stiff neck and spine. Within this 1 or 2 percent are the children who become paralyzed or die.

Minor cases may never be recognized as polio unless they occur as part of an epidemic. Diagnosis is based on examination of viral cultures and studies of antibodies (substances that the body produces to fight disease) in the blood. If the central nervous system (the spine and the brain) is involved, the child has a stiff neck and back and may not be able to sit up without supporting the trunk with both hands braced behind in a tripod fashion. The diagnosis is confirmed by the results of a spinal tap (in which spinal fluid is withdrawn from the spinal column), cultures, or antibody studies.

HOME CARE

The most important home treatment is prevention through immunization. The live virus vaccine (Sabin), which is given by mouth, is effective against all three types of polio, and it confers long-lasting immunity. The risk of paralysis from present-day vaccines is less than one in ten million—a far cry from the one in a thousand risk of exposure to naturally-occurring viruses.

PRECAUTIONS

● An infant is temporarily immune to each of the three types of polio for four to six months after birth only if the mother is immune (because she's had the disease or been vaccinated against it). The child needs a full series of vaccinations by mouth to achieve long-lasting immunity.
● Anyone who has received injections of the original, dead vaccine (Salk) must have boosters or two full series of the Sabin vaccine to guarantee immunity.
● Polio virus still exists in this country, and polio is epidemic in many other countries of the world. Since it is not possible to avoid it, immunization is essential.

MEDICAL TREATMENT

Your doctor's diagnosis will be made on the basis of a physical examination and the results of a spinal tap. A child with a suspected or known case of polio will be isolated. A child who is not immunized and has been exposed to the disease will be given gamma globulin to prevent or lessen the severity of the disease. A child who has contracted polio will be given aspirin, acetaminophen, other pain killers, and hot packs to reduce the pain. If polio causes paralysis, the child may need an artificial respirator, a tracheotomy (an opening into the windpipe through the neck), prolonged physical therapy, braces, or orthopedic surgery.

Related topics:

Immunizations
Viruses

Puncture wounds

SYMPTOM   A wound that is deeper than it is long or wide

HOME CARE   Wash the wound carefully and apply a nonirritating antiseptic.

If no foreign body remains in the wound, cover the area with a sterile bandage and inspect it regularly for signs of infection.

If a foreign body remains in the wound, take the child to the doctor.

PRECAUTIONS

☐ Redness, swelling, or stiffness of the joint at the site of a puncture wound is a **medical emergency**. Take the child to the doctor.

☐ A puncture wound in the abdomen, in the chest, or in a joint requires **immediate medical attention**.

☐ Never try to remove a foreign body (for example, needle, knife blade) from a puncture wound yourself.

☐ A puncture wound that is still tender after a day or two should be seen by a doctor.

☐ Make sure your child's tetanus immunization is always current.

Wounds that pierce the skin are classified as abrasions (scrapes), lacerations (cuts), and punctures. A puncture is a wound that is deeper than it is long or wide. Most puncture wounds in children are made by nails, needles, pins, knives, or splinters.

Because of their small opening and their depth, punctures present four particular dangers: the tetanus germ thrives in the absence of air, so a puncture is an ideal site for developing tetanus; a puncture wound is hard to clean and therefore susceptible to infection; punctures can penetrate deep into the body; and a puncture wound may harbor foreign bodies that are difficult to detect.

SIGNS AND SYMPTOMS

The presence of a puncture wound usually is obvious. The important aspects of the diagnosis involve determining whether the puncture has penetrated into a deeper structure (a joint, the abdominal cavity or chest cavity, the skull, or a tendon), whether it contains a foreign body (broken needle, wood or glass splinter, or shred of clothing), and whether it is infected.

HOME CARE

Wash the skin surrounding the puncture with soap and water and apply a non-irritating, nonstinging antiseptic such as solution—not tincture—of Merthiolate antiseptic. Be sure your child has been immunized against tetanus within the last five years. Make sure that the object that made the wound is intact and has not broken off at the tip. Inspect and feel the wound to determine if a foreign body can be detected under the skin. If no foreign body is present, cover the wound with a sterile bandage and inspect it twice a day for signs of infection (redness, discharge, swelling, increasing pain, and tenderness). Soak the wound frequently in warm water to help keep it clean. If there is a foreign body in the wound, take the child to a doctor.

PRECAUTIONS

● Puncture wounds in the abdomen or chest can be very serious. Take your child to a doctor. ● Punctures of a joint may cause infectious arthritis within hours. The knee joint is particularly susceptible; a puncture near a joint, especially the knee, should be seen by a doctor. Any signs of infectious arthritis (redness, swelling, increasing pain, inability to move the joint through its full range of normal motion) should be considered a **medical emergency**. ● Do not remove an object from a puncture wound, not even if it is a knife blade, a nail, a splinter of wood or glass, or a needle. Let your doctor remove it. You might cause further damage if you try to remove the object yourself. ● If a puncture wound remains tender for more than one or two days, it should be seen by your doctor.

MEDICAL TREATMENT

A puncture wound cannot be cleaned properly, even by a doctor. Your doctor will try to determine if any foreign bodies are present by feeling the wound or by X ray. If there is anything in the wound, it may need to be removed surgically; or the doctor may wait and observe the wound for awhile, perhaps instructing you how to soak it in Epsom salts solution for five to 10 minutes four times a day. Antibiotics will be prescribed if the wound is infected, and a tetanus toxoid injection will be given if the child's immunization is not current. If a wound has penetrated a joint, the abdomen, the chest, the skull, or a tendon, your doctor will hospitalize the child and explore the wound surgically.

Related topics:

Arthritis
Cuts
Immunizations
Scrapes
Tetanus

Rash

SYMPTOM   Red patches, blisters, or spots on the skin

HOME CARE   If the rash causes itching, have the child take warm baths, or apply a soothing lotion such as calamine.

PRECAUTIONS

- [ ] Do not be concerned about a rash that disappears within a few days and does not recur.

- [ ] Certain distinctive rashes are symptoms of specific diseases. A rash that is a symptom of a disease will disappear when the disease is identified and treated.

If a rash causes itching, it may help to have the child sit in a warm bath.

A rash is a skin eruption which appears as red patches, blisters, or spots. It is often accompanied by itching. A rash can affect a limited area or be widespread over extensive areas of the body.

A rash can be caused by exposure to the sun, heat, cold, chemicals in household products, or fabrics such as wool. Certain foods—strawberries, for example—also produce rashes in people who are sensitive (allergic) to that particular food. These rashes are often known as allergic rashes; the rash is a symptom of the allergy.

A rash can also appear as a symptom of a disease, in which case the rash is usually characteristic of the disease producing it. Distinctive rashes appear as symptoms of (among other diseases) measles, rubella (German measles), chicken pox, and shingles, all of which are infectious diseases. Certain sexually transmitted diseases such as herpes and syphilis also display distinctive rashes.

A rash often disappears when its underlying cause disappears or is successfully treated.

SIGNS AND SYMPTOMS

The rash itself is obvious, but the cause may not be so easily identified. A rash caused by a disease will be accompanied by other symptoms.

HOME CARE

You need not be too concerned about a rash that appears and then disappears within a couple of days and does not recur. If the rash causes itching you can apply a soothing lotion like calamine. Another suggestion is to have the child take a warm bath. A rash that recurs may indicate an allergy. If you cannot immediately identify the allergy-causing substance (a certain food, for instance), have the child checked out by a doctor. You can only avoid the allergy-causing substance in the future if you know what it is. If the child has a rash accompanied by other symptoms, consult the doctor.

PRECAUTIONS

● A rash that lasts for a few days and has no identifiable cause should be seen by a doctor. ● Certain types of rashes are warning signs of specific infectious or sexually transmitted diseases.

MEDICAL TREATMENT

The doctor may prescribe a soothing lotion for minor itching caused by a rash. In allergy-caused rashes the doctor will try to identify the allergy-causing substance. If the rash is caused by a disease, the doctor will diagnose and treat the disease.

Related topics:

Chicken pox
Diaper rashes
Eczema
Fifth disease
Food allergies
Hand, foot, and
   mouth disease
Heat rash
Herpes simplex
Hives
Impetigo
Measles
Molluscum
   contagiosum
Pityriasis rosea
Poison ivy
Ringworm
Rocky Mountain
   spotted fever
Roseola
Rubella
Shingles

Reye's syndrome

SYMPTOMS Severe vomiting
Unusual drowsiness
Overactivity or confusion in a child
  recovering from a viral infection

HOME CARE Do not attempt home treatment. Take the child to the doctor.

PRECAUTIONS

☐ There is a possible link of Reye's syndrome with the use of aspirin in treating a viral infection. Do not give aspirin to a child who has chicken pox or influenza. Acetaminophen, an aspirin substitute which has not been linked to Reye's syndrome, can be used instead. Sponge baths may help to bring down a fever.

☐ Reye's syndrome usually attacks children under the age of 18 who have just had a viral infection. Children between the ages of five and 11 are at highest risk.

☐ Reye's syndrome is fatal in 25 percent of cases; early diagnosis and treatment is vital, and a child who survives for three or four days usually recovers completely.

Reye's syndrome is a relatively rare but very serious noncontagious disease. It strikes children under the age of 18, and usually starts when the child is recovering from a viral infection, most commonly influenza or chicken pox. Reye's syndrome is a type of encephalitis, or inflammation of the brain. However, it is distinguished from other forms of encephalitis by the accompanying involvement of the liver. Although Reye's syndrome affects all organs and muscles of the body, it does most damage to the brain and the liver. It causes the brain to swell and fatty deposits to collect in the liver, so that the working of both organs is impaired. If the disease isn't diagnosed and treated early it can cause permanent brain damage, coma, or death. About 25 percent of cases of Reye's syndrome are fatal. Children between the ages of five and 11 who have just had a viral infection are at highest risk for Reye's syndrome. Most of the reported cases occur in the months of December through March.

It is not known precisely what causes Reye's syndrome. Some medical professionals think that, since it almost always follows a viral infection, Reye's syndrome itself may be a virus. It may be that the virus, in conjunction with some other unknown substance, produces a poison (toxin) that damages the body.

On the other hand, there is evidence of a possible link between Reye's syndrome and the use of aspirin in treating the viral infection which preceded the onset of the disease. Although it has not been proven that aspirin causes or promotes Reye's syndrome, doctors now caution against giving aspirin to a child with a viral infection, especially influenza or chicken pox.

Recent research suggests that the swelling of the brain that can accompany Reye's syndrome may be caused by a fault in the body's metabolism which prevents substances harmful to the brain from being flushed out.

SIGNS AND SYMPTOMS

Suspect Reye's syndrome if a child who has been recovering from a viral infection suddenly starts vomiting severely and becomes unusually drowsy, overactive, or confused. As the disease progresses it can cause convulsions and unconsciousness. Laboratory tests can confirm the diagnosis.

HOME CARE

If you suspect that the child has Reye's syndrome, consult a doctor immediately. Do not attempt home treatment.

PRECAUTIONS

● **Do not** give aspirin to a child with a viral infection, particularly chicken pox or influenza. Instead, sponge baths and aspirin substitutes such as acetaminophen can be used to treat fever and other symptoms. Aspirin substitutes have not been linked to Reye's syndrome. ● Reye's syndrome is fatal in 25 percent of cases. Early diagnosis and treatment is essential to the child's recovery.

MEDICAL TREATMENT

If the doctor suspects that the child's symptoms may be those of Reye's syndrome, tests will be ordered to confirm the diagnosis. Blood tests may reveal abnormalities that suggest liver damage. Younger children may have a very low blood sugar level. If the doctor does not suspect that there is increased pressure in the brain, a spinal tap may be done to rule out other kinds of diseases.

There is no known cure for Reye's syndrome, and treatment consists of supportive therapy to help the child withstand the disease until it runs its course. The child is usually hospitalized. As a rule, a child who survives for three or four days will recover completely.

Related topics:

Chicken pox
Convulsions
Encephalitis
Fever
Influenza

Ringworm

SYMPTOM   Scaly, red rash

HOME CARE   Apply a nonprescription antifungal ointment to the infected area until the skin is clear. If you do not know which preparation to use, ask your doctor.

PRECAUTIONS

☐ If a rash does not improve with home treatment, see the doctor. The rash may not be ringworm at all.

☐ If home treatment seems to make the rash worse, discontinue treatment and see the doctor. The child's skin may be sensitive to the medication you're using.

Ringworm is a skin infection that appears as oval, red, scaly patches that enlarge while healing proceeds from the center.

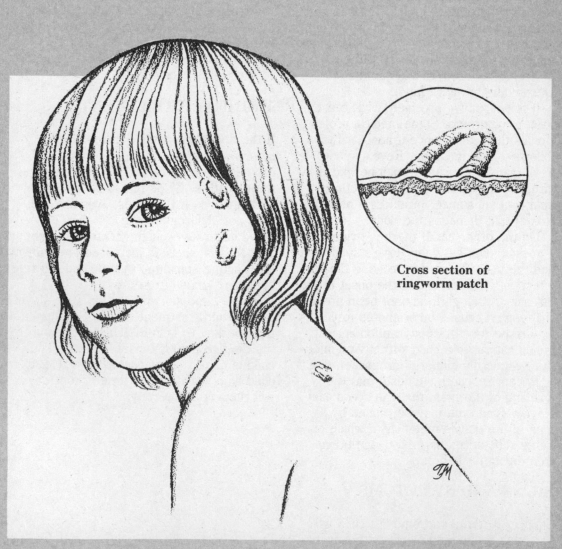

Cross section of ringworm patch

Ringworm is actually a skin infection caused by a fungus. Ringworm spreads by direct contact with an infected person or pet animal, or by indirect contact with contaminated objects such as combs, pillows, towels, clothing, even the floor.

SIGNS AND SYMPTOMS

Different funguses prefer different areas of the body. Ringworm of the scalp (*tinea capitis*) appears as scaly patches with stubs of broken-off hairs on the scalp. Ringworm of the body (*tinea corporis*) shows up as round or oval red, scaly patches that enlarge while healing proceeds from the center. Ringworm of the groin (*tinea cruris*) is characterized by a red or brown scaly rash on the crotch and the genital area and has a sharply defined margin of spread. Ringworm of the feet (athlete's foot, or *tinea pedis*) affects the feet and sometimes the ankles and legs.

The diagnosis of ringworm is based on your child's history and close inspection of the rash. The diagnosis is confirmed by laboratory tests.

HOME CARE

Antifungal ointments such as Whitfield's, haloprogin, chlortrimazole, tolnaftate, and undecylenic acid ointments can be applied to the infected area until the skin clears.

PRECAUTIONS

● Several other common rashes resemble ringworm. If a rash does not improve after several days of home treatment see your doctor. ● The preparations used to treat ringworm may cause another rash on sensitive skin. If the rash worsens or changes in any way, stop home treatment and see your doctor.

MEDICAL TREATMENT

Your doctor can confirm a home diagnosis of ringworm by examining your child's rash under ultraviolet light, and by culturing a skin scraping and examining the results under the microscope. The doctor may prescribe an antifungal ointment to be applied to the skin, or a medication such as griseofulvin fungicide for the child to take by mouth.

Related topics:

Athlete's foot
Rash

Rocky Mountain spotted fever

SYMPTOMS
Headache
Fever
Loss of appetite
Rash

HOME CARE This condition requires medical attention.

Watch carefully for symptoms in a child who has been bitten by ticks, and if you suspect the disease take the child at once to the doctor.

PRECAUTIONS

☐ Never remove ticks from a dog with your fingers; use tweezers.

☐ Use a tick repellent to keep your dog clear of the ticks.

☐ Do not allow your child to touch wild rabbits.

☐ If your child is bitten by a tick, observe his or her health closely for a week afterward.

☐ Note that Rocky Mountain spotted fever **always needs medical attention;** it is fatal in 40 percent of cases that are left untreated.

Children who are exposed to ticks should be checked carefully for signs of tick bites or symptoms of Rocky Mountain spotted fever.

Tick

Rocky Mountain spotted fever is an acute, noncontagious condition involving a rash and fever. It is transmitted by the bite of a wood tick, rabbit tick, or dog tick. The name of the disease is misleading: it occurs in all states, and is just as common in eastern and midwestern states as in the Rocky Mountain states.

The disease is caused by a microorganism called rickettsia that is midway between a virus and a bacterium. The incubation period—the time it takes for the symptoms to develop once the child is exposed to the rickettsia—is two to eight days. Rocky Mountain spotted fever is fatal in about 40 percent of cases in which the victim receives no treatment.

SIGNS AND SYMPTOMS

Rocky Mountain spotted fever starts with vague symptoms of headache, fever, and loss of appetite. One to five days later, a rash appears on the ankles and wrists and spreads rapidly to involve the entire body. The rash's pale rose-colored, flat or slightly raised spots often become reddish-purple. As the disease progresses, the fever worsens and severe muscle pain develops. The disease can be suspected if a rash and other symptoms follow a tick bite. The diagnosis cannot be confirmed, however, until the second week of the illness when the antibody (a substance produced by the body to fight invading disease) levels in the blood rise because the body is trying to fight the disease. Usually, the illness lasts about two to three weeks if complications do not arise.

HOME CARE

There is no home treatment. All you can do is watch carefully for symptoms of Rocky Mountain spotted fever in a child who is bitten by ticks. If symptoms appear, take the child to the doctor at once.

PRECAUTIONS

● If your dog has ticks, remove the ticks cautiously with tweezers, not with your fingers. A crushed tick can contaminate a scratch in the skin and transmit the microorganism that causes Rocky Mountain spotted fever. ● Use tick repellents on pets. ● Do not allow your child to handle wild rabbits. ● If your child is bitten by a tick, observe his or her health carefully for a week afterward.

MEDICAL TREATMENT

If there is a strong reason to suspect that the child has Rocky Mountain spotted fever, the doctor may start your child on antibiotics even before the diagnosis is confirmed. Tetracycline and chloramphenicol are the medicines used for initial treatment. The doctor may recommend that a child with this disease be hospitalized for up to ten days.

A vaccine is available that is partially effective against Rocky Mountain spotted fever. However, this vaccine is not recommended for routine use, and is only advised for those living or traveling in heavily tick-infested areas.

Related topic:

Insect bites
   and stings
Rash

Roseola

SYMPTOMS
High fever
Runny nose
Slight redness of throat
Slight enlargement of neck lymph glands
Rash

HOME CARE To help control fever, give aspirin or acetaminophen and have the child take lukewarm baths.

PRECAUTIONS

☐ The child does not seem to be very ill.

☐ Roseola does *not* cause cough, vomiting, diarrhea, eye or ear discharge, or extreme fatigue or collapse. Any of these symptoms should be brought to a doctor's attention.

☐ Fever caused by roseola typically cannot be consistently kept down with aspirin or acetaminophen.

☐ Another common illness that produces a high fever but few other symptoms is infection of the urinary tract.

A high fever precedes the splotchy, red rash of roseola.

Roseola is an acute, infectious disease characterized by a high fever followed by a rash. It is not known which virus causes the disease. Roseola occurs almost exclusively in children between the ages of six months and three years. The incubation period—the time it takes for symptoms to develop once a child has been exposed to the virus—is seven to 17 days. One attack of roseola provides lifelong immunity.

SIGNS AND SYMPTOMS

Roseola begins suddenly with a fever of 104°F to 106°F. It is one of the more common causes of convulsions with fever, which occur at the onset of the disease. It rarely produces any other symptoms, although sometimes roseola can cause a runny nose, mild redness of the throat, and minimal enlargement of the lymph nodes of the neck. Generally, the fever persists for three or four days and cannot be kept down consistently with aspirin or acetaminophen. Meanwhile, the child appears to be less ill than the degree of fever suggests. The fever disappears abruptly; at the same time, a splotchy, red rash appears on the trunk and spreads to the child's arms and neck. The rash disappears in one or two days, and the child is well again. Complications are rare.

Roseola is difficult to identify until the fever drops and the rash appears.

HOME CARE

Give aspirin or acetaminophen and use lukewarm baths to help control the fever.

PRECAUTIONS

● Another common illness that produces a high fever but few other symptoms is infection of the urinary tract. This is more common in girls. ● Coughing, vomiting, diarrhea, discharge from the eyes or ears, and extreme fatigue or collapse are not associated with roseola. If these symptoms occur, consult a doctor.

MEDICAL TREATMENT

The doctor will conduct a careful physical examination to rule out other illnesses which cause a high fever. The doctor may order blood or urine tests if he or she is concerned about other illnesses, but usually a few days' observation will confirm the diagnosis of roseola.

Related topics:

Convulsions with
   fever
Fever
Rash
Urinary tract
   infections

Rubella

SYMPTOMS
Swollen lymph nodes
Rash on face, spreading to body
Low-grade fever
Slight loss of appetite
Slight redness of throat and whites of
   eyes

HOME CARE
Give aspirin or acetaminophen to relieve fever.

Keep your child isolated from pregnant women.

PRECAUTIONS

☐ Rubella contracted during the first three months of pregnancy presents a 50–50 chance of damage to the unborn baby. Before trying to become pregnant, a woman should be tested to find out if she is immune to rubella. If she is not immune, she should be vaccinated at least three months before trying to become pregnant.

☐ A pregnant woman who has been exposed to rubella should consult an obstetrician immediately.

☐ Remember that a pregnant woman who is immune to rubella, because she had the disease earlier or has been immunized against it, will not pass rubella to her unborn child by being exposed to the disease.

☐ All children should be immunized against rubella.

An early symptom of rubella is swelling of the lymph nodes in front of and behind the ears, at the base of the skull, and on the sides of the neck.

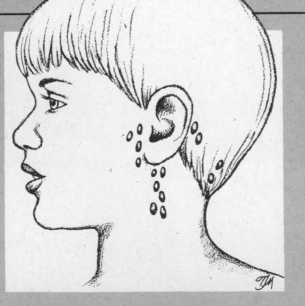

Rubella, or German measles, is one of the mildest contagious diseases of childhood. However, it can damage the unborn baby of a pregnant woman who contracts the disease. Women who contract rubella during the first three months of pregnancy have a 50–50 chance of delivering an infant who has cataracts, a cleft palate, heart problems, or who is permanently deaf or mentally retarded.

Rubella is caused by a specific virus and can be transmitted by direct contact with an infected person or by contact with articles contaminated by urine, stool, or secretions from the nose or throat of the infected person. The incubation period—the time it takes for symptoms to develop once a person has been exposed to rubella—is 14 to 21 days. One attack provides lifelong immunity.

SIGNS AND SYMPTOMS

Characteristic symptoms of rubella are swollen, tender lymph nodes in front of and behind the ears, at the base of the skull, and on the sides of the neck. In a day or two, a fine or splotchy dark-pink rash appears on the face; the rash spreads over the rest of the body within 24 hours. The rash usually lasts about three days and may or may not be accompanied by a low-grade fever (100°F–101°F), slight reddening of the throat and the whites of the eyes, and slight loss of appetite.

The patient is contagious for the period from seven days before the onset of the illness until four or five days after the appearance of the rash. Infants born with rubella may be contagious for as long as a year after birth.

No other disease causes both a rash and tenderness and enlargement of the particular lymph nodes involved in rubella. The diagnosis of rubella can be confirmed by culturing throat secretions, blood, or urine to identify the virus, or by blood test results that show an increased level of the antibodies, protective substances that the body has produced to fight the infection.

HOME CARE

Give aspirin or acetaminophen to reduce fever or discomfort. Do not let your child come in contact with pregnant women.

PRECAUTIONS

● Before becoming pregnant, a woman should either be immunized against rubella or should receive a blood test to find out if she is immune to the disease. If she is not immune, she should be immunized at least three months before trying to become pregnant. ● All children should be immunized against rubella. ● A pregnant woman who has been exposed to rubella should consult her doctor immediately. ● Be aware that a pregnant woman who is immune to rubella (having had the disease earlier or having been immunized) will not pass rubella to her unborn child by being exposed to the disease.

MEDICAL TREATMENT

Because it is so mild, doctors do not need to treat rubella in children. However, the doctor will establish the diagnosis by means of a physical examination and laboratory tests.

Related topics:

Glands, swollen
Immunizations
Rash

Scabies

SYMPTOMS Severe itching
Small red dots or black/gray lines on skin

HOME CARE Give nonprescription antihistamines to relieve itching.

Follow the doctor's instructions for treating the scabies, and make sure that all family members are treated at the same time.

Launder the infected child's undergarments, bedding, and towels to destroy the mites.

PRECAUTIONS

☐ If mites attack the skin around a nursing mother's nipples, scabies can occur on the baby's face.

☐ Secondary infection can occur when the child scratches.

☐ Consult a doctor before using any medications for scabies.

☐ Consult a doctor before applying any medication to the face of a baby with scabies.

☐ Lindane ointment, which is sometimes prescribed to treat scabies, is poisonous and should be kept out of the reach of children.

☐ If treatment does not clear up scabies, the person may be reinfested; consult the doctor.

☐ Scabies is easily transferred from one person to another, and all family members should be treated at the same time.

Lindane ointment or lotion to treat scabies is poisonous and must be kept out of the reach of children.

Scabies is a skin infection caused by the mite *Sarcoptes scabei*, a crawling insect barely visible to the eye. These mites burrow under the skin to lay eggs. The eggs hatch quickly and continue to tunnel for two weeks until they mature. Mature mites congregate around hair follicles, mate, and begin the cycle all over again. Scabies is easily transmitted to others and can be spread by direct human contact. It is rarely spread by animals.

The infestation of the mites typically occurs in between the fingers and toes, on the palms of the hands and undersides of the wrists, in the armpits, at the waistline, and, in males, on the penis. Because mites may also attack the skin around a woman's nipples, scabies sometimes occurs on the face of a breast-fed infant.

SIGNS AND SYMPTOMS

The burrowing of the insects and the skin's allergic reaction to their presence cause relentless itching. When the child scratches to relieve the itching, secondary infection can set in.

The diagnosis is based on the appearance and location on the skin of the small, red dots that mark the openings to the mites' burrows. The diagnosis also is suggested by gray or black lines on the skin marking the insects' tunnels. However, these signs on the skin can be obscured quickly by scratching.

HOME CARE

Mites can be destroyed by applying a lindane ointment or lotion or an ointment or lotion containing benzene hexachloride or crotonyl-N-ethyl-o-toluide. Before you use these medications, discuss them with your doctor. The medication is applied to all skin surfaces except the head and the face. If your infant appears to have scabies on the face consult your doctor before applying any medication. Because scabies is so easily transmitted from person to person, all family members should receive treatment at the same time. Treatment can be repeated once or twice. Nonprescription antihistamines may be used for temporary relief of itching.

PRECAUTIONS

● If marks on the skin and itching continue after treatment, the infected person may have been reinfested, or may have a persistent allergic reaction or secondary infection. Do not keep treating the condition in the hope that it will clear up; see your doctor. ● Destroy mites on undergarments, bedding, and towels by laundering these items. ● **Lindane ointment or lotion is poisonous**; be sure to keep it out of the reach of children.

MEDICAL TREATMENT

Your doctor will prescribe oral antibiotics to treat a secondary infection and antihistamines to relieve an allergic reaction.

Related topics:

Head lice
Impetigo

Scoliosis

SYMPTOMS Visibly curved spine
Hip-shot standing position

HOME CARE Check the child's posture periodically.

PRECAUTION

☐ Scoliosis can worsen rapidly. See your doctor if you suspect scoliosis.

Severe scoliosis can be seen from the back when the child stands up and even mild scoliosis is evident when the child bends forward at the waist. Bending forward causes the chest to rotate, making one side of the back more prominent.

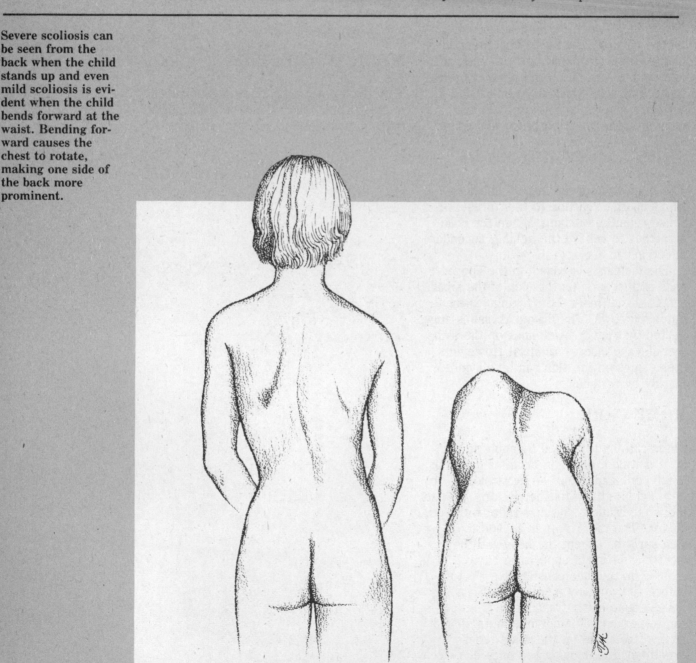

Scoliosis is also known as curvature of the spine. In profile (a side view) a normal spine, or vertebral column, traces an S curve from top to bottom of the back; viewed from the front or the back, the spine is straight from top to bottom. In scoliosis, the spine curves toward one side or the other when viewed from the rear. That curve toward one side produces a second, compensating, curve in the spine to keep the head straight.

One type of scoliosis (idiopathic scoliosis), which more frequently affects girls than boys, has no known cause. It develops during adolescence and stops getting worse when the child stops growing. The other types of scoliosis can develop at any age and can be caused by damage to the vertebrae (bones of the spine) from infection, a tumor, injury, radiation therapy; abnormal development of the vertebrae or ribs; or weakness in the muscles of the trunk. Scoliosis can also result from a difference in the length of the legs. Unlike other forms of the disease, this type of scoliosis does not result in a fixed curvature of the spine; the vertebral column straightens when the child lies down.

SIGNS AND SYMPTOMS

In severe cases of scoliosis the curvature of the spine can easily be seen when the child stands up. Even a slight curvature may be easy to recognize because the child stands in a hip-shot position, with one hip more prominent than the other. Scoliosis in almost any degree can be observed when the child bends forward at the waist with the knees straight. In this position scoliosis causes the chest to rotate, making one side of the back more prominent.

HOME CARE

The important aspect of home treatment is to watch for the onset of the condition by observing your child's posture periodically, particularly during periods of rapid growth.

PRECAUTION

● Any curvature of the spine is abnormal. Since scoliosis can become severe in a matter of months, your child should be checked as soon as you notice any abnormality. The child should then continue to see the doctor regularly.

MEDICAL TREATMENT

After confirming the presence of the condition, your doctor will often refer you to an orthopedist (bone specialist) who is skilled in treating scoliosis. The specialist will X- ray the spine.

Idiopathic scoliosis occasionally corrects itself during growth. However, it must be checked several times a year. Correction of idiopathic scoliosis may require the use of a back brace or surgery of the spine. Differences in leg length will be treated by placing lifts in the child's shoes or by surgery.

Exercise and physical therapy are not known to be helpful in treating any type of scoliosis.

Scrapes

SYMPTOM   A surface skin wound that is longer and wider than it is deep

HOME CARE   Wash the wound with soap and water and look carefully for embedded dirt or any other foreign matter.

Stop bleeding by covering the wound with gauze and applying gentle pressure.

If there's no dirt in the wound, apply a nonstinging antiseptic, cover the scrape, and keep it covered until completely healed.

If necessary, scrub gently to remove embedded dirt. Liberally apply antibiotic ointment to help keep the scab flexible. Keep the area covered.

PRECAUTIONS

☐ Do not treat at home any scrape that involves the full thickness of the skin; take the child to the doctor.

☐ If dirt is left in a scrape, it may cause infection or become sealed under the skin.

☐ A scrape on an area such as a joint that is subject to constant movement should be swabbed periodically with ointment to prevent cracking.

☐ A scrape that bleeds evenly over its entire surface requires medical attention.

☐ Keep your child's tetanus immunization up to date.

Scrapes are the most common and least dangerous injuries of childhood and seldom need a doctor's care unless the full thickness of the skin is involved.

A scrape (abrasion) is a shallow break in the skin caused by an injury. Scrapes are distinguished from cuts and lacerations in that they are not as deep as they are long or wide. Scrapes are, certainly, the most common and least dangerous injuries sustained by children. Most scrapes do not involve the loss of a full thickness of skin and heal with little or no scarring. However, any embedded dirt, sand, gravel, or blacktop may be permanently sealed under the skin if it's not removed before the abrasion heals.

SIGNS AND SYMPTOMS

Scrapes are easy to identify. As long as the full thickness of the skin has not been injured, the entire surface of the scrape will bleed unevenly and some large and small areas will not bleed at all. When the surface of a scrape does not bleed uniformly, it is classified as a first- or second-degree abrasion and can be treated at home. A third-degree abrasion bleeds uniformly over its entire surface and must be seen by a doctor because it could leave a scar.

HOME CARE

Wash the wound with soap and water, then examine it for any embedded dirt or other foreign matter. Inspect the wound carefully under good light, if necessary with a magnifying glass. To stop the bleeding, place a square of sterile gauze over the scrape and apply gentle pressure directly to the wound.

If there is no dirt in the wound, apply a nonstinging antiseptic, cover the scrape with a sterile bandage, and keep it covered until it heals completely and the scab falls off by itself. If the abrasion is in an area that is moved constantly (at a joint, for example), swab the scab periodically with an antibiotic or antiseptic ointment to keep it flexible and to avoid cracking.

If dirt is embedded in the wound, scrub gently. Sometimes, dirt will work its way out of the wound if you keep the abrasion covered and apply liberal amounts of antibiotic ointment twice a day.

PRECAUTIONS

● Do not treat an abrasion that involves the full thickness of the skin. Have the doctor look at it. ● Remove dirt from an abrasion, both to guard against infection and to prevent the dirt from being permanently sealed under the skin. ● It is unlikely, but not impossible, that tetanus will follow a scrape; since minor abrasions are seldom treated by a doctor, take the precaution of keeping the child's tetanus boosters up to date. ● Impetigo may begin at the site of an abrasion; if it occurs, refer to the section on *Impetigo*.

MEDICAL TREATMENT

If an abrasion is deep and badly soiled, your doctor may apply a local anesthetic to the region and scrub out the dirt with a brush or a substance that will dissolve the dirt.

Related topics:

Cuts
Immunizations
Impetigo
Puncture wounds
Tetanus

Shingles

SYMPTOMS   Listlessness
Fever
Pain and tenderness along a nerve
Blistery rash
Enlarged lymph nodes

HOME CARE   Give acetaminophen, not aspirin, to relieve pain.

PRECAUTIONS

☐ People who have shingles may transmit chicken pox. Consult the doctor if your child has not had chicken pox, or is at high risk from the complications of chicken pox, and is exposed to someone with shingles.

☐ A child who is taking steroid medications is at high risk from contracting chicken pox from someone with shingles.

☐ If shingles involves the eye, consult an eye specialist.

Shingles is an acute infection that produces crops of blisters on the skin. It's caused by the varicella zoster virus which also causes chicken pox, and people who develop shingles have had chicken pox at some time in the past. Presumably, after a bout of chicken pox, the varicella zoster virus lies inactive in the body until, for some reason, it is reactivated to cause shingles. Shingles is unusual in children under ten years of age, but it becomes increasingly common as the child gets older. One attack of shingles almost always provides lifelong immunity.

SIGNS AND SYMPTOMS

The initial symptoms of shingles are listlessness, fever, and pain, and tenderness along the path of a nerve. Shingles usually erupts on the chest, back, or abdomen, but it can occur along a nerve in the head or face, and it can involve an eye. In a few days red pimples appear on the skin, and nearby lymph nodes enlarge. The pimples turn into blisters that dry out and form scabs in five to six days. New outbreaks may continue to appear for up to a week; both rash and pain disappear within one to five weeks.

The diagnosis is based on the typical appearance of the rash—which is confined to the length of one or two nerves—and the pain. Before the rash appears the pain, which is sometimes intense, may be similar to that caused by pleurisy (inflammation of the lining of the chest cavity), an acute abdominal condition, or heart pain. In doubtful cases diagnosis of shingles is made on the basis of the results of blood tests.

HOME CARE

The only effective treatment consists of giving acetaminophen, not aspirin, to reduce the pain.

PRECAUTIONS

● If shingles involves the eye, consult an eye specialist. ● People who have shingles may transmit chicken pox. If your child is at high risk from the complications of chicken pox (for example, if the child is taking steroids, which suppress the body's immunity to disease) and is exposed to someone with shingles, the child should see a doctor.

MEDICAL TREATMENT

Your doctor may give zoster immune globulin (ZIG) or immune serum globulin (ISG) to a child who runs a risk from contracting chicken pox and who has been exposed to shingles.

Related topics:

Chest pain
Chicken pox
Glands, swollen
Rash
Stomachache, acute

Shock

EMERGENCY SYMPTOMS

Apply emergency treatment immediately.

EMERGENCY TREATMENT

1. Give essential life-saving first aid: take steps to stop bleeding and make sure the child's airway is open.

2. Get professional help immediately. Call police or paramedic squad.

3. Keep the child lying flat with the head lower than the body (unless there is a head injury).

4. If there is a head injury, have the child lie flat without elevating the feet.

5. Keep the child warm.

6. Do not offer food or water.

SYMPTOMS

Weakness
Feeling faint
Rapid, weak pulse
Paleness
Cold, clammy skin
Cold sweat

Chills
Dry mouth
Nausea
Rapid, shallow breathing
Restlessness
Confusion

PRECAUTION

☐ **Shock can be fatal** if the victim does not get immediate professional emergency care.

If you suspect a child is in shock, keep the child lying flat with the head lower than the body.

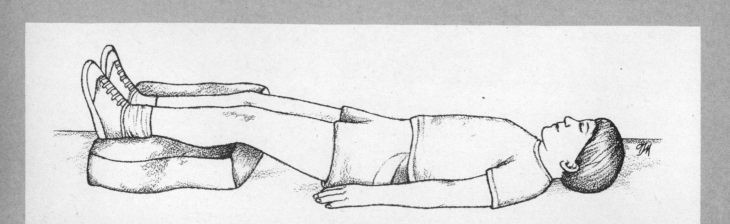

Shock is the term used to describe a sudden drop in blood pressure or a collapse of the circulatory system, which seriously reduces the blood supply to all parts of the body. Shock is an extremely dangerous condition; if it is not treated quickly it is usually fatal.

Generally, shock occurs when a great deal of blood or body fluid has been lost. It can also occur when blood vessels dilate (expand) and cause blood to pool or collect in one part of the body instead of circulating normally. The danger of shock exists in virtually every case of serious accident, injury, burn, or poisoning. Shock can also follow any of the following: severe infections; wounds or broken bones; hemorrhage (severe and uncontrolled bleeding); insect stings (in people who are allergic to the insect's venom); excessive vomiting or diarrhea; heart attacks; or reaction to certain drugs.

SIGNS AND SYMPTOMS

Signs of shock include weakness; feeling faint; rapid, weak pulse; paleness; cold, clammy skin; cold sweat; chills; dry mouth; nausea; rapid, shallow breathing; restlessness; and confusion. If these symptoms are not treated, the victim may lose consciousness.

HOME CARE

Shock is a **medical emergency** requiring immediate professional attention. After giving immediate life-saving first aid—for example, taking steps to stop bleeding and making sure the child's airway is open— you must call for professional help at once. Keep the child lying flat, with the head lower than the body (unless the head has been injured). If there is a head injury, have the child lie flat without elevating the feet. Keep the child warm. Do not give food or water.

PRECAUTION

● Shock is a very dangerous condition which is usually fatal if not treated immediately by professionals. If you suspect that the child is in shock, call at once for emergency help.

MEDICAL TREATMENT

Emergency medical treatment for shock will probably include administration of fluids or blood into a vein. The victim will be hospitalized.

Related topics:

Burns
Diarrhea in
   children
Diarrhea in infants
Fractures
Insect bites and
   stings
Poisoning
Vomiting

Shortness of breath

SYMPTOM   Breathing rate higher than normal

HOME CARE   None, except for shortness of breath caused by anxiety. Ask your doctor for advice.

PRECAUTIONS

☐ Do not be concerned if your child breathes more rapidly during a fever; fever increases the breathing rate.

☐ High doses of aspirin increase the breathing rate.

☐ Contact your doctor if your healthy child breathes rapidly while at rest.

Breathing is the process by which the body is supplied with oxygen and relieved of the waste product carbon dioxide. When the body's demand for oxygen is not met or it retains too much carbon dioxide, shortness of breath results. Shortness of breath usually follows prolonged physical exertion, but it also may accompany fever because the elevated temperature speeds up the body's chemical reactions which, in turn, increase the amount of carbon dioxide in the body and the demand for oxygen.

Shortness of breath also may be a sign of disease. It indicates that something is interfering with the intake and transport of oxygen. It may be due to croup; inflammation of the bronchial tubes or the epiglottis in the throat; asthma; pneumonia; inhalation of a foreign body; or spontaneous collapse of a lung (pneumothorax).

Inadequate transport of oxygen causing shortness of breath may signal the presence of heart disease, severe anemia, or carbon monoxide poisoning from automobile exhaust fumes or a defective heater.

A rapid rate of respiration may be a consequence of aspirin poisoning, which stimulates the breathing centers in the brain, or uncontrolled diabetes and dehydration (loss of body fluids). Anxiety sometimes causes the false sensation of shortness of breath.

SIGNS AND SYMPTOMS

The diagnosis of shortness of breath depends on the rate of breathing. To determine if your child is actually short of breath count the number of breaths per minute when the child is at rest. The average, normal rate of breathing for newborns is 40 breaths per minute; for one-year-olds, it is 30; and for those over eight years old it is 20. If the rate of breathing for your child at rest is double the normal rate, he or she is short of breath.

Your child's fever may hinder your ability to judge whether respiration is normal. If your child seems to be short of breath and has a fever, allow two or three extra breaths per minute for each temperature degree above normal, or time the breathing after the temperature has returned to normal.

HOME CARE

Except for air hunger caused by anxiety, no home treatment for shortness of breath should be attempted. Ask your doctor's advice and see the section on *Hyperventilation* in this book.

PRECAUTIONS

● A fever increases a person's rate of breathing. If the fever is treated with aspirin and the amount given is too much or given too often, the rate of breathing will increase even more. If your child who is taking aspirin becomes short of breath, double-check the dose of the aspirin to see if it's too high. ● Rapid breathing while your child is resting often signals a serious problem. Contact your doctor promptly whenever it occurs.

MEDICAL TREATMENT

Your doctor will perform a complete examination paying particular attention to the lungs, heart, throat, epiglottis, and blood pressure, and ordering chest and neck X rays. Blood and urine tests will be ordered to determine if the underlying cause of the shortness of breath is diabetes. You may be asked whether your child has been exposed to poisonous gases, such as carbon monoxide, or whether the child is being treated with aspirin for some other health condition. The specific treatment of shortness of breath depends on its cause.

Related topics:

Anemia
Asthma
Croup
Dehydration
Diabetes mellitus
Fever
Hyperventilation
Pneumonia
Poisoning

Sickle cell anemia

SYMPTOMS Weakness
Fatigue

OTHER SYMPTOMS Fever
Swelling of the joints
Pain

HOME CARE See your doctor for instructions about home care.

PRECAUTIONS

☐ Sickle cell trait and sickle cell disease occur most often in those of African descent and is found in a number of black Americans. Children of black parents or other parents with a family history of sickle cell disease should be tested before the age of one year.

☐ A child with sickle cell disease may get frequent infections and illnesses. Treat all infections immediately.

☐ If a child with sickle cell disease runs a high fever, call the doctor.

☐ A child with the disease should have frequent checkups.

☐ A child with the disease may need special treatment before surgery or dental work.

☐ No special treatment is needed if the child has sickle cell trait.

Sickle cell anemia, also called sickle cell disease, is an inherited blood disease. It is caused by an abnormality in the hemoglobin, which is a form of protein that helps the red blood cells to carry oxygen through the bloodstream. The abnormal hemoglobin makes the red blood cells become rigid and sickle-shaped (hence the name hemoglobin S). The deformed blood cells have difficulty passing through the blood vessels. In addition, normal blood cells are constantly destroyed and replaced by the body, but these abnormal cells are destroyed more quickly than normal ones. The replacement process cannot keep up with the destruction of the sickled cells, and this causes recurrent anemia.

Sickle cell trait and sickle cell disease are most common among people of African descent. The disease is also found in people from certain areas of India, Greece, Italy, and the Middle East.

A child may be born with sickle cell trait or sickle cell disease. A child with the trait has about 40 percent hemoglobin S and 60 percent normal hemoglobin. The child will function normally and will show no signs of the disease. However, the child carries the trait in his or her genes, and either the trait or the disease may appear in the next generation. If the child marries someone who also has the trait, the chances of their child having the disease are greatly increased.

SIGNS AND SYMPTOMS

In a child who has sickle cell disease, almost all the hemoglobin in the child's bloodstream is hemoglobin S. The child may often show symptoms of anemia, which include weakness and constant tiredness. In certain circumstances, such as when the child has an infection, a sickle cell crisis may occur. These crises may also occur for no apparent reason, or as a result of flying in an unpressurized airplane or traveling to altitudes over 6,000 feet. Other stresses on the body such as injuries or surgery can also cause a sickle cell crisis.

In a crisis, the abnormal red blood cells are destroyed rapidly, causing severe anemia. At the same time, other sickled cells may lodge in the blood vessels and cause fever, swelling of the joints, and severe pain. Sickle cell crises can damage body organs and such damage can eventually cause death.

To find out if a child has this disease, a blood test called a "sickle prep" is first performed to look for sickled cells in the blood. If abnormal cells are found, a more complicated test is done to separate the types of hemoglobin in the blood. The amount of hemoglobin S compared to the amount of normal hemoglobin will tell if the child has the trait or the disease.

HOME CARE

Sickle cell anemia requires medical treatment.

PRECAUTIONS

● All black parents, and any other parents who know there have been cases of sickle cell disease in their families, should have their children tested for the problem before they are a year old. ● All infections should be treated immediately, and high fevers should also be reported to the doctor right away. ● A child with this disease should have frequent checkups and may need special treatment before having dental work or surgery. ● A child who has sickle cell trait needs no special treatment.

MEDICAL TREATMENT

Each year, the doctor will carefully examine the child's liver, kidneys, heart, lungs, nervous system, and eyes. The doctor will probably prescribe antibiotics immediately if the child gets any infection. Blood transfusions may be needed to prevent anemia, and a vaccination against pneumococcus bacteria will be given as a precaution.

In a sickle cell crisis, the child should be hospitalized. Intravenous fluids and pain medications will be given until the crisis passes.

Related topic:

Anemia

Sinusitis

SYMPTOMS   Yellow or milky discharge from the nose
Fever
Pain
Stuffy nose
Cough
Red, swollen eyelids
Headache

HOME CARE   Protect the child against sinusitis by giving decongestant cold remedies for a cold and having the child use nose drops, or by treating an allergy with antihistamines.

Give aspirin or acetaminophen for pain. Warmth applied to the face also helps relieve pain.

PRECAUTIONS

☐ A child with symptoms of sinusitis plus high fever should see a doctor.

☐ See a doctor if the child has a pus-like discharge or other symptoms of sinusitis on one side of the nose only.

Sinuses are air-filled cavities within the face's structure that connect to the nasal passages. The sphenoidal sinuses are not shown here because they are located behind the ethmoidal sinuses.

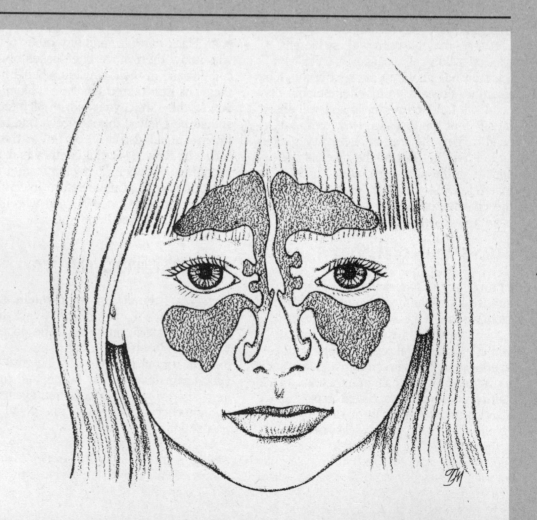

Sinusitis is inflammation or infection of the sinuses, the air-filled cavities in the face that connect with the nasal passages. Around the nose are four pairs of sinuses (the maxillary, frontal, sphenoid, and ethmoid sinuses). The maxillary sinuses, which lie below the eyes, and the ethmoid sinuses, which lie between the eyes, are present in infancy. The sphenoid sinuses, located behind the roof of the nose, become fully developed between the ages of three and five years, and the frontal sinuses, situated above the eyes, between six and ten years.

Because the sinuses are continuations of the nasal cavity, they are affected by any viral infection of the nose or any allergic reaction that occurs in the nose. Sometimes, a virus or an allergy attacks the openings to the sinuses and causes a bacterial infection within the sinuses. Bacterial infection of the sinuses can also follow a bacterial infection of the nose. A bacterial infection of the sinuses is true sinusitis.

SIGNS AND SYMPTOMS

The symptoms of sinusitis include fever (sometimes as high as 105°F), pain, stuffy nose, and cough. Depending on the location of the infection, headache may occur in the back of the head (infection of a sphenoid sinus), at the temples and over the eyes (infection of the ethmoid and frontal sinuses), or above and below the eyes (infection of the maxillary sinuses). Small children who have an infection in the ethmoid sinus develop red and swollen eyelids. However, the key to diagnosing sinusitis is the discharge from the nose.

With sinusitis, discharge from the nose is yellow, milky, or opaque. Pus in the sinuses can be revealed through an X ray, but it's easily confused with a thickening of the lining of the sinuses because of a common cold or an allergy.

HOME CARE

You can promote sinus drainage and protect against sinus infection by treating a cold with decongestants (taken by mouth) and nose drops, or by treating an allergy with antihistamines taken by mouth. These measures also encourage drainage after sinusitis has developed. To relieve pain and fever, heat may be applied to the affected sinuses, and aspirin or acetaminophen given to the child.

PRECAUTIONS

● A high fever (103°F to 104°F) plus signs of sinusitis indicate a potentially serious infection. See your doctor. ● A pus-like discharge or signs of sinusitis on one side of the nose suggest that a foreign object may be lodged in the nose or that the inside of the nose may be deformed. See your doctor.

MEDICAL TREATMENT

After identifying the infecting bacteria the doctor may prescribe antibiotics for the child to take by mouth. Suction may be used to drain the sinuses of older children with sinusitis. Surgical drainage is rarely indicated in children.

Related topics:

Common cold
Coughs
Fever
Headaches

Sore heels

SYMPTOM   Pain and tenderness

HOME CARE   Pad the heels of the child's shoes and temporarily restrict activities such as running and jumping.

PRECAUTIONS

☐ Inability to move the foot up and down may indicate a torn Achilles tendon and needs medical attention.

☐ Have the child see a doctor if home treatment does not promptly relieve the pain of Sever's disease.

☐ Pain may recur following a new injury. Repeat the treatment.

Sore heels are common among teenagers and are often caused by injury from the heels pounding the ground during sports activities. Restricting the child's activities and padding the heels of the shoes should relieve the pain.

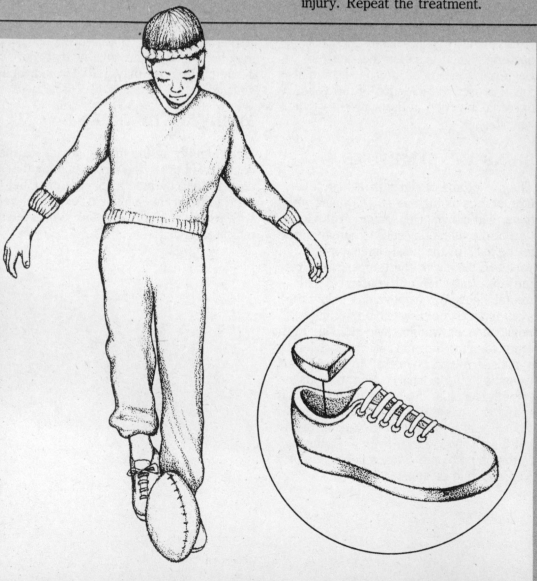

Painful heels are a common complaint before and during adolescence. Almost 90 percent of the time the pain is due to injury of the bony growth plate near the back of the heel bone (calcaneus). The injury is called Sever's disease and may be due to a direct blow caused by the heels pounding the ground, or to the calf muscles pulling on the Achilles tendon and the back of the heel bone.

SIGNS AND SYMPTOMS

In Sever's disease, one or both heels hurt when walking and are tender to the touch on both sides and the bottom of the heel bone (about one-half to one inch away from the back of the heel). The heels are not swollen or red; the skin over the heels shows no abnormality. The diagnosis is based on the presence of pain and tenderness at the heel and the absence of other symptoms. Note that other problems that cause pain at the heel also cause other symptoms. For example, infection of the heel bone (osteomyelitis) produces severe pain that intensifies over time, redness and swelling of the infected heel, and a low-grade fever. Blisters, plantar warts, and wounds of the heel can also cause sore heels.

HOME CARE

To relieve pain from Sever's disease, pad the heels of all of your child's shoes with a quarter-inch heel pad and temporarily restrict activities that involve running and jumping. Even if a child has pain in only one heel, be sure to pad the heels of both shoes.

PRECAUTIONS

● If your child can't move the affected foot up and down (by rising on tiptoes), he or she may have a torn Achilles tendon. Do not attempt home care. The child should see a doctor. ● With the proper home treatment Sever's disease should subside in four to six weeks; however, pain should cease as soon as the heels of the shoes are padded, and if the pain isn't promptly eased you should take your child to the doctor. ● Pain may recur following a new injury. Don't worry; just repeat the treatment.

MEDICAL TREATMENT

After a careful examination to rule out other causes of pain, your doctor will follow the same steps as you do in home treatment. If Sever's disease is severe, the doctor will immobilize the ankles. X rays are seldom required.

Related topics:

Blisters
Puncture wounds
Warts

Sore throat

SYMPTOMS
Pain
Swollen neck glands
Difficulty in swallowing

HOME CARE
Have the child gargle with salt water and drink extra fluids.

Give aspirin or acetaminophen to relieve pain.

Keep the child isolated until the cause of the sore throat is diagnosed.

PRECAUTIONS

☐ A child with a sore throat accompanied by any of the following symptoms should be seen by a doctor:
- swollen or tender neck glands
- persistent difficulty swallowing
- pus-like discharge from eyes or nose
- earache
- sinus pain
- breathing difficulty
- chest pain
- rash
- stiff neck
- weakness or exhaustion
- confusion
- prolonged vomiting

☐ Any child with a sore throat and fever that are still getting worse after 24 to 36 hours should be seen by a doctor.

☐ A child with a sore throat should be kept away from other children, particularly infants, until a diagnosis has been made.

In theory, and in the medical school classroom, a sore throat is one of the simplest childhood problems to diagnose and to treat. Medical textbooks state that a sore throat is usually caused by a virus and, therefore, does not require treatment with antibiotics because viruses do not respond to medication. A sore throat that is not caused by a virus is generally due to streptococcus bacteria. These organisms can be identified by culturing throat secretions, and a strep throat can be treated with penicillin or, if the child is allergic to penicillin, with erythromycin.

In practice, however, the diagnosis and treatment of a sore throat is not so straightforward. Viral infections sometimes are complicated by streptococcal infections. A throat culture may isolate streptococci organisms even though the illness is not being caused by these organisms, and about 5 percent of throat cultures will not show streptococci even when they are present and are, in fact, the cause of the sore throat. Some bacterial illnesses that cause a sore throat will respond to antibiotics, but the infecting bacteria cannot be identified through an ordinary throat culture.

SIGNS AND SYMPTOMS

It is difficult to be certain that an infant or toddler has a sore throat because the child cannot communicate, but swollen glands in the neck or difficulty swallowing are clues. Determining the cause of a sore throat depends on the results of a throat or other type of culture; on a complete blood count; and on the doctor's skill in performing the physical examination, knowledge of the illnesses in the community, and professional judgment.

HOME CARE

Older children may gargle with warm salt water to relieve a sore throat; all children should drink extra fluids and eat their usual diet if they can. Give aspirin or acetaminophen to reduce pain or fever and isolate the child from other children, particularly infants, until the cause of the problem is found.

PRECAUTIONS

● Take the child to a doctor if a sore throat is accompanied by any of the following symptoms: moderately or severely swollen and tender neck glands; difficulty swallowing that cannot be relieved by aspirin or acetaminophen; pus-like discharge from the eyes or nose; moderate or severe earache; tenderness over the sinuses; breathing difficulty; chest pain; reddish-purple rash or a rash resembling scarlet fever (fine, slightly raised red spots resembling coarse red sandpaper); stiff neck; weakness or exhaustion; confusion; or continual vomiting. ● If a sore throat and a fever continue to worsen after 24 to 36 hours, consult a doctor.

MEDICAL TREATMENT

Your doctor will conduct a complete physical examination and order a throat culture and, perhaps, other laboratory tests. Depending on the results of these tests, your doctor may treat a sore throat with antibiotics. Regardless of the treatment prescribed, you should report any new symptoms to your doctor. Also consult the doctor if there's no improvement in the child's condition after 48 hours.

Speech problems & stuttering

SYMPTOMS
Marked delay in achieving speech
Continued stuttering or stammering

HOME CARE
Speak to and listen to your baby in order to encourage speech.

Correct a child's speech gently, but never punish or ignore the child for incorrect speech or try to make the child practice speaking.

Do not get angry or anxious if the child stutters, and don't let other children tease or ridicule the child.

PRECAUTIONS

☐ Consult your doctor if your child's speech patterns do not appear to be developing according to the normally accepted timetable.

☐ Children learn to speak by imitation; speak, sing, and read to your child.

☐ A child who is not speaking clearly should not be forced, deliberately misunderstood, teased, or have attention drawn to his or her speech.

☐ Consult a doctor if your child speaks only in a monotone, has a marked nasal quality to his or her speech, or seems to be regressing rather than improving in vocabulary or pronunciation.

☐ Stuttering between the ages of two and five years old is not a problem unless it persists for several months.

☐ Severe, constant, or prolonged stuttering requires professional attention.

You can encourage your child's speech development by talking and listening and by introducing reading and singing activities.

Children learn to speak by imitation, but they may learn at different rates depending on their intelligence, their hearing, and their control of the muscles involved in speaking. Speech may be delayed or impaired if the speech centers in the brain are not normal, or if there is any abnormality of the larynx, throat, nose, tongue, or lips.

A child's normal speech development depends on how often the child hears speech and how much he or she is encouraged to speak. The average baby begins to babble and make letter-like sounds at four to six months of age. By eight months, the child has achieved a typical baby vocabulary using such "words" as "goo," "ba-ba," and "da-da." By 12 months, the baby will usually be using two-syllable "words" meaningfully ("ma-ma" for mother, "ba-ba" for bottle), and by two years old will be connecting words purposefully ("go bye-bye," "want cookie"). A child of five years can generally speak five-word sentences, and by the age of six can make all the sounds of the alphabet, except perhaps the sounds for *s* and *z*.

Children between two and five years of age often lack fluency and may stutter or stammer at times. If the lack of fluency or the stuttering or stammering continues, the child may have a speech problem. Speech that does not develop normally may also be due to partial or complete deafness, mental retardation, inadequate exposure to language, brain damage, physical abnormalities, or malfunction of the speech centers (aphasia).

SIGNS AND SYMPTOMS

Any marked delay in a child's achieving speech or an impairment of speech raises the suspicion of a speech or hearing problem.

HOME CARE

If your baby is to learn to speak adequately, he or she must be spoken to and listened to. Incorrect speech should be corrected, but a child should not be scolded, deliberately ignored, or forced to practice speaking. Stuttering in children aged two to five years old can be disregarded unless it is still a problem several months after its onset. It should not provoke anger or anxiety, suggestions that the child speak more slowly or more clearly, or laughter and taunts from brothers and sisters. Stuttering warrants professional attention if it is severe, constant, or prolonged.

PRECAUTIONS

● If your child's speech does not develop more or less in accordance with the timetable above, consult your doctor. ● Do not refuse to understand your child or try to force him or her to speak more clearly. ● Do not call the child's attention to stuttering. ● Read, sing, and speak to your child whenever possible. ● Notice if your child speaks only in a monotone or with a marked nasal quality, or if the vocabulary and ability to pronounce words are diminishing instead of improving.

MEDICAL TREATMENT

Your doctor will perform a complete physical examination, checking the child's throat, palate, and tongue, and testing the child's hearing. If your child is under the age of five you may be referred to a speech pathologist for evaluation and treatment if: stuttering is severe, constant, or unduly prolonged; the child seems to be severely frustrated in his or her efforts to speak clearly; or you need assistance in handling your child's development of speech. If your child substitutes sounds or stutters after the age of five or six, your doctor may suggest he or she be seen by a speech specialist.

Related topic:

Deafness

Sprains and dislocations

SYMPTOMS

Sprains
Pain
Swelling
Tenderness
Stiffness
Internal bleeding

Dislocations
Visible malformation
Inability to use joint

HOME CARE

A dislocation should not be treated at home.

A sprain can be treated by immobilizing and then resting the affected area.

Cold compresses applied to the area help relieve swelling.

Aspirin or acetaminophen can be given for pain.

PRECAUTIONS

☐ A sprain that does not improve rapidly may indicate a bone fracture and should be examined by a doctor.

☐ After a dislocation has been corrected, the joint may remain unstable for some time.

☐ A severe sprain that is improperly treated can result in a permanently weak joint.

☐ A sprain that is still swollen or painful to move is not healed.

☐ Elastic bandages do not adequately support or protect a sprained ankle.

All joints of the body are surrounded by ligaments, the tough connective tissues that hold bones together. These ligaments can be partially or completely torn when the joint is forcibly twisted beyond its normal range of movement. A partially or completely torn ligament is called a sprain.

If the ligaments are badly torn the bones of the joint may become dislocated (slip out of position). Besides the usual symptoms of a sprain, a dislocation causes a visible malformation of the area, and marked or total loss of function of the dislocated parts. Even after the dislocation has been corrected, the joint remains unstable for weeks.

Sprains are common during childhood, but dislocations other than a dislocated elbow are rare. Sprains most often occur in the fingers ("jammed" or "baseball" fingers), toes, ankles, neck, and back. Dislocations can also occur in the fingers, toes, kneecaps, and shoulders.

SIGNS AND SYMPTOMS

A sprain causes pain which is sometimes severe, swelling, tenderness, decreased movement of the joint, and internal bleeding. A mild or moderate sprain generally can be suspected if a joint is tender after it has been twisted or overextended.

Because dislocations produce a visible malformation, they are seldom missed. Furthermore, the inability to use the joint is an obvious sign of a dislocation. Fractures of the bones of the joint cannot be ruled out without X rays.

HOME CARE

A dislocation should not be treated at home. Minor sprains, particularly of the fingers, toes, and ankles, may be treated safely at home by immobilizing the hand or foot involved and then resting it. The sprained part should be kept elevated. Cold compresses applied for one to four hours after injury help minimize swelling. Aspirin or acetaminophen will temporarily relieve the pain. If a sprain does not improve rapidly a bone may be fractured; the child should be seen by a doctor.

PRECAUTIONS

● Do not attempt to correct a dislocation, even of the fingers. Dislocations are often accompanied by a fracture. ● What appears to be a sprained wrist in a child may actually be a fracture of the forearm bones near the joint; what appears to be a sprained thumb may actually be a fractured navicular bone in the hand. ● A severe sprain may take as long as a fracture to heal and if not treated properly can result in a permanently weak joint. ● A sprain is not healed if it is still swollen or if it is painful to move. ● Elastic bandages do not adequately support or protect a sprained ankle.

MEDICAL TREATMENT

Your doctor will carefully examine the injured joint and will take X rays if a dislocation or a fracture is suspected. A minor sprain may be X-rayed, or the joint immobilized and its rate of healing observed. If the rate of healing is not rapid enough, an X ray will be ordered.

Related topics:

Dislocated elbow
Dislocated hips
Fractures
Knee pains

Stomachache, acute

SYMPTOMS   Sudden abdominal pain
Cramping pain
Diarrhea
Vomiting

HOME CARE   Apply mild heat to the abdomen.

Treat constipation by changing the child's diet or with a glycerin suppository.

PRECAUTIONS

☐ Do not try to relieve stomach pain by giving a laxative or placing ice on the stomach.

☐ If you cannot diagnose the child's pain as being due to a cause such as constipation, digestive tract upset, or emotional stress, take the child to the doctor.

☐ If the stomach pain is accompanied by fever and painful urination, the child should see a doctor.

☐ If pain is accompanied by a fever and a cough, see a doctor.

☐ If any stomach pain persists or gets worse, consult a doctor.

☐ Severe, crampy stomach pain accompanied by blood or mucus in the stool requires a doctor's attention.

☐ Be concerned if the stomach pain causes the child to bend forward while walking.

☐ Severe pain that follows injury to the abdomen or lower chest may indicate internal injury and requires a doctor's attention.

The abdomen contains the stomach, small and large intestines, liver, spleen, pancreas, kidneys, urinary bladder, gall bladder, and organs of reproduction. Disease or injury involving any of these organs can cause abdominal pain and, consequently, a "stomachache" can test the diagnostic ability of a parent or a doctor. Fortunately, almost all stomachaches in children are caused by one of four problems: constipation; acute digestive tract upset (caused by viruses, bacteria, or improper diet); emotional stress; or urinary tract infection.

Other less frequent causes of a stomachache are appendicitis, pneumonia, infectious mononucleosis, and hepatitis.

SIGNS AND SYMPTOMS

The diagnosis first involves ruling out appendicitis. If appendicitis can be ruled out, consider other possiblities.

Your child probably is constipated if he or she has recently had no bowel movement or a hard movement; if the pain is intermittent (crampy) on the left side of the body and follows eating; and if the abdomen is soft but not tender to the touch.

Your child probably has digestive tract upset if he or she has eaten too much or has been exposed to someone who has acute gastroenteritis; if the pain is intermittent and occurs around the upper abdomen or navel; or if diarrhea follows vomiting.

Your child's stomachache is probably due to emotional stress if he or she is or has been upset and if the pain does not worsen.

If your child's pain cannot be explained by any of these causes take the child to the doctor.

Your child's stomachache may be due to urinary tract infection if the child has a fever and frequent, painful urination. The child should see a doctor.

HOME CARE

Treat constipation with a change in diet or a glycerin suppository. Unless it is severe (acute pain lasting for more than 24 hours), digestive tract upset will go away on its own; however, an anti-nausea medication (ask your doctor for suggestions) can relieve the vomiting, and mild heat applied to the abdomen can relieve the pain. A stomachache due to emotional stress will ease with relief from the stress, but one that arises from a urinary tract infection requires the attention of a physician. If any stomach pain persists or worsens, take your child to your doctor.

PRECAUTIONS

● Never give a child a laxative or place ice on the abdomen to treat abdominal pain. ● Steady, worsening pain usually is more serious than intermittent, crampy pain. However, severe and regular crampy pain may indicate a serious problem, particularly if there is also blood or mucus in the child's stools. ● Abdominal pain that forces a child to bend forward as he or she walks is a cause for concern. ● Abdominal pain combined with fever and a cough suggests pneumonia. ● Severe, worsening abdominal pain that follows an injury to the abdomen or lower chest suggests internal injury and requires a doctor's attention.

MEDICAL TREATMENT

Your doctor's first task is to determine the cause of the pain by taking a detailed medical history, performing a complete physical examination, and, in many cases, ordering a series of laboratory tests or X rays. If the diagnosis remains doubtful your doctor may observe your child for a few hours or ask for a consultation with another physician.

Stomachache, chronic

SYMPTOM Recurrent abdominal pain unaccompanied by other symptoms

HOME CARE Home treatment depends on the cause of the stomachache.

To treat constipation, give the child a high fiber diet including plenty of fruits and juices. For immediate relief, use a glycerin suppository. In the case of intolerance to milk, temporarily remove milk and milk products from the diet.

Try to remove any source of stress that is causing the stomachache.

Record the pattern of the pains so that you can explain the condition to the doctor if necessary.

PRECAUTIONS

- ☐ Stomach pain due to emotional stress is not a product of the child's imagination; it is as real as a pain produced by a physical condition and should be treated accordingly.

- ☐ Do not try to relieve stomach pain by giving laxatives or by placing ice on the stomach.

Examining your child's abdomen may help you determine the cause of a stomachache. For example, an abdomen that is soft but not tender may indicate constipation.

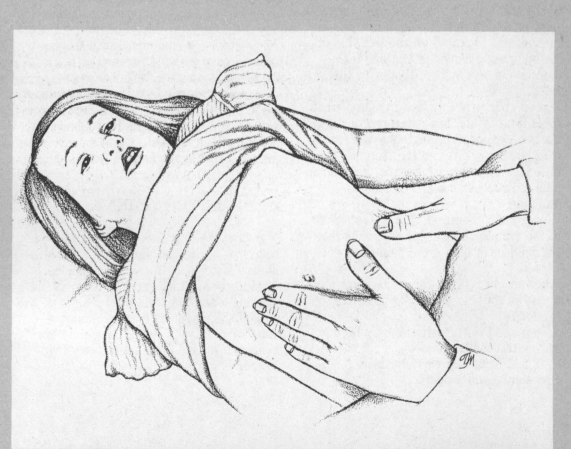

Intermittent (crampy) abdominal pain is quite common in children and may continue for weeks, months, or years. In some cases the pain occurs as often as two or three times a day, in others as infrequently as two or three times a year. Of course, one of a series of recurrent stomachaches may seem to be a bout of acute abdominal pain, and some conditions that cause abdominal pain can occur over and over again. However, chronic stomach pain usually is due to constipation, intolerance of cow's milk (lactase deficiency), or emotional stress. Less common causes are urinary tract problems (obstruction, chronic infection); peptic ulcer; sickle cell anemia; lead poisoning; ulcerative colitis; regional enteritis (Crohn's disease); tumors; ovarian problems; worm infestations (pinworms, Giardia); intolerance of foods other than milk; and internal hernias. Recurrent abdominal pain is not due to appendicitis.

SIGNS AND SYMPTOMS

To pinpoint its cause, recurrent abdominal pain must be associated with other symptoms such as vomiting, diarrhea, constipation, blood or mucus in the stools, fever, failure to gain weight, painful urination, ingesting inedible substances (pica), or anemia. Also important is the pattern of the pain—where it is, when it occurs, how long it lasts.

In general, recurrent abdominal pain that is accompanied by no other symptoms or has no set pattern is probably not serious.

HOME CARE

If constipation is the cause of the pain, correct it by changing your child's diet or using a glycerin suppository. If milk seems to be the cause, eliminate milk and milk products from the diet for one or two weeks; then add milk to the diet again and observe the effects. If emotional stress is responsible, try to eliminate the stress. Most important, note and record the pattern of recurrent abdominal pain and any other symptoms that occur before consulting your doctor.

PRECAUTIONS

● Recurrent abdominal pain due to emotional stress is real and requires treatment just as much as pain due to an identifiable physical condition. ● Do not try to relieve stomach pain by giving laxatives or placing ice on the stomach.

MEDICAL TREATMENT

Your doctor will take a careful history of your child's recent health and perform a complete physical examination. Frequently the doctor will order urine, stool, and blood tests. If the cause of the pain still is not clear, X rays of the stomach, large and small bowels, and the urinary tract may be required. If X rays provide no clues to the problem your child may be hospitalized for extensive blood tests and an internal abdominal examination.

Strep throat

SYMPTOMS

Headache
Fever
Sore, red throat
Vomiting
Abdominal pain
Swollen lymph glands in neck
Sandpaper rash

HOME CARE

Give aspirin or acetaminophen to relieve pain and fever and take the child to the doctor.

PRECAUTIONS

☐ Keep infants away from groups of children, some of whom may be carriers of the strep bacteria.

☐ If one child has a strep infection, your other children should receive a throat culture whether they are sick or not.

☐ Even if the child appears to be better, do not discontinue treatment until the child has taken all the medication prescribed by the doctor.

☐ A strep infection imparts immunity only to the particular type of bacteria that caused it; there are over 60 types of streptococcus organisms.

Strep throat requires a doctor's attention. The doctor will examine the child's throat and order a culture to identify the strep germ.

Strep throat is a highly contagious infection of the throat, usually caused by the group A strain of beta-hemolytic streptococci bacteria. Although some strep germs do not cause rashes, most types can produce a toxin (poison) that causes the rash that typifies scarlet fever (also commonly called scarlatina). There are at least 60 different types of streptococcus organisms. After an attack of strep throat the individual is immune to further attack from that one type of streptococcus organism only.

A streptococcal infection can be serious. Among its complications are rheumatic fever, nephritis (inflammation of the kidneys), middle ear infection, sinusitis, pneumonia, and transient (temporary) arthritis.

The incubation period (the time it takes for symptoms to develop once the child has been exposed to the bacteria) of strep throat is two to five days, and the disease is passed from child to child by means of the throat or nasal secretions of an infected person. It may also be spread by a carrier who has no symptoms of the illness. (A carrier is a person who harbors the disease-causing organism and can pass it on to others, but does not get sick him- or herself.) At times, as many as half the children in any one area may be carriers of the disease.

SIGNS AND SYMPTOMS

The onset of strep throat is sudden. It begins with a headache, fever up to 104°F, sore and red throat, vomiting, abdominal pain, and swollen lymph nodes in the neck. If the infecting organism is rash-producing and the child is not immune, he or she will develop a rash within 24 to 72 hours. The rash is typical of scarlet fever, with fine, slightly raised red spots resembling coarse red sandpaper. It appears on the base of the neck, in the armpits and groin, and then on the trunk and extremities. The child's face is flushed, but the lips are pale. When the rash subsides in three to 20 days, the skin flakes and peels.

The diagnosis of a strep throat cannot be confirmed without a throat culture that isolates streptococcus organisms. However, cultures are only 90 to 95 percent reliable. The diagnosis of scarlet fever is based on the appearance of the rash.

HOME CARE

The only home treatment recommended is to give aspirin or acetaminophen to relieve fever and pain. A streptococcal infection should be treated by your doctor.

PRECAUTIONS

● Infants are immune to the scarlet fever toxin for four to six months if their mothers are immune. The infants are *not* immune to a streptococcal infection, which may be very serious but may not produce typical symptoms. Consequently, keep infants away from groups of children, some of whom may be carriers of the streptococci bacteria. ● If one child in your family has a streptococcal infection, your other children should receive a throat culture whether they are sick or not. ● Follow the full course of antibiotic treatment prescribed by a doctor, giving your child all the medication prescribed even if the child seems to be well before all the medicine is finished.

MEDICAL TREATMENT

Strep throat is diagnosed by means of a physical examination and the results of a throat culture. Penicillin (or another antibiotic for those who are allergic to penicillin) is usually prescribed for ten days to cure the streptococcal infection. Antibiotics prevent rheumatic fever and may prevent inflammation of the kidneys. A child who develops complications may have to be hospitalized.

Styes

SYMPTOMS   Swelling, pain, and redness of the eyelid
Formation of pus and a "head"

HOME CARE   Bathe a stye with warm water several times a day.

Aspirin or acetaminophen help reduce pain.

Apply antibiotic ointment to prevent reinfection.

Cysts only require treatment if they are infected; then treat them like styes.

PRECAUTIONS

☐ Do not confuse styes with cysts or insect bites.

☐ Styes do not cause redness of the white of the eye.

☐ See a doctor if a stye recurs, or if it is accompanied by any of the following: fever, headache, loss of appetite, or lethargy.

☐ Washcloths and towels used by the infected child should be kept separate from those used by other family members.

A stye is a boil that occurs in the oil or sweat glands on the upper or lower eyelids.

Styes are boils that occur in the oil or sweat glands in the upper or lower eyelids. Styes are usually caused by staphylococcus organisms, and they can spread from person to person through direct contact. Styes tend to occur in crops, because the bacteria in the pus that forms in the stye spread easily to infect other glands in the eyelids.

SIGNS AND SYMPTOMS

Styes develop like boils. The area at the edge of the eyelid becomes increasingly red, painful, tender, and swollen. After two to three days, pus forms, and the stye "points"; that is, a yellow head appears at the edge of the lid near the base of the eyelashes. Styes usually break spontaneously, drain, and heal. Occasionally, a stye will heal without pointing or draining.

Styes differ from insect bites and cysts in that they are painful and tender. They occur near the margins of the eyelids, and they usually come to a head. Insect bites itch, are not painful, and do not come to a head. Cysts are lumps or swellings that show through the under surface of the eyelids as pink or pale yellow spots. They usually are not tender. Sometimes, however, they become infected and, like styes, are red, tender, and painful. Unlike styes, cysts persist for some time and do not come to a head.

HOME CARE

Place cotton balls or a washcloth soaked in warm water on the eyelids for ten to 20 minutes several times a day. Give aspirin or acetaminophen to reduce pain. Apply antibiotic eyedrops (available by prescription) several times a day to prevent the formation of additional styes. Do not treat cysts unless they are infected; then, treat them in the same way you would a stye.

PRECAUTIONS

● The whites of the eyes do not become red as a result of a stye. ● One large or several small recurring styes, or a stye that accompanies such symptoms as fever, headache, loss of appetite, or lethargy, should be seen by a doctor. ● Styes can be contagious. Keep the infected child's towel and washcloth separate from those used by other family members.

MEDICAL TREATMENT

Your doctor may prescribe antibiotics to treat one large or several small recurring styes. It is rarely necessary to open and drain a stye. The doctor may take a culture of the nose and throat secretions to find out where the bacteria are located.

Your doctor may surgically remove an infected cyst. However, cysts often disappear spontaneously in months or years. Your doctor will treat an infected cyst in the same way as a stye.

Related topics:

Boils
Conjunctivitis
Insect bites and
  stings

Sudden infant death syndrome

Quick Reference

SYMPTOMS   None

HOME CARE   If an infant is diagnosed as high risk, the doctor will make recommendations for home care to guard against SIDS.

PRECAUTIONS

☐ Have your doctor demonstrate how to revive an infant who has stopped breathing.

☐ Courses in cardiopulmonary resuscitation (CPR) are available through community organizations and should be taken by every parent.

☐ Certain factors, including premature birth, low birth weight, and lack of medical care during pregnancy, make some babies more at risk than others.

☐ SIDS is more common in families in which it has occurred before.

☐ Whether the baby is breast- or bottle-fed has no relation to the occurrence of SIDS; neither does the position in which the child sleeps.

All babies sometimes have periods when they stop breathing for a second or two. Occasionally, the nonbreathing period will last for a longer time. This is called "periodic breathing." But if the infant's automatic breathing mechanism does not start again, and if no one is there to revive the baby, the child will die. This is called Sudden Infant Death Syndrome, or SIDS, because the cause is not well enough understood to give it a more specific name. SIDS usually occurs at night, when an infant is asleep, and is most common between the ages of one and four months. It is most common in the winter months and affects boys more often than girls. Although the cause of death is not known, some experts believe SIDS is related to an abnormality or an underdevelopment of the respiratory control center of the brain. In many cases, the infant has a mild respiratory infection, such as a cold, when death occurs.

There are several factors that make SIDS more likely for some babies than for others. If a child's parents are under 20 years of age when the child is born or if they are poor, the risk of SIDS is increased. If the mother did not receive medical care during the pregnancy, was ill during the pregnancy, or smoked or abused drugs during the pregnancy, the risk is also increased. Twins, triplets, and infants who are born prematurely or are below normal weight at birth are especially susceptible. Although SIDS is not actually inherited, the risk is greater for infants whose parents have lost a child to SIDS before and for infants from families in which SIDS has occurred before.

It has been determined that the baby's sleeping position does not play a part in SIDS, nor does whether a child is breast-fed or bottle-fed.

SIGNS AND SYMPTOMS

There are no warning signs. SIDS can only be identified for certain after death, when an autopsy does not reveal any other cause of death. An infant who has stopped breathing and has been revived, or who is considered at risk for other reasons, may be given a pneumogram. In this test, a machine is attached to the infant for 48 hours to record breathing patterns. The periods of nonbreathing are evaluated based on their number, their length, and how often they occur. The doctor can then determine if special treatment is necessary.

HOME CARE

There is no specific treatment for SIDS, unless a diagnosis of high risk is made by a doctor.

PRECAUTIONS

● Every parent should know how to revive an infant who has stopped breathing. This is especially important when an infant is at high risk of SIDS. Courses in cardiopulmonary resuscitation (CPR) are available from the Red Cross and other community agencies. ● Have your doctor show you how to revive a baby who has stopped breathing.

MEDICAL TREATMENT

If your baby has stopped breathing or turned pale or blue, and has been revived, or if a pneumogram has shown abnormal breathing patterns, there are two ways to protect the child from SIDS.

The first is to attach monitors to the infant whenever he or she is put down to sleep. Each time the infant stops breathing for an amount of time set on the monitor, an alarm goes off. These devices are not completely reliable, and they can be disruptive to the whole family if they're used at home.

The second possibility is to give the child regular doses of a drug called theophylline, which stimulates the respiratory center of the brain and is usually used to treat asthma. In some infants, use of theophylline protects against nonbreathing periods. The long-term results of giving theophylline to infants is not yet known, so the drug is prescribed with caution. An infant who is being given theophylline as protection against SIDS must be watched closely and have blood tests and pneumograms regularly.

Sunburn

SYMPTOM Red, blistering, painful skin

HOME CARE Prevent sunburn by regulating the child's exposure to the sun and using an appropriate sunscreen.

If the child does get burned, apply cold water compresses, then cocoa butter, burn ointment, or a paste of baking soda and water to the burned area.

Give aspirin or acetaminophen for pain, and antihistamines for itching.

Avoid breaking the blisters of sunburn.

PRECAUTIONS

☐ The sunscreen used on a child should contain para-aminobenzoic acid (PABA), titanium dioxide, methyl anthranilate, or sulisobenzone.

☐ Sunscreens come off in water. Follow the instructions for reapplying the product after the child has been swimming.

☐ Remember that children and babies can be burned by sun coming through a window.

☐ Use sunburn medication sparingly; it can be absorbed through the skin and cause side effects.

☐ Skin damage from overuse of sun-lamps is often seen in teenagers.

☐ Some medications increase sensitivity to the sun, and a child who is taking such a medication should use a sunscreen and limit exposure to the sun.

☐ A child who has a sunburn accompanied by fever or extreme fatigue or weakness needs a doctor's care.

☐ Fair-skinned babies and children can burn even on cloudy days or in shade.

Sunburn is a heat burn, usually of the first degree. Babies and children who have fair complexions are particularly susceptible to sunburn, even on cloudy days or in shade. Occasionally, sunburn causes a skin rash which resembles hives or the rash caused by poison ivy. This condition is called sun poisoning.

SIGNS AND SYMPTOMS

Sunburn causes the skin to become inflamed, blistered, and painful, and the diagnosis is usually immediately obvious. The rash caused by sun poisoning, however, may not appear for several days after exposure to the sun.

HOME CARE

Apply cold water compresses, then cocoa butter, commercial burn ointments, or a paste made of baking soda and tap water to the burned area. Do not break the blisters. Give the child aspirin or acetaminophen to relieve pain and nonprescription antihistamines to reduce itching.

PRECAUTIONS

• The most important aspect of home treatment is prevention. A child should begin exposure to the sun slowly and gradually increase the length of exposure. • Apply sunscreens to filter out damaging rays of the sun, but remember that sunscreens offer only limited protection; the child who is out in the sun for too long can still get sunburned. For a child, select a sunscreen that contains para-aminobenzoic acid (PABA), titanium dioxide, methyl anthranilate, or sulisobenzone. • Remember that all sunscreens wash off when the child goes swimming or even perspires. Follow the instructions on the product's package for reapplying the sunscreen. • Sunscreens may cause a mild rash on some people. If a rash appears, switch to another product. • Infants and children may receive a severe burn from the sun coming through the windows especially in the car. Be sure children are protected by sunscreens. • Medication applied to large areas of sunburn can be absorbed into the body and produce side effects. Use medication sparingly. • Injury to the skin from overexposure to ultraviolet light from sunlamps is common among teenagers. • Some medications (for example, tetracycline, chlorpromazine, griseofulvin, and coal tar ointments) increase the sensitivity of the skin to sunburn. If the child is taking one of these medications, be extra careful about protecting him or her from the sun. • Take the child to a doctor if he or she has a sunburn plus a fever or extreme fatigue and weakness.

MEDICAL TREATMENT

Your doctor will treat your child's sunburn the same as any other type of burn. A child who has a severe burn will be hospitalized for treatment.

Related topics:

Blisters
Burns

Swallowed objects

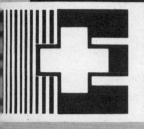

EMERGENCY SYMPTOMS

Choking
Inability to breathe or cry

EMERGENCY TREATMENT

Call police or paramedic squad.
See section on *Choking*—p. 80.

SYMPTOMS

Gagging
Pain in throat or chest
Difficulty swallowing
Abdominal pain
Vomiting

HOME CARE

A small, smooth object that the child has swallowed should pass out of the body in the stool without treatment; examine the stools until the object is passed.

In the case of a larger object, examine each stool to see if the object has been passed. If it does not appear within one week, notify the doctor.

PRECAUTIONS

☐ Do not give the child a laxative in an effort to speed passage of a swallowed object.

☐ No medication or other agent is available to speed up or make safer the passage of a swallowed object through the system.

☐ An object lodged in the esophagus must be removed promptly, preferably by a doctor.

☐ Any object that has not left the body within one week should be reported to the doctor.

Over 95 percent of the penny-, nickel-, or dime-size foreign objects that are swallowed by children cause no trouble and pass from the body in the child's stool. However, objects that are the size of a quarter or larger may become lodged in the esophagus (the tube through which food passes on its way to the stomach). Sharp objects (pins, needles, bones, matchsticks, nails, glass splinters) may lodge in the tonsils, throat, or esophagus. Objects longer than a toothpick may not be able to pass out of the stomach and may have to be removed surgically.

SIGNS AND SYMPTOMS

Depending on where the object is lodged, it may cause choking (see section on *Choking* immediately), gagging, pain, discomfort in the throat or chest, or difficulty swallowing. Once a foreign object passes into the stomach it does not produce any symptoms unless it obstructs or penetrates the digestive tract. Then abdominal pain, vomiting, and fever may develop. If the child has swallowed a metal object it will be visible on an X ray, but wood, plastic, or glass will not. Usually, however, the diagnosis is suggested by the circumstances and the symptoms that do appear.

HOME CARE

If the swallowed object is small and smooth, no treatment is necessary. If the object is long, sharp, or large, examine the child's stools carefully for several days to be sure the object has passed from the body. Each bowel movement must be passed through a sieve until the object is passed. If the child has been trained, place in the toilet bowl a basin fashioned of window screening. Then, after the child has passed a stool wash it through the screening with hot water.

PRECAUTIONS

● An object lodged in the esophagus must be removed **within hours**, preferably by a doctor. ● No known food, drink, or medication will speed up the passage of a foreign object through the body. ● If an object has not passed from the child's body within one week, see your doctor. Try to bring a duplicate of the swallowed object to show your doctor. ● Do not give your child a laxative in an effort to speed passage of a swallowed object.

MEDICAL TREATMENT

Your doctor will carefully inspect the throat and observe the way your child swallows. The doctor may order X rays of the throat, neck, chest, or abdomen. If an object is wedged in the throat or esophagus, your doctor will remove it with a surgical instrument. If the object is in the stomach the doctor will watch the child's condition for three or more weeks before trying to remove it surgically. If the object is in the intestines and does not pass within a week the doctor may remove it surgically.

Related topic:

Choking

Swimmer's ear

SYMPTOMS   Itching or clogging of ear canal
Discharge from ear canal
Pain
Fever
Swollen and tender lymph nodes

HOME CARE   To relieve pain, give aspirin or acetaminophen and apply warm compresses to the outside of the ear.

Try to prevent swimmer's ear in a susceptible child by drying the ear canals after each swimming session; to do this, place a few drops of rubbing alcohol or glycerin in each ear.

After administering any ear drops, keep the child's head tilted for a little while so that the drops can penetrate deeply into the ear canal.

PRECAUTIONS

☐ Severe pain, fever, or swollen glands, or failure to respond to home treatment within a few days indicate that the child should see a doctor.

☐ Earplugs of lamb's wool coated with petroleum jelly keep water out better than rubber plugs and can be made at home.

☐ Never clean inside a child's ear canal.

Swimming in fresh water or pools can cause swimmer's ear in which frequent exposure to moisture causes the ear canal to soften, swell, and crack so that germs can enter and cause infection.

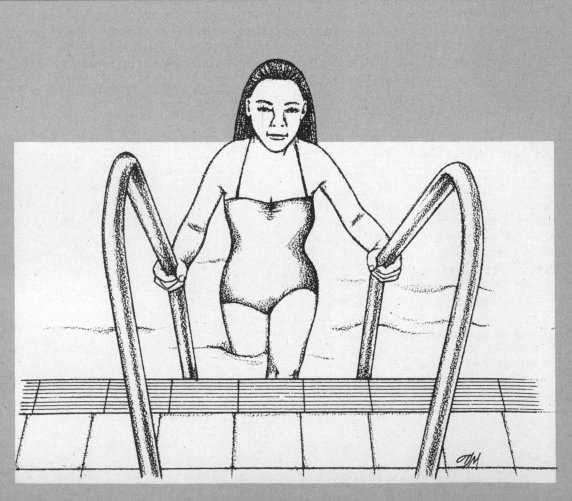

Irritation or infection of the ear canal is known as swimmer's ear. Swimmer's ear may arise from a middle ear infection that has caused the eardrum to rupture and allowed infected material (pus) to drain into the outer canal. The condition can also occur if an injury to the ear canal becomes infected. Usually, however, swimmer's ear is caused by swimming in fresh water or pools. Frequent and sustained moisture in the ear softens, swells, and cracks the ear canal, allowing germs to penetrate the canal and cause infection.

SIGNS AND SYMPTOMS

A mild case of swimmer's ear may appear as an itching, clogged ear canal with or without discharge; hearing may be diminished. A severe case may cause intense pain, fever, and swollen and tender lymph nodes in front of, behind, and below the ear. Without discharge from the ear, the diagnosis is based on internal examination of the ear.

HOME CARE

Under your doctor's direction, treat a mild case of swimmer's ear by administering ear drops containing antibiotics and steroids four times a day. Give aspirin or acetaminophen or apply warm compresses to the outside of the ear to reduce pain. If your child has had several bouts of swimmer's ear, dry the ear canals at the end of each swimming session by dropping in a few drops of rubbing alcohol or glycerin. This may prevent the condition from recurring.

PRECAUTIONS

● If a child has severe pain, fever, or swollen glands, or does not respond to home treatment in a few days, take the child to your doctor. ● Rubber earplugs will not keep water out of the ear canals. Earplugs made at home from lamb's wool and coated with petroleum jelly may be more effective. ● Do not clean ear canals by using bobby pins, cotton swabs, or any other object. ● If ear drops do not penetrate deeply into the ear canal, they will not be effective. After administering the drops, be sure to keep the child's head tilted for a little while to give the drops time to penetrate properly.

MEDICAL TREATMENT

In addition to ear drops, your doctor may prescribe antibiotics for the child to take by mouth. If the ear is not too tender, the doctor will clean the ear canal.

Related topics:

Draining ear
Earaches
Glands, swollen

Teething

SYMPTOMS
Drooling
Fretfulness
Sleeplessness
Loss of appetite
Pain or discomfort
Chewing fingers or objects

HOME CARE Give the baby zweiback toast, teething biscuits, or a teething ring to bite on; this will help the teeth erupt.

To ease pain give aspirin or acetaminophen, rub the gums with a cold object, or have the child bite on a cold object.

Distract the baby with activities.

PRECAUTIONS

☐ Do not be too quick to assume a baby's symptoms are caused by teething; look for other causes.

☐ Do not try to force-feed a child whose eating and drinking habits change during teething.

☐ Diarrhea and constipation are not related to teething unless there has also been a significant change in the child's diet.

☐ Teething does not cause fever, cough, or discharge from the nose.

☐ Drooling from teething may cause the face to become chapped, but any other rashes are due to other causes.

☐ Overuse of teething ointments and solutions that contain local anesthetics can be harmful.

☐ A baby may be fretful, wakeful at night, or unwilling to eat for many reasons other than teething.

A baby usually cuts 20 teeth during the first three years of life. All 20 are temporary (deciduous) and are partly formed within the gums at birth. The age and sequence of the eruption of the teeth varies from child to child. Usually, however, the lower central front teeth (incisors) are the first to break through the gums. This can occur before birth or as late as one year of age. The upper four central front teeth (incisors) and the lower side incisors on either side of the lower central front teeth usually follow. The four one-year molars appear next (in the gums inside the cheeks), then the four canines, (the cone-shaped pointed teeth on either side of the upper and lower front teeth), and finally the four two-year molars.

SIGNS AND SYMPTOMS

Teething commonly is accompanied by drooling, fretfulness, wakefulness at night, unwillingness to eat, discomfort, or chewing on fingers or objects. The drooling and chewing are quite normal; fretfulness, wakefulness, and unwillingness to eat can have many causes.

A few days before teeth erupt, they push at the gum ahead of them and can be seen or felt. Before molars erupt, they frequently cause a blue blood blister at the site of the tooth.

HOME CARE

Teething pain can be eased by rubbing the baby's gums with a cold object. Biting on zwieback toast, teething biscuits, and teething rings help the teeth erupt, and biting on cold objects (ice wrapped in cloth, frozen teething rings) numbs the gums and eases the pain of teething. Aspirin or acetaminophen also may help relieve pain. In the daytime, keeping the child amused and occupied may make him or her forget the pain.

PRECAUTIONS

● Young children cut teeth on and off for three years. During this period, do not assume that every symptom the child has is due to teething; look for other possible causes. ● Diarrhea and constipation are related to teething only if there is an extreme change in the child's diet. ● If the child's eating and drinking habits change during teething, do not try to force-feed. ● Fever, cough, and nasal discharge are not symptoms of teething. ● Drooling because of teething may produce chapping on the face; other rashes are not related to teething. ● Overuse of commercial teething ointments and solutions that contain local anesthetics can cause anemia (deficiency of red blood cells).

MEDICAL TREATMENT

Before assuming symptoms are caused by teething, your doctor will check for other causes.

Related topics:

Anemia
Toothache

Testis, torsion of

Quick Reference

SYMPTOMS
Increasing pain and swelling of testis
Discoloration of the skin of the scrotum
Nausea
Vomiting
Lower abdominal pain
Fever

HOME CARE Torsion of the testis is an emergency and requires immediate professional care.

PRECAUTIONS

☐ Do not attempt to treat this condition at home. The child must see a doctor **immediately**.

☐ If pain near a testis increases and the testis is swollen, tender, or discolored, take the child to a doctor at once.

☐ Lower abdominal pain or pain in the groin may indicate torsion in a boy who has an undescended testis that has not been corrected.

☐ If pain increases following an injury or bruise to the testis, suspect torsion.

☐ **Never** delay treatment of torsion of the testis. Hours count.

For unknown reasons, a testis, the male sex gland, may become twisted, shutting off the blood supply. Although the condition is more apt to affect boys who have an undescended testis, it is quite common among boys whose testes are in the normal position in the scrotum, the pouch of skin behind the penis. The condition may also follow a minor injury.

SIGNS AND SYMPTOMS

A testis that is twisted first becomes slightly swollen and tender. Within a few hours it is intensely painful, and very tender and swollen. The testis and the surrounding skin become discolored (red or blue), and the boy may be nauseated or vomit and have lower abdominal pain and a fever.

Torsion (twisting) of a testis that has descended into the scrotum may be confused with an infection (orchitis), a strangulated hernia, or a bruise of the scrotum. Torsion of a testis that has not descended and lies in the groin may be confused with a strangulated hernia, an injury, or infected lymph glands in the groin. Torsion of an undescended testis that lies within the abdominal cavity is difficult to diagnose but may be suspected whenever abdominal pain occurs. This is an emergency situation and requires immediate medical treatment.

Torsion of a part of a testis (appendix of the testis) causes similar, although less intense, symptoms. Nevertheless, this too is considered an emergency. Both conditions are treated the same way.

HOME CARE

Do not attempt home treatment. Torsion of the testis is an emergency that requires immediate surgical correction.

PRECAUTIONS

● Take your child to a doctor immediately if pain near a testis increases and the testis is tender, swollen, or discolored. **Do not** delay; hours count. ● Suspect torsion of the testis in a boy with an uncorrected, undescended testis if he has lower abdominal pain or pain in the groin. ● An injury or a bruise of the scrotum and testis is not uncommon and will cause instant pain that gradually subsides. If pain increases following an injury or a bruise, suspect torsion of the testis.

MEDICAL TREATMENT

Your doctor will arrange immediate surgery to untwist the testis and to anchor it in the scrotum in order to prevent further episodes. If surgery is not performed within 24 hours of the onset of symptoms the testis may be damaged permanently.

Testis, undescended

SYMPTOM   Failure of one or both testes to rest in the
                scrotum at birth

HOME CARE   Check periodically to see if the testis has
                descended. If it does not, consult the
                doctor.

PRECAUTIONS

- [ ] An undescended testis that is not treated may become twisted, injured, or possibly cancerous.

- [ ] If an undescended testis is not corrected before age seven, body heat may cause it to become damaged and unable to produce sperm.

- [ ] An undescended testis should not be confused with a migratory or retractile testis which needs no correction.

- [ ] An undescended testis may be mistaken for a hernia or a swollen lymph gland. Have the doctor make the diagnosis.

- [ ] An undescended testis should be treated between the ages of four and seven.

- [ ] Do not worry the child by discussing the condition.

In the male unborn baby the two testes, the sex glands, lie just beneath the kidneys. Before birth, they travel down into the groin and come to rest in each side of the scrotum. In 1 to 2 percent of full-term male infants and 20 to 30 percent of premature male infants one or both testes have not completed their descent by the time the baby is born. The testis or testes are then referred to as "undescended."

An undescended testis may lie within the abdomen or the groin. In a boy's first months or years of life an undescended testis may successfully complete its migration to the scrotum. However, this does not always happen.

A testis that remains undescended is at risk of becoming twisted, injured, or cancerous (malignant). If the condition is not corrected by the time a boy reaches age seven, an undescended testis may be damaged by the heat of the body; it may shrivel (atrophy) and lose its ability to produce sperm.

SIGNS AND SYMPTOMS

The condition exists if one or both testes do not rest in the scrotum at birth. However, an undescended testis must be distinguished from a migratory or retractile testis. A migrating or retractile testis has completed its descent into the scrotum, but has risen temporarily into the groin. A migratory or retractile testis returns to its normal position as a boy matures, and it needs no correction. If the size of the scrotum is normal, the testis is migrating; if it is small, the testis is undescended. An undescended testis sometimes can be felt in the groin, but it may be mistaken for a hernia or a swollen lymph gland.

HOME CARE

If a testis appears to be missing from the scrotum after birth, check periodically to see if it has descended of its own accord. To check for an undescended testis, place the child in a tub of warm water and pull his knees up toward his chest. If the testis is migratory it will often descend into the scrotum. If the testis is undescended, it will not.

PRECAUTIONS

● Don't worry the child by discussing the condition. An undescended testis can usually be corrected. ● Do not postpone correction of an undescended testis. It should be corrected when the boy is between four and seven years old. ● A boy with an undescended testis has an increased chance of an inguinal hernia.

MEDICAL TREATMENT

Your doctor will examine the child's scrotum and groin carefully and check for the presence of a hernia, which often accompanies an undescended testis. Some doctors give hormone injections to encourage the testis to descend, but most prefer to perform surgery when the child is between the ages of four and seven, and not to use hormones at all.

Related topics:

Glands, swollen
Hernia
Testis, torsion of

Tetanus

SYMPTOMS   Muscle stiffness, especially of jaw and
neck
Difficulty in swallowing
Pain in extremities
Muscle spasms
Convulsions

HOME CARE Prevent tetanus by having your child adequately immunized against the disease.

Treat all wounds, even minor ones,
promptly.

PRECAUTIONS

☐ Tetanus can be fatal; be sure your
child is properly protected by immunization.

☐ Tetanus can enter the body through a
cut or puncture wound as well as a
scratch, burn, insect bite, or other
minor wound; all such wounds should
be treated at once.

☐ All family members should be vaccinated against tetanus.

☐ If a mother has not been immunized
against tetanus, her newborn baby is
susceptible to tetanus.

☐ Tetanus can infect a newborn baby
through the stump of the umbilical
cord. In the case of a home delivery
of a baby, be sure strict antiseptic
techniques are used during and after
the birth.

Tetanus (lockjaw) is a disease of the nervous system and is caused by the *Clostridium tetani* germ. The germ grows in the absence of oxygen and normally lives in soil, dust, and the intestines and intestinal wastes of animals and humans. It easily enters the body through deep puncture wounds or cuts, but can also enter through a scratch, scrape, burn, or insect bite. The germ incubates (the time between exposure and development of symptoms) for three to 21 days. Tetanus is frequently fatal.

SIGNS AND SYMPTOMS

Once the infection is full-blown, it causes muscle stiffness, especially of the jaw and neck (giving rise to the name lockjaw); difficulty in swallowing; pain in the extremities; muscle spasms throughout the body; and convulsions. When a child develops muscle spasms and convulsions days or weeks after sustaining a wound, he or she probably has tetanus. However, tetanus may be confused with a disorder called neonatal tetany (a generally harmless condition in babies) or in older children with a drug reaction, poisoning, meningitis, encephalitis, or rabies. The diagnosis can be confirmed by laboratory tests to isolate the *Clostridium tetani* germ.

HOME CARE

Prevention is the key to home care. Have your child immunized against tetanus in infancy and make sure he or she receives the booster shots necessary to guarantee immunity for life. Be sure to take proper care of wounds, even trivial ones, until they heal.

PRECAUTIONS

● If a mother has not been immunized against tetanus, her newborn baby is susceptible. If a mother is immune, her baby may be temporarily immune. ● In newborns, the tetanus germ can enter the body through the stump of the umbilical cord. If a baby is delivered at home, be certain that strict antiseptic techniques are employed during and immediately after the birth. ● Be certain that all members of the family have received the initial series of tetanus immunizations and the necessary boosters. In general, clean wounds, such as those from kitchen utensils, require boosters every ten years; dirty wounds, such as those from rusty nails, barbed wire, and others that happen outdoors, require boosters every five years. For example, if your child has a wound from a rusty nail, check to see if he or she has received a booster within the last five years.

MEDICAL TREATMENT

Your doctor will take prompt care of wounds and administer a tetanus booster to a child who has been immunized, or human tetanus anti-serum (a substance containing antibodies to fight tetanus) to one who has not. If tetanus has developed, your doctor will hospitalize your child and order intensive treatment involving anti-serum, antibiotics, sedation, and intravenous fluids. When recovered, your child should be immune to subsequent attack.

Thrush

SYMPTOM   White, flaky patches on tongue and inside areas of mouth

HOME CARE   Follow the doctor's instructions for treating thrush.

Sterilize objects that are placed in the baby's mouth.

PRECAUTIONS

☐ Thrush often follows antibiotic treatment and may also accompany nutritional deficiencies or long-term illness.

☐ A nursing mother may have to use medication on the breasts to avoid reinfecting the child.

☐ A nursing mother should be treated for diseases that could reinfect her child.

☐ White plaques that occur only on the tongue are probably not due to thrush.

☐ A doctor should see a child who gets recurring bouts of thrush.

☐ Inadequate sterilization of the baby's things can cause thrush.

☐ Overuse of nonprescription products can burn the membranes of the mouth.

Thrush is a mouth infection caused by the *Candida albicans* fungus. It is common in babies immediately after birth, and in infants and toddlers. Thrush frequently follows antibiotic treatment, or accompanies nutritional deficiencies and chronic illnesses.

SIGNS AND SYMPTOMS

Thrush causes white, flaky patches that resemble milk curds to appear on the tongue, roof of the mouth, gums, and the insides of the cheeks and lips. These white patches (plaques) do not easily wipe away. Generally, thrush produces no other symptoms. The diagnosis is confirmed by laboratory tests to identify the *Candida albicans* fungus.

HOME CARE

To treat thrush, the doctor will prescribe nystatin solution and show you how to place the recommended dosage into each of the child's cheeks four times a day after the child has nursed or eaten. To prevent reinfection, sterilize objects that are placed in the baby's mouth. A nursing mother may have to use nystatin cream on each breast to avoid reinfecting her baby.

PRECAUTIONS

● White plaques confined to the tongue are not due to thrush. They are normally the result of nursing. ● If thrush occurs with a fever or cough see your doctor. ● If thrush recurs frequently, it may be because the baby's things are not being adequately sterilized; consult your doctor.

MEDICAL TREATMENT

Your doctor will try to determine if the child has some condition that increases his or her susceptibility to thrush. The nursing mother may be examined or treated for diseases of the nipples or vagina that may reinfect the infant. (The *Candida albicans* fungus can cause what is commonly known as a vaginal yeast infection, and a mother can pass the infection to the baby.)

Thyroid disorders

SYMPTOMS

Underactive thyroid
Excessive sleepiness
Choking while nursing
Severe constipation
Noisy breathing
Retarded growth
Protruding tongue
Hoarse cry
Thick, dry skin
Goiter (in some cases)

Overactive thyroid
Irritability
Restlessness
Behavior problems
Hand tremors
Increased appetite without weight gain
Excessive sweating
Protruding eyeballs
Goiter (in some cases)

HOME CARE Take your child for regular checkups. Be aware of signs that might indicate thyroid malfunction.

PRECAUTIONS

☐ Some symptoms of underactive thyroid may appear in older children whose thyroid is normal. Only a doctor can diagnose thyroid malfunction.

☐ A cyst on the neck should be seen by a doctor; it could be an abnormally positioned thyroid gland.

The thyroid gland is located in the neck just below the Adam's apple; it produces hormones that control the body's temperature, energy production, growth, and fertility. The thyroid gland may become underactive (resulting in hypothyroidism) or overactive (hyperthyroidism). Either condition can occur in infancy or at any age thereafter.

SIGNS AND SYMPTOMS

Hypothyroidism. When the thyroid is underactive at birth, it's not usually apparent for a few weeks. When the condition finally does become apparent, it causes excessive sleepiness, choking while nursing, severe constipation, and noisy breathing. After three to six months it is obvious that the child's growth rate is retarded. In addition, the child has a protruding tongue; thick, dry skin; and a hoarse cry. When the thyroid becomes underactive later in childhood it slows growth and causes constipation, sleepiness, and thick, dry skin. An underactive thyroid may or may not be associated with goiter (enlargement of the thyroid gland).

Hyperthyroidism. Overactive thyroid usually develops between the ages of ten and 15. Sometimes, however, it may occur in children as young as one or two. An overactive thyroid causes irritability, restlessness, behavior problems, tremors of the hands, increased appetite without weight gain, excessive sweating, and protruding eyeballs. Overactive thyroid is sometimes accompanied by goiter.

Because all symptoms of over- and underactive thyroid can result from other conditions not related to the thyroid, laboratory tests are essential to the diagnosis. In some states all newborn infants must be tested for thyroid malfunction before leaving the hospital.

HOME CARE

Home care involves taking your child to your doctor for routine checkups and watching for the symptoms of a thyroid malfunction.

PRECAUTIONS

● Symptoms of underactive thyroid may occur in older children, especially adolescents, who have normal thyroid function. Only your doctor can determine if the thyroid is malfunctioning. ● A child who has a cyst on the neck should not have it removed until the doctor has determined that the cyst is not actually the thyroid gland in an abnormal position.

MEDICAL TREATMENT

Your doctor will establish the diagnosis on the basis of a physical examination, which includes measuring the child's blood pressure, and laboratory tests that measure thyroid and pituitary hormone levels in the blood. The doctor may also order a test to determine how well the thyroid absorbs radioactive iodine; this may be necessary to evaluate function and look for tumors of the thyroid.

Treatment of an underactive thyroid involves prescribing synthetic thyroid or thyroid hormones for the child to take by mouth. Treatment of an overactive thyroid involves either medication or surgical removal of part of the thyroid gland.

Related topic:

Goiter

Tics

SYMPTOM Jerky, spasmodic muscle movement

HOME CARE Try to find out what type of stress is causing the problem.

Do not nag or punish the child, or call attention to the tics.

PRECAUTIONS

☐ Everyone in the child's environment must cooperate in ignoring the tics.

☐ Tics that persist for more than a few weeks or accompany other symptoms or unusual types of behavior may indicate a potentially serious problem and require professional attention.

☐ Tics can be caused by physical conditions, and the diagnosis should be made by a doctor.

Repeated, jerky, spasmodic movements of isolated groups of muscles are called tics.

Tics occur in preschool and school age children as a result of undue pressure and emotional stress. They increase when a child is upset or excited and stop temporarily when he or she is diverted or asleep.

SIGNS AND SYMPTOMS

Usually, tics involve twitching the mouth, wrinkling the forehead, blinking the eyes, sighing, coughing, or sniffing. The head, shoulders, hands, or arms may jerk uncontrollably. Tics can happen several times a minute or only once or twice a day, and they persist for weeks or months.

Tics are usually obvious, but they may have to be distinguished from allergies, which often lead to twitching the nose, blinking the eyes, and coughing. A more serious but rare form of tics is Gilles de la Tourette's disease. The disease may resemble tics at the outset, but it progresses to violent twitching of the face and arms and sometimes other parts of the body. The spasmodic movements are accompanied by explosive sounds such as a barking cough or indistinct words or unintentional obscenities. Because Gilles de la Tourette's disease is so unusual and because it is fairly mild to start with and becomes progressively worse, early diagnosis is not possible.

HOME CARE

Do not pay undue attention to tics. You may aggravate or prolong the condition if you react by calling your child's attention to the tics, demanding that the child stop, nagging, or punishing the child. Your best plan is to identify and then relieve any obvious stressful situation at home, at school, or among your child's friends.

PRECAUTIONS

● Ignoring tics requires the cooperation of brothers and sisters, parents, relatives, neighbors, and teachers. ● If tics are the only sign of emotional tension in a child they may be due to the customary stresses of childhood. However, if tics persist for more than a few weeks or occur with other symptoms or patterns of disturbed emotional behavior, they may signal a potentially serious problem. Seek professional advice.

MEDICAL TREATMENT

Your doctor will examine the child carefully to make sure that the tics are not due to a physical illness. The doctor will evaluate stressful situations in your child's environment, and advise you how to handle them. Your doctor may require consultation with a neurologist (specialist in nervous system disorders) to diagnose and treat Gilles de la Tourette's disease.

Related topic:

Hay fever

Tonsillitis

SYMPTOMS　Sore, red throat
Inflamed tonsils, often with spots
Fever

HOME CARE　Treat as you would treat a cold or sore throat.

Give aspirin or acetaminophen for fever and pain.

Give the child plenty of fluids.

PRECAUTIONS

☐　Drooling accompanying a sore throat should be brought to the attention of your doctor **immediately**.

☐　Between the ages of three and nine, children often have enlarged tonsils and adenoids; this enlargement is normal and should not be confused with infection.

☐　White, cheesy material on the tonsils is normal and does not indicate infection.

☐　If a child is eating poorly, the cause is something other than enlarged tonsils.

☐　A quinsy sore throat always requires medical treatment.

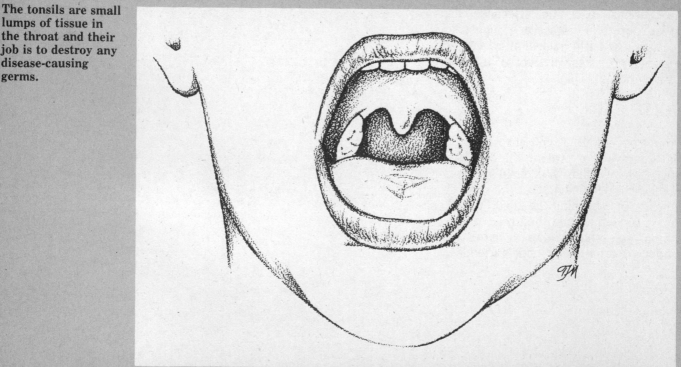

The tonsils are small lumps of tissue in the throat and their job is to destroy any disease-causing germs.

The tonsils (in the throat) and the adenoids (in the back of the nose) are part of the lymphatic system, and their function is to destroy disease-causing germs. They may become infected with disease-causing germs from a common cold, strep throat, infectious mononucleosis, diphtheria, or tuberculosis.

SIGNS AND SYMPTOMS

The child will complain of a sore throat and will have a fever. The throat will appear red and sometimes there are spots on the tonsils. Acute infection of the tonsils is diagnosed from the appearance of the throat and the results of a throat culture or blood count. This enlargement of the tonsils rarely produces symptoms by itself but, in extreme cases, can make it hard for the child to swallow. Enlargement of the adenoids can result in mouth breathing, hearing loss and middle ear infection, snoring, nasal speech, and bad breath. Adenoids can be examined with special instruments or seen on an X ray.

A unique infection of the tonsils is quinsy sore throat (peritonsillar abscess). In quinsy a large abscess forms behind a tonsil, producing intense pain and a high fever (103°F or 104°F). The abscess eventually pushes the tonsil across the midline of the throat. The child will have difficulty speaking ("hot potato speech") and swallowing and will drool.

HOME CARE

Treat tonsillitis the same way as a common cold, a sore throat, or hay fever. A throat culture will usually be required to help your doctor identify the illness. Give aspirin or acetaminophen and plenty of fluids. A peritonsillar abscess requires treatment by a doctor.

PRECAUTIONS

● If drooling occurs with a sore throat, the child should be seen by a doctor **immediately**. ● Enlarged adenoids and tonsils are common in healthy children three to nine years of age. ● Tonsils often contain a white, cheesy material. This is normal and does not indicate infection. ● Tonsils and adenoids may be infected without becoming enlarged. ● Enlarged tonsils do not cause poor eating habits.

MEDICAL TREATMENT

The decision to remove tonsils and adenoids surgically requires careful evaluation. Some doctors insist that they should never be removed; others recommend routine removal. Both groups are mistaken.

The tonsils can be removed as part of the treatment of: a quinsy sore throat; frequent infections (for more than a year) of the tonsils; a tonsillar tumor; or a diphtheria bacilli-infected tonsil.

Upper airway obstruction resulting in sleep apnea (temporary halt in breathing) is an indication for removing the adenoids (adenoidectomy). The adenoids can also be removed to correct: a nasal obstruction that has led to facial peculiarities such as a pinched face, narrow nostrils, or constantly open mouth; snoring; or a nasal voice. In some cases, it also may be wise to have adenoids removed if their enlargement is causing a hearing loss or frequent middle ear infections. Alternatives to adenoidectomy include prolonged use of decongestants and antibiotics.

Your doctor will treat a peritonsillar abscess with antibiotics; occasionally surgical drainage is necessary.

Toothache

SYMPTOMS Pain
Redness and swelling of the gums

HOME CARE Give aspirin or acetaminophen for pain.

Apply an ice pack to the jaw.

PRECAUTIONS

☐ Have your child see the dentist regularly from age two or three on.

☐ Do not apply heat to the site of a toothache.

☐ Provide extra fluoride if the water in your area is not fluoridated. Ask your dentist about this.

An icepack on the jaw may ease a child's toothache, but a warm compress may make the pain worse.

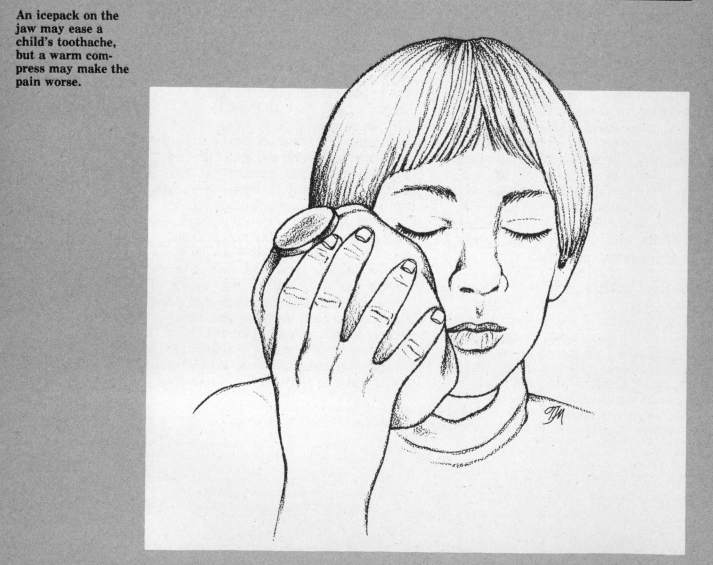

In common with earaches and the onset of labor, children's toothaches always happen at the least convenient time—after pharmacists have closed their doors and doctors and dentists have closed their offices.

A toothache can be caused by an injury to a tooth, an infection between the gum and the tooth, or an abscess of the root of the tooth due to extension of a cavity (even a filled one) into the tooth's pulp.

SIGNS AND SYMPTOMS

The source of a toothache is obvious if the gum near the tooth is red, swollen, and tender, or if a cavity is visible. If the source of the pain is in doubt, tapping gently with a tongue depressor or the handle of a spoon will cause sharp pain in the tooth responsible.

HOME CARE

Temporary treatment is to ease the pain of the toothache with aspirin or acetaminophen. An ice pack on the jaw may help, but heat may make the toothache worse. Call your dentist.

Part of home treatment is prevention. Your child should see a dentist regularly, beginning at age two or three. The child should brush his or her teeth at least daily and use floss if possible. Through adolescence, fluoride must be provided each day. If you live in an area where the water is not fluoridated, supplementary fluoride is needed. Talk to your dentist about this.

PRECAUTIONS

● Take your child to a dentist regularly to avoid any emergency situation involving a toothache. ● Do not apply heat to the site of a toothache.

MEDICAL TREATMENT

Your doctor may prescribe a pain killer, or an antibiotic if an infection is present, but treatment of the tooth is left to the dentist.

Related topics:

Gumboils
Teething

351

Toxic shock syndrome

SYMPTOMS   High fever
Vomiting
Diarrhea
Sunburn-like rash
Peeling of skin on soles and palms
Blurred vision
Confusion

HOME CARE   Toxic shock requires **immediate** medical attention. Do not attempt home care.

PRECAUTIONS

☐ Although rare, toxic shock can be fatal.

☐ This disease develops very suddenly and progresses rapidly.

☐ Toxic shock is not limited to menstruating women. It has also occured in nonmenstruating women, men, and children.

☐ Tampon use may promote an environment favorable to the growth of the bacteria. If tampons are used, they should be used alternately with napkins whenever possible, changed frequently, and not used at night.

☐ Women are at greater risk for toxic shock just after delivering a baby than at other times.

☐ Toxic shock can affect patients recovering from burns or surgery, or persons with boils or abscesses.

Toxic shock syndrome (TSS) is a rare and sometimes fatal disease that occurs when a poison (toxin) produced by the *Staphylococcus aureus* bacterium enters the bloodstream. The poison causes leaks in cell walls that allow blood to seep into the tissues of the body. This seepage can lead to a dangerous drop in blood pressure, shock, and possibly death.

The disease develops very suddenly and progresses rapidly. Although most of the victims recover, a severe case of toxic shock syndrome can lead to liver and heart damage. This damage occurs because low blood pressure and weakening of the cell walls allow foreign substances to invade the heart and liver.

Toxic shock syndrome was first officially defined in 1975 and is considered by many to be a new disease. Since the bacterium can be present in the body without producing the toxin, it is still not known what triggers the disease. Toxic shock syndrome has been linked to the use of tampons during menstruation, but scientists are still trying to determine what the link is. Research is also continuing to discover exactly which toxin produced by *Staphylococcus aureus* causes TSS.

It is known that the tampons themselves do not cause TSS. However, they may promote in some unknown way the growth of the staph bacteria. Researchers are exploring the theories that: (1) the new "superabsorbent" tampons may swell so much during use that they block the blood flow entirely, and thus create a breeding ground for bacteria; (2) because these tampons are so absorbent women tend to leave them in longer, increasing the likelihood of infection; and (3) the tampon applicators may scratch the vagina, allowing bacteria to enter the bloodstream.

This disease, however, is not limited to menstruating women. It also has been seen in nonmenstruating women, in men, and in children. Women who have just had a baby are also at greater risk because the vagina is more susceptible to bacteria.

TSS also affects those recovering from surgery or burns and persons suffering from boils or abscesses. Thus, the bacteria can enter the body in ways other than the vagina.

SIGNS AND SYMPTOMS

Toxic shock symptoms include high fever, vomiting, diarrhea, rash that resembles sunburn, peeling of the skin on the soles of the feet and palms of the hands, blurred vision, and confusion. Because the disease frequently occurs during or just after menstruation, these symptoms in a girl who menstruates should be brought to the immediate attention of a doctor.

HOME CARE

If a child or adolescent has symptoms resembling those of toxic shock, consult a doctor at once.

PRECAUTIONS

● This disease is not restricted to menstruating women; it can also occur in men and in children, and in the presence of certain medical conditions. ● Tampon use is clearly a risk factor for the disease. A girl using tampons should change them every three to four hours and use tampons alternately with sanitary napkins whenever possible. She should not wear tampons at night, since they might be left in for prolonged periods while she sleeps. ● Women who have just given birth are at greater risk for toxic shock syndrome.

MEDICAL TREATMENT

Because there is no quick and definite test for toxic shock syndrome, diagnosis depends largely on the doctor's ability to recognize the symptoms. It's possible to test for the presence of the *Staphylococcus aureus* bacteria, but the presence of the bacteria does not necessarily mean that the person has the disease. If toxic shock is identified, it can usually be treated successfully. In most cases the patient is hospitalized for supportive treatment similar to that used in cases of poisoning. The treatment may include fluids and blood transfusions administered into the vein to raise blood pressure. An ice blanket may be used to bring down the fever, and antibiotics may be prescribed.

Related topics:

Boils
Burns
Shock

Toxoplasmosis

SYMPTOMS   Minor illness produces few symptoms
Severe illness causes high fever

HOME CARE   Prevention is the best home care.

PRECAUTIONS

- [ ] Toxoplasmosis can damage a pregnant woman's unborn child.

- [ ] A pregnant woman should avoid eating raw or undercooked meat.

- [ ] A pregnant woman should not handle or change a cat's litter box during the pregnancy.

- [ ] It's not necessary to get rid of the family cat if someone in the household is pregnant. Do not, however, introduce a new pet, especially a cat, during the first three months of the pregnancy.

Although toxoplasmosis is rarely serious, it can cause damage to an unborn baby. If you are pregnant, do not change the cat's litter box or acquire a new pet until after the baby is born.

Toxoplasmosis afflicts all mammals (including people), many birds, and some reptiles. It's caused by a one-celled parasite (called toxoplasma) that is one-third the size of a red-blood cell. Although blood tests show that as many as half the adults in this country have had the infection at one time or another, few people outside the medical community are even aware of it. Like German measles, toxoplasmosis can severely damage an unborn baby during the first three months of pregnancy; however, it is rarely serious for any other age group.

Toxoplasmosis is contracted from eating raw or undercooked meat, or by direct contact with the feces of chickens, cats, or dogs. The disease is not spread among humans, except from a pregnant woman to her unborn baby.

A woman who contracts toxoplasmosis during the first three months of pregnancy can transmit the infection to the unborn baby. As a result she may miscarry, the baby may be stillborn, or the infant may be born with water on the brain (hydrocephalus) or a small head (microcephaly). The newborn may be mentally retarded, or have convulsions, anemia, jaundice, or eye damage.

SIGNS AND SYMPTOMS

Most people with toxoplasmosis have no symptoms. Some have temporary swelling of the lymph nodes, and a few have symptoms resembling those of infectious mononucleosis. Rarely is the illness severe. When it is, it causes a high fever (103°F or 104°F) and can lead to pneumonia, encephalitis, and heart disease. One attack, however mild, seems to give lifelong immunity.

Toxoplasmosis is not usually diagnosed. It may be suspected from a blood count that shows numerous white blood cells of a certain type, but it can be confirmed only by complicated tests that evaluate the blood levels of the antibodies, the protective substances that the body has produced to fight against the toxoplasma organisms.

HOME CARE

Prevention is the best method of home care. A pregnant woman should take the precautions listed below.

PRECAUTIONS

● A pregnant woman should not expose herself to toxoplasma organisms by eating raw or undercooked meat. ● A pregnant woman should not change a cat's litter box or acquire a new pet during the first three months of her pregnancy. However, congenital toxoplasmosis (occurring during pregnancy) is so rare that many experienced physicians have never seen a case. It hardly seems necessary, therefore, for a pregnant woman to avoid eating meat altogether or to get rid of household pets.

MEDICAL TREATMENT

Drugs are available to treat severe cases of toxoplasmosis, but they are highly toxic (poisonous) and cannot be given to pregnant women.

Related topics:

Glands, swollen
Infectious
    mononucleosis

Ulcers

SYMPTOMS Abdominal pain
Vomiting blood
Blood in stool

HOME CARE The only home care recommended in the case of a suspected ulcer is to give the child an antacid by mouth.

The child should be under a doctor's care.

PRECAUTIONS

☐ Ulcers do not usually cause ordinary stomachaches in children.

☐ Intense, highly motivated children, particularly those with family problems, may be susceptible to ulcers.

☐ If a child is under stress, his or her abdominal pain is more likely to be caused by the stress than by an ulcer.

☐ When more than one member of a family has ulcers, the cause is more likely to be shared stress than a hereditary factor.

☐ Black, tarry stools can be caused not only by blood in the stool but also by iron supplements and some foods.

Ulcers are less common in children than in adults, but they are by no means rare and may even occur in newborns. Like adults, children get ulcers in the stomach or in the duodenum (the first part of the small intestine). Duodenal ulcers, in fact, are five times more common than stomach ulcers.

Ulcers are more common in intense, highly motivated children, particularly those who have family conflicts. Ulcers also can be caused by prolonged treatment with steroid medications, extensive burns, diseases of the brain, severe infections such as meningitis, or blood poisoning.

SIGNS AND SYMPTOMS

An older child with ulcers has upper abdominal pain before meals or at night, and the pain is often relieved by eating. Preschoolers with ulcers have pain near the navel; the pain comes and goes and is aggravated by eating. Children of any age may vomit bright red or dark brown blood or have blood in the stools (appearing as tarry stools). Ulcers are seldom the cause of ordinary stomachaches in children—although they often get blamed for such pains. The diagnosis of an ulcer can be made only by X rays (upper gastrointestinal series) or, less commonly, by endoscopy which involves viewing the stomach directly by means of an instrument passed down the esophagus, the passageway from the mouth to the stomach.

HOME CARE

Temporary relief for pain can be provided by giving the child an antacid by mouth. Other home treatment is not recommended. The child should be under a doctor's care.

PRECAUTIONS

● Not all black (tarry) stools contain blood. Iron supplements and some foods can cause black stools. The stool should be tested. ● Abdominal pain in a child who is under emotional stress is more likely to be caused by the stress than by an ulcer. ● Several members of a family may have ulcers because they share the family's life-style and tensions, not because ulcers are hereditary.

MEDICAL TREATMENT

Your doctor will take a careful health history of your child, perform a physical examination, and may order X rays. Your child's stools will be tested for blood, and a blood count will reveal any evidence of secondary anemia. The doctor will probably prescribe antacids between meals and at bedtime or antispasmodic drugs before meals. The doctor will also advise you on changes in the diet and ways to relieve the child's emotional stress.

Changes in the diet usually involve avoiding caffeine in cola drinks, tea, and coffee, and aspirin (including cold remedies that contain aspirin). Treatment usually can be discontinued in a few weeks or months.

Urinary tract infections

SYMPTOMS
Frequent, urgent, or painful urination
Dribbling of urine
Bedwetting
Inability to control urination
Abnormal urine
Fever
Abdominal or back pain
Chronic diarrhea
Vomiting
Redness of external genitals

HOME CARE
Do not attempt home treatment. If symptoms are present the child should see a doctor.

PRECAUTIONS

☐ Urinary tract infection (UTI) is ten times more common in girls than in boys.

☐ Home treatment of a UTI can cause a low-grade, chronic infection.

☐ In many cases a UTI produces fever but no other symptoms and is not evident in the course of a medical examination.

☐ A urine sample should be collected at the midpoint of urination.

☐ An infant suspected of having a UTI should be examined at once to find the underlying cause of the infection.

Infections of the urinary tract (UTIs) are common during childhood and occur ten times more frequently in girls than in boys. About 5 percent of all girls will have one or more urinary tract infections before reaching maturity.

In many cases, except during infancy, there is no physical abnormality to account for the development of a urinary tract infection. However, in 5 percent of the girls and over 50 percent of the boys the UTI is due to an underlying anatomical abnormality somewhere along the urinary tract that results in a partial or total block in the flow of urine. Most UTIs are caused by germs, such as *E. coli bacilli*, that do not cause disease in other locations. *E. coli bacilli* live harmlessly in the bowels of all children and adults but cause infection when they enter the urethra (the tube that leads to the urinary bladder). Other causes of UTI are inflammation of the vagina, foreign bodies in the bladder or urethra, and possibly severe constipation.

The urinary tract is a series of interconnected tubes, and an infection in one part easily spreads to another. For this reason, this discussion does not distinguish among infection of the collecting basins of the kidneys (pyelonephritis and pyelitis), infection of the bladder (cystitis), and infection of the urethra (urethritis).

SIGNS AND SYMPTOMS

A urinary tract infection may produce either no symptoms at all (silent UTI), or any combination of the following: urgency or frequency of urination; painful urination; dribbling of urine; bedwetting; daytime incontinence (inability to control urination); foul-smelling, cloudy, or bloody urine; fever; abdominal or back pain; vomiting; chronic diarrhea; or redness of the external genitals. If the infection is untreated, the symptoms generally disappear in a few days or weeks, but often return later.

The diagnosis of UTI depends upon a careful physical examination, plus urine tests. In boys, the diagnosis involves a search for an obstruction in the urinary tract. In girls, the search for an obstruction is undertaken only after two or three bouts of UTI or one bout with an infection that is resistant to treatment. In an infant, whether boy or girl, investigation for the underlying cause is always undertaken immediately.

HOME CARE

Any attempt at home treatment is potentially dangerous and may result in a low-grade, destructive infection with no outward symptoms.

PRECAUTIONS

● A urinary tract infection, particularly one of a series of infections, commonly produces fever, but few or no other symptoms; the doctor's physical examination reveals nothing unusual. ● To obtain a urine specimen for analysis or culture, cleanse the genitals and collect the portion at the midpoint of urination. In this way, the urine sample will not be contaminated.

MEDICAL TREATMENT

Your doctor will conduct a complete physical examination, including taking your child's blood pressure and ordering urine tests. If the urine specimen shows an infection, the doctor will put the child on antibiotics for ten to 14 days. Urine samples will be retested during and after the course of antibiotics.

After your child has recovered from a urinary tract infection, your doctor may recommend X rays to determine if there is a physical abnormality. Sometimes, further X rays and direct examination of the urethra and bladder are necessary. To treat recurrent UTIs that are not due to obstruction, your doctor may prescribe the use of antibiotics constantly or on and off for months or years. To correct an obstruction, your doctor may perform surgery.

Related topics:

Bedwetting
Constipation
Diarrhea
Fever
Nephritis
Stomachache, chronic
Vaginal discharge
Vomiting

Vaginal bleeding

SYMPTOM   Bleeding that is not due to normal
menstruation

HOME CARE   If the condition causes a burning sensation
on urination, have the child urinate while
in a bathtub of water.

Bleeding due to minor bruises or lacerations can be treated at home. All other
abnormal vaginal bleeding requires medical
attention.

PRECAUTIONS

☐   If a girl is less than nine or ten years
old and has vaginal bleeding with or
without breast development, she
should be seen by a doctor.

☐   If there is any suspicion of sexual
molestation, contact your doctor
immediately.

☐   Any girl whose mother took diethylstilbesterol (DES) during pregnancy
should be seen by a gynecologist at
the beginning of puberty whether or
not bleeding is present.

☐   A baby girl may have a bloody discharge from the vagina during the
first two weeks of life.

A baby girl may have a bloody discharge from the vagina during the first two weeks of life; this is usually due to the withdrawal of her mother's hormones after birth. The most common cause of vaginal bleeding is, of course, menstruation, which begins at puberty, any time between the ages of nine and 17. "Precocious" puberty may begin before age nine, even as early as five or six. With both normal menstruation and precocious puberty, the first menstrual flow is preceded by development of the breasts.

Vaginal bleeding any time after the immediate post-birth period in a girl whose breasts have not developed, or bleeding between menstrual periods, is most often due to injury. Wounds in the vaginal area, even those of considerable size, heal rapidly with no infection or scarring.

Less common causes of vaginal bleeding are inflammation of the vagina, a foreign body in the vagina, prolapse (slipping from the usual position) of the lining of the urethra (the tube leading to the urinary bladder), and tumors of the vagina or the uterus.

SIGNS AND SYMPTOMS

The signs are obvious, and diagnosis of the cause of abnormal vaginal bleeding often can be made by inspecting the vaginal area. The inspection should determine whether blood is coming from the vaginal opening, the urethra, a laceration of the surrounding tissues, or the rectum.

HOME CARE

Unless they are extensive or due to sexual molestation, bruises and lacerations of the vagina and the surrounding area usually can be treated at home. No antiseptic is necessary, and burning on urination can be minimized by having the child urinate while in a bathtub or water. All other causes of vaginal bleeding require your doctor's attention.

PRECAUTIONS

● If a girl is less than nine or ten years old and has vaginal bleeding with or without breast development, she should be seen by a doctor. ● If there is any suspicion of sexual molestation, contact your doctor immediately. ● Girls whose mothers received the drug diethylstilbesterol (DES) during pregnancy may have a deformity of the vagina (adenosis) that causes bleeding. Whether or not they have vaginal bleeding, all girls whose mothers took DES should be examined by an experienced gynecologist (a specialist in the diseases and health of women) at the beginning of puberty. Although the medical profession originally overestimated the chances of a girl whose mother took DES getting cancer, the possibility does exist; all girls with adenosis of the vagina should be carefully monitored.

MEDICAL TREATMENT

Treatment of vaginal bleeding depends upon its cause. Your doctor will determine what is causing vaginal bleeding by performing a careful examination, sometimes involving the rectum. Your doctor may require a culture of any vaginal discharge or an X ray of the pelvis. A girl whose mother received DES will be referred to a gynecologist. A prolapsed urethra requires surgical correction.

Related topics:

Bruises
Menstrual
  irregularities
Vaginal discharge

Vaginal discharge

SYMPTOM   Discharge that is irritating, pus-like,
              bloody, or foul-smelling

HOME CARE   Have the child take sitz baths to which a
cup of vinegar has been added.

Check for signs of pinworms or urinary
tract infection.

Teach your daughter simple preventive
measures such as wearing cotton underpants, avoiding the use of chemical products, and practicing proper techniques for
cleaning herself after using the bathroom.

PRECAUTIONS

☐ Any girl whose mother took diethylstilbesterol (DES) while pregnant
should be examined by a gynecologist
at the beginning of puberty, whether
or not vaginal discharge is present.

☐ The use of vaginal sprays or chemicals in the bath water can cause
vaginal discharge.

☐ Discharge from the vagina is normal
during the first two weeks of a baby
girl's life and for one to two years
before a girl starts menstruating. This
discharge does not irritate or have a
foul odor.

Mucus discharge from the vagina is normal during the first two weeks of a baby girl's life and during the one to two years before a girl starts menstruating. Such vaginal discharge may be quite heavy, but it does not have an unpleasant odor and it does not irritate the skin.

Vaginal discharge that irritates nearby membranes, smells foul, and causes itching, soreness, or pain may be caused by using chemicals in the bath (bubble bath, water softeners) or vaginal hygiene sprays, wearing panties made from synthetic materials, or poor toileting habits. It can also result from pinworms, a urinary tract infection, masturbation, foreign bodies in the vagina, or poor hygiene. Also, vaginal discharge can be caused by vaginal infection (vaginitis) due to viral or bacterial microorganisms or yeasts.

SIGNS AND SYMPTOMS

Vaginal discharge that occurs during puberty and is not irritating or foul-smelling is normal. Vaginal discharge that is pus-like, irritating, foul-smelling, or bloody is not normal. The cause of the problem usually must be determined by your doctor.

HOME CARE

Some of the simple causes of abnormal vaginal discharge can be prevented. Have your daughter avoid using vaginal sprays or chemicals in bath water, wear cotton rather than synthetic underpants, and wipe herself from front to back after going to the bathroom. Look for signs of pinworms or urinary tract infections. Taking sitz baths in a tub of water to which a cup of vinegar has been added may be helpful.

PRECAUTION

● Girls whose mothers received the drug diethylstilbesterol (DES) while pregnant may have a deformity of the vagina (adenosis) that causes vaginal discharge. Such girls should be examined by a gynecologist at the beginning of puberty whether or not they have vaginal discharge. Although the medical profession originally overestimated the chances of a girl whose mother took DES getting cancer, the possibility does exist. Any girl with adenosis of the vagina should be carefully monitored.

MEDICAL TREATMENT

Your doctor will take a detailed health history and conduct a physical (including rectal) examination. The doctor may require a culture of the discharge, and sometimes an X ray of the pelvis. Your doctor may also order urine tests.

Treatment depends upon the cause of the problem, but it may involve the use of antibiotics, worm medicine, fungicides, medicated suppositories, or hormone ointments.

Related topics:

Gonorrhea
Herpes simplex
Menstrual
  irregularities
Pinworms
Toxic shock
  syndrome
Urinary tract
  infections
Vaginal bleeding

Viruses

SYMPTOMS   Vary according to the virus

HOME CARE   In the case of illness caused by an intestinal virus, give aspirin or acetaminophen to relieve pain and fever. Refer to the appropriate section for treatment of diseases caused by a specific virus.

PRECAUTIONS

☐ Because there are so many different types of viruses, diagnosis can be very difficult.

☐ Immunity against any one virus is short-lived, so a child can have one virus infection right after another.

☐ Call the doctor if your child has any of the following symptoms: stiff neck or back; severe headache and vomiting; extreme weakness or collapse; confusion.

☐ The following are *not* symptoms of Coxsackie or ECHO viruses: rash resembling red sandpaper or red goosebumps; pus-like discharge from eyes, nose, or ears; reddish-purple spots; tender, red, enlarging lymph nodes; severe earache; blood in stool; severe cough; breathing difficulty.

A virus is a germ, smaller than a bacterium, that can live only within a living cell. Many common illnesses are caused by a particular virus, among them mumps, chicken pox, measles, rubella, mononucleosis, cat scratch fever, hepatitis, warts, molluscum, and roseola. Two large groups of other viruses—the respiratory viruses and the intestinal viruses—cause a variety of similar illnesses in children.

The respiratory viruses include the adenoviruses, parainfluenza viruses, rhinoviruses, influenza viruses, and the respiratory syncytial virus. The intestinal viruses (enteroviruses) inhabit the intestinal tract and are divided into Coxsackie viruses (of which 30 varieties are known so far), enteric cytopathogenic human orphan (ECHO) viruses (with 31 known types), and the three polio viruses. Coxsackie viruses are responsible for hand, foot, and mouth disease, herpangina, and pleurodynia. Herpangina lasts three to six days and produces a fever, sore throat, swollen neck glands, and painful ulcers on the soft palate, tonsils, and throat. Pleurodynia is an inflammation of the nerves between the ribs, and it causes intense pain, aggravated by breathing, on one side of the chest.

ECHO viruses may cause diarrhea. Coxsackie and ECHO viruses may cause symptoms of a common cold, a fever with or without a rash, encephalitis (inflammation of the brain), or paralysis.

The Coxsackie and ECHO viruses have an incubation period of three to five days or more, and they can be spread via the mouth or in the stool. Immunity against any one of them is short-lived. Therefore, a child can have one virus right after another.

SIGNS AND SYMPTOMS

Because of the large number of viruses and the multiplicity of symptoms, diagnosis of the specific virus is very difficult and usually not necessary. Herpangina can be identified by the look and location of the ulcers. Pleurodynia resembles pleurisy and pneumonia, but it produces no cough.

A rash due to a virus tends to be generalized, flat, and pink rather than red and splotchy, but rashes vary considerably from child to child.

HOME CARE

Only the symptoms of illnesses caused by intestinal viruses can be treated. To reduce pain and fever, give aspirin or acetaminophen. However, **do not** give aspirin to a child with chicken pox or influenza.

PRECAUTION

● Coxsackie and ECHO viruses *can* cause: stiff neck or back; severe headache and vomiting; paralysis; extreme weakness or collapse; or confusion. If your child has these symptoms, call your doctor. Coxsackie and ECHO viruses do *not* cause the following symptoms: a rash that looks like red sandpaper or red goosebumps; pus-like discharge from the eyes, nose, or ears; reddish-purple spots; tender, red lymph nodes that continue to enlarge; severe earaches; blood in the stools; severe cough; or breathing difficulties.

MEDICAL TREATMENT

A diagnosis may be difficult to reach. It usually depends upon a careful history and physical examination, aided by knowledge of what illnesses are currently going around in the community. Complete blood counts and throat cultures may be needed to exclude other illnesses, and a chest X ray or spinal tap may also be necessary. Viral cultures or antibody studies confirm the presence of specific diseases, but the results of these tests take days or weeks.

Vision problems

SYMPTOMS
Tilting or cocking head
Looking out of corner of eye
Squinting
Crossed eyes
Sensitivity to light
Headaches
Dislike of reading
School problems

HOME CARE   Have your child's eyes examined regularly, and be aware of the signs that might suggest the child has a vision problem.

PRECAUTIONS

☐ A child's vision should be checked annually from the age of four or younger.

☐ If your child holds books very close to his or her eyes when reading or cannot see the television screen from a distance, have the child's eyes checked.

At each checkup, the doctor will examine the insides of the child's eyes using an instrument known as an ophthalmoscope.

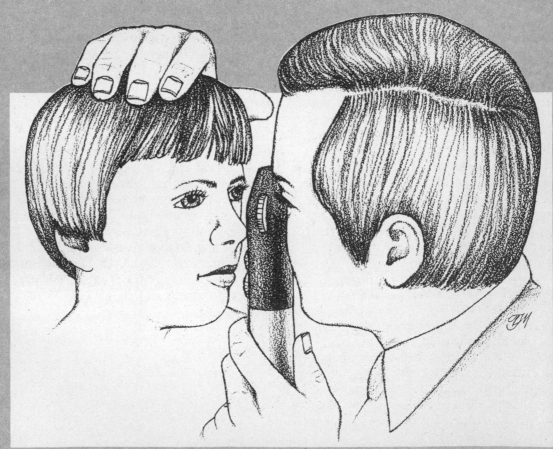

By age four or five, 5 to 10 percent of all children have a problem with vision. By the end of adolescence, the percentage has climbed to 30.

The usual vision problems that occur among children and adolescents are near-sightedness *(myopia)*, lazy eye *(amblopia ex anopsia)*, farsightedness *(hyperopia)*, and astigmatism. Nearsightedness, or the inability to see distant objects clearly, is hereditary. It is rarely present at birth but develops as the child grows. Lazy eye develops during the first six or seven years of life. Farsightedness (inability to see nearby objects clearly) and astigmatism (blurred vision at all distances) occur at an early age and don't usually grow worse with time.

SIGNS AND SYMPTOMS

There are clear symptoms that may indicate poor vision. If your child habitually tilts his or her head or looks out of the corners of his or her eyes, if the eyes cross or move away from normal, or if the child squints or is excessively sensitive to bright lights, there could be an eyesight problem. Holding objects close to examine them, failure to recognize familiar people at a distance, headaches following use of the eyes, problems in school, and a dislike of reading may also signify poor vision.

At birth, a baby who has normal eyes can focus on an object and visually follow movement. If an infant's eyes seem to make random, searching movements, he or she may have defective vision.

Vision can be tested at different ages in a variety of ways. During the first week of life an infant should be able to fix his or her eyes on a bright light. By two months of age, the child's eyes should follow that light as it moves through a 180-degree arc. By seven or eight months the child should be able to recognize and respond to facial expressions. After age three, a child's eyes can be tested by having him or her focus on charts that use pictures or the letter E pointed in different directions. Finally, around age five or six, the child's eyes can be tested using a standard Snellen eye chart.

HOME CARE

Be alert to the symptoms that can indicate impaired vision, and have the child's eyes examined periodically.

PRECAUTIONS

● A child who cannot see the television screen from a distance or who holds books close to the eyes may be near-sighted. ● A child's vision should be checked annually, beginning no later than age four.

MEDICAL TREATMENT

At each annual eye checkup, your doctor will examine your child's eyes inside and out with an ophthalmoscope, and test the child's vision using a chart of letters in rows of diminishing sizes. If an abnormality is suspected, your doctor will refer your child to an eye specialist for more detailed examination and correction of the problem.

Related topics:

Crossed eyes
Lazy eye

Vomiting

SYMPTOM Forceful ejection of the contents of the stomach

HOME CARE Solid foods, milk, or aspirin tablets aggravate vomiting and should not be given.

Have the child sip ice water, carbonated beverages, tea with sugar, flavored gelatin water, commercial mineral or electrolyte mixtures, or apple juice.

If you do not know why the child is vomiting, consult the doctor. Note if abdominal pain, fever, or headache accompany the vomiting.

PRECAUTIONS

☐ Prolonged or severe vomiting can cause dehydration, which can be very serious in infants.

☐ If vomiting and diarrhea occur at the same time, control the vomiting first.

☐ Abdominal pain, whether it is accompanied by vomiting or not, may indicate appendicitis.

☐ Some phenothiazine drugs that are given to control vomiting in adults can have serious side effects in children and should not be given.

☐ If the child is on medication, vomiting may hinder the action of the medication.

A child who is vomiting should be encouraged to sip ice water, carbonated beverages, and juices.

Vomiting is a common occurrence during childhood. In most instances it is merely a nuisance, but at times it can hinder the work of medications, cause the child to lose so much fluid that dehydration (loss of body fluids) occurs, or indicate a problem that requires medical attention.

Most infants spit up and occasionally vomit. If this vomiting does not hinder weight gain, it is neither harmful nor abnormal. Excessive vomiting, however, may indicate an intolerance of formula, milk, or some foods. Frequent forceful vomiting during an infant's first two months suggests an obstruction at the end of the stomach (pylorospasm or pyloric stenosis).

In children, a viral infection of the digestive tract (gastroenteritis or intestinal flu) or an infectious disease elsewhere in the body can cause vomiting. Less common causes are abnormalities of the brain (concussion, migraine, meningitis, encephalitis, tumors); poisoning; appendicitis; severe emotional distress; jaundice; foreign bodies in the digestive tract; abdominal injuries; and motion sickness.

SIGNS AND SYMPTOMS

The vomiting itself is obvious, and the doctor concentrates on identifying its cause. It's also important to evaluate the degree of dehydration caused by persistent vomiting.

HOME CARE

If your child is vomiting, avoid giving solid foods, milk, or aspirin tablets. These substances aggravate the vomiting. Allow the child sips of cold, clear liquids (ice water, carbonated beverages, tea with sugar, flavored gelatin water, commercial mineral and electrolyte solutions, or apple juice). Commercial preparations of orthophosphoric acid, fructose, and glucose also may be given. If the child can keep down a teaspoon of liquid every five minutes, he or she will retain two ounces of fluid in an hour.

PRECAUTIONS

● Watch for signs of dehydration in your child. ● If vomiting and diarrhea are happening at the same time, control the vomiting first, then treat the diarrhea. ● Some phenothiazine drugs that are used to control vomiting in adults may cause serious central nervous system side effects in children; do not use them for children. ● Remember that abdominal pain (with or without vomiting) could be appendicitis.

MEDICAL TREATMENT

Your doctor will determine the cause of the vomiting by obtaining a detailed health history and performing a careful physical and neurological examination. The presence and degree of dehydration will be assessed, and if the child is seriously dehydrated he or she will be hospitalized for administration of intravenous fluids.

Related topics:

Appendicitis
Concussion
Dehydration
Diarrhea
Encephalitis
Food allergies
Gastroenteritis,
    acute
Headaches
Jaundice
Meningitis
Motion sickness
Poisoning
Stomachache,
    acute
Stomachache,
    chronic
Swallowed objects
Viruses

Warts

SYMPTOM

Rough, raised growth anywhere on the skin

HOME CARE

As a rule, leave warts alone.

With the approval of your doctor, you can use an appropriate commercial product to safely remove most warts other than those on the eyelids or face.

PRECAUTIONS

☐ No treatment is successful in all cases, and warts may spread during treatment or recur afterwards.

☐ At home, do not treat warts on the eyelids or face or warts that involve the cuticles or extend under the nails.

☐ If the surrounding skin becomes red or painful, discontinue home treatment.

☐ Most warts are harmless unless they are annoying, bleed often, or become infected.

A wart is a growth on the skin caused by a specific virus. Although warts may differ in appearance, they are caused by the same virus.

Warts can be spread by direct contact or by scratching. Plantar warts which appear on the soles of the feet can be contracted by walking barefoot where someone who has them recently walked.

For 67 percent of the children who have them, warts disappear on their own within two or three years; for 95 percent, the warts will be gone within ten years. Still, some warts must be treated. Plantar warts usually require treatment because they cause pain. Warts that extend under the nails may produce permanent deformities if they are not treated. Warts on the face and eyelids are removed for cosmetic reasons. All other warts are harmless and can be ignored unless they are annoying, bleed frequently, or become infected.

SIGNS AND SYMPTOMS

The common wart is a rough, raised growth that ranges in size from one-eighth inch to one inch and occurs anywhere on the skin. A juvenile wart is a small (one-sixteenth to one-fourth inch), smooth, pinkish wart that is common on the hands. Warts on the soles of the feet are plantar warts. They may be pressed into the foot (sometimes to a depth of a quarter-inch or more) and are often surrounded by a callus. Groups of plantar warts are known as "mosaic warts." Many warts are unmistakable, but some are not. When they are tiny, plantar warts may be mistaken for small brown splinters on the sole of the foot. Also you may not be able to see them if they're surrounded by a callus.

HOME CARE

Leave warts alone. If they have to be removed, it is probably safest to have a doctor do it or instruct you in the use of an appropriate ointment. Usually, treatment must continue for many days or weeks.

PRECAUTIONS

● If excessive pain or redness occurs on the surrounding skin, stop treatment. ● Do not treat any warts on the face or eyelids at home. ● Warts that involve the cuticles or extend under the nails should not be treated at home.

MEDICAL TREATMENT

No treatment is successful in all cases. Treatment may even spread warts or they may recur following treatment. In general, your doctor will remove warts with acids, podophyllin, electric cauterization (burning away), surgery (curetting), liquid nitrogen, solid carbon dioxide, or phenol.

Related topic:

Viruses

Whooping cough

SYMPTOMS

Runny nose
Low-grade fever
Severe, strangling ("whooping") cough
    followed by vomiting of mucus

HOME CARE

Make sure your child is adequately immunized against whooping cough.

Isolate the child from other young children.

If the vomiting is severe, feed the child small meals several times a day.

PRECAUTIONS

☐ Whooping cough is often fatal in infants. All infants should be immunized against this disease.

☐ Whooping cough is more common than many parents and doctors believe, and 90 percent of cases are never diagnosed.

☐ A child who has been exposed to whooping cough should see a doctor.

☐ A mild cough may indicate mild whooping cough, which the child can spread to others.

☐ Any cough that is getting progressively worse after two weeks should be brought to the attention of your doctor.

☐ Whooping cough is highly contagious and the infected child should be kept away from other people.

☐ Whooping cough can be caused by several germs, and the disease caused by one type does not give immunity against the others.

Whooping cough is a highly contagious infection of the respiratory tract, usually caused by the bacterium *Bordetella pertussis,* but sometimes by *Bordetella parapertussis* or *Bordetella bronchiseptica.* Whooping cough caused by one organism does *not* provide immunity against whooping cough caused by other germs, and the vaccine that's available provides immunity only against infection from the most common organism, *Bordetella pertussis.* The incubation period—the time it takes for symptoms to develop once the child has been exposed to the disease—is seven to 14 days. Whooping cough can be serious in infants under one year, and as many as 50 percent of these infants die. Newborns are not immune.

SIGNS AND SYMPTOMS

In a child who has not been immunized, whooping cough begins with a runny nose, low-grade fever (100°F to 101°F), and a cough that gradually worsens over the next two to three weeks. Then, the cough becomes characteristic: it is worse at night than during the day and paroxysmal (several coughs occur at once without inhaling in between). At the end of a spasm the child makes a "whoop" or strangling sound as air is sucked into the lungs; vomiting of thick mucus follows. The severe, strangling cough persists for another two to three weeks and gradually subsides in three to six more weeks. But the cough may return with new respiratory infections.

In an unimmunized child, the diagnosis is unmistakable. The diagnosis may not be obvious, however, in infants who never develop a "whoop," and in an immunized child the diagnosis may be impossible. The child who has been immunized may have full or partial immunity, but without boosters the immunity declines over the years. A child who is partially immune may have a mild case of whooping cough that produces none of whooping cough's identifiable characteristics. In the absence of characteristic symptoms, laboratory tests don't help. All the organisms that cause whooping cough are difficult to grow on cultures and more modern techniques

for the isolation of these organisms are not readily available. Because it may be difficult to diagnose and because both doctors and parents mistakenly believe the disease is rare, over 90 percent of cases of whooping cough are never detected, or even suspected.

HOME CARE

A child who has whooping cough should be isolated from young brothers and sisters. If the vomiting is severe, feed the child several small meals a day.

PRECAUTIONS

● Infants should be immunized against whooping cough. Risks from the disease far outweigh the risks from the immunization. Infants are not naturally immune to the disease, and the mortality (death) rate among infants who contract whooping cough is high. ● A child who has a mild cough may have a mild form of whooping cough, in which case he or she could spread the disease. Avoid unnecessary exposure to others. ● If your child has been exposed to whooping cough, take the child to a doctor. ● Report to a doctor any cough that is getting progressively worse at the end of two weeks.

MEDICAL TREATMENT

Your doctor will try to establish a diagnosis with the help of a complete blood count and cultures of the secretions from the nose and throat. Most often, however, the child's medical history and the doctor's clinical judgment are all that you can depend on. All infants with whooping cough are hospitalized, while older children may or may not be, depending on the child's condition.

Your doctor may prescribe the antibiotic erythromycin for ten to 14 days to make the disease less contagious. If given early enough, the medication may shorten the course of the illness. If your child has been exposed to whooping cough, he or she can be given erythromycin by mouth, a booster shot of vaccine, or a large dose of human antipertussis serum.

Related topics:

Coughs
Immunizations
Vomiting

Index

with chicken pox, 78, 79
contact dermatitis, 47
diaper, 116–17, 197
eczema, 140, 141
with fifth disease, 152, 153
with head lice, 192, 193
heat, 196–97, 283
with hepatitis, 203
hives, 213
from infections, 116, 117
with infectious mononucleosis, 222, 223
with measles, 244, 245
pityriasis rosea, 270, 271
poison ivy, 276, 277
purpura, 200, 201
ringworm, 286, 287
with Rocky Mountain spotted fever, 288, 289
with roseola, 290, 291
with rubella, 292, 293
with shingles, 300, 301
with sore throat, 312, 313
with strep throat, 322, 323
with sunburn, 329
with toxic shock syndrome, 352, 353
RBCs. See red blood cells
reading difficulties, and dyslexia, 134, 135
rectum, protrusion of, 108, 109
red blood cells, abnormal, 35, 307
redness
of earlobe, with earring problems, 138, 139
of eyelids, 144, 145, 146, 147
with sinusitis, 308, 309
with styes, 324, 325
of eyes, 144, 145
with common cold, 86, 87
with conjunctivitis, 90, 91
with rubella, 292, 293
of genitals, with urinary tract infections, 358, 359
of gums
with herpes simplex, 206, 207
with leukemia, 242, 243
with toothache, 350, 351
of joint, with puncture wounds, 280, 281
of lymph glands
with cat scratch fever, 74, 75
with chicken pox, 78, 79
of skin
with boils, 60, 61
with burns, 72, 73
with diaper rashes, 116, 117
with infected glands, 59, 172, 173
with sunburn, 328, 329
red streaks, with blood poisoning, 50, 57, 58, 59, 106, 107, 173
regional enteritis, 121
with stomachache, chronic, 321
remission, in leukemia, 243
resorcin, for acne, 32, 33
respiratory infections, 45, 67, 87, 108, 109, 162, 163, 225, 237, 245, 246, 247, 272, 273, 373
respiratory tree, 99
restlessness
with shock, 302, 303
with thyroid disorders, 344, 345
retarded growth, with thyroid disorders, 344, 345
Reye's syndrome, 14, 17, 18, 284–85
and chicken pox, 79
and influenza, 224, 225
rheumatic fever, 42, 43, 243
with strep throat, 323
rheumatoid arthritis, 42, 43, 243
Rh factor, 231
rhinoviruses, 365
rickets, 64, 65

rickettsia, 289
rickettsial pox, 229
rifampin, and meningitis, 247
ringworm, 51, 141, 270, 271, 286–87
Rocky Mountain spotted fever, 229, 288–89
roseola, 290–91, 365
rubella, 20–21, 110, 111, 143, 153, 283, 292–93, 365
arthritis of, 43
and jaundice in newborns, 231
and pregnancy, 21, 110, 111, 292, 293
vaccine, 19, 20, 21, 257, 292, 293
rubeola. See measles
runny nose
with fifth disease, 152, 153
with food allergies, 156, 157
with measles, 244, 245
with roseola, 290, 291
with whooping cough, 372, 373

Sabin polio vaccine, 20, 278, 279
salicylic acid, for acne, 32, 33
salicylic acid shampoo, for cradle cap, 100, 101
salivary glands, and mumps, 256, 257
Salk polio vaccine, 20, 278, 279
salmonella bacteria, 133
salmonella infections, 43
salt tablets and heatstroke, dangers of, 198, 199
salt water gargle, for sore throat, 312, 313
salty tasting skin, and cystic fibrosis, 108, 109
Sarcoptes scabei, 295
scabies, 294–95
scaliness
of scalp
with baldness, 50, 51
with cradle cap, 100, 101
of skin
with athlete's foot, 46, 47
with diaper rashes, 116, 117
with earring problems, 138, 139
with eczema, 140, 141
with pityriasis rosea, 270, 271
with ringworm, 286, 287
scalp depression, with concussion, 88, 89
scarlatina, 323
scarlet fever, 153, 323
and nephritis, 259
Scheuermann's disease, 49
scoliosis, 296–97
and backaches, 49
scrapes, 37, 107, 173, 221, 281, 298–99, 340, 341
"screamer's nodes," 215
scrotum, discoloration of, with torsion of testis, 336, 337
scurvy, and spontaneous bruises, 71
sea sickness, 254, 255
seborrheic dermatitis. See cradle cap
secondary infections, 47, 188, 189, 225, 264, 265, 277, 294, 295
sedatives, 88, 89
seizures
absence, 97
complex partial, 97
generalized convulsive, 97
generalized non-convulsive, 97
with lead poisoning, 240, 241
simple partial, 97
See also convulsions with fever
self-starvation. See anorexia nervosa
serum hepatitis, 202, 203
Sever's disease, 310, 311
shampooing
for cradle cap, 100, 101
for head lice, 192, 193
shigella bacteria, 133

shingles, 77, 283, 300-301
shock, 72, 73, 181, 199, 302–3, 353
emergency procedure, 302, 303
insulin, 115
toxic, 352–53
shortness of breath, 219, 304–5
with anemia, 34, 35
with asthma, 44, 45
with bronchiolitis, 67
with chest pain, 76, 77
with high blood pressure, 208, 209
with influenza, 225
sick headache, 191
sickle cell anemia, 35, 243, 306–7
and stomachache, chronic, 321
sickle cell crisis, 307
sickle cell test, 35, 307
sigmoidoscopy, 121
silent urinary tract infections, 359
silver nitrate solution
and blocked tear duct, 147
for gonorrhea in newborns, 177
silver sulfadiazine cream, for burns, 72, 73
simple hernia, 205
simple partial seizures, 97
"singer's nodes," 215
sinus infections. See sinusitis
sinusitis, 87, 191, 308–9, 323
sinus pain, with sore throat, 312, 313
sitting up, difficulty in, with encephalitis, 142, 143
sitz baths, for vaginal discharge, 362, 363
skin, 32, 33, 46, 47, 54, 55, 56, 57, 60, 61, 70, 71, 72, 73, 100, 101, 106, 107, 116, 117, 138, 139, 140, 141, 164, 165, 186, 187, 196, 197, 200, 201, 206, 207, 212, 213, 220, 221, 252, 253, 264, 265, 270, 271, 276, 277, 280, 281, 282, 283, 286, 287, 290, 291, 294, 295, 298, 299, 328, 329, 370, 371
skull fractures, 129, 131
and meningitis, 246, 247
See also concussion
sleep apnea, 349
sleep, fitful, with colic, 85
sleepiness
after convulsions without fever, 96, 97
with encephalitis, 142, 143
with thyroid disorders, 344, 345
sleeplessness, with teething, 334, 335
sleepwalking, 260, 261
slipped femoral epiphysis, 211
slow breathing, 112, 113, 118, 119
slow development, with lead poisoning, 240, 241
slow pulse, with concussion, 88, 89
smallpox, 21
smegma, 83
smelling salts, 150, 151
sneezing
with bronchitis, 69
with common cold, 86, 87
with hay fever, 188, 189
with nosebleeds, 263
soft spot in skull, 27
with dehydration, 112, 113, 118, 119
solid food, and vomiting, 119, 120, 121, 368, 369
solution of Merthiolate, for puncture wounds, 281
sore glands, 91
See also glands, swollen
sore heels, 310, 311
soreness, of muscles
with backaches, 48, 49
with growing pains, 179
with polio, 278, 279